MAR 0 4 2009

mer's

# CANCÚN
# & THE
# YUCATÁN

## spend less see more

## 1st Edition

☞ P9-DNW-529

by Christine Delsol

Series Editor: Pauline Frommer

WILEY
Wiley Publishing, Inc.

Published by:

## Wiley Publishing, Inc.

111 River St.
Hoboken, NJ 07030-5774

ISBN 978-0-470-28789-7
Editor: Melinda Quintero
Production Editor: Suzanna R. Thompson
Cartographer: Andy Dolan
Photo Editor: Richard Fox
Interior Design: Lissa Auciello-Brogan
Production by Wiley Indianapolis Composition Services
Front and back cover photo © Bertrand Gardel/Hemis/Alamy Images
Cover photo of Pauline Frommer by Janette Beckmann

For information on our other products and services or to obtain technical support,
please contact our Customer Care Department within the U.S. at 800/762-2974,
outside the U.S. at 317/572-3993 or fax 317/572-4002.

Wiley also publishes its books in a variety of electronic formats. Some content that
appears in print may not be available in electronic formats.

Manufactured in the United States of America

5   4   3   2   1

# Contents

# List of Maps

## About the Author

**Christine Delsol** recovered from her first memory of Mexico—a bullfight during a childhood trip with her Mexican *Californio* grandmother—and has been traveling to the country at every opportunity for 30 years. She has spent most of her career in newspapers, winning an Associated Press award for feature writing and, as travel editor of the *San Francisco Chronicle,* two Lowell Thomas awards from the Society of American Travel Writers. She left the *Chronicle* a year ago to write full time but still con-

tributes an online column about Mexico. Christine lives with her husband, another newspaper creature, in the San Francisco Bay Area and has an absurdly well-traveled 21-year-old daughter.

## Acknowledgments

Thanks are due to **Jeanne Cooper,** for her contribution to chapter 8, "The Essentials of Planning."

## An Invitation to the Reader

In researching this book, we discovered many wonderful places—hotels, restaurants, shops, and more. We're sure you'll find others. Please tell us about them, so we can share the information with your fellow travelers in upcoming editions. If you were disappointed with a recommendation, we'd love to know that, too. Please write to:

*Pauline Frommer's Cancún & the Yucatán,* 1st Edition
Wiley Publishing, Inc. • 111 River St. • Hoboken, NJ 07030-5774

## An Additional Note

## Star Ratings, Icons & Abbreviations

Every restaurant, hotel, and attraction is rated with stars ★, indicating our opinion of that facility's desirability; this relates not to price, but to the value you receive for the price you pay. The stars mean:

**No stars:** Good
★ Very good
★★ Great
★★★ Outstanding! A must!

Accommodations within each neighborhood are listed in ascending order of cost, starting with the cheapest and increasing to the occasional "splurge." Each hotel review is preceded by one, two, three, or four dollar signs, indicating the price range per double room. Restaurants work on a similar system, with dollar signs indicating the price range per three-course meal.

| Accommodations | | Dining | |
|---|---|---|---|
| $ | Up to $50/night | $ | Meals for $7 or less |
| $$ | $51–$75 | $$ | $8–$12 |
| $$$ | $76–$125 | $$$ | $13–$17 |
| $$$$ | Over $126 per night | $$$$ | $18 and up |

In addition, we've included a kids icon  to denote attractions, restaurants, and lodgings that are particularly child friendly.

## Frommers.com

Now that you have this guidebook to help you plan a great trip, visit our website at **www.frommers.com** for additional travel information on more than 4,000 destinations. We update features regularly to give you instant access to the most current trip-planning information available. At Frommers.com, you'll find scoops on the best airfares, lodging rates, and car rental bargains. You can even book your travel online through our reliable travel booking partners. Other popular features include:

- Online updates of our most popular guidebooks
- Vacation sweepstakes and contest giveaways
- Newsletters highlighting the hottest travel trends
- Podcasts, interactive maps, and up-to-the-minute events listings
- Opinionated blog entries by Arthur Frommer himself
- Online travel message boards with featured travel discussions

I started traveling with my guidebook-writing parents, Arthur Frommer and Hope Arthur, when I was just four months old. To avoid lugging around a crib, they would simply swaddle me and stick me in an open drawer for the night. For half of my childhood, my home was a succession of hotels and B&Bs throughout Europe, as we dashed around every year to update *Europe on $5 a Day* (and then $10 a day, and then $20 . . .).

We always traveled on a budget, staying at the Mom-and-Pop joints Dad featured in the guide, getting around by public transportation, eating where the locals ate. And that's still the way I travel today, because I learned—from the master—that these types of vacations not only save money, but offer a richer, deeper experience of the culture. You spend time in local neighborhoods, meeting and talking with the people who live there. For me, making friends and having meaningful exchanges is always the highlight of my journeys— and the main reason I decided to become a travel writer and editor as well.

I've conceived these books as budget guides for a new generation. They have all the outspoken commentary and detailed pricing information of the Frommer's guides, but they take bargain hunting into the 21st century, with more information on using the Internet and air/hotel packages to save money. Most important, we stress "alternative accommodations"—apartment rentals, private B&Bs, religious retreat houses, and more—not simply to save you money, but to give you a more authentic experience in the places you visit.

Highlights of each guide are the sections that deal with "The Other" side of the destinations, the one visitors rarely see. These sections will actively immerse you in the life that residents enjoy. The result, I hope, is a valuable new addition to the world of guidebooks. Please let us know how we've done! E-mail me at editor@frommers.com.

Happy traveling!

*Pauline Frommer*
Pauline Frommer

# 1

# The Best of Cancún & the Yucatán

An ancient civilization & a brazen new culture make Mexico's last frontier a land of never-ending fascination

THE YUCATAN PENINSULA SOMETIMES SEEMS A COUNTRY ALTOGETHER separate from Mexico. That's partly a legacy of the Maya's determined, centuries-long resistance to being scooped up as part of Spain's booty, and you still feel more than a hint of "in it, but not of it" to the present-day Yucatán. The other-ness goes beyond history, though; the very earth is a mystery, an impossibly flat, porous limestone slab whose rivers run below rather than above the surface and grudgingly yield their contents through sporadic breaches in the stone ceilings. Dependence on these life-giving cenotes, or wells, gave rise to a complex view of the cosmos that nearly 5 centuries of Catholicism have failed to stamp out.

The Yucatán's aloofness from the rest of Mexico, and its closer ties with Europe, Cuba, and the United States, produced a culture unlike any other in Mexico. Still, it's the ancient Maya legacy you see at every turn, and the one that tourism marketers emphasize.

So, what do we make of Cancún in this context? It, too, is unlike the rest of Mexico (with the possible exception of Los Cabos), but equally different from the rest of the Yucatán. Brash and beautiful, blessed by an accident of nature, Cancún is a culture unto itself, as irresistible as it is infuriating.

The tension between the excess and artifice of Cancún and the humility of Yucatán's interior somehow makes the region all the more compelling. It is never one thing or the other, at least not for long. And no matter what you like or dislike about the Yucatán, once you've been there, you always have a stake in it.

## THE STATES OF THE YUCATAN PENINSULA

### QUINTANA ROO

Cancún might as well be the name of the Yucatán's eastern state. Before Quintana Roo finally became a state in 1974—not coincidentally, the year Cancún's first resorts opened—this was just the scary east side of what originally was one big territory of Yucatán. Even after they had control of the inland, *conquistadores* dreaded entering Quintana Roo's jungles for fear of disappearing forever (and not without some justification). Today, of course, Quintana Roo is the peninsula's cash cow, its sublime Caribbean beaches hosting more tourists and more resort developments every year and still managing to make every visitor feel it's his or her secret hideaway. This is the land of dreamy beaches; secluded cenotes; picturesque Maya ruins; and, increasingly, resorts that charge more for 1 night than you pay for your monthly mortgage. The southernmost reaches of the state, bumping up against Belize, still have an outback feel.

## YUCATAN

Yucatán state is the triangular wedge in the middle of the Yucatán that divides the peninsula roughly into thirds. The lure of a mysterious "lost" civilization made it a travel destination when travel was still the privilege of the wealthy. Travelers are just as captivated today, only there are more of us, and boutique hotels and eco-tours have joined untouched ruins, authentic and inexpensive handicrafts, and Maya villages arrested in time as reasons to venture so far away. Its northern coast, with coarser sands and murkier green water than the Caribbean, is not considered as desirable and therefore is wide open to claim as your own for a day or two. While more tranquil, less crowded, and less expensive than travel on the Caribbean coast, the Yucatán is also somewhat less attuned to U.S. travelers' needs and quirks. Most of the time, that's all the more reason to love it.

## CAMPECHE

In colonial times, Campeche was the place to be, whether you were a Spanish conqueror or a roving pirate; the only ones who didn't have it so good were the Maya who were alternately killed and enslaved. Campeche city is a vision of colonial architecture, one of only three walled cities built by Europeans in this hemisphere, and yet it gets a fraction of the visitors that Quintana Roo or even Yucatán do. When Mérida was the only major city on the peninsula, Campeche was no farther away from "civilization" than Tulum was. Now, with all the focus on Cancún up there on the northeast corner of the Caribbean coast, Campeche is the other end of the world. It is, if anything, more relaxed than Yucatán, though far fewer people speak English and, outside of Campeche city, it can be a challenge to get any consistent responses to questions about hours or services.

# THE BEST BEACHES

**AKUMAL BAY**   The lazy crescent of Akumal Bay laps a wide swath of soft white sand shaded by coconut palms in the center of town. It's one of the few places in the Riviera Maya where you'll regularly find sea turtles swimming beside you. See p. 162.

**PLAYA DELFINES**   One of Cancún's longest and widest beaches escapes the high-rises along the spectacular east shore to display a perfect Caribbean landscape of glittering dunes and striated shades of aqua water; on a peaceful early morning, you can watch the wild dolphins that give the beach its name. See p. 45.

**PLAYA NORTE**   You can sink up to your ankles in the powdery sand at Isla Mujeres' northern tip, and you can wade out in the placid, perfectly crystalline water for 37m (120 ft.) before it reaches your chest. See p. 83.

**TULUM**   Stretching south from the Maya's unique seaside city are some of the Caribbean's most beautiful beaches, becoming more sublime and less populated the farther you go. See "Active Tulum" on p. 172.

# THE BEST ARCHAEOLOGICAL SITES

**CALAKMUL**    Both a vast Maya city and a biosphere reserve where you encounter more howler monkeys than tourists, Calakmul boasts the Yucatán's tallest pyramid and was a rival to Guatemala's Tikal. See p. 262.

**EDZNA**    This huge but barely excavated city gets fewer visitors in a year than Chichén Itzá does in a day, leaving you to absorb the natural and architectural beauty—resembling Palenque or Tikal more than anything in the Yucatán—on a whole different level. See p. 261.

**EK BALAM**    Archaeologists, who began work only in 1997, continually unveil history-altering finds in a city that might eventually prove to be as big and as important as Chichén Itzá. Ek Balam's main pyramid, one of the few that visitors are still allowed to climb, is 6m (20 ft.) higher than El Castillo at Chichén Itzá. See p. 240.

**UXMAL**    Yes, Chichén Itzá and Tulum are must-sees, so see them you must. But many less famous ruins stay with you longer. Deep in a sparsely populated jungle, Uxmal was second in size and influence only to Chichén Itzá, yet its graceful proportions and intricate stone work reveal no military ambition or human sacrifice. See p. 215.

# THE BEST DIVING & SNORKELING

**AKUMAL**    The first place where divers waded into the Mexican Caribbean not only offers easy reef diving with abundant sea life but is surrounded by cenotes where the earth opens to underground rivers. Local operators specialize in cenote diving; snorkelers can get an introduction to the spectacular cavern system at Hidden Worlds Cenotes Park (p. 164) or explore the lovely Laguna Yal-Kú (p. 162); the more adventurous can visit more than a dozen secluded cenotes just north of town. See p. 165.

**COZUMEL**    Cradled by 32km (20 miles) of the Great Maya Reef, made famous by Jacques Cousteau in the 1960s, Cozumel is still considered one of the world's great dive destinations. Nondivers can get an eyeful in dozens of snorkeling spots where the underwater mountains of coral rise close to the surface. See p. 118.

**PUERTO MORELOS**    This quiet fishing village's snow-white beaches are protected by a pristine section of the Great Maya Reef 183m (600 ft.) offshore. Divers gravitate to the Ojo de Agua (Eye of Water), where fresh water wells up from a cenote below the sea floor, while novice snorkelers can see an abundance of colorful sea life less than a meter (3 ft.) from the surface right in front of town. See p. 154.

# THE BEST MUSEUMS

**CASA 6**    Visitors step into colonial life as the Spanish merchant elite in Campeche knew it, in a 17th-century home with its interior courtyard, sitting room, bedroom, and kitchen re-created to look just as it would have been 350 years ago. See p. 254.

**LA CASA DEL ARTE POPULAR MEXICANO** Cancún's overlooked museum, hidden away in a nondescript marina building, boasts one of the most comprehensive displays of Mexican folk art in the country, set up in lifelike dioramas including a chapel scene with life-size wax figures modeled after real people from throughout Mexico. See p. 46.

**MUSEO DE LA CULTURA MAYA** Interactive displays decoding Maya architecture and customs, a three-level exhibit representing the sacred *ceiba* tree, and a glass floor that allows you to walk over replicas of ancient cities make Chetumal's innovative museum one of the best places in the country to get insight into the ancient Mayas' intricate spiritual and temporal worlds. See p. 180.

**MUSEO REGIONAL DE ANTROPOLOGIA** Ensconced in Mérida's most sumptuous colonial mansion, the Museo Regional de Antropología displays artifacts of the ancient Maya's daily life, including limestone jaguars, deformed skulls, and sacrificial offerings—all surrounded by European Beaux Arts architectural flourishes. See p. 198.

## THE BEST YUCATECAN CUISINE

**CASA TIKINXIK** *Tikin xic* fish from this classic *palapa* restaurant on Isla Mujeres's best west-side swimming beach is a mandatory pilgrimage for seafood lovers. A fresh whole fish is marinated in sour orange juice and chilies, then grilled in a banana leaf over an open flame. See p. 81.

**LABNA** Marked by a towering Maya-style entrance, this downtown Cancún landmark serves not just the piquant regional favorites *poc chuc* (marinated pork strips grilled and served with pickled onions) and *pollo pibil* (spiced chicken baked in banana leaves), but also lesser known specialties such as *papadzules* (hard-boiled eggs rolled inside tortillas and smothered in a pumpkin seed–and–fried tomato sauce). See p. 39.

**LA PIGUA** The best example of Campeche's signature *pan de cazón* (tortillas layered with shredded baby shark meat, black beans, and tomato sauce) comes from this distinctive glass restaurant modeled after a traditional oblong Maya house. See p. 252.

**YAXCHE** Just off Playa del Carmen's Quinta Avenida, Yaxché honors Maya culinary traditions and offers intriguing contemporary tweaks—think cream of *xcatic* pepper and potato soup and grilled shrimp fajitas marinated in *achiote*—in a setting of reproduction stelae and murals of Maya gods and kings. See p. 142.

## THE BEST "OTHER" EXPERIENCES

**KEEPING PACE WITH THE TURTLES** Thousands of endangered sea turtles come ashore along Mexico's Caribbean coast to lay their eggs each spring. Visitors can join local conservationists in Cancún, Cozumel, and Akumal to help protect the exhausted mothers returning to the water or usher the tiny hatchlings safely on their first journey to the sea. See p. 51, 124, and 165, respectively.

**A MAYA VILLAGE**    Deep in the tropical forest, families living much as the ancient Maya did in round thatch huts will show you their jungle paths, mangrove lagoons, and hidden cenotes; bestow ancient blessings; and serve you lunch in an open-air *palapa*. See p. 144.

**THE *HACENDADO* LIFE**    Sotuta de Peón isn't just a restored hacienda; it's an entire *henequén* plantation and processing plant for the "green gold" that made Mérida fabulously wealthy a century ago. You can witness the whole process and try your hand at combing the fiber and spinning it into twine—then cool off after your labors in a cenote. See p. 199.

**SPEAK YOUR PIECE**    Sometimes all you have to do to get in with the locals is speak English. The Mérida English Library's "Conversaciones con Amigos" ("Conversations with Friends") is a regular weekly social event that allows English and Spanish speakers to practice their second languages together (p. 200), while Isla Mujeres' La Gloria English School asks for a commitment of a few hours to work with students in the classroom who need to practice their new English skills (p. 88).

# THE BEST WEEKLONG ITINERARIES
## Creatures Great & Small

Swimming with sea turtles, gliding among flamingos, and snorkeling with whale sharks are the highlights of this eco-adventure tour, which takes in cenotes, jungles, and the Great Maya Reef. It's a bit of a whirlwind but allows a little sleepy-village down time.

### Days ❶ & ❷: Playa del Carmen

Pick up a rental car from the Cancún airport and stop at Croco Cun (p. 47) on your way to Playa del Carmen for the night.

Take a dive trip to Cozumel the next day. The Tank-Ha Dive Center (p. 145) is one of the few operators who will take you to Cozumel in the dive boat; most require you to take the ferry and meet the dive boat on the island. If you're not a diver, book a tour with Alltournative to visit the Maya village of Pac Chen, where you'll hike through the jungle, glide over a cenote on a zipline, rappel down into another for a swim, and kayak a lagoon where howler monkeys scold you from the mangroves, all followed by lunch prepared by village women in an open-air *palapa* (p. 144). Drive to Akumal for the night.

### Days ❸ & ❹: Akumal

Start your mornings swimming with the turtles in Akumal Bay. In the afternoons, shift your sights inland, to Laguna Yal-Kú for snorkeling (p. 162), or the cenote Jardín del Edén, frequented (but not *too* much) by both snorkelers and divers (p. 157). At the end of day 4, drive to Valladolid on the road leading inland from Tulum.

## Days ⑤ & ⑥: Valladolid

Get up with the roosters and drive north to Río Lagartos for a boat trip into the Ría Lagartos flamingo reserve (p. 241). Afterward, have lunch and soak up some real small-town atmosphere. If you have time and energy on the way back to Valladolid, stop at Ek Balam (p. 240). The next morning, stop at Cenotes Dzitnup (p. 240) on your way to Chiquilá on the north coast, where you'll get the ferry to Isla Holbox (p. 96). Make it an early night.

## Days ⑦ & ⑧: Isla Holbox

If it's summer, snorkeling with the whale sharks that congregate just off Holbox's shores will be the biggest thrill of your trip—maybe of any trip (p. 101). In other months, book a boat tour to Isla Pájaros, Isla de la Pasíon, and the Ojo de Agua cenote, or see if you can arrange for a boat to Cabo Catoche, Holbox's best snorkeling spot, at the island's northeastern tip (p. 102). The next morning, allow about 3½ hours to catch the ferry back and drive to Cancún's airport.

# Into the Maya Heartland

The hint of Maya history and culture that flavors the Yucatán's resort areas is part of everyday life in the interior and on the west coast. This itinerary requires some road time, but it's easy driving. Your rewards are grand but sparsely visited ruins; lively traditional towns; haunting haciendas; and the splendid city of Mérida, cultural nexus of the entire peninsula.

## Days ① & ②: Valladolid

Rent a car at Cancún's airport and drive to Valladolid on the toll road. Stroll around the plaza or, if you arrive late, have a bite and enjoy some live music at Las Campanas, which stays open until 2am (p. 238).

Get to Ek Balam (p. 240) when it opens to see the huge but undiscovered ruins at their most peaceful time. Back in town, get lunch from the food vendors in Valladolid's central plaza, relax in the shade, make a leisurely circuit of the shops, and peek into the cathedral. Go to the second floor of El Ayuntamiento (City Hall) to see the dramatic murals, then head down the street to the Museo San Roque's display of artifacts from Ek Balam. Cool off at Cenote Zací a few blocks farther on (p. 239). Then go for a sunset walk down beautiful Calzada de los Frailes to the Ex-Convento de San Bernardino de Siena.

## Days ③ & ④: Campeche

On the way out of town in the morning, stop at Cenotes Dzitnup and Samulá (p. 240). If you haven't been to Chichén Itzá (p. 227) before, make time to stop there on the way and plan to arrive in Campeche after dark. After all that time on the road, stretch your legs with a walk along the *malecón*—you'll have plenty of *campechanos* for company.

Get to the ethereally beautiful ruins of Edzná (p. 261) at opening time the next day, and stop for lunch at Hacienda Uayamon on your way back to town (p. 253). Back in the city center, drive or take a taxi to the 18th-century Fuerte San Miguel and its Museo de la Cultura Maya, with artifacts from ruins throughout the state (p. 257). Spend the rest of the day relaxing in the plaza and visiting the *baluartes* (bastions) and their small museums. Be sure to take a walk along the one remaining fragment of the original city wall, and visit Casa 6 to see how the Spanish elite lived during colonial times (p. 254). If it's a weekend, join in a game of Campechean bingo in the plaza at night (p. 253).

### Days ❺ & ❻: Mérida

Work your way to Mérida on the inland route, Hwy. 261, making a quick stop at Kabah (p. 218), the most interesting of the smaller Puuc Route cities, before arriving at Uxmal (p. 211). If you don't stay for the evening light-and-sound show, stop at Hacienda Yaxcopoil on your way to the capital (p. 212). Even after a full day of travel, the lower evening temperatures and the activity around Mérida's Plaza Grande and nearby squares might lure you out for a stroll.

Get to the sprawling Mercado (p. 201) in the morning on the next day, and visit the Museo de la Ciudad in its splendid new home (p. 197). Return to the plaza, relax a bit and visit Casa de Montejo (p. 196) and the Palacio de Gobierno (p. 196) with its

haunting murals. Next door to the cathedral, visit the MACAY to see works by the region's best contemporary artists (p. 196). Save the evening for one of the city's free cultural events.

### Day ❼: Izamal

Drive to Hacienda Sotuta de Peón (p. 199) for the first tour to see how *henequén* is produced and how the *hacendados* once lived. When you leave, head east toward Tecoh, then north through Acanceh and Seyé to Hwy. 180 and drive east to the exit for Izamal (p. 231). In the "Yellow City," stop at the Casa de Cultura for informative exhibits on regional handicrafts and pick up a walking tour map; spend the rest of the afternoon visiting local artists' studios. Afterward, walk up to the Ex-Convento de San Antonio de Padua at sunset to see it at its ethereal best. If you didn't get a place to stay in or near Izamal, you can easily drive back to Mérida for the night.

### Day ❽: Izamal to Cancún Airport

The Cancún airport is about 4 hours from Mérida or 3½ from Izamal.

## A Family Affair

Never mind that Cancún and the Riviera Maya are best known for their nightlife, spas, and shopping; the region's beaches, exotic animals, and abundance of exciting activities captivate kids of all ages. This itinerary plucks some of the most beguiling offerings on land and sea without overtaxing youthful attention spans or requiring hard road time.

### Days ❶ & ❷: Cancún

Start your trip with a stay in Cancún's Zona Hotelera; you won't need (or want) a car until Day 5. Start with beach time, either at your resort or at Playa Ballenas or Playa Delfines (p. 45). You might spend part of the day taking a jungle tour or renting a kayak or

WaveRunner on Laguna Nichupté (p. 53); for real thrill junkies, try some of AquaWorld's more outrageous offerings (p. 55). An alternative: spend the day at Parque Nizuc, which includes the Wet'n Wild water park, an aquarium, and a dolphin-swim program (p. 50). Later in the day, go to La Isla Shopping Village, with its Interactive Aquarium, boat tours through the canals, and rock-climbing wall (p. 61).

On day 2, after some morning beach time at Playa Linda, ride the Torre Escénica Giratoria (Rotating Scenic Tower) (p. 50) at the adjacent Embarcadero Marina and visit La Casa del Arte Popular (p. 46). Even kids with the shortest attention spans will enjoy the realistic settings and the fascinating toy room. Swashbuckle your way through dinner on the Captain Hook Pirate Cruise (p. 66).

### Days ❸ & ❹: Isla Mujeres

Take a morning ferry to Isla Mujeres (p. 70). After you settle in, preferably in town, stop by the Casa de la Cultura to check out the kids' activities (p. 87). Spend the rest of the day in the calm, shallow waters at Playa Norte.

The next day, rent a golf cart and head down the island's west side. At Tortugranja, you can feed young turtles being cared for until they are big enough for release (p. 86). Stop at Playa Lancheros for grilled *tikin xic* fish and pens of languid nurse sharks and sea turtles (p. 81). Get in some leisurely snorkeling at Garrafón de Castilla beach club (p. 89), unless you prefer the ziplines, climbing tower, "snuba" tours, and see-through canoes at Garrafón Natural Reef Park (p. 89). Continue to the island's southern tip to see the lighthouse and the last vestige of Isla's only Maya ruin, then drive back up the east side. Leave time for beach-combing on the beautiful wild beaches, and keep an eye out for the "Crayola House" and the landmark conch-shaped house as you pass the *colonias*.

### Days ❺ & ❻: Akumal

Take the morning ferry to Cancún and get a taxi or a bus to the airport to pick up your rental car. On the way to Akumal, stop at Croco Cun, where kids love getting touchy-feely with baby crocs, iguanas, boas, and spider monkeys (p. 47). Other options are horseback riding at Rancho Loma Bonita (p. 60) or farther down the coast at Rancho Punta Venado (p. 146), or a detour to Dolphin Discovery in Puerto Aventuras (p. 147).

The next day, start with a swim in Akumal Bay in the center of town, where sea turtles will swim with you more often than not. If it's turtle nesting season, stop at the Centro Ecológico Akumal to sign up for the 9pm turtle walk (p. 165). Later, drive to the northern end of town to snorkel with turtles, rays, and tropical fish in Laguna Yal-Kú (p. 162). On the way back, stop at La Buena Vida restaurant in Half Moon Bay for dinner in a lookout tower with eagle-eye views of the Caribbean and the jungle (p. 162).

### Day ❼: Tulum

Hit the Tulum ruins at opening time to beat the crowds and heat (p. 166). Tulum is Maya Ruins 101 for kids, extensively excavated and small enough to cover in an hour (but allow time to explore the beach). Hundreds of resident iguanas, and the occasional coati or other exotic creature, will entertain even the most disengaged youngster. In the afternoon, go to Hidden Worlds Cenotes Park (p. 164) for an introduction to snorkeling in the area's vast network of cenotes—or strike out on your own for one of the low-key cenotes nearby (p. 156). Return to your hotel in Akumal for the night.

### Day ❽: Akumal to Cancún Airport

Cancún's airport is less than 1½ hours away from Akumal.

# 2 Cancún

CANCUN MIGHT WELL BE THE LEAST MEXICAN CITY IN ALL OF MEXICO—this despite the fact that it generates one-third of the entire country's tourism revenues. Just as "cultural tourism"—focusing on a country's communities and traditions—was becoming tourism marketers' favorite bullet point in the 1960s, Mexico, which had little *but* cultural tourism until then, unveiled its glittering, entirely prefabricated beach resort, which sprawls for 23km (14 miles) like the love child of Miami and Las Vegas. Since the first hotels opened in 1974 on what had once been a deserted island visited only by local fishermen, droves of tourists have flocked here for the privilege of lounging on talcum-powder beaches lapped by turquoise waves.

Cancún today offers upwards of 25,000 rooms and has an estimated population of close to 700,000 residents, making it not only the Yucatán Peninsula's most prosperous city but one of the Caribbean's top destinations, surpassing even Jamaica, Puerto Rico, and the Dominican Republic. At the heart of the development is a narrow, dog-legged spit, barely wide enough for a single boulevard lined by imposing resorts, vaguely resembling pyramids, palaces, and Cubist sculptures. It's a culture unto itself, an idyllic Caribbean cocoon: easy to get to, largely English speaking, requiring no exchanging of dollars for pesos. Hotels, stores, and restaurants belong to international chains with familiar names. Those who come here enjoy lazing on the legendary Caribbean beaches; shopping in glittering retail centers; letting off steam in thumping, all-night discos; and fortifying themselves in fine restaurants to do it again the next day. This is vacationing at its purest.

The one demand Cancún makes is on your wallet. And among the megaresorts, hotel and restaurant tabs are at least on a par with U.S. resorts. Budget travelers therefore head downtown, to El Centro, as it is called, where Cancún's Mexicans make their homes, do their shopping, and let off steam. An ample supply of budget hotels makes it a reasonable alternative to the Hotel Zone, but even Hotel Zone vacationers are finding their way to downtown's lively fusion of Mexican, Yucatecan, Maya, Caribbean, and North American lifestyles.

## DON'T LEAVE CANCUN WITHOUT . . .

PLAYING TAG WITH THE WAVES AT PLAYA DELFINES  Cancún's longest, widest beach also seems to have the bluest skies and deepest turquoise waters—everything that's wonderful about Cancún, in superlatives. See p. 45.

**EATING *POC CHUC*** Or *pollo pibil.* Or *sopa de lima,* or any of the unique blends of piquant Maya flavors with European cooking techniques that make up today's Yucatecan cuisine. See "Yucatecan Cuisine" on p. 35.

**GOING UNDER** Half of Cancún's reason for existence lies beneath the water's surface. You don't have to be a diver (though you'll probably want to be after your first glimpse of the underwater scenery). Snorkeling is easy and cheap, and inventive entrepreneurs have come up with whole new ways to put you below the water line without even getting wet. See "Snorkeling & Scuba Diving" on p. 58.

**HAVING A WILD NIGHT** Coco Bongo isn't just Cancún's hottest club. It's a Vegas revue, a Broadway musical, Cirque du Soleil, and an open bar all in one big brassy package. See p. 64.

**GOING TO TOWN** Real life in Cancún happens in El Centro, in the restaurants and pubs of Avenida Yaxchilán, the cantinas under the bull ring, and the communal living room known as Parque Las Palapas where people come to meet their friends, make some music, and eat *botanas* (appetizers) from the food stalls. See "Dining for All Tastes: El Centro" on p. 37 and "Nightlife: El Centro" on p. 65.

# A BRIEF HISTORY

Many think of Cancún as being in the heart of Maya territory, but in truth the flourishing cities of the Classic period (A.D. 250–900) lie primarily east and south of today's resort mecca. Quintana Roo's eastern coast hosted some of the kingdoms of the Postclassic period (A.D. 900–1511), but Cancún's main activities appear to have been fishing and serving as a navigational and lookout point on trade routes between Chichén Itzá, Tulum, Cozumel, and Isla Mujeres.

The Spanish conquistadors' incursion in 1521 unsettled the entire peninsula. Despite many years of resistance from the native Maya, the Spaniards took control soon after the city of Mérida was founded in 1542, and the Maya who lived here became second-class citizens. Their status didn't improve after independence (1821), when they were virtually enslaved in debt peonage to the landowners, who used Maya workers to cultivate tobacco, sugarcane, and *henequén* (agave rope fiber known today as sisal). In 1847, the Maya rose in a bloody revolt that continued sporadically until 1901, when a tentative peace was established. Quintana Roo didn't come under official government control for another 30 years, and some of the territory's Maya still do not recognize Mexican sovereignty.

Despite this tragic and bloody history, it was to the Yucatán Peninsula that the Mexican government turned in 1968, when it decided to create a megaresort that would outshine Acapulco, the reigning beach destination. A computer analysis by the country's tourist development agency, FONATUR, came up with an island off the northeastern corner of the Caribbean coast, in the undeveloped federal territory of Quintana Roo (named after Andrés Quintana Roo, a Mexican loyalist influential in the War of Independence). Though bits of ancient Maya ruins dotted the scrub jungle and deserted shore, the only settlement in the 1960s was Puerto Juárez on the mainland, a fishing village with a few hundred residents.

# A Tale of Two Hurricanes

By 1988, when Hurricane Gilbert swept through, Cancún had more than 200,000 residents, with more than 12,000 hotel rooms and 11,000 more on the drawing boards. The storm's destruction barely slowed the explosive growth; existing resorts were promptly remodeled and reopened, followed by dozens of new ones. But the decision to slash hotel rates to lure tourists back, combined with the drinking age of 18, had the unintended effect of making Cancún the spring-break capital of North America. Images of binge-drinking college hordes replaced idyllic scenes of couples and families playing tag with impossibly turquoise waves.

Ironically, another—and far more destructive—hurricane was the occasion for turning this image around. On Oct. 18, 2005, Hurricane Wilma parked on top of the region, battering it with 240kmph (150mph) winds. The bridges linking the Hotel Zone with the island collapsed, electricity and water were out for 10 days, and the world's most celebrated beaches were scoured down to rock. Tens of thousands of tourists were stranded in shelters for as much as a week by the most destructive natural disaster in Mexican history, surpassing even the 1985 Mexico City earthquake.

The government, insurance companies, and major resort hotel chains mobilized a massive recovery effort. Restoration of more than 11km (7 miles) of white-powder beach with sand pumped 35km (22 miles) from the ocean bottom grabbed all the attention, but a more important transformation was in the works. Within 3 months, 18,000 of the 22,000 hotel rooms were ready for guests. Crews built new roads, installed better street lamps, planted thousands of palms, and installed modern sculptures. In rebuilding, in some cases from the ground up, resorts took pains to distance themselves from the spring-break crowd, going bigger, better, and more luxurious than ever, with price hikes to match.

Cancún (its Maya name, Kan Kun, means "nest of snakes") was an unlikely choice in some respects: 1,820km (1,131 miles) from Mexico City and 322km (200 miles) from Mérida, the nearest major city; no real highway through the coastal marshes, mangroves, and virgin jungle; lack of capital and manpower. But it was close to some of the world's most famous Maya sites, and the natural beauty, most famously the magnificent, powder-fine beaches, was a certain draw. And its northern location made it an easy trip for snowbirds from the U.S. East Coast.

Construction began in 1970 on the bridges that now link Cancún Island, then a deserted sandbar studded by coconut palms, to the mainland. The government filled in part of Nichupté Lagoon to make room to build roads and hotels, then built a downtown and an airport on the mainland. The island's tourism zone—the Zona Hotelera—was built without permanent residential areas, focusing on hotels, shopping centers, golf courses, and marinas. The urban area was built on the mainland north of the island to house construction workers.

Quintana Roo became a state in 1974, the year the first resort hotels opened. By 1976, Cancún was firmly established in the tourism firmament, with 18,000 inhabitants, 1,500 hotel rooms, and 100,000 visitors. Despite natural disasters, a national depression leading to the 1982 peso devaluation, and the tourism slump following the September 11, 2001, terrorist attacks in the U.S., Cancún has repeatedly bounced back to prosper anew. Financial crises in 1982 and 1994 drew even more international tourists taking advantage of the favorable exchange rates; when hurricanes struck, Cancún rebuilt on an even grander scale.

## LAY OF THE LAND

There are really two Cancúns: Ciudad Cancún on the mainland, and the island's Zona Hotelera, or Hotel Zone.

In Ciudad Cancún, the area of interest to tourists is downtown, roughly 9 square blocks known as El Centro. Most of its moderately priced hotels, restaurants, shops, pharmacies, dentists, banks, travel and airline agencies, and rental-car firms are within walking distance of one another. The wide main street, Avenida Tulum, is an extension of Hwy. 307, the main coastal highway that travels south through the Riviera Maya to the state capital of Chetumal near the Belize border. Heading north on Avenida Tulum leads to Hwy. 180 to Mérida, the road to Puerto Juárez and the Isla Mujeres ferries.

Avenida Tulum is studded by traffic circles where major streets veer off to other neighborhoods. (Take the wrong exit on one of these circles and within minutes you're miles away from where you wanted to be.) At one of those circles, Avenida Cobá crosses Tulum and soon becomes Bulevar Kukulcán, the main artery through the Zona Hotelera.

The 23km-long (14-mile) island where the Hotel Zone is located is shaped like the number seven and separated from the mainland by Laguna Nichupté

---

### Coming or Going?

Finding an address in Cancún can be a challenge, so study a map and get precise directions before attempting to find a building for the first time.

Rather than the traditional Mexican city built around a central plaza, Ciudad Cancún was designed as a collection of *supermanzanas* (subdivisions) separated by large avenues, each with its own parks. Many addresses still include the number of the building lot and *supermanzana*. Even more confounding, many streets actually are pairs of parallel streets with the same name.

Few of the Zona Hotelera's resorts and businesses have numbered addresses. The vast majority are on Bulevar Kukulcán, so their location is described in relation to their distance, from 2 to 22km, from the boulevard's northern end in Ciudad Cancún. Fortunately, the boulevard's central divider displays markers at nearly every kilometer. Not so fortunately, several buildings will have the same address, and when you encounter an address like Km 12.5, you're in for some guesswork. The eagle-eyed have the advantage.

(Nichupté Lagoon). It is attached to the mainland by two bridges, Puente Nichupté in the north and Puente Nizuc in the south. Bulevar Kukulcán, a four-lane divided avenue, continues eastward (along the top of the seven of the island shape) for several miles, passing condominium complexes, hotels, and shopping complexes, until it reaches Punta Cancún (Cancún Point) and the Centro de Convenciones (Convention Center).

From Punta Cancún, Kukulcán shoots south for 13km (8 miles). The sandy spit is so narrow that it required tons of landfill to make room for even this one road; you could see the Caribbean on one side and Nichupté Lagoon on the other if it weren't for the mammoth hotels, shopping centers, restaurants, bars, and dance clubs flanking the boulevard. At Punta Nizuc (Nizuc Point, home to Club Med), Kukulcán jogs west and rejoins the mainland, crossing Hwy. 307 and cutting through light tropical forest before ending at Cancún International Airport.

# GETTING TO & AROUND CANCUN

## BY AIR

All major U.S. and Canadian airlines, as well as Mexicana and Aeromexico, Mexico's international carriers, fly to **Cancún International Airport,** a modern and constantly expanding facility. Connecting service is offered from almost every city in North America, and nonstops (usually, but not always, more expensive) take off from all major hubs. Many airlines add nonstop flights and increase the frequency of service during winter months. Several European and South American airlines also offer nonstop or connecting flights.

Prices vary by season (and for other nebulous reasons), but the intense competition generated by Mexico's second-busiest airport means that even in high season flying to Cancún is cheaper than flying anywhere else in the country, with the occasional exception of Mexico City. With airfares fluctuating minute to minute, it's folly to try to predict prices, but for purposes of comparison, the lowest available fares for one-stop, round-trip flights to Cancún in December 2008 when booked at least a month in advance ranged from $228 to $380 from five cities across the United States. Nonstop flights, when available, were $340 to $406. Just to make things more confusing, fares usually drop during high season (except over the Christmas holidays) because of increased competition.

The best way to cut air costs is to abandon the weekend-to-weekend vacation mentality, if at all feasible. Fares are lower on Tuesday, Wednesday, and Thursday than they are the rest of the week—sometimes startlingly lower. For several recent trips from the West Coast to Cancún, I found the difference between booking on Saturday and booking on Wednesday, when fares tend to bottom out, was at least $150. In one case, the spread was $425. And if you can tolerate an overnight flight, you'll usually find the fares lower than on daytime or early-evening flights. See chapter 8 for information on where to book flights.

### Getting to & from the Airport

If you aren't renting a car, you can book authorized taxi, shuttle, or private-car service to Cancún or the Riviera Maya through the airport website with a credit card or PayPal (www.cancun-airport.com/transportation.htm). You can buy a ticket when you arrive, but you'll likely have to wait longer, and you will pay more; online reservations are discounted 10%. The most economical option, shared van **shuttles** that leave daily every 20 minutes from 7am to 11pm, are available only by advance reservation and often sell out a week in advance. Shuttles cost $9 to Cancún (30–45 min.) and $23 to $35 to the Riviera Maya. **Taxis** to Cancún are quicker (about 30 min.) because they don't have to make multiple stops and cost $41 for one or two people or $45 for three or four. If your plans allow you to buy a round-trip taxi ticket, you'll save 25% over the cost of two separate one-way trips. **Private vans** cost $45 (round-trip $68) for three to seven passengers, $50 (round-trip $86) for eight to ten. Only the authorized transportation companies are allowed to pick up passengers at the airport, and if you haven't booked ahead, the only way to hire one is by buying a fixed-rate ticket at the taxi counter. You can pay for your taxi or private van in U.S. dollars or pesos.

## GETTING AROUND

Three words about driving in Cancún: Just say no. Downtown is a nightmare of congested traffic circles and badly marked one-way streets with eager police lurking in the shadows. The Hotel Zone, with basically only one road, is simpler but presents its own logistical quagmire, and congestion is only part of it. There are no left turns and no going around the block if you miss your destination on the first pass; you have to find the right *retorno* and double back—sometimes more than once, if you don't know exactly where you're going.

Most people who spend their entire vacation in Cancún find that they can see and do everything they wish by simply relying on public transportation (see below), taxis (p. 16), and their own two feet. But if you're planning to explore further than Cancún, renting a car will allow you to see more and do it on your own schedule. All the major rental companies have stalls inside the airport terminal.

### By Bus

Cancún's public bus system, one of the best in Mexico, should be the basis of your transportation strategy, augmented by an occasional taxi ride. Buses are in good repair, cost just 6.50 pesos (less than 65¢), run every few minutes, and are reasonably quick. The Hotel Zone, especially, is a snap to navigate, since Bulevar Kukulcán is the only route. Downtown's more complex, but virtually everything you'll want to see is within walking distance once you get to Avenida Tulum. If you're lucky, an impromptu serenade will break out during your ride.

**Routes 1 and 2** run between the Hotel Zone and Avenida Tulum. From the Hotel Zone, R-1 runs north along Tulum to Puerto Juárez, the Isla Mujeres ferry terminal; R-2 crosses Tulum and ends at Mercado 28 downtown. Buses heading from downtown to the island display a "Zona Hotelera" sign. For short trips within the Hotel Zone, you can also try other routes, which turn off before going downtown. Bus stops, usually displaying a blue sign with a picture of a bus, line Bulevar Kukulcán and the major downtown streets. If you see the bus you want coming when you're between signs, the driver will usually stop if you wave. You're expected to pay with peso coins, but the driver might accept a dollar bill in a pinch (you won't get change). Keep your ticket in case you are asked for it later.

Ideally, you'll know where your destination is so you can watch for it through the window. If the driver isn't slowing to a stop as you approach, move to the door and pull the ringer cord—or just yell *"Alto"* ("Stop"). If you don't know where your stop is, ask the driver as you board and he'll call it out—if he remembers. If you know some basic Spanish, ask other riders if they know where your stop is.

## By Taxi

At certain times, a taxi makes the most sense—you're loaded down with snorkeling gear; you need to get from the disco to your hotel at the south end of the island at 4am; you have no idea how to get to that great little restaurant you heard about. Always agree on the fare before getting into the car. Prices are set by zone, but where one zone ends and another begins isn't easy for a visitor to discern. In the Hotel Zone, local residents pay about half of what tourists pay, and guests at higher-priced hotels pay about twice what those in budget hotels are charged. This isn't chicanery, but the official rate structure set by the taxi union.

Most hotels post fares so you know what you should be paying. Drivers are required to carry a rate card in their taxi, so if you aren't sure what you are being charged (or why), ask to see it. Minimum fares within the Hotel Zone are about 500 pesos ($5) and go up to about 1,000 pesos ($10); rides within the downtown zone cost about 15 pesos ($1.50) but go up to 500 pesos ($5) if you cross into another zone. It costs an average of 700 pesos ($7) to go between downtown and the Hotel Zone. Taxis also have an hourly rate for travel within Cancún, and there's some room for negotiation. If you're planning just one or two excursions outside the city, hiring a taxi by the hour or day will usually cost less than renting a car.

# ACCOMMODATIONS, BOTH STANDARD & NOT

The **Zona Hotelera**—which was, after all, created to lure upscale travelers and has attained ever more extravagant heights with post-Wilma development—can bruise the budget, but it is possible to soften the blow. Booking a package that bundles together the costs of airfare and hotel can reduce hotel tabs to manageable proportions, as can traveling in low season. Renting an apartment or condo may be an even better solution. Not only do they usually cost less than a hotel—especially for families and groups—but the kitchens in these rentals allow you to rein in food costs by preparing some of your own meals.

To find the kinds of bargain prices Mexico is known for, head for town. **El Centro** offers comfortable, moderately priced hotels, and other lodgings. You give up the beachfront convenience, but you gain an interlude among the people who actually live in Cancún, a more adventurous mix of bars and restaurants, and lower prices for everything you do.

## AIR/HOTEL PACKAGES

Cancún is prime territory for package deals, and they should be your starting point. Even in the unlikely event that you don't find one that meets your needs—solo travelers, in particular, usually won't benefit from packages, which are based on double occupancy—it will give you a point of comparison when shopping for prices. The basic package includes airfare and hotel, with the option of adding rental cars, airport transfers, tours, sports activities, and travel insurance for less than the price of purchasing them separately. Contrary to common wisdom, the percentage of savings over published rates booked separately tends to be greatest during high season. This is when competing airlines add seasonal service and

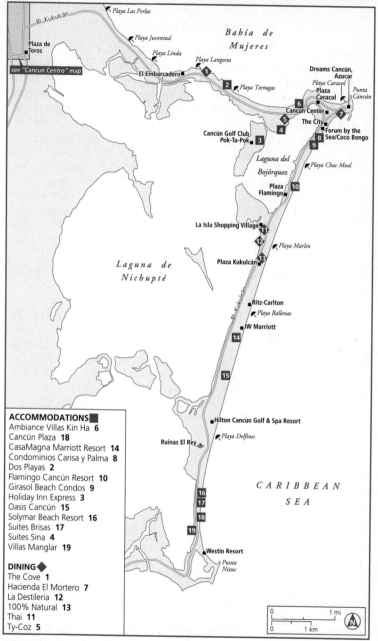

Playa Las Perlas

Bl. Kulkulcán

Playa Juventud

**Plaza de Toros**

*see "Cancun Centro" map*

Playa Linda

Playa Langosta

**El Embarcadero**

*Bahía de Mujeres*

Playa Tortugas

**Dreams Cancún, Azucar**
Playa Caracol
**Plaza Caracol**
Punta Cancún

**Cancún Center**
**The City**
**Forum by the Sea/Coco Bongo**

**Cancún Golf Club Pok-Ta-Pok**

*Laguna del Bojórquez*

Playa Chac Mool

**Plaza Flamingo**

**La Isla Shopping Village**

Playa Marlin

**Plaza Kukulcán**

*Laguna de Nichupté*

Bl. Kulkulcán

**Ritz-Carlton**
Playa Ballenas
**JW Marriott**

**Hilton Cancún Golf & Spa Resort**
Playa Delfines
**Ruinas El Rey**

*CARIBBEAN SEA*

**Westin Resort**
Punta Nizuc

## ACCOMMODATIONS ■
Ambiance Villas Kin Ha **6**
Cancún Plaza **18**
CasaMagna Marriott Resort **14**
Condominios Carisa y Palma **8**
Dos Playas **2**
Flamingo Cancún Resort **10**
Girasol Beach Condos **9**
Holiday Inn Express **3**
Oasis Cancún **15**
Solymar Beach Resort **16**
Suites Brisas **17**
Suites Sina **4**
Villas Manglar **19**

## DINING ◆
The Cove **1**
Hacienda El Mortero **7**
La Destileria **12**
100% Natural **13**
Thai **11**
Ty-Coz **5**

0    1 mi
0    1 km

## Parsing Packages

Not all packages are created equal. So it's extremely important to read all the fine print and make comparisons before booking. Some suggestions on how to proceed:

1. **When looking at different companies online, make sure that you're making an "apples-to-apples" comparison.** Go all the way through to the booking page to get the true rate. Prices on the initial search page usually don't include mandatory taxes and fees.

2. **To save the most, don't futz around with the package.** If you search for a different flight than the one included in the initial offer, it often increases the cost. Upgrading to a better room category certainly will; initial price quotes are always for the most basic rooms.

3. **Carefully reread the package inclusions before turning over your credit card number.** Some packages include airport transfers or some form of travel insurance at no extra cost, but most don't. An insidious ploy of some packagers is to add these or other extras, along with their additional charges, by default. If you don't want the extras, it's up to you to remove them.

4. **Move quickly.** The price you're looking at is good only for that instant in time. Because of changes in airfares or hotel occupancy rates, you could see a different price if you go back to the site an hour later; the price might even be updated while you are looking at it. A package can disappear altogether if the hotel has filled up. Since different packages are based on different flights, the best deal one minute can be a runner-up the next. Once you've narrowed down the contenders, run a quick double-check—then grab it.

sharply elevated room rates allow for more discounts. And purchasing a package may be the only way to obtain flights and rooms that are otherwise sold out.

Lodging available through travel packages ranges from generic all-inclusives to exclusive luxury resorts, varying by company, season, and availability. Travel agents can book package trips, and they have access to some deals from wholesalers that aren't available to individual travelers. GoGo Worldwide Vacations, for example, sells only through agents and has some exclusive deals with hotels and resorts that aren't available through direct-to-public packagers. For most of the major packagers, though, you'll save money by booking them yourself.

Some packagers consistently offer better savings than others, and within each company some deals are better than others. There's only one way to determine how much of a bargain any particular deal is: Compare the total package price—including taxes and fees, which often aren't quoted upfront—with prices available directly through the hotel's and airline's websites. Even when the saving is minimal, you'll benefit from the convenience, access to an agent if something goes

# Cancún El Centro

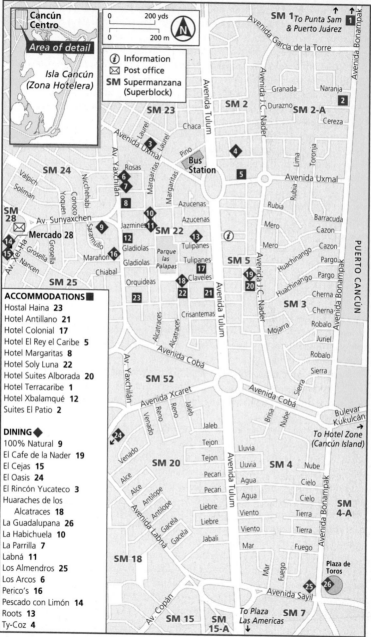

**Cancún Centro**
Area of detail
Isla Cancún (Zona Hotelera)

0 — 200 yds
0 — 200 m

N

*(i)* Information
✉ Post office
**SM** Supermanzana (Superblock)

To Punta Sam & Puerto Juárez
SM 1

Avenida García de la Torre
Avenida Bonampak

Avenida J.C. Nader
Granada    Naranja
Durazno    **SM 2-A**
Cereza

Avenida Tulum
**SM 2**

**SM 23**
Chaca
Pino
**Bus Station**

Avenida Uxmal

Lima    Toronja
Rubia    Rubia    Barracuda
Mero    Cazon
Mero    Cazon
Huachinango    Pargo
Pargo
Huachinango
Cherna
Cherna
Mojarra    Robalo
Juriel
Robalo
Sierra

PUERTO CANCÚN

**SM 24**
Valpich    Nichchehabi
Soliman    Yoquen    Conoco
Rosas
Avenida Uxmal
Margaritas    Margaritas
Azucenas
Azucenas
Jazmines
Gladiolas
Gladiolas
Orquideas
Crisantemas

Avenida J.C. Nader

**SM**
**28**
✉
Mercado 28
Av. Sunyaxchen
Saramullo
Grosella
Av. Grosella
Av. Nancen
Marañon
Chiabal
**SM 25**

Av. Yaxchilán

Marañon
**SM 22**
Parque las Palapas
Tulipanes
Tulipanes
Claveles

**SM 5**
**SM 3**

**ACCOMMODATIONS** ■
Hostal Haina **23**
Hotel Antillano **21**
Hotel Colonial **17**
Hotel El Rey el Caribe **5**
Hotel Margaritas **8**
Hotel Soly Luna **22**
Hotel Suites Alborada **20**
Hotel Terracaribe **1**
Hotel Xbalamqué **12**
Suites El Patio **2**

**DINING** ◆
100% Natural **9**
El Cafe de la Nader **19**
El Cejas **15**
El Oasis **24**
El Rincón Yucateco **3**
Huaraches de los Alcatraces **18**
La Guadalupana **26**
La Habichuela **10**
La Parrilla **7**
Labná **11**
Los Almendros **25**
Los Arcos **6**
Perico's **16**
Pescado con Limón **14**
Roots **13**
Ty-Coz **4**

Av. Yaxchilán
Alcatraces    Alcatraces
Avenida Coba

**SM 52**
Avenida Xcaret
Reno    Reno    Jaleb
Venado
Jaleb
Venado
Tejon
Tejon
Alce    Alce
Antilope    Antilope
Avenida Labná
Gacela    Gacela
Avenida Copán
**SM 18**
**SM 20**

Avenida Tulum

Lluvia
Lluvia    **SM 4**    Nube
Pecari    Agua    Cielo
Pecari    Agua    Cielo
Liebre    Viento    Tierra
Liebre    Viento    Tierra
Jabali    Viento    Tierra
Mar    Fuego

Avenida Cobá
Birsa    Nube
Sierra

Bulevar Kukulcán →
To Hotel Zone (Cancún Island)

Avenida Bonampak

**SM**
**4-A**

Mar    Fuego
Plaza de Toros
Avenida Sayil
**SM 7**
**SM 15**    **SM 15-A**
To Plaza Las Americas ↓

wrong when you're on foreign soil, and any extras the company includes, such as airport transfers. For greatest savings, look for last-minute deals and other specials.

Vacation packages are available from specialized vacation companies, airlines and the Big Three (Expedia, Orbitz, and Travelocity) online booking agencies. The listings that follow are all established, reputable firms, and their deals run the gamut from great values to overpriced. They appear in order of average savings per night for a couple, based on my research of air/hotel packages offered from New York in spring and fall, compared with the cost of booking the same flights and rooms separately on airline and hotel websites.

**BookIt.com** (☎ 888/782-9722; www.bookit.com) came out on top with an average saving for a couple of $121 per night over separate direct bookings. The average doesn't tell the whole story, though. For spring trips booked less than a month in advance, the average saving was a whopping $244 per night; in effect, the hotel room was usually free. On the other hand, deals for low-season stays booked 6 months ahead averaged out to about the same cost as separate direct bookings with the airlines and hotels. The website is quick and easy to use, and ample property details on the search page reduce the clicking around required to decide which to select for further investigation. This site offers the widest range of choices for all-inclusive resorts, which dominate the listings.

**Expedia** (☎ 800/397-3342; www.expedia.com), with an average savings of $92, did the best of the Big Three online travel agencies. Flights bundled with the hotels were among the least expensive available from any of the packagers, resulting in lower total package prices. The site strong-arms you into disabling all your browser's privacy filters, which is annoying. Once you comply, though, it runs smoothly and allows you to sort search results in a variety of ways, including previous travelers' ratings.

**Mexicana Vacations** (☎ 800/380-8781; www.mexicanavacations.com), which turned up average savings of $89 a night per couple, is the best of the airline vacation sites, which generally are hobbled by a limited pool of hotels and the sometimes tortuous itineraries required to get you to your destination on their routes. The Mexican carrier's packages offer good flight schedules and plenty of hotel choices across the whole price spectrum. **Aeromexico Getaways** (☎ 800/676-0820; www.aeromexico.com) offers a similar lineup of packages—in fact, it uses the same booking engine—but with a few exceptions, its prices are higher.

**American Airlines Vacations** (☎ 800/321-2121; www.aavacations.com) did almost as well, saving an average of $74 a night. As the U.S. airline with the greatest number of flights to Latin America, it comes up with reasonable itineraries and has nearly as many hotels to choose from as Mexicana. Fewer of American's choices fall into in the budget category, though.

**Orbitz** (☎ 800/504-3248; www.orbitz.com), whose packages also saved an average of $74, offers more choices than the airlines do, both in flight schedules and hotels. Its packages include a couple of inexpensive downtown hotels that most U.S. packagers don't offer. The website has a nifty feature that allows you to enter a hotel name on the initial search form if you are interested in a specific property. Orbitz sporadically tacks on its own special offers, such as 25% early-booking discounts or 10% to 20% off food and beverages.

**Apple Vacations** (☎ 800/517-2000; www.applevacations.com) produced an average savings of $6 per night but did very well from the West Coast of the U.S., averaging $47 savings from San Francisco. Formerly available only through travel agents, the major player in Cancún packages now offers online booking direct to the public. Though its website is painfully slow, it offers a better than average range of accommodations, from popular lower-priced properties (including a few in El Centro) to luxury icon Ritz-Carlton. Airport transfers are included in the package price, another nice plus. An added bonus: Apple representatives are available at most departure airports to help with check-in and also in Cancún, where they provide destination briefings, and are available throughout your stay to make sure all goes as planned.

**Vacation Travel Mart** (☎ 800/288-1435; www.vacmart.com) is another example of a company that may better serve travelers in the Western and Midwestern U.S. than on the East Coast. Its deals also saved an average of $31 per night from New York City, but $41 from San Francisco. Its deals are skewed toward midrange and high-end properties. Nearly half of the packages listed require you to call for prices. The option of placing a 24-hour hold on a reservation before paying is a nice touch, but the website is a little clunky. Cancún packages are mixed in with Riviera Maya properties, with no option for sorting them, and hotel information doesn't include an address or map; the "location" section is basically a promotional blurb.

**Funjet Vacations** (☎ 888/558-6654; www.funjet.com), with average savings of $41, is prolific, often turning up more than 100 package options per search. It's one of only two sites that display the total cost, including taxes, upfront (airport transfers included in the price). It has some annoying quirks, though: A $200 insurance policy is added to every package by default, and it's easy to overlook until you get to the checkout page. Also, some packages use overnight flights, putting you on the ground the morning *after* you're supposed to check in to your hotel. It does adjust the check-in date—changing the length and cost of your stay—after you get to the final booking page. By then, you've wasted a lot of effort trying to fix things with the "change flight" option, which invariably adds to the total cost.

**Best Day Travel** (☎ 800/593-6259; www.bestday.com) packages offered average savings of $31 per night. It has the most extensive selection of hotels I've seen, including many budget properties that other packagers don't offer, so you could end up spending considerably less for your vacation here than with packagers offering greater nightly savings at more expensive properties. The zippy site also includes a precise and easy-to-read map for every property. Unfortunately, Riviera Maya destinations are mixed in with the Cancún packages; with more than 100 pages of results, that means a lot of sifting.

## CONDOS & VACATION RENTALS

With their extra space and layouts more like home, condos are especially suited to families and groups, or for longer stays. Most are in massive, beachfront highrises with restaurants, swimming pools, bars, gyms, and activities (watersports usually carry an extra charge). While decor varies—most online agencies provide plenty of photos—you can expect ocean or lagoon views, air-conditioning, fully equipped kitchens, and cable TV. Some also have telephones, dishwashers, DVD players, stereos, or computers with Internet access. As a bonus, homeowners and rental agents often provide local tips you wouldn't get from staying in a hotel.

## Your Home Away from Home

Most budget-priced condos are in older high-rise buildings, the bulk of them in the more peaceful southern half of the Hotel Zone. Though they cut a less than graceful profile on the Cancún skyline, they may boast lush landscaping and gorgeous beaches; aesthetics and upkeep of individual units vary. Pricing also can be quixotic, as owners charge different rates depending on the view, the number of guests, and their own estimation of the unit's desirability. Expect to pay about $60 to $110 a night for a studio in low season, $80 to $160 in high season. One-bedroom units can start at about $45 to $71 a night, but average $135 to $170 a night. Two bedrooms generally start at $115 and average about $155 in low season, $185 in high season. When you get into three- and four-bedroom units, which start at about $250 to $350, many of the offerings are pricey penthouses and villas, which pushes the average cost to about $360 a night in low season and $525 high, but some can sleep 10 people comfortably. (Don't take owners' statements of sleeping capacity at face value; get specifics on square footage, layout, and available beds, then decide for yourself.) Nightly prices at the low end of these ranges are usually for weekly rentals, and some are rented only by the week. You might find room for negotiation if your trip is beginning within a few weeks; owners would rather rent at a lower rate than have their condos stand empty.

Some of the buildings with affordable condos include:

**Solymar Beach Resort** ★★★ (Bl. Kukulcán Km 18.7; ☎ 998/885-1811; www.solymarcancun.com), sprawling along the island's southern reaches, is a condotel with 245 rooms, studios, and multistory villas. The roomy condos, separate from and a distinct cut above the hotel operation, are well managed by several private owner associations that work to ensure renters get a unit that meets their needs. The condos tend to be bright and contemporary, with bold color accents and some traditional touches. Most have generous balconies. Some of the owners live on-site year-round and keep a close eye on things, functioning as concierges, socializing with guests, and creating an unusual sense of community. A staggered stairway leads to the beach through lush grounds that include an infinity pool and forever views of the Caribbean. The hotel offers condo renters an all-inclusive option, which I'd skip in favor of sampling better food at Cancún's diverse restaurants.

**Girasol Beach Condos** ★★ (Bl. Kukulcán Km 9.5; ☎ 998/883-5045), one of Cancún's first condotels, is a V-shaped tower firmly rooted in the 1980s. The lobby could use some sprucing up, but its large, clean hotel-type rooms and condos with well-equipped kitchenettes are quite pleasant. A typical studio layout includes a small galley kitchen, a king or queen bed and a double futon, a dinette set tucked in a corner, and a divided bathroom. Generally, you'll find fresh paint and tile; the best units may have sponge-painted walls, modern bathrooms, and marble or granite counters. Decor ranges from clean, modern lines to fussy pink satin bedspreads. All units have large balconies with views over one of Cancún's most stunning beaches. The staff is efficient and congenial, and the grounds include a wading and an infinity pool, a soccer field, and tennis courts.

**Suites Brisas** ★ (Bl. Kukulcán Km 19.5; ☎ 998/885-0302; www.suites brisas.com), a relatively small, low-rise building at the southern end of the island between the Hilton and Club Med, rents one- and two-bedroom condos with no pretensions to luxury. Most are clean and well kept, though occasional problems with jammed doors or ant invasions have been known to occur. Some go for tropical flair, with sunny colors and lots of rattan, while others sport white walls and Danish modern furniture. A delightful, plant-filled terrace nook may appear in the same unit that has dated kitchens and loud flowered curtains. The front of the building sits close to Bulevar Kukulcán and gets some traffic noise, but the other side overlooks a long, white stretch of beach.

**Cancun Plaza** (Bl. Kukulcán Km 20.5; ☎ 998/885-0072; www.cancun plaza.com), a fading, vaguely Mediterranean-style six-story building on the same stretch of beach as the Suites Brisas, has about 150 utilitarian units with a hint of Motel 6 about them. These often appear at the low end of the price range, perhaps because not all have kitchens or balconies (though all rooms have ocean views). Beds range from sublime to lumpy. Showers don't always get as hot as you'd like, and the walls are thin, but rooms are cleaned and towels are replaced every day. And the big pool has a large wading area ideal for small children. Cancun Plaza has no front desk. Upkeep is dependent on individual owners; get references and do some research before booking.

**Condominios Carisa y Palma** (Bl. Kukulcán Km 9.5; ☎ 998/883-0211; www.carisaypalma.com) is a pair of imposing towers in the midst of Punta Cancún's clubs and restaurants. All units have private terraces with ocean or lagoon views, though the latter are subject to the sounds of revelry until early morning. Most units are large, clean, and in good repair, whether they have airy modern motifs with rattan furniture and stainless-steel kitchens or college-dorm white walls and furniture. Some kitchens are larger than others; ask questions and compare photos if this is important to you. Although it stands on the same beach and has the same magnificent views as the Girasol next door, it seems to have more problems with loud air-conditioning, malfunctioning toasters or lights, and tour and timeshare hustlers. This complex is best suited to visitors planning to spend their vacation on the beach by day and in the clubs by night.

*One note:* The line between hotels and vacation rentals in Cancún is a blurry one. While some properties offer condos and villas exclusively, many are "condotels"—a hybrid that looks and feels like a traditional hotel but sells studio to four-bedroom condos to private owners in addition to renting standard hotel rooms. The condos may go into a hotel-managed rental pool when the owners aren't staying there, but some owners list them with agencies, rent them directly through their own efforts, or form associations to handle rentals. Thus, the same unit might be offered through multiple sources. In any case, you'll pay for overnight stays (or, in some cases, weekly or monthly stays) just as in a traditional hotel and when your condo is in a hotel, you get the benefit of the hotel facilities, maid service, and even room service.

When renting through an online agency, you typically view photos and descriptions, choose the condo and dates you are interested in, and submit a request. The agency will respond with more details. You should expect plenty of photos, with a full description of the property, including exact location, and the agency's services. The best impose high maintenance standards, offer an orientation upon arrival, and provide contact information in case you need help.

Allow plenty of time to make arrangements. Response to e-mail can take several days and might not come at all. Some of the blame falls on the vagaries of Mexican e-mail systems (sending your own e-mail rather than using a website form is usually more reliable), but I've also learned that e-mails written in English may simply be ignored if the staff member who catches it speaks only Spanish. If you have any doubts about the transaction, follow up with a phone call. International calls can be expensive, so it's a bonus if the agency has a U.S. number. And consider it a red flag if no phone number is provided.

## Condo Clearinghouses

Among the dozens of mostly reliable online sources of budget-priced condo rentals, the following stand out for their quick responses and personalized service.

Some of the best deals come from **Cancún Condos** (☎ 786/533-2721 U.S., 998/206-3521 Mexico; www.cancun-condos.net), one of several owners' associations at Solymar Beach Resort (p. 22) which books condos in other properties as well (see below). Its members are well familiar with each of the 90 condos they manage. Accurate photos on the website show a sample of each type of condo; when you decide what you want, a coordinator quickly sends pictures of the best currently available units and then works with you to choose the right one for your needs. At the low end of the price range—$59 in low season, $75 high—are lagoon-side studios with a double bed and a futon. With bed space for four, this would work for a family but would squeeze four adults. The considerably roomier master suites ($99–$169 a night) would be comfortable for four adults. Penthouses ($129–$259) easily accommodate up to eight people, while a villa of palatial proportions ($250–$350) can sleep 10. Christmas and Easter week rates are about 25% higher and carry a 15% surcharge for stays of less than 4 nights. The association monitors each unit to be sure it is painted, the furniture is in good shape, and everything works. They also only work with condos that have ocean or lagoon views, fully equipped kitchenettes, safety boxes, phones, and cable or satellite TV. Cleaning services are provided every other day. The association's office at the complex is staffed daily 9am to 6pm.

Cancún Condos also has connections with Cancun Plaza, where it rents studios and master suites for similar rates, and at Suites El Patio, a sweet little downtown guesthouse (see "Hotels: El Centro" on p. 30). You'll get kitchenettes rather than full kitchens, but prices are just $29 to $40 a night in low season, $33 to $50 high.

For a wider variety of vacation rentals in all price ranges, **Cancún Hideaways** (☎ 817/468-0564 U.S., www.cancun-hideaways.com) is a fine option—it manages units in five Hotel Zone complexes and four downtown (which require minimum rentals of 2 weeks or more). Owner Maggie Rodriguez, who was born in Mexico and lived in Cancún when it was still growing into Mexico's top destination, has run a travel agency out of Arlington, Texas, for 18 years. She now spends most of her time in Cancún, living and conducting business out of the vacant condos to make sure they are "like brand new" before being rented again, right down to the leaky faucets and nonfunctioning outlets that renters neglect to report. She owns some of the condos herself, while others are owned by family members and friends.

The latest addition to Rodriguez's lineup is an amazing deal: $560 for 2 weeks or less in brand-new, two-bedroom, two-bathroom condos at Puerto Cancún, the luxury development rising along the Bahía de Mujeres downtown. The "city within a city" is destined to become a Hotel Zone in itself, with resorts, residences, a marina, shopping center, golf course, and ecological reserve. Minimum rental is 2 weeks, but even if you actually stay for only 1, you'll beat the cost of staying in most hotels. Many of Rodriguez's renters are retirees who rent by the month, but she also offers nightly rates at the Solymar (p. 22; studios $55–$149, penthouse $129–$240, villa $250–$450) and the Royal Mayan (doubles $90–$140, four-person suites $150–$310, six-person villas $215–$485), an older but top-rated condotel in the middle of the island that has a little Maya ruin at its doorstep.

A realty firm with its office in the Hotel Zone, **Cancún Prime Realty** (☎ 998/883-0111; www.cancunprimerealty.com), primarily handles property sales but also lists vacation rentals for owners who are not using them. The company works with local property management companies that advise owners on furnishing their condos, inspect each one before guests arrive, and are available to renters during their stay. The offerings change constantly, but in recent listings the best deals were for roomy two-bedroom or larger apartments that families or groups can share for as little as $25 per person per night. For less than $45 per person in low season, up to 10 people can share a four-bedroom, four-bathroom, upper-floor condo in the Portofino at Punta Cancún, the Hotel Zone's newest luxury condominium complex, with sweeping ocean and lagoon views, an outdoor whirlpool overlooking the Caribbean, a washer and dryer, and a stainless-steel kitchen with granite countertops and double sinks. Prices for studios at the Suites Brisas (p. 23), the Carisa y Palma, and the Dos Playas condotel ($70 a night in low season to $170 over Christmas) tend to be slightly higher than you can find elsewhere.

## Going Direct to the Source

Services that allow private owners to bypass agents and rent directly to the public are becoming increasingly important to the Cancún condo-rental scene. Prices are sometimes lower, especially on "rental by owner" sites where you'll most likely find that rare detached home in the Hotel Zone or a house next to a downtown park. But you might encounter problems with upkeep, as no outside source inspects the properties or imposes any standards for furnishings or maintenance. Still, you can sometimes find excellent deals at the following sites, which charge owners an annual fee, which at least filters out scammers and flakes.

**HomeAway** (www.homeaway.com) has by far the greatest number of listings in Cancún. Sprinkled among dozens of Cancún condos are a few downtown houses. One property is a modest, two-bedroom home with Maya design touches in a quiet residential area with a garden that opens onto a park, renting for $490 to $590 a week most of the year. Condo rates typically start at about $75 a night or $400 a week, though the majority are large or luxury units that top $3,000 a week. The site has ample photos, but descriptions don't divulge the address, and few tell you what building the condo is in. You'll need to contact the owner to get specifics. HomeAway is unique in providing reviews from previous renters for many listings. Since they were sent to the property owners, almost all tend to be positive, but they do provide further detail on the character of the place.

HomeAway also owns **VacationRentals.com** (www.vacationrentals.com), **Vacation Rentals by Owner** (www.vrbo.com), and several other vacation rental sites. These operations are analogous to classified ad listings, so it's up to you to contact the owners and make arrangements. The HomeAway agencies guarantee up to $5,000 of your payment if the listing turns out not to be legitimate, but any other problems are yours alone.

Cancún listings are less plentiful at **Owner Direct Vacation Rentals** (www.owner direct.com), but I've found beachfront studios for $78 a night or $550 a week and one-bedroom condos for as little as $125 a night or $650 a week. Some are in the same condo complexes that appear in agency listings, but many others are in more upscale developments. The same Maya-style house listed at HomeAway showed up here for $105 to $180 a night, as did a plain but bright two-bedroom house on the Pok-Ta-Pok golf course in the Hotel Zone for $175 a night. Owner Direct doesn't offer any guarantees, but it provides more hand-holding than most other services. Once you submit your request, the company's staff handles the inquiries and walks you through the entire transaction.

Of course, the elephant in the room is **Craig's List** (www.craigslist.org), the online behemoth that claims nine billion hits per month. To find condos on Craig's List, you must first chose a geographical area, go to the housing menu, and choose "Vacation Rentals." I have turned up a total of nearly 100 Cancún rentals by searching classified postings just from owners in Mexico, New York, Houston, and San Francisco Bay Area. ***Note:*** A search on "Cancún" will return results from Riviera Maya and other listings that mention Cancún in the description. The caveat here is that anyone can post for free and say anything he or she likes; it takes some investigation to figure out exactly what you're dealing with. Some good deals are out there, especially from timeshare holders staring at a deadline. But the fact is, prices fall into the same range you'll find through the online agencies, and the condos are in many of the same properties. Unlike the agency listings, they don't come with property inspections, quality control, customer service, or any kind of guarantee, which puts Craig's List in the last-resort category.

## Highs & Lows

Cancún and the Riviera Maya are notorious for wildly fluctuating prices, with low-season rates often dipping below half of the high-season rates. High season is roughly late December through March, with a sharp spike during Christmas and New Year's weeks. Low season is May through November or early December, with a more modest rise in July and August, when Mexicans and Europeans generally take long vacations. But each hotel has its own price structure, and some have as many as eight different price periods.

*Money-saving tip:* The period just before the high-priced Christmas holidays is the lowest season. Although some hotels boost prices in November (before an even more precipitous hike for Christmas and New Year's weeks), many charge their lowest rates until a few days before Christmas. Traveling on December 15 can cost half as much as going a week later. The weather won't be much different, and you'll be ahead of the crowds.

## BOOKING SERVICES

A plethora of travel information sites operate out of Cancún and offer reservations at a discount. All claim to have the most complete hotel listings and the best rates, but when it comes to reservations, the majority of them link to the same booking engine (another Cancún enterprise). I have used **Best Day Travel** (www.bestday.com) and have been happy with the service. Other sites include **Cancuntravel.com, DoCancun** (www.docancun.com), and **Cancun.com.**

The Cancún sites have a couple of advantages over the giants such as Hotels.com, which can usually—but not always—get you $5 to $15 off the hotel's published rates. With the rare exception, the local sites beat Hotel.com's rates by $10 to $30 a night and sometimes more. Just as important, they book many smaller, low-priced hotels that Hotels.com doesn't offer. You can usually expect to pay $5 to $30 a night less than published rates at a full range of Cancún hotels.

## HOTELS
### Zona Hotelera

Most Hotel Zone resorts belong to international hotel chains, ranging from Holiday Inn to Ritz-Carlton, and despite efforts to distinguish themselves in decor, landscaping, and service, a certain sameness pervades. Winter prices at these luxury properties generally run from about $200 to more than $500 a night (slightly discounted in the off season and for those who use packages), putting them beyond the range of most budget travelers. The island, however, does have some more modest hotels sprinkled among the showplaces.

**$–$$$**   The **Flamingo Cancún Resort** ★★ (Bl. Kukulcán Km 11, opposite Flamingo Plaza shopping center; ☎ 998/848-8870; www.flamingocancun.com; AE, MC, V), one of Cancún's best-known budget hotels, has something of a double personality. The "party zone" is the interior courtyard, dominated by a meandering pool with multiple bridges. This section, on the resort's Bulevar Kukulcán side, can feel hemmed in by the guestroom wings and crowded by the *palapa* bar where it's spring break every day. The "grown-up zone" is the newer, and quieter, part of the hotel on the ocean side. The spacious rooms are light and breezy, and the simple rectangular pool has plenty of breathing room. Whether you get an ocean, lagoon, or street view, though, is the luck of the draw. For the heart of the Hotel Zone, the Flamingo's 200 rooms qualifies as intimate, and even the published rates ($126–$179; $199 Christmas week) would be a bargain. But you can pretty much ignore the published rates, as rates with online booking engines start at only $79 in high season, and a multitude of package deals can bring the cost down to $30 a night or even less. An all-inclusive option costs about twice the standard plan for a double, and the food is better than at most budget all-inclusives.

**$$**   My favorite find in the Hotel Zone is **Suites Sina** ★★★ (Quetzal no. 33, Club de Golf; ☎ 998/883-1017; www.cancunsinasuites.com.mx; AE, MC, V), tucked away in a quiet residential neighborhood next to the Pok-Ta-Pok golf course. Most travelers aren't aware that, in addition to the suites, it also offers four basic but comfortable motel-type rooms that go for an unbelievable (for the Hotel Zone) $60 a night, year-round. They don't have the garden views, balconies, or terraces that the suites do, but the garden and pool are just down one flight of stairs. And lounging over a drink in the central garden on a sultry evening is a treat—the panorama of glittering resort palaces across Nichupté Lagoon looks like the landing of the mountainous space ship from *Close Encounters of the Third Kind*. Coming home to this oasis of calm makes you realize just how tumultuous the rest of the Hotel Zone is, yet restaurants, grocery stores, and a bus stop are a short walk away. If you decide to upgrade, the 33 well-furnished suites come complete with full kitchens and huge bedrooms. One-bedroom suites, which can sleep six, cost $120; two bedrooms are $160. Post-hurricane renovation added a pool bar (one drink included in price of stay) and a restaurant that serves breakfast ($6–$9) every day but Monday. The solicitous front-desk staff speaks English, and the owner lives on-site, which always makes a difference.

**$$–$$$**   Hidden away on the lagoon side at the quiet southern end of the Hotel Zone, **Villas Manglar** ★★★ 🄺 (Bl. Kukulcán Km 19; ☎ 998/885-1808; www.villasmanglar.com; MC, V) feels more like a private apartment complex than a hotel. It has managed to remain a fisherman's secret; if you're driving south, turn in at the Marina Manglar and head for the glass doors to the left of the 24-hour market. There's no hotel sign, but the fresh tile floor and vaulted beam ceilings are a giveaway. The two-story building, set below street level in a verdant tropical lagoon populated by ibis, spoonbills, white pelicans, and other wildlife, has eight large units surrounding a sparkling pool and a *palapa* where continental breakfast is served. Each large room has a king-size bed and two couches that can double as twin beds or be configured as another king, making Villas Manglar ideal for families with children. Rooms can also be connected for larger groups. This is one of the few budget hotels ($60–$120, depending on season) that has hair dryers and big thick towels. Fishing for tarpon, snook, and bonefish keep loyal guests coming back, so be sure to ask at the front desk about fishing and diving trips (p. 54).

**$$–$$$**   The best things about **Dos Playas** (Bl. Kukulcán Km 6.5; ☎ 998/849-4920; www.dosplayas.com; AE, MC, V) are the grounds, with palm- and *palapa*-studded lawns scored by flower-lined stone paths leading to a long, pretty public beach frequented by Cancún residents. The pool is clean but small for a 111-room hotel; lounge chairs and towel space are at a premium. The building itself is pure mid-century modern motel, and the rooms are hit or miss—some are perfectly adequate and well kept while others are dreary and in need of rehab. The friendly concierge staff, though, earns kudos for helpfulness. Published rates range from $91 low season to $121 high ($154 holidays), but the starting rate at most online booking agencies is around $65, and the hotel also shows up in a number of discount packages. The low rates draw young people who just want a cheap bed and shower and like having watersports and Isla Mujeres ferries at the embarcadero next door. If that describes you, Dos Playas will fit the bill. Just be prepared to assert yourself if you don't like the room you're assigned. Pass on the all-inclusive option; the mediocre food isn't worth the extra money.

**$$$** With its suburban shopping-mall architecture and standard motel layout, you wouldn't choose **Holiday Inn Express** ✸ (Paseo Pok-Ta-Pok 21–22; ☎ 800/000-0404 toll-free Mexico, or 998/883-2200; www.hiexpress.com; AE, DC, MC, V) for the classic Cancún experience, but it has virtues beyond a starting price of $81 (up to $124 in high season) for a double, including a buffet breakfast. Set in the residential area along the Pok-Ta-Pok golf course (guests get a discount) on the lagoon side of the island, the hotel is removed from Bulevar Kukulcán's congestion and provides free Wi-Fi and transportation to its beach club 5 minutes away. The 119 spacious rooms are bright and sleek, and all have balconies or terraces overlooking the garden with a large, gleaming pool as its centerpiece. This is reasonable alternative if you want plenty of creature comforts and prefer to digest the Cancún scene in small doses.

**$$$–$$$$** **Ambiance Villas Kin Ha** ✸✸✸ 🅺🅸🅳🅢 (Bl. Kukulcán Km 8.5; ☎ 866/340-9082 toll-free U.S., or 998/891-5400; www.ambiancevillas.com; AE, MC, V) is almost too good to be true. It sits an easy walk away from the heart of Bulevar Kukulcán's action on a large, seldom crowded beach, widely considered to be Cancún's finest. And it offers some of the largest and most comfortable lodging on the island for $97 to $140, depending on season, for a standard double room, including an ample buffet breakfast. Even better, when the hotel isn't full, potential guests who walk in or call can get last-minute promotions that aren't available even through the website; during high season, a $140 standard room was being offered for $90 to guests who could check in within the week. Ambiance Villas also appears in many package offerings, typically for $30 to $40 per night off rack rates. The bright rooms, simply decorated in light-wood furniture, all have balconies or patios. It has two restaurants, a lobby bar, boutique, convenience store, bilingual concierge service, and tour desk—all services not usually seen at these prices. Compared to its high-rise neighbors, Ambiance Villas' three stories of arched windows among palm trees rising from acres of lawn provide a breath of fresh air. This is a great place for families, with the wide beach, a large free-form pool with a large wading area, and free organized youth activities. The owners, who live on-site, discourage the spring break contingent. Huge (72–176 sq. m/775–1,895 sq. ft.) one- to three-bedroom suites with living and dining rooms and full modern kitchens are also available ($200–$897, depending on size and season).

**$$$–$$$$**   The all-inclusive **Oasis Cancún** 🧒 (Bl. Kukulcán Km 16.5, north of Grand Oasis; ☎ 998/287-3855; www.oasishotels.com; AE, MC, V), in the middle of the island's action zone, is the quintessential spring-break hotel and a constant presence on the packagers' lineups. Rack rates zigzag between $88 and $167 per adult throughout the year's eight pricing periods, though its Internet rates may vary $10 to $20 either way. Package deals can shave another $20 or so off the nightly rate. A huge (more than 700 rooms) complex of vaguely pyramid-shaped buildings with eight restaurants, nine bars, and one of Latin America's largest swimming pools, the Oasis is popular with young party types who are well into their first tequila before they reach the front of the check-in line. The somewhat dated rooms make a laudable attempt at Mexican color and decor. All have terraces or balconies with views of the Caribbean, the lagoon, or the meandering gardens, which connect the property to the more upscale Grand Oasis next door. If you avoid spring break, the resort's low prices, marina, nonstop activities, and long, long beach make it an option for families.

**$$$$**   For a taste of luxury without a fatal blow to the budget, my choice for a splurge would be **CasaMagna Marriott Resort** ★★ 🧒 (Bl. Kukulcán, Retorno Chac L-41; ☎ 998/881-2000; www.marriott.com; AE, DC, MC, V). Not only are its rates, at $160 to $256, at the bottom of the luxury range, but guests have use of the pools, gym, spa, and restaurants at its adjacent sister property, the sumptuous JW Marriott. Its own facilities are fine, but for a dose of real opulence, head next door to JW's three-level, Maya-inspired spa, which has a special kids' program, oceanview showers, and a fitness center where you can do your cardio facing sunrise over the ocean or sunset over the lagoon—if you can tear your gaze from your own individual plasma TV. One of JW's three free-form, oceanview pools is a 5.4m (18-ft.) PADI-certified pool with an artificial reef for scuba and snorkeling lessons. CasaMagna is tops for families: Kids stay free, and the Kid's Club for both Marriott properties ($25 a day, including lunch and a backpack) is at CasaMagna, offering sand-castle building, scavenger hunts, movies, and other activities every day from 10am to 4pm. Some packages make the CasaMagna a downright bargain, especially for last-minute bookings when the hotel isn't full. I've seen deals that reduce the price to as low as $83 a night, compared with the regular $245 rate, for an April stay booked less than 2 weeks in advance. The best deals for October stays booked 6 months in advance produced rates as low as $114 and $128 when the regular rate was $190.

## El Centro

The obvious drawback to staying downtown is that you're a 5- to 10-minute cab or bus ride from the beach, though some larger hotels offer privileges at Hotel Zone beach clubs. The advantage is that you can easily find comfortable digs in smaller, locally owned hotels for as little as $50 to $75 a night. Meals, groceries, cab rides, Internet cafes, tours, exchange rates (at banks and shops), and other services also cost correspondingly less than in the Hotel Zone. And it's refreshing to be in a city built for residents instead of made to order for tourists.

As is generally true in Mexico, amenities can be quixotic. Washcloths are a rarity, and while soap is always provided, shampoo is not a given. You'll have a TV more often than not, but the selection of stations varies. Air-conditioning is generally provided but occasionally costs $5 to $10 more than a room with only a fan. The unreliable hot water and sagging mattresses that would put a gleam in a chiropractor's eye are largely things of the past, but water pressure might not always be up to U.S. travelers' expectations and the mattresses now, ironically, tend to be too hard for some tastes. Good bedside reading light is still elusive.

Lower-priced lodgings often don't have online reservation systems; you'll have to e-mail to inquire about availability and complete the reservation. The response isn't always immediate, so allow ample time. It's also a good idea to reconfirm a few days before your stay. In most of these places, there's no such thing as a standard room; look at the one you're assigned before signing the registration card, and if there's something you don't like, ask to see what else is available. ***Money-saving tip:*** Unlike the Hotel Zone, where prices are generally quoted in dollars, downtown hotels quote both dollar and peso rates. For ease of calculation (and added profit), most hotels convert the price at 10 pesos to the dollar. The actual exchange rate is more than 10.50 pesos, so you can save money by paying in pesos.

**$**    Family-run **Hostal Haina** ★★★ (Orquídeas 13, btw. Yaxchilán and Margaritas; ☎ 998/898-2081; www.hainahostal.com; no credit cards), is really more of a bed-and-breakfast than a hostel. Yes, it has dorm rooms—two comfortable ones with bunk beds ($11 per person)—but in addition are six darn nice private rooms, equipped with cable TV and small fridges. Some have one bed and others have two; all have large windows looking onto the tidy flower garden. Best of all is the price: the five air-conditioned rooms cost 390 pesos (about $37) double; the one with fan only is 350 pesos ($34). A hearty continental breakfast is included, and guests also have use of a colorful, tiled communal kitchen and dining room, a TV room, and a back patio. The front desk is staffed 24 hours a day. I also very much like the locale, on a quiet residential street half a block off of Avenida Yaxchilán, the downtown entertainment strip. Every weekend, local artists display their work at the Jardín del Arte (art park) across the street.

**$**    The **Hotel Colonial** ★ 🅺 (Tulipanes 22 at Av. Tulum; ☎ 998/884-1730, 884-1535; www.hotelcolonialcancun.com; MC, V) lives up to its name, with a mission-arch entry painted terra cotta and blue leading to a courtyard where tall palms and other foliage surround a fountain. Some of the 50 unpretentious rooms have concrete brick walls and riotously colored bedspreads, while others are toned down (if not exactly sleek), but all are fresh and comfortable. The only drawback here is the rather dim bathroom lighting. Rooms come with one or two beds (children stay free) and are a great deal at 500 pesos (about $48) in low season and 550 pesos in high season (rooms with fan only are 400–450 pesos/$38–$43). The location is hard to beat, on the pedestrian stretch of trendy Avenida Tulipanes, across from Roots jazz club and half a block from Parque Las Palapas.

**$–$$**    The hacienda-style **Suites El Patio** ★★ 🅺 (Av. Bonampak 51 at Cereza; ☎ 998/884-3500 or 884-2401; www.cancuninn.com; MC, V) is an oasis on the busy thoroughfare that runs from the Hotel Zone to the Puerto Juárez ferry terminal. The former residence turned guesthouse has just 18 units surrounding a courtyard full of trees, flowers, and a picturesque tile fountain. More tile work, carved wooden wardrobes, and Talavera ceramics give many of the large, airy rooms a rustic flavor, and bathrooms offer plenty of counter space. Rates run $40 to $80 for a maximum of three adults or two adults and two children, with discounts for longer stays and full payment in advance. Some rooms with kitchenettes are suitable for extended stays. Continental breakfast is served in the courtyard or in a library stocked with board games and books on Mexican culture. The genteel air, congenial and knowledgeable staff, locked front gate, and in-room spa services make this an especially good choice for women traveling alone. Restrictions on visitors, food or drink in guest rooms, and bare feet on the patio have raised some guests' hackles, so be aware of these going in. Avenida Tulum is a quick 2-block walk, and the bus to the Hotel Zone stops just out the front door.

$$   The unassuming street facade of the **Hotel Terracaribe** ★★ (Av. López Portillo 70 at Av. Bonampak; ☎ 998/880-0448 or 211-3014, -3015, -3016, -3017, -3018; www.terracaribe.com; AE, MC, V) barely hints at the gleaming, stylish interior that could have been lifted from one of Playa del Carmen's trendier efforts. Recent remodeling—the new pool and 12-room tower annex were completed in December 2007—gave this basic business hotel an avant-garde slant, and the new rooms' crisp white walls, floors of sand-colored marble tile, and neutral-toned spread and curtains are soothing after a hot, busy day. Those facing the courtyard have glass doors opening onto small balconies. Upscale touches include big, thick towels, in-room safe boxes, great reading light, sturdy wooden hangers, and constantly replenished toiletries (hair dryers are available on request). The spotless bathrooms, though on the small side, have roomy showers with terrific pressure. Rooms in the original building, surrounding a sheltered tropical courtyard, are a little larger and perfectly agreeable if not quite as bright or as chic; they're slated for a makeover in the style of the tower rooms. The pool and Jacuzzi get steady but not raucous use from a mix of mostly Mexican business travelers and families and European tourists. Guests also get free van transportation to the Playa Cabana beach club in the Hotel Zone with a 50% discount on food and drink. It's more than you'd expect for doubles starting at $55 with one queen bed, $65 for two. Suites (separate living room, bathrobes and slippers, and small refrigerator) run $75 to $100. The one downside is the location: The Terracaribe, on a busy road leading from the Hotel Zone to the Puerto Juárez ferry terminal, is a short drive or bus ride from most of Cancún's attractions. The neighborhood is slightly shabby but feels quite safe, an impression confirmed by expatriates living in the area.

$$   After seeing the blocky, rather severe profile of **Hotel Antillano** ★ (Av. Tulum at Claveles 1; ☎ 998/884-1132; www.hotelantillano.com; AE, MC, V) rising from clamorous Avenida Tulum, walking into the bright, open-air lobby on a side street is a sign of better things to come. The clean, airy rooms let you forget you are on downtown's main street, and red-tile floors and wooden furniture bring a light touch of Caribbean style. A cozy lobby bar opening onto the pool patio serves snacks and tropical drinks and offers live music in the evenings. The pool gets midday sun but is shaded much of the day. The hotel does a decent job of buffering noise from Avenida Tulum, but rooms overlooking the courtyard or Avenida Claveles are quieter. And you definitely don't want a room over the lobby bar when the mariachis rev up at night. The hotel has a beach club on the island with showers, toilets, lounge chairs, games, and a restaurant that discounts food and drinks for guests. Rates hold at 690 to 830 pesos ($63–$75) throughout the

year and include a modest breakfast buffet. Some lower-priced singles are available, as are suites with kitchenettes and large, separate dining areas (830 pesos–1,040 pesos/$83–$104).

**$$**    Eco-hotels are all the rage along the Caribbean coast's beaches and jungles, but **Hotel El Rey del Caribe** ★★★ (Av. Uxmal 24, SM 2-A, btw. Tulum and Nader; ☎ 998/884-2028; www.reycaribe.com; MC, V) is the real deal. The owners, who live on-site, use solar collectors, rainwater cisterns, a water-recycling system, and composting toilets to minimize environmental impact. And since your room key operates the air conditioner, you can't cavalierly take off and leave it churning away for naught. The 25 spare but roomy suites, costing $65 to $75 in low season and $85 December 21 to April 14, have fully equipped kitchenettes, good showers (though the hot water is slow to come up), cable TV, and phones. What makes the place irresistible, though, is the luxuriant courtyard, where hammocks hang near a lovely small pool and wrought-iron tables and chairs are tucked into the tropical foliage. My sister declared her massage in the little *palapa* spa better than any she's had in the United States—an almost unconscionable bargain at about $32 for 50 minutes (tip big). Hotel El Rey del Caribe is actually a B&B, and most standard breakfast choices (eggs with ham and cheese, hot cakes, cereal with yogurt and fruit, organic coffee) are included, and other items are available for an extra charge.

**$$–$$$**    Smack in the middle of downtown's nightlife, **Hotel Margaritas** ★ (Av. Yaxchilán 41, SM 22 at Jasmines; ☎ 998/881-7870; www.margaritascancun.com; AE, MC,V) is a budget hotel (642–856 pesos/$60–$80 most of the year, up to 960 pesos/$95 holidays) that wants to be something more, and the result is endearing. An employee intercepted me at check-in to invite me back to the lobby after settling in to let her know if all was to my liking; she then gave me a map and a brief orientation of the area and insisted that I let her know if I needed anything during my stay. Some rooms show signs of wear—dings in the cabinets, a battered soap dish in the shower—but they have plenty of space, lots of natural light, unusually comfortable beds, and all rooms have a small balcony. The otherwise ordinary decor is brightened by colorful bedspreads and a painted "headboard" formed by an arch set into the wall. I especially appreciated the good light above the bed, acres of bathroom counter space, and Internet computers on the ground floor (many hotels offer only free Wi-Fi, leaving non-laptop-toting travelers out of luck). The open-air restaurant, serving a good selection of satisfying Mexican, Yucatecan, and international dishes (most under $10) is a pleasant place to linger and watch life on the street. On the down side, you might have to dodge time-share sales pitches in the lobby, and a certain amount of noise filters in from surrounding restaurants and clubs.

**$$–$$$**    It's hard to believe the gleaming, modern **Hotel Suites Alborada** ★★★ (kids) (Av. Nader 5 at Claveles; ☎ 998/884-1584 or 994-4347; www.suitesalborada.com; MC, V) has been in business since 1976, and even harder to believe so few travelers know about it. The ones who do, though, keep coming back—some of them for 30 years. The family-owned hotel's nine units are one- and two-bedroom apartments that wouldn't be out of place in an IKEA showroom, but the sheltered courtyard is pure Tropics. One-bedroom apartments cost $65 a night for two people in low season, $85 in high season, and $95 Christmas and New Year's weeks; two-bedroom apartments are $105 to $150 for four people. Extra guests cost $8.50 to $15 each, depending on season. The fully stocked kitchenettes are ample, and bathrooms have a designer feel with such touches as glass-block partitions. The hotel is a block away from the clamor of Avenida Tulum but within easy reach of its conveniences. With its unassuming concrete and stonework facade blending into a commercial complex shared with the lively and inexpensive El Café and other businesses, Suites Alborada is easy to miss but worth seeking out. The restaurant on-site is a great option for a light breakfast or lunch (p. 37).

**$$–$$$**    Entering **Hotel Xbalamqué** ★★ (Av. Yaxchilán 31; ☎ 998/884-0699; www.xbalamque.com; AE, MC, V) is a little like wending your way through the line of Disneyland's Indiana Jones Adventure ride: eye-popping stone archways, replicas of Maya statues and stelae, murals of ancient warriors and legends, walls of reliefs that would be at home in a museum. You'll even swim through stone arches in the ivy-draped waterfall pool. This is downtown's closest approximation of a Hotel Zone resort, right down to the beauty salon, full-service spa with Maya healing treatments, yoga studio, and traditional *temazcal* (sweat lodge). But with just 92 rooms, its scale is more personal, and its room rates ($75 low season, $96 high) are a lot easier to take. The simple room decor invokes Mexican tradition of a more recent era, with heavy wooden furniture and inlaid tile floors. The salonlike El Pabilo *cafebrería* (coffee shop/bookstore, p. 67) serves dinner 6 nights a week and hosts live music in the evenings. The hotel offers guests half-price passes to The City's beach club in the Hotel Zone. Make no mistake, this isn't the Ritz. You don't get hand towels or washcloths, hallways are rather dim, mattresses are on the hard side, and its location in club central makes asking for a quiet courtyard room a wise choice. But no other downtown hotel is this much fun just to look at, and the floor-to-ceiling city view from upstairs corridors is one of the best in Cancún.

**$$$**    The vaguely colonial, vaguely Victorian, and thoroughly contemporary **Hotel Sol y Luna** ★ (Calle Alcatraces 33; ☎ 998/887-5579, 887-5528; www.soly lunahotel.com; MC, V) is a quiet, sophisticated boutique hotel poised between Parque Las Palapas and Suites Colonial. Each of the 11 uncluttered rooms (eight with private terraces) is different, but all mix bold colors, themed artwork and traditional pieces of furniture. One has the self-conscious, Playa del Carmen kind of chic of neutral colors, white bed covers, and monochromatic bathrooms, while another invokes tradition with two-tone green-and-yellow walls bordered with stenciled leaves. There's a nod to luxury, with magnifying mirrors, hair dryers, minifridges, and a full lineup of Teva toiletries. Rooms cost $90, including breakfast, most of the year but spike to $120 in August. All but the ground-floor rooms have views over the park. At this writing, the new owners had not yet decided whether to reopen the hotel's restaurant.

# DINING FOR ALL TASTES

Those who find typical Mexican fare too robust will have no problem in Cancún. You can find just about any type of cuisine you can think of here, from exotic international dishes to Big Macs. Even if Mexican isn't high on your list, don't shy

# Yucatecan Cuisine

When the first Spaniards landed in the Yucatán in 1519, they found Indians cooking with corn, beans, chilies, tomatoes, and squash, often combined with wild game. The conquerors introduced beef, pork, lamb, nuts, fruits, cheese, and sugar cane (by way of the Caribbean), fully expecting local women to adopt European cooking techniques. Imagine their dismay when Yucatecans incorporated the new ingredients to produce new versions of native food instead of replicating Spanish dishes.

Today, the Yucatán boasts one of Mexico's most distinctive regional cuisines, a complex blend of European, Mexican, and Caribbean flavors and cooking techniques. Some of the most recognizable flavors come from *achiote* (an earthy, mildly tangy paste made from the annato seed), native sour oranges, lime juice, pumpkin seeds, and pickled onions. Turkey *(pavo)* is still the most common meat eaten in Yucatecan homes.

The Yucatán's three trademark dishes are *pollo* or *cochinita* (chicken or pork) *pibil,* meat marinated in achiote, bitter orange, and spices, then barbecued in banana leaves; *poc chuc,* pork slices marinated in sour orange juice and served with a tangy sauce and pickled onions; and *sopa de lima* (lime soup), made with turkey or veal broth and shredded chicken marinated in local limes, with the addition of sizzling tortilla strips. (For more about local dishes, see "Menu Terms" on p. 297.)

In recent years, the Yucatán's traditional cuisine has taken on flavors contributed by immigrants from Lebanon, France, Cuba, and even the United States. At the same time, international dishes prepared here—particularly in Cancún, where most of the world's cuisines are represented—are borrowing native Yucatecan ingredients. The evolution of new exotic flavors make eating in the Yucatán a never-ending adventure.

away from the regional specialties that appear on many menus. With little heritage of its own, Cancún has appropriated traditions from all over Mexico, and cuisine is no exception. If your experience of Mexican food has been limited to tacos, burritos, and the occasional chalupa, biting into *chiles en nogada* or mole will be a revelation. Most important, don't leave Cancún without sampling some Yucatecan dishes, with their lively Maya spices and cooking techniques applied to European-style dishes that crossed the ocean with the Spanish. *A bonus:* Mexican and Yucatecan dishes are usually the least expensive items on the menu.

Most of Cancún's finest restaurants are in the Zona Hotelera on the lagoon side of Bulevar Kukulcán in the high-end hotels. U.S. franchises such as Hard Rock Cafe, Planet Hollywood, Ruth's Chris Steak House, and Rainforest Cafe are well represented here. Seafood is big in Cancún, but it's usually the most expensive choice; lobster, in particular, rarely lands on a menu for less than $30. With prices equal to or higher than comparable U.S. restaurants, eating on the island can quickly bust your budget. Fortunately, a single entree, perhaps with an appetizer, is more than enough for two average appetites, and most restaurants are happy to provide extra plates. Some of the priciest restaurants even take pride in dividing an entree before it leaves the kitchen, just to ensure an artful presentation worthy of their reputations. Another strategy is making a meal of an appetizer and soup or salad. Or plan a foray to that must-try restaurant at lunch time, when entrees typically cost $5 less than at dinner. It might be a little smaller and come with fewer side dishes, but it will be ample and just as tasty.

El Centro is a whole different story, full of distinctive local haunts that charge moderate prices. Even the few upscale choices cost about half of what they would on the island. This is where you'll find the personality and sometimes raucous spirit Mexico is known for. And instead of toning down the bold flavors for tourists, downtown restaurants cater to local tastes, offering a culinary playground for adventurous palates.

## ZONA HOTELERA

**$–$$**    With just three tables on the front patio, **Ty-Coz** ★★★ 🧒 (Plaza San Francisco Quetzal, Bl. Kukulcán Km 7.7; no phone; Mon–Sat 7am–7pm; cash only), is basically a take-out place specializing in hearty, deli-style sandwiches ($4–$7) on crusty baguettes or flaky croissants. A welcome value in the expensive Hotel Zone, this is the offspring of the venerable downtown restaurant, where you can get the full deli/coffeehouse experience (p. 38).

**$–$$**    Mexico's vegetarian and natural food restaurants used to be mostly expat enterprises, but **100% Natural** ★★ 🧒 (Plaza Kukulcán, Bl. Kukulcán Km 13; ☎ 998/885-2904; www.100natural.com.mx; daily 7am–11pm; AE, MC, V) is 100% Mexican. Seemingly infinite combinations of fresh tropical juices embellished (optionally) with aloe vera, *nopal* (cactus), *chaya* (a spinachlike leafy vegetable), pollen, and other health boosters (about $3) require their own separate menu. Hot cakes, omelets, or fruit plates ($5.50–$9) provide a day's worth of fuel; I couldn't come close to finishing the cornucopia of exotic fruit topped with sweet yogurt and granola. Sandwiches, salads, pasta, and simple Mexican fare, with plenty of vegetarian options, are good lunch and dinner choices (up to $15). The restaurant's four locations include one downtown at avenidas Sunyaxchen and Yaxchilán (☎ 998/884-0102 or 884-3617). Locals and visitors alike linger here through the morning, nursing salubrious potions in the serene, palm- and hibiscus-lined courtyard anchored by a stone fountain that tweaks colonial tradition with three tiers of fresh fruit and vegetables instead of cherubs.

**$–$$$$**    One of the more reasonably priced restaurants in the Hotel Zone, **The Cove** ★ 🧒 (Playa Langosta, Bl. Kukulcán Km 5; ☎ 998/881-7473; www.thecove cancun.com; daily 7am–midnight; MC, V), specializes in Caribbean-style seafood but also offers *tampiqueña* steak, sandwiches, hamburgers, and an excellent chicken breast with three-pepper sauce for $10. Main courses start at $6.50 for a club sandwich. A stunning, multilevel view of the pretty beach makes up for sometimes spotty service. Extended families finishing their meals spread out on the deck to spend the afternoon visiting while the kids frolic in the sand.

**$$–$$$$** An admitted Thai food snob, I was skeptical about **Thai** ✦ (La Isla Shopping Village, Bl. Kukulcán Km 12.5; ☎ 998/883-1401; www.interactivedolphins. com/restaurants.html; daily 6pm–1am; AE, MC, V). It's not only behind an aquarium but in a shopping mall, of all places. Faster than you can say, "Beam me up," the open-air waterfront restaurant transports you to Thailand's coast with lantern-lit dining cabanas in the jungle and stilt houses rising from the water. The chef, cooks, and waitresses hail from Thailand and serve fresh, authentic recipes that let underlying flavors shine through the perfectly balanced seasoning. Starters ($8.50–$9) include spring rolls, satay, and deep-fried shrimp; the curries ($20–$25) and the rice and noodle dishes ($15–$20) are ideal for sharing. The most popular dish is Pla De Phuket, a crispy fish filet in a tamarind chili sauce ($20). Doors open at sunset; by 10pm the bar fills with a mix of young locals and visitors partying against the backdrop of dolphins frolicking on the other side of the glass wall shared with the aquarium (p. 65).

**$$$–$$$$** Fronted by a plot of blue agave plants, **Hacienda El Mortero** ✦ (NH Crystal Cancún, Bl. Kukulcán Km 9; ☎ 998/848-9800; daily 6–11pm; AE, MC, V) is a lovely, evocative replica of an 18th-century *henequén* hacienda, with tables arranged to make the most of views of the flowering garden, the sea, and one of Cancún's most beautiful beaches. At night, the small tables around the interior courtyard's stone fountain are a romantic place to sample creative dishes such as chicken breast stuffed with *chaya* and cooked in an *achiote* sauce ($17). Premium grilled meats and seafood cost up to $36; fortunately, main dishes are ample and varied enough for sharing. Small touches such as light, flaky corn chips and rice cooked with *huitlacoche,* the black corn mushrooms widely used in traditional Maya recipes, elevate even a modest dinner here to an experience. A mariachi band winding through the columned archways in the evenings adds to the genteel, old-time atmosphere.

**$$$–$$$$** Inventive tweaks on traditional Mexican cooking are only part of the reason to go to **La Destilería** (Bl. Kukulcán Km 12.5; ☎ 998/885-1086; www.cmr.ws; daily 1pm–midnight; AE, MC, V). Just as compelling is the chance to sample 150 types of tequila and browse displays that turn the restaurant into a tequila museum outlining tequila's history, growing, and distilling process. The dining room, perched over Nichupté Lagoon, is arranged around a Herradura-brand still. Hearty affordable starters include quesadillas filled with squash blossoms and *huitlacoche* ($7.75) and tortilla soup with chilies, *chicharrón,* cheese, and avocados ($4.70 small/$6.50 large). I recommend making a meal of these to save money for the guided "tequila tour" ($5) and sample tastings (at extra cost) offered several afternoons a week. Some main dishes, such as shrimp in tamarind and chipotle sauce ($16) or chicken breast stuffed with squash blossoms and topped with Oaxaca cheese and *mole poblano* ($19), are within reach, but approach the fresh fish and seafood at your budget's peril.

## EL CENTRO

**$** Sharing a building (and phone number) with Suites Alborada (p. 33), **El Café de la Nader** ✦✦✦ 👶 (Nader 5; ☎ 998/884-1584; Mon–Sat 7am–10pm; cash only), offers a clean, cool respite for local business people and clued-in tourists who lounge around a stone fountain on the tiled patio sheltered by sailcloth awnings. The *pan dulce* (sweet bread), baked twice a day, is a morning favorite with coffee or tea. Afternoon fare revolves around tacos ($1.75–$2.75) and quesadillas ($2.60–$3.70) made of fresh, handmade tortillas filled with chorizo, rib meat, turkey breast, and other unusual fillings, as well as the usual suspects. It's a little off the well-trodden sightseeing paths but worth the short detour for the cheap, fresh food, and speedy service.

$    A fresh, peppery smell greets you when you open the door to the deli-style **Ty-Coz** ★★★ (kids) (Tulum at Uxmal; ☎ 998/884-6060; Mon–Sat 7am–7pm; cash only), tucked behind the Comercial Mexicana supermarket. Its huge vegetarian or classic deli combination sandwiches ($4–$7) come on baguettes or croissants. Though the cafe invokes French tradition, one specialty is a "Very German" plate of cold meats, cheeses, baguette or croissant, garlic mayo, and . . . marmalade. The flaky croissants *(cuernos),* which have a devoted following, go well with the fresh coffee and espresso. Wood paneling and artwork on the walls give the place a coffeehouse feel. It's become so popular that a tiny satellite branch (p. 36) recently opened in the Hotel Zone.

$–$$    In the time it took me to read the menu behind the cafeteria-style counter, the staff of **Huaraches de los Alcatraces** ★★ (kids) (Alcatraces 31; ☎ 998/884-3918; Tues–Sun 8am–6:30pm; cash only), tucked away off the quiet southeast corner of Parque de Las Palapas, had already dispensed two orders for more decisive customers. The array of Mexican comfort food includes giant quesadillas stuffed with chilies, potatoes, *nopales,* or 11 other fillings for a mere $2, and full dinner plates such as beef *tampiqueña,* chile relleno, or enchiladas with two side dishes for $5.50 to $8.25. *Huaraches,* not leather sandals but big, slightly crispy, oval-shaped tortillas, come with green-chili salsa, your choice of meat, sour cream, and cheese, making them more of a meal than most people need for $3.75.

$–$$    The city blocks west of the bus station are full of inexpensive restaurants serving the area's numerous hostels, and **El Rincón Yucateco** ★★★ (kids) (Uxmal 35, btw. Chaca and Laurel; ☎ 998/892-2459; Mon–Sat noon–11pm; cash only) is one of the best. Recognizable by two tiers of thatched roof camouflaging a concrete hole in the wall, it serves outstanding *sopa de lima, panuchos* (bean-stuffed fried tortillas topped with turkey or chicken), *cochinita pibil,* and other Yucatecan dishes for $5.50 to $8. The $10 Yucatecan combo is a veritable menu (grilled pork sausage, tortillas stuffed with hard-boiled eggs, *panuchos,* beans) unto itself. Tables often make their way out onto the sidewalk as diners pack the little dining room, but take heart: For about $2.40, they'll deliver.

$$    The gleaming white interior and dressed-up diners are a bit of a surprise at **Los Almendros** (Av. Bonampak Sur 60 at Sayil; ☎ 998/887-1332; daily 11am–10pm; AE, MC, V), which sits across from the bullring and next to the police station. Like its more famous sibling in Mérida, it specializes in Yucatecan cuisine. The crisp *salbutes* (fried tortillas topped with chicken or turkey), for $6.50, are especially good, but the restaurant also does right by the classic *poc chuc* and *cochinita pibil.* Their Lomitos de Valladolid (cubed pork cooked in fresh crushed tomatoes) and

## La Cuenta, Por Favor

If your previously attentive waiter seems to be ignoring you after the plates are cleared, don't blame the service. Mexico's rules of etiquette consider it rude to bring the check until you ask for it. It's okay to summon any waiter and ask, *"La cuenta, por favor,"* or you may simply catch someone's eye and pantomime a scribbling motion against the palm of your hand. The standard **tip** *(propina)* for good service is between 10% and 15% of the total bill, unless it shows that a service fee was included. While not common in Mexico, it does happen, usually in upscale restaurants, so look before you tip.

Pavo en Escabeche de Valladolid (turkey in a tangy broth with marinated onions) are less common regional treats, even in Yucatecan restaurants.

**$–$$$**    The shape of the stone arch towering over the entrance to **Labná ★★★** (Margaritas 29 at Jasmines; ☎ 998/892-3056, 884-3158; www.labna.com; daily noon–10pm; AE, MC, V) is echoed in the dining room's vaulted ceiling. A mural of Maya pyramids in the type of rainforest that has disappeared from the Yucatán and photos from the hacienda era of the 1900s set the mood for a happy collision of unfamiliar flavors: *sopa de lima, poc chuc,* and pork or chicken *pibil.* But don't overlook the Yucatán's lesser known dishes, such as turkey in pumpkin-seed sauce seasoned with *achiote,* or *papadzules,* hard-boiled eggs rolled inside tortillas and smothered in a pumpkin seed–and–fried tomato sauce. Only one of the Yucatecan entrees costs more than $10, though some Mexican "haute cuisine" items reach $16. For culture mavens, happiness is tucking into the Yucatecan Tour combo ($12) on a weekend afternoon, during a traditional *trova* (guitar trio) performance by local musicians.

**$–$$$**    One of the great things about **Roots ★★★** (Tulipanes 26; ☎ 998/884-2437; Tues–Sat 7pm–1am; MC, V), downtown's stylish jazz and supper club, is its *antojitos* or "small ones," a selection of tapas-style dishes such as shrimp or mushrooms with ajillo peppers, chicken wings, and sandwiches ($7.90–$13). Even better, the cold-cut platter and the pâté-and-cheese platter at the high end of the range come in less expensive small sizes. The sophisticated menu's main dishes won't break the bank, either; the most expensive item, filet mignon, costs $16. The intimate coffeehouse atmosphere and congenial, efficient staff make you want to linger as local residents start filling the tables . . . and that's a good thing, since evenings bring live music that lasts into the wee hours (p. 65).

**$–$$$**    Most seafood restaurants have at least one chicken or vegetarian dish on their menus, but **El Oasis ★★** 🄺 (Yaxchilán 3; no phone; Mon–Sat 7am–4pm; cash only) is for the hardcore. If you don't eat seafood, you're limited to chicken nuggets on the children's menu. A lot of locals come for the tacos (shrimp, fish, marlin, or crab, about $1.60 apiece) and douse them liberally with sweet, smoky tamarind sauce—this is one of the few places that has it. The place has grown

## La Plaza de Toros: No Bull

One of the best places to kick back and relax with the locals is at Cancún's bullring, **Plaza de Toros** (Av. Bonampak at Calle Sayil, a block from Bl. Kukulcán, Centro)—and I don't mean at a bullfight, which are mostly a tourist attraction rarely attended by Cancún residents. Spending a Thursday or Friday afternoon in the cantinas tucked into the outside wall of the bullring, on the other hand, is a cherished local tradition. These cantinas are not the seedy Mexican dives of legend but lively restaurant-bars where locals gather to have lunch, visit, and watch soccer matches while downing hot Spanish sausage dipped in guacamole or chili strips in melted cheese. The ritual gets going at about 2:30pm. On Fridays, people often come for lunch and drink straight through the afternoon into din-ner. Free bar bites, such as Aztec soup (a deep red, smoky brew great with lime juice), *chicharrones,* and fresh salsa, stave off total oblivion.

The best-known cantina, **La Guadalupana** (☎ 998/887-0660; AE, MC, V) looks like a grown-up version of a college beer hall. The menu offers a wide array of *botanas* (appetizers) such as sausage and empanadas ($3–$6), and traditional entrees such as *arrachera* beef (about $13). You might have to knock back a few before you're ready for the *sobre ruedas,* whose main ingredient is blood, or *las criadillas* (bull testicles). Each can-tina is a little different—La Faena, a few doors down from La Guadalupana, resembles a family-style Italian restaurant—but most offer a *vuelta al ruedo,* a circular sample platter named after the bullfighting tradition of the matador circling the ring to brandish the vanquished bull's tail or ears for the crowd's approval. Mariachis work the restaurants, com-ing in to play one free song and then soliciting special requests for a fee. They tend to approach the tables with women first and often skip over the large groups of men, who make up the majority of the crowd.

If you do want to see a bullfight, they take place every Wednesday at 3:30pm and include an hour of entertainment with *charros* (Mexican cow-boys), a mariachi band, and flamenco dancers. Travel agencies sell tickets, which cost $40, or you can buy them at the bullring (☎ 998/884-8372; cash only).

from a little storefront to the current large *palapa* with a stone floor and TV screens. House specialties, including oysters, paella, shrimp brochettes, and fish filets in a Caribbean sauce, cost about $9 to $14.

**$$–$$$$**    If you skip the lobster, you can sample fresh local seafood quite rea-sonably at **El Cejas** ✦ (Av. Xel-Ha side of Mercado 28; ☎ 998/887-1080; daily 9am–9pm; MC, V). Fish filets come fried with garlic or with ajillo-pepper sauce, prepared with oranges or olives, breaded, au gratin, and stuffed, for $8 to $12. The restaurant's specialty is a lineup of crabs, bare or stuffed, that go for $11 to

$12. Shrimp, conch, and other shellfish run $11 to $12, but if you venture into lobster and crayfish you're looking at $15 to $28. This is a plastic-tables-and-chairs place, far from fancy but wildly popular with Cancún residents, who share seafood plates, swill beer, and sing lustily with the wandering musicians who play for change. Next-door rival **Pescado con Limón** (☎ 998/887-2436; daily 11:30am–7:30pm; MC, V) has slightly lower prices, with specialties—octopus cooked in its ink or Veracruz style, and fajitas—running $7.50 to $10.

**$$–$$$$**    A favorite since the city's infancy, **La Habichuela** ✖ (Av. Margaritas 25; ☎ 998/884-3158; www.lahabichuela.com; daily 1pm–midnight; AE, MC, V) is the upscale sister to Labná (p. 39) next door. Starry-eyed couples flock to the Green Bean's impossibly romantic courtyard garden, where lacy wrought-iron chairs and tables stand incongruously among the Maya sculpture reproductions, native plants, and trees that replicate jungle-draped ruins. The focus is on Caribbean flavors, including Yucatecan specialties such as cream of *habichuela* soup ($5.70), chicken mole ($13), and marinated *tampiqueña*-style grilled beef ($17). Grilled seafood and steaks are excellent but hardly unique; go for the local specialties. If you don't have room for dessert, at least try the Xtabentún (about $5), a Maya liqueur made from honey and anise.

**$$$–$$$$**    Sure, it's touristy. It's campy. And it's overpriced. But there's a reason **Perico's** (kids) (Yaxchilán 61 at Gladiolas; ☎ 998/884-3152; www.pericos.com.mx; daily 1pm–1am; AE, MC, V) is a Cancún institution: It's a lot of fun. With its huge, stained-glass sign over the *palapa* roof, it looks like a cross between a '70s fern bar and a *South Pacific* set, and the gaudy interior decor resembles an oversized puppet theater. It's worth going at least once, even if only for appetizers ($4.60–$8.60) and a drink, just to see your order arrive on the head of a waiter impersonating a Zapata revolutionary. The fairly standard menu offers chicken, with your choice of preparation and side dishes, for about $13; fajitas, meat, and seafood are $16 to $27. The food's more palatable than the prices, but that's almost beside the point. You're here for the conga lines, loud mariachi and marimba bands, and free tequila shots.

# WHY YOU'RE HERE: CANCUN'S BEACHES

Although nightclubs, boutiques, and 400-thread-count sheets have stolen much of the limelight, you have only to wiggle your toes in the powdery white sand lapped by turquoise waves to remember why Cancún exists. The fine, lightweight sand—composed of crushed seashells, coral, and fossils of microscopic plankton rather than rock—remains powdery and cool to the touch even in the most ferocious heat and humidity. Since they are the city's bread and butter, the beaches tend to be clean and well groomed.

Water temperatures top 27°C (80°F) from June to November and cool off only a few degrees in winter and spring. Many locals avoid swimming during the cooler months, but the water is plenty warm for most visitors.

Despite the city's sexy reputation, including several clothing-optional resorts, Cancún has no nude beaches. Topless bathing is quietly accepted if not widespread, though women sunbathing on hotel property may be asked to put their tops back on.

## Going Public

Signs mark the entrances to public beaches, which can quickly fill on Sundays and holidays when local families traditionally enjoy a day out. From north to south:

**Playa Las Perlas,** Km 2.5. In front of Barceló Club Las Perlas at beginning of the Hotel Zone, midway between downtown Cancún and the Nichupté bridge.

**Playa Juventud,** Km 3. In front of Villas Juveniles youth hostel.

**Playa Linda,** Km 4. West of Nichupté Bridge. Parking at Embarcadero marina.

**Playa Langosta,** Km 5.

**Playa Tortugas,** Km 6. Public entrance next to Fat Tuesday's.

**Playa Caracol,** Km 8.5. Across from Mayafair Plaza; public entrance through small wooden gate next to Fiesta Americana Grand Coral Beach resort or through Xcaret bus terminal.

**Playa Gaviota Azul,** Km 9. Near Plaza Forum and The City Beach Club.

**Playa Chac Mool,** Km 10. Across from Señor Frog's.

**Playa Marlin,** Km 13. Public entrance behind Kukulcán Plaza.

**Playa Ballenas,** Km 14.5. Public entrance on sidewalk along Le Méridien Hotel wall.

**Playa Delfines,** Km 18. South of Hilton Cancún Beach. Parking on Bl. Kukulcán above beach.

Cancún has two distinct beach zones. The northern Hotel Zone (the top of the seven) faces Isla Mujeres across the Bahía de Mujeres. The waters, while not quite as intensely turquoise as those on the open Caribbean, are calm and ideal for swimming. South of Punta Cancún, the east-facing beaches on the sea along the stem of the "seven" shape have no buffer from seasonal wind, formidable currents and waves, and aren't always safe for swimming (see "Water Safety," later in this section). The saltwater Nichupté Lagoon, on the west side of the island, has little beach to speak of and is lined with restaurants and watersports.

From Bulevar Kukulcán, nearly all of the Caribbean beachfront is obscured by high-rise resorts that claim their own patch of paradise. Most provide guests with such facilities as *palapa* shelters, volleyball courts, exercise classes, bars, restaurants, showers, restrooms, towels, and lifeguards. Some downtown hotels offer privileges at beach clubs with similar facilities. Though all Mexican beaches are government owned and open to everyone, the resorts are private property. Some resorts provide entrances for the public, and most of the rest will tolerate, if not welcome, nonguests traipsing through their lobbies. Few go so far as to turn them away. Fortunately, public-access beaches stipple the island (see "Going Public,"

# Cancún Zona Hotelera Beaches & Attractions

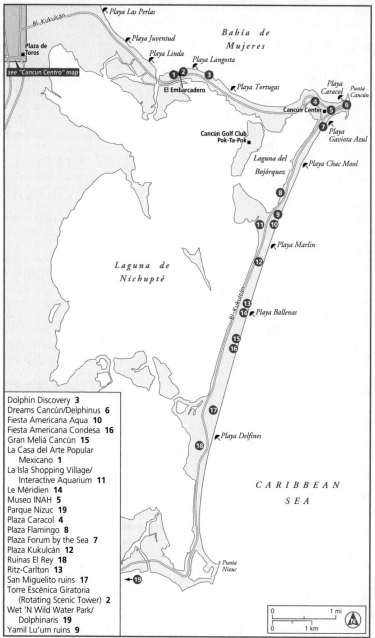

Bl. Kukulcán

Playa Las Perlas

Playa Juventud

Bahía de Mujeres

Plaza de Toros

Playa Linda

see "Cancun Centro" map

Playa Langosta

El Embarcadero

Playa Tortugas

Playa Caracol

Punta Cancún

Cancún Center

Playa Gaviota Azul

Cancún Golf Club Pok-Ta-Pok

Laguna del Bojórquez

Playa Chac Mool

Laguna de Nichupté

Playa Marlin

Bl. Kukulcán

Playa Ballenas

Playa Delfines

CARIBBEAN SEA

Punta Nizuc

Dolphin Discovery **3**
Dreams Cancún/Delphinus **6**
Fiesta Americana Aqua **10**
Fiesta Americana Condesa **16**
Gran Meliá Cancún **15**
La Casa del Arte Popular
   Mexicano **1**
La Isla Shopping Village/
   Interactive Aquarium **11**
Le Méridien **14**
Museo INAH **5**
Parque Nizuc **19**
Plaza Caracol **4**
Plaza Flamingo **8**
Plaza Forum by the Sea **7**
Plaza Kukulcán **12**
Ruinas El Rey **18**
Ritz-Carlton **13**
San Miguelito ruins **17**
Torre Escénica Giratoria
   (Rotating Scenic Tower) **2**
Wet 'N Wild Water Park/
   Dolphinaris **19**
Yamil Lu'um ruins **9**

0             1 mi
0             1 km

p. 42), and you can usually find an entrance near your chosen spot. Once on the beach, you can walk as far as you like in either direction.

## NORTHERN BEACHES

Protected by Isla Mujeres, the tranquil surf and shallow waters near the shoreline make these palm-fringed beaches the choice for swimmers, snorkelers, and families with children. Most offer kayaking, jet-skiing, water-skiing, and boat and other rentals, as well as docks for water taxis, shuttles to Isla Mujeres, and numerous day-trip departures. Most are also well supplied with restaurants and bars. These beaches are smaller than those on the east side and hugely popular, so privacy is at a premium. An overview, from west to east:

Just as the land begins stretching into the Caribbean south of El Centro, you first encounter **Playa Las Perlas,** a small beach near some grand private homes. Lined by palm trees and Lego-block hotel complexes, Las Perlas' negligible waves offer some of Cancún's safest swimming, making it popular with locals. Facilities are pretty much limited to hotel restaurants and bars on the beach. Most of the watersports activities are available only to guests, but it's the kind of place where you can drop your Boogie board or join a pickup volleyball game.

Just north of the channel where Nichupté Lagoon's waters flow into the Caribbean, **Playa Linda** is tucked into curving sands near the bridge linking the island to the mainland. It also offers fine swimming and watersports, along with changing rooms and restaurants. The beach's small size and tuft of palm trees give it an intimate feel, but that intimacy can become rather cramped and busy with the ferries and submarine tours to Isla Mujeres, the Captain Hook Pirate Dinner Cruise ships, and the Rotating Scenic Tower all located at adjacent El Embarcadero marina. But it makes great people-watching, which might include practice swordplay when the pirate ships are docked.

If you book a Dolphin Discovery tour (p. 56), you'll leave from **Playa Langosta,** near the football-field-size Mexican flag visible from most of the Hotel Zone. The small beach is popular with local families, and watching kids jump off the dock after the boats pull out is entertainment in itself. While this beach has no public facilities, it has plenty of *palapas,* restaurants, and bars. It can get crowded with tourists from surrounding all-inclusive resorts, especially during spring break.

Neighboring **Playa Tortugas** brings in crowds with snorkeling and sailboard rentals and one of the loveliest views of the Bahía de Mujeres. By Cancún standards, though, it is peaceful and somehow doesn't feel like a tourist trap. The beach is often filled by local families lazing away an afternoon. To find a more secluded patch of sand, head past the rocks to the quiet beach on the right. With broader sands and deeper water than neighboring beaches, it offers better swimming for grown-ups but also has shallow areas for children. Waves here are larger than those at the beginning of the Hotel Zone, luring water-skiers, jet-skiers, and parasailers. In addition to the open-air restaurants, an indoor crafts market stands at the edge of the sand.

**Playa Caracol** is the closest beach to Punta Cancún, where bay waters meet the Caribbean, and is blessed with clear, turquoise water dotted by sailboarders, water-skiers, catamarans, and parasailers. Unfortunately, massive developments loom over the sand, and rocks jutting out from the water where the point begins make it dicey for serious swimming. Still, this is one of the island's most crowded beaches. A short stroll to the west, though, leads to a less populated stretch of beach where shallow water leads out to a smooth, sandy bottom ideal for children or beginning swimmers. And you can't beat it for conveniences, from bars and restaurants to watersports rentals to tours to the Isla Contoy bird sanctuary—not to mention the gargantuan Xcaret office complex and bus station.

## EASTERN BEACHES

It's no mystery why the luxury resorts positioned themselves on the expansive (in some cases extending for miles), mostly treeless sands on the island's east-facing beaches, becoming pricier as they march south. Seaward beaches have the iconic, translucent Caribbean waters that morph from pale aqua in the morning to deep turquoise in the afternoon to peachy hues in the evening. Unfortunately, they also have the winds, high waves, and dangerous currents that preclude swimming much of the time. The beaches south of Km 14 are generally considered the best, but nearly all have beach restaurants and bars, and present postcard-perfect settings for sunbathing, strolling, bodysurfing, and watersports within walking distance of Cancún's vaunted shops and restaurants. And, of course, there are those incomparable Caribbean sunrises. From north to south:

The northernmost beaches, **Gaviota Azul, Chac Mool,** and **Playa Marlin,** don't exude the glamour of those near the exclusive resorts farther south, but all three offer expansive views and space to get away from crowds. They tend to have the highest wave action, making them popular for windsurfing and parasailing. Chac Mool is one of Cancún's few beaches that occasionally has good surfing conditions. Gaviota and Chac Mool have changing rooms and showers. Chac Mool's shallow, clear waters are great to walk and play in, as long as you don't venture too far out. Playa Marlin, with miles of sand, offers your best shot at privacy, and strollers can head about ½-mile north to Yamil Lu'um, the smallest of Cancún's ruins.

Known for its panoramic views of Cancún and such family-friendly activities as swimming, tubing, boating, and water-skiing, the powdery sands of **Playa Ballenas** stretches along some of the Hotel Zone's toniest resorts. (Hotel waiters sometimes make their way onto the beach to offer bar service.) Though its classic Caribbean beauty makes it one of the most popular patches of sand on the spit, it rarely feels crowded. There are large rocks near Bulevar Kukulcán, but the beach soon widens and extends for several miles. Several hotels have installed ropes and buoys to help swimmers make their way safely in and out of the water in rough surf.

If you're in a mood for a serving of history with your sun and sand, make your way to tiny **Playa San Miguelito.** You can model your sand castle after the fragment of ancient Maya ruins that rises from a patch of jungle between Bulevar Kukulcán and the Royal Mayan resort.

**Playa Delfines,** where Bulevar Kukulcán curves into a small hill, is the only beach really visible from the road, and the sight will pull you up short: Escaping from the march of high-rises is a perfect Caribbean landscape of dunes, glittering sand, striated shades of aqua, and a sky sprinkled with multicolored parasails. One of Cancún's longest and widest beaches, it's the local favorite but has plenty of room for everyone. A lookout (El Mirador) offers mesmerizing views and the waves below it occasionally strike the right balance for surfers. The sand here is

## Water Safety

Though ideal for sunbathing, Cancún's legendary east-side beaches often have dangerous currents that make swimming unsafe, even when the surf looks placid. Lifeguards are stationed at many beaches, and they are trained to recognize potentially dangerous conditions. If a lifeguard signals you, take the advice to heart. Marinas and hotel beaches use a warning system of colored flags: **red** or **black** mean dangerous conditions; **yellow** means use caution; and **green** or **blue** mean ideal for swimming. Don't take these lightly; Cancún's ambulance crews respond to near drownings every week.

coarser and darker than the fine stuff on more northerly beaches, and swimming is dangerous. But with no hotels nearby, it's a peaceful place for sunbathing or, in early morning, watching the wild dolphins who give the beach its name.

Within shouting distance of Palancar Reef, second largest in the world, **Punta Nizuc** at the southern end of the Hotel Zone has a broad, white crescent of beach bordered by mangrove jungle. Between Club Med and the Westin Resort & Spa is Cancún's best spot for snorkeling and diving among yellow- and blue-striped grunt and brain coral. **Playa Punta Nizuc,** near the Parque Nizuc water park, has placid waters, though there is often more seaweed than swimmers like.

# THE TOP SIGHTS & ATTRACTIONS

The Caribbean and its long, talcum-powder beach is sight enough for many Cancún visitors, and those in need of a culture fix tend to head down the coast or to the Yucatán's Maya interior. Still, when sun-and-sand overload sets in, exploring the city can easily provide a week's worth of diversions, especially if you seek out its more subtle side.

## MUSEUMS & MARINE EXHIBITS

An entrancing display of folk art fills several rooms at **La Casa del Arte Popular Mexicano** ✹✹✹ (Bl. Kukulcán Km 4.5, Zona Hotelera; ☎ 998/849-4332; $5; Mon–Sat 9am–7pm, Sat–Sun 11am–7pm), hidden away on the second floor of the undistinguished Embarcadero building. Masks, toys, dolls, pottery, and intricate tapestries from the country's best artisans create a series of dioramas, including a full tiled kitchen typical of Puebla, a Michoacán home, and a traditional market. The life-size wax figures in the chapel scene were so lifelike and so expressive that it was unnerving. The free audio tour (available in English) said they were created from masks the museum director made of people he met throughout Mexico. The collection, which also includes rain sticks, crosses, musical instruments, regional folkloric costumes, religious artifacts, gourd art, crafts, and artwork, is remarkable considering the museum's modest size. All of Mexico's diverse regions are repre-sented, from nativity scenes sculpted from Oaxaca's clays to the intricate *árbol de la vida* (tree of life: large, hand-painted clay pieces that defy description) to sculp-tures crafted in Metepec in Mexico state. Surprisingly little known, this is one of the most comprehensive displays of its kind in the country. And its shop has the best souvenirs I've seen in the region.

A small but interesting look into the pre-Hispanic history of the enigmatic Maya is tucked into the south side of the Cancún Convention Center. **Museo INAH** (Bl. Kukulcán Km 9, Zona Hotelera; ☎ 998/883-0305), operated by the National Institute of Anthropology and History, contains hundreds of relics from Quintana Roo's archaeological sites, including stelae, jewelry, masks, and intentionally deformed skulls. The museum closed after Hurricane Wilma, and at the time of this writing it had not announced a reopening date.

It's popularly referred to as a crocodile farm, and it does look a lot an old-timey Florida roadside attraction, but **Croco Cun** ★★★ (kids) (Carretera Cancún-Tulum Km 31; ☎ 998/850-3719; www.crococunzoo.com; $17 adults, $11 children, free for kids under 6; daily 9am–5pm, until 6pm Mar–Aug) is a lot more than that. If your vacation won't be taking you off road, this "interactive zoo" on the road to Puerto Morelos is your best chance for nose-to-nose encounters with some of the Yucatan's most fascinating natives. And yes, that does include crocodiles—you can even hold one of the babies, which are disarmingly cute and surprisingly benign. You'll walk through crocs in all stages of development (the 227kg/500-lb. patriarch remains secure in his pit), part of a privately funded captive breeding program that releases offspring in coastal habitats. Croco Cun did start as a crocodile farm, and it takes pride in its role in increasing the toothy reptiles' numbers in Nichupté Lagoon from 200 when Cancún was developed to 7,800 today. But its conservation mission has expanded, and it now houses specimens of many of the reptiles and some of the mammals indigenous to the area. You can pet fat iguanas, wind a boa around your shoulders, and feed spider monkeys that leap onto your shoulder, all the while learning about these creatures' adaptations to the local environment. The immensely informative tours are guided by volunteers who are studying veterinary medicine. These are knowledgeable and safety-conscious young people, and their dedication is infectious. Many tour buses stop here, but they don't get the full 90-minute tour, which is offered in English or Spanish.

Better marine life displays can be found in most of the aquariums you'll encounter in your travels, but at the **Interactive Aquarium** (kids) (La Isla Shopping Village, Km 12.5, Zona Hotelera; ☎ 800/012-0856 toll-free Mexico, or 998/883-0411; www.interactivedolphins.com; $13 adults, $10 children; daily 9am–7pm) you do get to pet manta rays, nurse sharks, sea turtles, and other marine creatures in open exhibition tanks. Guides diving in the main tank, which is an artificial reef teeming with tropical fish, point out the sea life and answer questions using underwater microphones. A 20-minute dolphin show, held daily at 6 and 7pm, is included with admission. For $65 ($100 for two, $10 for three) you can join the Shark Encounter, donning diving gear to be lowered into the aquarium's huge shark tank. You'll spend 30 minutes underwater, feeding bull, brown, and nurse sharks from small slots protected by your acrylic cage. You can also pet and swim with the dolphins for about the same price (see "Active Cancún," p. 53).

## MAYA ARCHAEOLOGICAL ZONES

They're no substitute for visiting Chichén Itzá or Tulum, but vestiges of pre-Columbian settlements scattered throughout Cancún are a welcome reminder of the Maya coastal trade empire that once stretched from Honduras' Bay islands to the salt beds of northern Yucatán state. Remnants of ancient watchtowers and lighthouses suggest the Maya used Cancún as a Caribbean lookout on the route between Tulum, Cozumel, and Chichén Itzá. These stops make a rewarding break from the rigors of snorkeling, shopping, or chasing a tan. And if one of the famous archaeological sites isn't on your itinerary, the ruins here make a decent introduction to the ancient Maya world.

The collision of ancient and modern is at its most striking at **Ruinas El Rey** (Blvd. Kukulcán Km 17.5 across from Playa Delfines, Zona Hotelera; ☎ 998/883-2080; $4; daily 9am–4:30pm). Standing among the broken columns, stepped platforms, and stairways of a palace (Structure 4), you'll see the crowning glass pyramid of the Hilton Cancún Golf & Spa Resort looming beyond the piles of stone. In fact, the ruins were incorporated into the golf course. This might be the most peaceful spot on Bulevar Kukulcán; it's so quiet that you'll hear the scuttling before you see the perfectly camouflaged, plump iguanas that have colonized the ancient foundations by the hundreds. Many of the objects in the INAH archaeological museum (p. 47) were recovered from these 16 buildings.

Though the Maya lived in Cancún as early as 200 B.C., El Rey ("The King") was built much later. A ceremonial center and possibly an astronomy lookout, the city reached its apex during the Postclassic period (A.D. 1250–1521). Its two main plazas and two ceremonial walkways are unusual among Maya cities, which typically have one of each. Archaeologists stop short of definite conclusions but presume the site was a royal burial ground. The original Maya name, Kin Ich Ahau Bonil, means "king of the solar countenance," and skeletons uncovered in the pyramid (Structure 2) appear to have been kings. Two small altars are all that remain of a temple that once topped the pyramid. The Maya commonly built pyramids on top of older structures, and partially buried in the middle of the pyramid is a stairway and a balustrade from an earlier building. The best-preserved building is Structure 3B, a temple where you can make out traces of an original painting in what is believed to have been a king's tomb.

Though El Rey is the most complete archaeological site in the Hotel Zone, a visit takes only about an hour. Many structures are marked by plaques with information in Spanish, Mayan, and English.

Two much smaller but beguiling sites on the island are a little trickier to get to. **Yamil Lu'um** (Bl. Kukulcán Km 12.5, Zona Hotelera), south of Playa Chac Mool, consists of two structures, believed to be a temple and a lighthouse, built between A.D. 1200 and 1500. The site stands between the Westin Lagunamar and the Park Royal resorts above the beach on Cancún's highest point—the name means "hilly land." To get there, ask the concierge at one of those properties to let you through, or approach it from the beach; it's a short walk north of Playa Marlin. Half a kilometer north of El Rey, unrestored temples and pyramids surround a ceremonial square at **San Miguelito** (Kukulcán Km 16.5, Zona Hotelera), near the beach of the same name. The site, which dates to sometime between A.D. 900 and 1521, stands in the jungle in front of the Royal Mayan resort.

Other smaller remnants of Maya buildings dot the island in unlikely places, such as fragments of the tiny, badly deteriorated temple of Ni Ku on the grounds of Dreams Cancún Resort & Spa, and two more on the Pok-Ta-Pok golf course.

You'll have to leave the hotel zone to see the northern Yucatán's tallest pyramid. **El Meco** (Carretera Puerto Juárez-Punta Sam Km 2.7; $3; daily 8am–5pm) is about 6km (3½ miles) north of Ciudad Cancún on the Bahía de Mujeres, between Puerto Juárez and Punta Sam. It opened to the public only in 2001 and is still sparsely visited, so wandering among the 14 buildings and vestigial columns and stucco walls protruding from the dry jungle makes a tranquil interlude. Sadly, visitors are no longer allowed to climb the pyramid El Castillo. El Meco emerged late in the 10th century on the site of an even earlier, primitive fishing town, to become the main departure point for Isla Mujeres and an important reference point for sailors. As the story goes, the name comes from a coconut rancher who owned the land in 19th century. *El meco* means bow-legged, and the rancher was, well, bow-legged. The original Maya name is lost.

Today's highway cuts El Meco in two. The side that is open to the public includes the large central plaza that served as the city's ceremonial heart. El Castillo, with snakes carved into its base and an outer staircase leading to the top, looks onto two smaller buildings believed to have been a temple and an administrative building. The best-preserved building is a small temple in the northern part of the park. Archaeologists are still exploring the region between the highway and the coast, which has the remains of an ancient dock. This, as much as the tall pyramid, marks El Meco's significance, since its most important activity was shipping religious and commercial items to Isla Mujeres.

## HOTELS

More than ever since the post-Wilma rebuilding effort, the Hotel Zone's imposing and sometimes outlandish architecture has become one of Cancún's main attractions, literally and figuratively overshadowing its famous beaches. Bulevar Kukulcán's display of sleek glass pyramids, gargantuan *palapas,* block-long palaces, and Lego-brick towers is impossible to ignore, so why try? Just because you don't drop the equivalent of a mortgage payment to spend the night doesn't mean you can't stop in for a margarita and drink in the creative opulence at the same time. It's a little like gawking at the derivative excesses of the Vegas Strip or the manic march of skyscrapers across Dubai—an awe-inspiring and enlightening glimpse into the culture of a certain place and time. For sheer eye candy, here are some of the best (from north to south).

With its privileged perch at the tip of Punta Cancún, **Dreams Cancún Resort & Spa** is the only resort surrounded by the sea on three sides; one low-slung, vaguely pyramidal wing sloping into its own saltwater lagoon is a variation on the angular, contemporary Mexican design. The **Fiesta Americana Aqua** (Km 12.5), which reopened only in spring 2008 after extensive renovations, is a love letter to Modernism with a curving, all-glass facade, crystal cube fountain, and watery turquoise-and-white interiors.

The crystal-chandelier, polished-marble formality of the **Ritz-Carlton** (Km 14) shows Spanish influence in its elaborately tiled roofs, wrought-iron railings, and trickling fountains. Next door, **Le Méridien** (Km 14) gets many visitors' votes as Cancún's classiest luxury hotel, blending French Art Deco and traditional Maya details in an artful mix of wood, glass, and mirrors. You have to wonder what Cancún's ancient inhabitants would have made of the **Gran Meliá Cancún**'s (Km 16.5) minicity of five concrete-and-glass pyramids, the central one a nine-story affair enclosing a jungle greenhouse with five-story pillars supporting a smoked-glass skylight. At the **Fiesta Americana Condesa** (Km 16.5) next door,

## Getting Out of Town

One reason Cancún was anointed Mexico's reigning tourist destination was its proximity to the Yucatán's trove of natural, historical, and cultural riches. If you're not planning an excursion on your own, you can easily get out of town for the day with a tour operator. Cancún's sidewalks are swarming with so many competing tour operators that it's tempting to simply put yourself in the hands of your hotel concierge. I can recommend **Alltournative** (Hwy. 307 Km 287, Playa del Carmen; ☎ 800/507-1092 toll-free U.S., or 984/803-9999; www.alltournative.com), a socially and environmentally conscious outfit that runs adventurous and enlightening excursions into Maya jungle communities ($92–$115), as well as dive tours; and **Eco Colors** (Calle Camarón 32, SM 27, Cancún; ☎ 998/884-3667; www.ecotravelmexico.com), which runs day trips ($48–$205) to Isla Holbox, Sian Ka'an, and Maya ruins.

what has to be the world's largest *palapa* and hotel towers sculpted like ancient cliff dwellings form an envelope for pure extravagance.

## WORTHWHILE TOURIST TRAPS

It is the very definition of touristy, but you won't get a better view in all of Cancún than from the **Torre Escénica Giratoria (Rotating Scenic Tower)** (El Embarcadero, Bl. Kukulcán Km 4.9, Zona Hotelera; ☎ 998/849-7777; $9; daily 9am–4pm). The 80m (263-ft.) tower has a rotating cabin and audio descriptions in English and other languages. For 10 minutes, you'll get a 360-degree view of downtown, Isla Mujeres, the Caribbean coast, and the open sea.

    **Parque Nizuc Water Park** [kids] (Bl. Kukulcán Km 25, Zona Hotelera; ☎ 998/881-3030; www.wetnwildcancun.com; $45 adults, $39 children; daily 10am–5pm), at the southern tip of Cancún Island, is all about water. The main attraction is Atlántida, where the chance to swim with dolphins thrills young and old alike (see "Active Cancún," p. 53). When that's over, you can also snorkel with stingrays, nurse sharks, and other tropical fish at Baxalha. And if those aren't enough, you can thoroughly douse yourself at Wet'n Wild. It's not terribly different from dozens of other water parks around the world, though it does have a smashing tube ride and some big, wild slides. Admission includes a food coupon, and is free with purchase of a dolphin swim.

## THE OTHER CANCUN

Culinary-minded tourists can join local students working toward diplomas at the **Taller Gourmet** ✹✹ (Av. Sunyaxchen 64-B at Yaxchilán, Centro; ☎ 998/898-4612; www.tallergourmet.com), which has turned out sous chefs and line cooks for the Hotel Zone's high-end restaurants. Topics range from menu planning to sautéing to salsas, stews, Mexican pastry, and the all-important maize. The cuisines of Oaxaca, Michoacán, Veracruz, the Yucatán, and other regions share the roster with European and Asian cooking. When school is in session, September through April, visitors who call ahead are welcome to attend single sessions of regularly scheduled classes from 9am to 12:30pm weekdays for 475 pesos ($46). Chef Federico López, who studied at the Culinary Institute of America, will also create a special class outside of regular school hours for groups of visitors who call ahead to make arrangements. Regular school classes are in Spanish, though López says he will try to explain in English if tourists are sitting in, and he will conduct the special group classes in English.

Many of Cancún's beachfront resorts participate in the city's coordinated **sea turtle rescue program** ✪✪✪ and invite their guests to help release new hatchlings back into the sea during nesting season. You don't always have be a guest to join in, though. The **Ritz-Carlton** (Bl. Kukulcán Km 14, Zona Hotelera; ☎ 998/881-0808; www.ritzcarlton.com), for example, welcomes anyone who wants to volunteer. The resort added a new staff position, the Kanan-Ak ("turtle guardian" in Mayan), who ushers volunteers through a wildlife encounter like no other. Depending on the timing of your visit, you might patrol the beach at night in search of nesting turtles while the Kanan-Ak talks about efforts to safeguard the diminishing sea turtle population. As the hatchlings emerge, you may carry the babies to the beach at sunset (to avoid threats from land predators) and see them on their way to their new life in the ocean. In a brief ceremony accompanying this ritual, you listen to ocean sounds in a seashell and entrust the babies to Ixchel, a Maya goddess who takes the travelers under her protection.

The ideal introduction to real life in Cancún is **Parque de las Palapas** ✪✪✪ (bounded by Margaritas, Gladiolas, and Tulipanes, Centro). Cancún's version of the classic central square, or *zócalo*, was rebuilt after being chewed up by Hurricane Wilma, and the new plaza has more concrete than character. On the plus side, it is cleaner, and artists still hang their paintings in two small satellite parks, Parque Los Artesanos and Jardín del Arte, on weekends. If Parque de las Palapas looks less

---

## Turtle Season

Thousands of sea turtles arrive on the beaches of each year in May and June to lay their eggs. In the natural order of things, the eggs would incubate in the sand until hatching 40 or 50 days later. But tourists jumping for volleyballs and tractors clearing land for a new resort tower have made beaches a perilous place for baby turtles, and four species were threatened with extinction when Cancún's marine turtle conservation program asked the beach resorts for help several years ago.

Cooperating resorts send specially trained staff out at night to protect the mother turtle until she returns to the ocean. They then collect the eggs, nests and all, to be taken to a nursery where biologists supervise the incubators and collect data on the program. When the hatchlings emerge, staff and volunteers take them back to their nesting sites on the beach and release them to find their way to the sea. Nesting season usually runs through September, but may last through October in some years.

inviting than the old park by day, it still comes alive at night with crowds of couples, families, balloon vendors, and huddles of giggling teenagers. Grab a seat under one of the white umbrellas and sample the $1 tacos, *cochinita pibil* sandwiches, and other treats from the food stalls that line one side of the park, while kids chase dogs, dance, zip around on toy SUVs, and swarm the play structures. The bandstand usually hosts live music and dance performances on weekends, but you can also get a great evening's entertainment from the impromptu and surprisingly polished efforts of young bongo and guitar players.

Your one-stop shop for a culture fix is the **Casa de la Cultura de Cancún** ★★ (Prolongación Av. Yaxchilán, SM 21, Centro; ☎ 998/884-8364; www.casadecultura cancun.blogspot.com). The "House of Culture" maintains a rotating exhibition of local artists' work and generates an exhausting schedule of art exhibits, traditional dances, poetry readings, literary events, and theater and musical performances at least three or four times a week. One month, for example, included a film on Diego Rivera, a dance by students of the Academy of Spanish Dance and Flamenco, and special programs for International Women's Day and International Theater Day . . . to name a few. Other events can also include round-table discussions on hot-button topics related to Cancún.

The Casa de la Cultura also offers a regular schedule of art, literature, music, theater, and dance workshops. Among these are "Salsa and Latin Dance," "Hatha Yoga," "Introduction to Music for Children," and "Mayan Language" classes. Keep in mind that this a local community center, so events are presented in Spanish and charge a nominal fee, if any. But visitors are welcome, and you can enjoy many events whether you know Spanish or not. Events are posted on the website; for a schedule of classes, e-mail casadelaculturadecancun@yahoo.com.mx.

There might be no more unlikely place to take Spanish classes than the one destination in Mexico where you could conceivably spend your entire vacation speaking only English; Cancún poses no threat to colonial cities such as Cuernavaca and Oaxaca, where language schools are a major source of tourism. But Cancún does have **El Bosque del Caribe** ★★★ (Av. Nader 52 at Uxmal, Centro; ☎ 998/884-1065; www.cancunlanguage.com), the only school here dedicated to teaching Spanish to foreigners. Eduardo Sotelo, a native of Cuernavaca who has run El Bosque with his Swiss-born wife for 13 years, interviews each student to determine the level of study and adapts the program to individual learning styles. This isn't the repetition and language labs of your high school days. You'll absorb Spanish through conversation, newspapers, literature, and music as well as textbooks and videos, and then put it to use on excursions to markets, museums, and restaurants.

You can take best advantage of this opportunity to delve into local life and do your lodging budget a favor at the same time by staying with a Mexican family. Participating families live in middle-class neighborhoods a few blocks from the school's downtown campus. Students pay $26 per night ($23 per person double) including two meals a day; bed and breakfast only is $23 single, $19 double. Other economical options don't include meals and are shared with other students, three-fourths of whom come from Europe, Brazil, and Asia ($20 single, $17 per person double). The school can also arrange private air-conditioned apartments. Apartment prices vary with the season and are quoted upon request.

Group courses have a maximum of six students but often are smaller, except in the busy months of July and August. Four weeks are recommended to advance from one level to the next, but the small-family atmosphere produces significant progress in as little as one week. Group courses cost $195 a week for 25 hours of class (5 hr. a day, Mon–Fri) or $145 for 15 hours, plus a one-time enrollment fee of $100. Either can be combined with a 4-day, open-water dive certification course ($435). The school also organizes dancing and cooking lessons for $5 to $10 extra and offers excursions to Maya ruins.

# ACTIVE CANCUN

With the Caribbean on one side and Nichupté Lagoon on the other, water is the element that dominates Cancún's active pursuits. Interrupting a sojourn under a *palapa* with the occasional dip in clear, turquoise water is all the exertion many Cancún visitors are seeking. But if you're looking for some adrenaline with your indulgence, hundreds of vendors, from big commercial outfits to modest beach-side concessions, stand ready to serve. Cancún is becoming the dolphin-swim capital of the world, and watersports entrepreneurs are constantly coming up with new innovations whether we need them or not, just to keep return guests from succumbing to the "been there, done that" mentality. Landlubbers needn't feel left out either—golfing and horseback riding are close at hand. But be forewarned: None of this fun comes cheap.

## WATERSPORTS & TOURS

The general rule is the bigger the thrill, the bigger the bill. If you want to become one of those color sprinkles dotting the sky over Cancún's most popular beaches, drinking in the ultimate ocean view, prices for **parasailing** are fairly uniform at about $50 per person. Mind you, that's for a 10-minute adrenaline rush (plus the boat ride to and from the launch point), making it one of the island's most expensive beach sports. But if you're not an acrophobe, the sensation of soaring over the Caribbean, your skin bare to the wind, is like no other. Independent operators work most of the public beaches, especially Ballenas, Chac Mool, Delfines, Playa Gaviota Azul, and Playa Marlin. The same beaches are good for **windsurfing,** and sailboards are rented at many hotels and most marinas. Expect to pay about $60 an hour, but if you aren't experienced, add another $60 for lessons (it usually takes about 6 hr. of instruction to get a good start).

The most frugal, and underrated, pursuit is **kayaking,** which remains so popular that many hotels now offer kayaks to guests free of charge. A kayak is a great vantage point for exploring Cancún's watery surroundings, whether it's spotting crocodiles, turtles, and tropical birds among Laguna Nichupté's mangroves or paddling around Punta Nizuc, where the edge of the Mesoamerican Barrier Reef system and its attendant confetti-colored fish are visible through 2.5m (8 ft.) of crystalline water. Rental outlets are plentiful along the beaches and at marinas, generally charging about $25 an hour (3-hr. lessons cost about $60).

**Jungle tours** have become a Cancún classic, probably because they combine two popular watersports for a relatively low fee. Usually accompanied by two guides, one in front and one in back, you pilot your own WaveRunner or small speedboat, winding through the mangroves lining Nichupté Lagoon to reach the Caribbean Sea at Punta Nizuc. Most include 45 minutes of snorkeling in the shallow reef (they're about 2½ hr. total; average cost $60 per person). It's fine as an introduction, taking in both the lagoon and the ocean, but the trips are a bit regimented and your group might include dozens of adventurers during busy seasons. After you've done it once, you'll probably prefer the freedom of renting jet skis and going snorkeling on your own.

A constantly rotating lineup of entrepreneurs rent **jet skis** and **WaveRunners** along both the beach and the lagoon sides of the island (drivers must be 18). Within the buoys that mark areas where jet-skiing is allowed, you can zoom along as fast as you like. The going rate hovers around $70 per hour for jet skis and $90 for WaveRunners. Check to see that the watercraft is in good condition before you accept the keys, and report any minor dings before you take it out, or you might be accused of causing the damage. **Banana boat** rides on elongated, dou-ble-pontoon rafts towed at warp speed by a motorboat are less common but are available through some hotels and at Playa Tortugas and Playa Ballenas (about $25 per person for a 20-min. ride). A few hotels and most of the marinas rent small, zippy **Hobie Cats** and **Sunfish** boats. Rates depend on the sailboats' seat-ing capacity and how long you keep it out, generally ranging from about $30 to $70 an hour. You can usually bargain for a better rate if you rent for a half or a whole day.

For the most part, Cancún's beaches aren't suited to **surfing;** the northern beaches on the Bahía de Mujeres are too placid, and the Caribbean beaches are too tumultuous. When conditions do conspire to produce good surf, it usually will be at Playa Chac Mool or at Playa Delfines, which became the official site of the Mexican Surf Festival (www.surfcancunmex.com) in 2006. I've heard reports of surf lessons being offered in a beach hut there, but I haven't seen it.

**Water-skiing** is best on the calm waters of Laguna Nichupté, though calm days bring some enthusiasts to Bahía de Mujeres, north of the island. Rentals and lessons, available at many marinas, cost about $70 per hour.

If you know what you're doing, you can find (or negotiate) lower prices for equipment rentals and lessons from mom-and-pop outlets along the beach. If you're a novice and just want a few hours of fun, or you're looking for a tour, you're better off with one of the established operators. Here are some well-regarded outfits that offer a variety of watersports:

The specialty at **Aqua Fun** (Bl. Kukulcán Km 16.2; ☎ 998/885-3260 or 885-2930; www.aquafun.com.mx) is the classic jungle tour, but it also offers a tour that explores Laguna Nichupté and the channels meandering through the mangroves. The family-owned business has operated a small marina on the lagoon, across from Royal Mayan, for 20 years. Its small speedboats are in top condition and have side-by-side seating, which most people prefer to the tandem-style WaveRunners. The experience is more personalized and relaxed than tours from larger outfits. Equipment rented includes WaveRunners, jet skis, snorkeling equipment, sail-boats; Aqua Fun also offers chartered fishing trips and jungle tours.

Fishing trips are the main business at **Marina Manglar** 🅺 (Bl. Kukulcán Km 19.8; ☎ 998/885-1808; www.villasmanglar.com), part of a small, pleasant budget hotel (p. 28) on Nichupté Lagoon. But the company's experienced guides, less-traveled sites, and individual attention (with special accommodations for chil-dren) also make it a good place for other sports. These include water-skiing, scuba diving, and wakeboarding.

## Where to Find Them

Many of the Hotel Zone's major hotels have their own watersports rental facilities, but independent beach concessions also rent rubber rafts, kayaks, and snorkeling equipment. Nichupté Lagoon is dotted with boat, jet-ski, sailboard, and water-ski rental outlets. Watersports rentals and deep-sea fishing charters are clustered around the following public marinas:

**Playa Tortugas,** Bl. Kukulcán Km 6.5; ☎ 998/849-4995

**Marina Barracuda,** Bl. Kukulcán Km 14.1, in front of the Ritz-Carlton; ☎ 998/885-3444

**Marina del Rey,** Bl. Kukulcán Km 15.6, in front of Grand Oasis Cancún; ☎ 998/885-0363

**Marina Punta del Este,** Bl. Kukulcán Km 10.3; ☎ 998/883-1210

**El Embarcadero,** Bl. Kukulcán Km 4; ☎ 998/849-4848

**Mundo Marina,** Blvd. Kukulcán Km 5.5; ☎ 998/849-7257

**Solo Buceo** (Dreams Cancún Resort, Bl. Kukulcán Km 9.5; ☎ 998/883-3979; www.solobuceo.com), despite its name, is far from "only diving." Divers swear by this friendly shop, run by the same family since 1982, because of its intimate group sizes and individual attention. It offers the same personal service on parasailing, WaveRunner rentals, guided tours, snorkeling trips, boat rentals, and deep-sea fishing.

If all the choices are overwhelming, or you have a family who can't agree on one activity, the larger, all-things-to-all-people outfits come into play. **Aquatours** (Bl. Kukulcán Km 6; ☎ 800/713-8862 toll-free Mexico, 800/417-1736 toll-free U.S., or 998/849-4748; www.aquatours.com.mx), an offshoot of Dolphin Discovery (p. 56), is one of the island's most pleasant places to hit the water. The large marina has garden areas and a shoreline walking path, so it handles a lot of people without feeling like a mob scene. In addition to a jungle tour (in boats with side-by-side seating) it offers snorkeling tours, daylong sailing trips to Isla Mujeres, and dinner cruises. Packages combining the jungle tour, dinner cruise, and a dolphin swim are available for $246 per person, $42 less than separate bookings.

**AquaWorld** (Bl. Kukulcán Km 15.2; ☎ 998/848-8300; www.aquaworld.com.mx), the biggest and busiest operator, is the Wal-Mart of Cancún watersports. It offers a little of everything, from kayak and WaveRunner rentals to jungle tours (on tandem-seat WaveRunners), a lagoon cruise, diving and snorkeling trips, and fishing charters. Some of its prices are lower than those at other marinas, but its professional, efficient service is virtually devoid of personal attention. For those sports, you'll be happier with a smaller company; the reason to come to Aquaworld is for the activities the others don't offer. Its Sky Rider is an oversized parasail with a seat for two people ($50 per person). Hour for hour, the Sub See Explorer is one of Cancún's better deals: The glorified glass-bottom boat carries passengers entirely below the water's surface to explore the coral reef in Captain Nemo fashion on a

2-hour trip that includes lunch, refreshments, and an hour of snorkeling for about $45. For amusement-park thrills, the Aqua Twister ($43) is a kind of Tilt-a-Whirl on a jet boat that executes full-speed sideways slides, fishtails, and 270-degree spins. Various combo packages are available for $193 to $226, including day cruises or dolphin swims, or you can choose three shorter activities for $132 per person.

**BOB Cancún** (El Embarcadero, Bl. Kukulcán Km 4.5; ☎ 988/849-4440; www. cancun-webs.com/bob.htm) does one thing only, but it's a doozy: the "breathing observation bubble," an electric-powered underwater scooter that looks like something the Jetsons would have driven to do their errands had they lived in Atlantis. In your clear bubble helmet, you can breathe normally without an air hose, nose to nose with neon-colored fish as you scoot through the coral reefs. The 45-minute submersion costs $68 and includes a DVD documenting your experience.

## DOLPHIN SWIMS

Think about it for a minute: Dolphins are mammals, which means they breathe through lungs. But they spend their life in water, so how do they sleep? Wouldn't they drown? The answers (they don't, and yes, they would) are just some of the insights you pick up when you spend an hour with the playful, brainy creatures in their element. Several companies in Cancún offer chances to swim, ride, dance with, and kiss these awe-inspiring animals.

My favorite is **Dolphin Discovery** (Bl. Kukulcán Km 5, Playa Langosta Mall; ☎ 866/393-5158 toll-free U.S., or 998/193-3360; www.dolphindiscovery.com), whose facility on Isla Mujeres (a 40-min. boat ride from Playa Langosta in the Hotel Zone is included) is as close to open sea as you can get. Of the three options, the best is the Dolphin Royal Swim, an hour that includes an educational video with a conservation theme, an orientation session, and plenty of time to frolic with the dolphins, hang onto their fins for a ride across the water, practice hands-free water-skiing on their backs, and collect a kiss at the end. The price is $149; a 45-minute Dolphin Encounter for nonswimmers is $69 ($59 for children under 12) and a Dolphin Swim Adventure, also 45 minutes, is $99.

**Dolphinaris** (Wet'n Wild Water Park, Blvd. Kukulcán Km 23; ☎ 998/881-3000; www.dolphinaris.com) offers a 50-minute Dolphin Swim Experience, allowing you to swim with and touch the dolphins in shallow water and watch their under-water antics through a diving mask. It costs $99 for one person or $119 for two. The Dolphin Swim Program adds some finny acrobatics and a foot-push, which propels you across the water on their backs, costing $135 for one or $155 for two (Internet discounts available). Tickets include admission to the water park, where you can view more dolphins in their aquarium. The 50-minute Primax swimming program at **Delphinus** (Dreams Resort, Kukulcán Km 7.5; ☎ 998/206-3304; www. delphinusworld.com) on Punta Cancún is similar to Dolphin Discovery's Royal Swim and costs $149, with Internet discounts available. Once you get past the novelty of swimming with dolphins in a shopping center, the **Interactive Aquarium** (La Isla Shopping Village, Bl. Kukulcán Km 12.5; ☎ 998/883-0411; www.interactive dolphins.com) emerges as a clear third choice. The facilities, while not as spacious or as natural as the others, are commodious by most standards, and the animals

## To Swim, or Not to Swim?

Mexico outlawed the capture of wild dolphins in its waters in 2002, and strengthened the law in January 2006 to ban import and export of marine mammals as well. The only dolphins added to the country's dolphin swim programs since then were born in captivity.

That may have eased concerns about the torture and death associated with wild captures, but notes stapled to Dolphin Discovery ads on copies of *Cancún Tips* magazine, distributed in most Cancún hotels, attest to the enduring controversy. Dolphin-swim programs are staffed by marine biologists who say the mammals are thriving under human care. They also conduct research, conservation, and education programs and are frequently summoned to rescue sick and injured animals. But animal-rights advocates maintain that keeping these intelligent mammals in captivity is nothing more than exploitation. They argue that dolphin-swim programs don't qualify as "public display" under the Marine Mammal Protection Act because their cost makes them inaccessible to most of the public.

For more information on a complex question, you might visit the website of the **Whale and Dolphin Conservation Society** at www.wdcs.org or the **American Cetacean Society**, www.acsonline.org. The **Conservation of Marine Mammals in Mexico (COMARINO)** was instrumental in getting the 2006 ban passed. Although its website, www.comarino.org, is in Spanish, you may e-mail questions to contacto@comarino.com.

---

are treated with sensitivity. But surrounding boutiques, jewelry stores, and nightclubs is an unavoidable reminder that this is not what dolphins are meant to do. A 30-minute educational program for nonswimmers and timid folks costs $65, while the advanced program with all the stunts is $135. Both include entrance to the aquarium.

## FISHING

Cancún's fecund waters virtually guarantee success on fishing trips. Approximately 500 species of fish, including more than a dozen species of sport fish, live in the waters around the island. You can charter deep-sea fishing boats at almost any travel agency, in most large hotels, and at many piers. Rates start at about $380 for 4 hours and go up to around $680 for 8 hours. This should include a captain and first mate, gear, bait, and beverages. Rates are lower if you depart from Isla Mujeres or from Cozumel. Veteran fishermen head to the Puerto Juárez ferry dock to try to negotiate an even better deal with local fishermen.

In addition to **AquaWorld** and **Aqua Fun** (see "Watersports & Tours," above), the following are reliable operators that charge fair prices.

**Scuba Cancún** (Bl. Kukulcán Km 5; ☎ 998/849-7508 or 849-5225), a family-run dive center, also has experienced captains that take anglers out, charging $450 to $749 for trips of 4 to 8 hours for six to eight people. If you can't fill the

## Gone Fishing

The actual seasons are longer than what's shown below—in some cases extending throughout the year—but these are the best times for catching some of Cancún's most prized fish:

**Blue marlin:** June, July, and August

**White marlin:** April to June

**Sailfish:** March to July

**Grouper:** October to December

**Wahoo:** November to January, April to June

**Amberjack:** September to December

**Dolphin fish, blackfin tuna:** April to May

**Bonita:** April to August

**Barracuda, kingfish:** October to December

boat, a shared fishing program is available for $99 per person (4 hr.) to $113 (6 hr.). The family program ($58 adults, $38 children) combines snorkeling, swimming, 2 hours of fishing, and lunching on the catch.

**Marina Manglar** (see "Watersports & Tours," above) mines largely unexplored fishing grounds in the shallows around Isla Blanca, about 40 minutes north of Cancún, primarily for tarpon, snook, and bonefish. The charge for two anglers is $375. Free door-to-door transportation included.

## SNORKELING & SCUBA DIVING

As a snorkeling and diving destination, Cancún's greatest virtue may be its proximity to Isla Mujeres and Cozumel. Cancún's underwater scenery can't compare with the spectacles around those islands, and excursions to those superior sites make up a good portion of the local dive shops' offerings. Still, Cancún's shallow reef, crystalline waters, and colorful marine life make diving and snorkeling popular in its calmer waters, and they are especially suited to beginners.

General consensus puts the best snorkeling and diving at Punta Nizuc, the northern tip of the Gran Arrecife Maya (Great Mesoamerican Reef), the largest reef in the Western Hemisphere and the second-largest in the world. Not only do hundreds of species of tropical fish put on a good show, but several sunken boats add some intriguing dive options. Other favored reefs, between Cancún and Isla Mujeres, are El Tunel, San Toribio, and San Miguel; Cancún has no shore diving. More experienced divers seek out nearby inland caverns and cenotes, or sinkholes, to explore the cool, freakishly clear waters that percolate from the subterranean channels scoring the Yucatán Peninsula. Punta Cancún, along with its offshore Chintales and El Bajito reefs, is another good bet for snorkelers, as is Playa Tortugas (though you have to be mindful of the currents).

Almost all of Cancún's resorts rent snorkeling masks and fins, and you should be able to find them for $10 to $15 at any dive shop and set out on your own.

But snorkelers can get more awe for their buck by joining an excursion with a knowledgeable guide. The companies listed here have strong reputations for service and offer guided trips that put those jungle tours' snorkeling interludes to shame. Some also arrange cenote trips for snorkelers.

Scuba divers will find Cancún's offerings okay for a quick fix, but if you have time, you'll be find it more satisfying to join a trip to Cozumel or the Riviera Maya. In any case, look for an outfit that will let you meet the dive master and view the equipment and certification.

A small, family operation owned by U.S. expatriates, **Manta Divers Scuba Center** (Bl. Kukulcán Km 13.5; ☎ 998/849-4050; www.mantadivers.com) keeps its groups small and makes a genuine effort to help divers experience the Caribbean's wonders. Two-tank reef dives cost $67, including equipment, while a PADI open-water certification course is $389. Experienced divers may do a night dive for $74, explore the wrecks of two U.S. Navy minesweepers for $79, or make a cenote trip to the Riviera Maya for $145. They also offer two-reef snorkeling trips, cenote snorkeling, and a Cozumel snorkeling trip for $45 to $98. Most intriguing is a whale shark expedition (June 15–Aug 31 only) for $175.

Another small operation, **Lemon Divers** (Bl. Kukulcán Km 2.5; ☎ 998/845-0977; lemondiver@yahoo.com), on the beach of Las Perlas Hotel, also limits group size and works with divers to create the trips they want. Owned by a PADI instructor, its boat captain and crew get high marks from all levels of divers. Two-tank dives are $60, including equipment, as is a one-tank night dive is $60. The open-water certification course here is $360. They also offer cenote dives for $115 and a "Sleeping Shark" trip for $125.

You can be sure of finding the best reefs with **Solo Buceo** (Dreams Cancún Resort, Bl. Kukulcán Km 9.5; ☎ 998/883-3979; www.solobuceo.com), and with its selection of trips to Cozumel or cenotes, you can visit a different dive site on every day of your vacation. Two-tank reef dives cost $70, while two-tank Cozumel trips or cenote dives near Akumal are $145. They also offer open-water certification courses ranging from $120 to $330.

In business since 1982, **Marina Punta del Este** (Bl. Kukulcán Km 10.3, in front of Hyatt Cancún Caribe; ☎ 998/849-7508; www.marinapuntadeleste.com) focuses on personalized service, and works only in small groups. A two-tank dive starts at $72; just $7 more gets you a trip to the sunken Mexican navy ship. A 4-hour lesson costs $88.

**Nautilus Diving Training Center** (Bl. Kukulcán Km 9; ☎ 998/884-0791; www.cancunscuba.com), located at the Best Western Cancún Clipper Club, has been in

## Resort Course, or Open Water?

Many resorts offer 1-hour dive courses for free. You'll learn the basics, but these courses do not qualify you for open-ocean diving. They are intended only to prepare you to dive in shallow water where you can surface safely and easily— enough to introduce you to the unimaginably beautiful world below the water's surface. If you're hooked, look into taking an open-water certification course.

business for more than 23 years has a reputation for being organized, attentive, and talented at finding startling quantities of undersea life. A two-tank dive costs $60, including equipment; wreck dives and night dives are $65. You can get full PADI certification for $375. Nautilus also offers cenote diving ($125) and Cozumel trips ($137, including equipment, national park fee, and all transportation).

## GOLF

Cancún is proud of, and famous for, both the challenge and the beauty of its golf courses, which are graced by mangrove stands, Maya ruins, and impossibly beautiful Caribbean views. Green fees here don't reach the heights of Pebble Beach or St. Andrew's, but it's not a sport for the faint of wallet. "Twilight" rates (which actually start as early as 1pm) can shave the cost of a round by $30 to $50. And if you plan ahead, online booking sites such as **Mexico Tee Times** (www.teetimes mexico.com) and **Internet Golf** (www.bookyourgolf.net) discount the regular fees by 10% to 30%, depending on season and time of play.

The original is still the best loved: **Cancún Golf Club at Pok-Ta-Pok** (Bl. Kukulcán Km 7.5; ☎ 998/883-1230; www.cancungolfclub.com). There are newer, more heralded greens, but you've got to love a course that has 1,000-year-old Maya ruins for a 12th-hole hazard and straddles Bulevar Kukulcán to sweep in both Caribbean and lagoon views. The 18-hole, par 72 course was designed by Robert Trent Jones, Jr. Green fees, including a cart, are $145 in low season to $175 in high season, with twilight rates (after 2pm low season, 1pm high) are $115 to $125. Check with your hotel to see if it offers special rates at Pok-Ta-Pok. The course's affiliations seem to shift with the winds and favors higher-priced resorts, but the last time I was there, the Holiday Inn Express was offering 20% discounts on golf and 15% on food and drinks.

The 60-hectare (150-acre) **Hilton Cancún Golf & Spa Resort** (Bl. Kukulcán Km 17; ☎ 998/881-8016; www.hiltoncancun.com/golf.htm), which meanders around Nichupté Lagoon, presents views of water at every turn, and its 16th hole skirts the El Rey archaeological site for haunting views of the Maya ruins. The impeccably manicured 18-hole, par 72 course was refurbished in 2006 with Papsalum Sea Isle grass and its tees leveled to USGA standards. Public green fees, which include a cart, range from $149 in low season to $199 in high season, but you'll pay $50 less by opting for 9 holes or playing after 2pm to take advantage of twilight rates.

## HORSEBACK RIDING

No, you won't be clopping down Bulevar Kukulcán. **Rancho Loma Bonita** (Carretera Cancún-Tulum Km 49; ☎ 998/887-5423 or 887-5465; www.rancholomabonita. com) is technically just over the dividing line between Cancún and the Riviera Maya, about 3km (2 miles) south of Puerto Morelos, but it's the closest place to Cancún for horseback riding. After being separated into groups based on experience level, you'll ride single file through mangrove jungle filled with wild peacocks, deer, turtles, and wild pigs, emerging about 45 minutes later at the ocean. Experienced riders (who pay an extra $10 and sign a waiver) are free to gallop at will along the beach. What keeps some people coming back over and over— besides the congenial guides—is riding into the Caribbean for a short swim on horseback, though you can opt out if you're not comfortable. Back at the corral,

## Body Work

Submitting to some judicious kneading or steaming is a brilliant way to replenish yourself after a day of swimming, sailing, and soaring. Resort spas are big business in Cancún, with ever more elaborate palaces of pampering that welcome the general public. Of course, you can easily drop $200 on that indulgence, which I hope is more than you're paying for 1 night's lodging. You could try to justify it by tallying up all the money you've saved by not actually staying in those tony resorts, or you could go to the **Centro Naturista** (in Hotel Xbalamqué, p. 34, Av. Yaxchilán at Jazmines; ☎ 998/887-7853) instead.

The Centro Naturista is hardly palatial, but its artful stone and tile floors and the light filtering through a wall of windows into the plant-filled main corridor suggest the privilege of an earlier era. You can get a natural marine-algae facial, formulated to Cancún's environment and adapted to your skin type, for 385 pesos ($37), or a 50-minute harmonizing massage for the same price. A 2-hour aromatherapy treatment costs 490 pesos ($47). And a 30-minute Maya ritual in a tile-and-brick domed *temazcal* will only set you back 120 pesos ($12).

a light Mexican-style lunch is served, and there's a swimming pool if you need to cool off. The tour lasts 2 hours and costs about $66 for adults, $60 for children (minimum age 6 years). The ranch is about a half-hour drive from Cancún, and transportation is available for an extra $10. Tours run three times a day; do yourself a favor and take the 9am tour to avoid the afternoon heat. If you go in the warmer months, you'll want bug spray. The ranch also offers WaveRunners, snorkeling, scuba diving, deep-sea fishing, and ATV tours.

## ATTENTION, SHOPPERS!

You can buy just about anything you can think of in Cancún. Its huge, air-conditioned malls are renowned throughout Mexico and have become attractions on par with the beaches and clubs; most are open daily from 9am to 10pm or later. Local residents treat malls like the main plazas of colonial cities and dress to the hilt to stroll with their neighbors. You'll find the stores, the brands, and even the food look pretty familiar (same goes for the prices). For the more traditional Mexican shopping experience—with haggling over prices and dodging hawkers—downtown is the best bet. Most mall retailers take major credit cards; markets deal in cash.

### MALLS

The newest and easily most appealing of the Hotel Zone's glitzy shopping malls is a collection of contradictions. The Downtown Disney look of the open-air **La Isla Shopping Village** ✰✰ (Bl. Kukulcán Km 12.5; ☎ 998/883-5025) might lead you to believe this is a hive of tourists and high-priced stores. You would be right . . . sort of. The 250-plus retailers occupy reasonable facsimiles of grand town houses that line a series of canals, bridges, and walkways but also operate out of kiosks where you might have a shot at exercising your bargaining skills. The "Caribbean village" architecture, with its fountains and mosaic floors, feels more like a brand-spanking new version of Venice. You can, with little effort, drop a fortune at Bulgari or Tommy Hilfiger, but you can also find Lancôme, Chanel, or Clinique cosmetics at duty-free prices (typically amounting to 25% less than U.S. prices) at Ultrafemme, or pick up a well-made cotton tank top or pair of shorts for $10 to at Miro. Good-quality silver bracelets can be purchased for $20 to $50 at one of the craft carts. Tourists do flock to La Isla, drawn like moths to the brilliantly lit signs and the flaming colors of the nighttime light shows at the pond-size, walk-through fountain that throws water jets 15m (50 ft.) into the air, but locals also make Cancún's version of the leisurely evening *paseo* here. Nighttime is the right time at La Isla, whether you stroll the streets, thrash in a thumping disco, catch a movie at the 10-screen theater, or sample its restaurants. Not a shopper? Take a boat tour on the canals, burn off some energy on a rock-climbing wall, arrange a diving or fishing expedition at the marina, or commune with the fishes (and dolphins) at the Interactive Aquarium (p. 47).

The other major malls are also cool, modern, and comfortable, but with little to distinguish one from another. The three-level, open-air **Plaza Forum by the Sea** (Bl. Kukulcán Km 9.5; ☎ 998/883-4426) has several name-brand shops and restaurants, including a Harley-Davidson showroom, but is noted more for its entertainment, which includes disco powerhouse Coco Bongo (p. 64). **Plaza Caracol** (Bl. Kukulcán Km 8.5; ☎ 998/883-4759; www.caracolplaza.com), next to the Convention Center, is known for such tony specialty shops as Gucci, Polo, and Cartier. The enclosed **Plaza Kukulcán** (Bl. Kukulcán Km 13; ☎ 998/885-2200; www.kukulcanplaza.com) boasts hundreds of shops, restaurants, and the only bar I know of with its own eight-lane bowling alley. In addition to names such as Benetton, Mont Blanc, Max Mara, and Versace. Plaza Kukulcán's new Luxury Avenue section houses exclusive shops such as Lladrò, Fendi, and Cartier. The smaller, dowdier **Plaza Flamingo** (Bl. Kukulcán Km 11.5; ☎ 998/883-2855) offers mainly clothing, jewelry, souvenirs, and party restaurant chains.

## HANDICRAFTS

Though Cancún has no handicrafts industry of its own, you can find a wide variety of woodcarvings, *huipiles* (traditional embroidered dresses), hammocks, pottery, textiles, and jewelry from throughout the country. Not surprisingly, prices are higher than they are in other parts of Mexico. Even the malls sell some handicrafts, but the Hotel Zone's best selection of Mexican goods is at **Plaza la Fiesta** ★ (Bl. Kukulcán Km 9; ☎ 998/883-2116), across from the Convention Center (and I'm not saying that just because a bottle of tequila is set up at a table near the entrance so shoppers can help themselves). Despite the name, this is not a shopping center but a warehouse-size megastore. A MEXICAN OUTLET sign above the door overpowers the smaller PLAZA LA FIESTA appearing near the roof. Thousands of products include leather goods, silver, handicrafts, and swimwear, and prices are reasonable if not cheap—$30 to $38 for men's *guayaberas* and $40 to $48 for women's long cotton dresses, some with intricate embroidery and crocheting. An ample supply of cement models of the Chichén Itzá pyramid and hundreds other souvenirs satisfy certain needs, as do the drugstore, tour desk, and grocery store.

The only place you can really haggle over prices in the Hotel Zone is the **Flea Market Coral Negro** (Bl. Kukulcán Km 9), next to the convention center. It's the closest thing the island has to a traditional Mexican market, with about 50 open-air stalls selling sombreros, traditional clothes, and Mexican candies. It stays open late into the evening. One stall, Tropical Mike's, is run by an expatriate from Rochester, New York, who mercifully refrains from following shoppers around, preferring to reel them in with flip comments like "Let me rip you off here, I'll give you a better price." Quality is decent, and prices are better than you'll find in the malls but generally not much better than those in Plaza la Fiesta, unless you bargain them down. The market also houses temporary tattoo and piercing stands and the famous hair braiders that young girls can't resist.

## MARKETS

To find a semblance of the traditional Mexican market, head for El Centro. Most stalls are open daily from about 9am to 9pm, though they tend to keep slightly shorter hours on Sunday.

Cancún's oldest craft market, **Ki-Huic** (Av. Tulum at Av. Cobá), has long been the traditional favorite, but the number of vendors has been dropping lately. Determined hagglers can find some good bargains here, but if you're going for the experience as much as the shopping, you'll find more of both at **Mercado 28** ★ (Av. Sunyaxchen at Av. Xel-Ha), Cancún's main open-air market. About 100 stalls sell many of the same items found in the Hotel Zone, at half the price. The dizzying array ranges from hammocks made in Mérida to silver from Taxco to *alebrijes* (carved wooden figures) from Oaxaca, along with cheesy souvenirs and more hair braiders. Locals do their daily shopping here, but tourists do get the harder sell. Don't forget to browse some of the shops around the periphery of the market. **La Esfinge** (Av. Xel-Ha 63; ☎ 998/884-5724), in particular, is a hoot, full of potions and herbs and scents designed to attract love, luck, and money.

After stocking up on crafts and souvenirs at Mercado 28, browse the adjacent **Plaza Bonita** for shoes, Indian imports, and "flotation systems" (water beds, as it turns out). The colorful outdoor mall, designed like a little colonial street painted in colors typical of Mexican homes and accented with wrought iron, also has boutiques, plenty of jewelry stores, ice-cream parlors, and several kids' clothing shops. Prices are higher than in the *mercado,* but way below the Hotel Zone.

# NIGHTLIFE

All the party-hearty stalwarts, such as **Carlos'n Charlie's** (Bl. Kukulcán Km 5.5; ☎ 998/849-4053; www.carlosandcharlies.com), **Planet Hollywood** (Plaza Flamingo, Bl. Kukulcán Km 11.5; ☎ 998/883-0921; www.planethollywood.com), and **Señor Frog's** (Bl. Kukulcán Km 12.5; ☎ 998/883-1092; www.senorfrogs.com), can be found in the Hotel Zone. But just as you come to Cancún for beaches that you can't find in Miami or L.A., why not seek out clubs unique to Cancún? Most are open daily at 9 or 10pm; get there before midnight to beat the worst of the crush. Weekends can be brutal (as can any night during spring break); if you want a good show and a little breathing space as well, try a Monday or Tuesday night.

# DANCE CLUBS
## Zona Hotelera

Its reputation for wildly spectacular (or spectacularly wild) shows is legendary, but nothing you've heard will prepare you for Cancún's hottest club, **Coco Bongo** ✪✪✪ (Bl. Kukulcán 9.5, 2nd floor of Plaza Forum by the Sea; ☎ 998/883-5061; www. cocobongo.com.mx; $50 open bar; daily 10:30pm–5am). Equal parts disco, Vegas revue, and Cirque du Soleil, it's most popular with the younger crowd but has a respectable baby-boomer contingent. Despite its capacity for 3,000 revelers, the vertiginous levels of bleachers scaling the walls are strangely reminiscent of a Victorian theater, an illusion boosted by the lack of a defined dance floor. Scantily dressed girls and guys in camouflage pants gyrate rather desultorily on the bars at opening time but soon give way to a sophisticated live show on the elevated stage. Performers might impersonate anyone from Frank Sinatra to Elvis to Madonna to Jim Carrey in *The Mask,* melding seamlessly with film clips, music videos, and closed-circuit shots of the stage and gape-jawed guests, all projected on 6m (20-ft.) screens. Just for variety, bartenders juggle flaming drinks, trapeze artists fly overhead, and confetti occasionally showers the crowd, most of which is dancing on the bars and tables before the spectacle is over. The 4-hour shows change regularly and grab themes from old-style Vegas to kabuki to reality TV. The cover charge sounds steep, but considering that it includes an all-night open bar and the equivalent of two Broadway shows, it's a bargain. The place can get painfully crowded on weekends (and any night during spring break), but weeknights can be downright sane.

Acrobats and brain-searing light shows are trademarks of **The City** ✪ (Bl. Kukulcán Km 9; ☎ 998/848-8380, or 984/803-5603 beach; www.thecitycancun. com; $35–$45 open bar; daily doors at 10pm), a cavernous place with nine bars and roughly a hundred rotating ceiling lights that would do Disney's Space Mountain proud. Cancún's (if not Latin America's) biggest night club is best known for its roster of top international DJs such as Paul Van Dyk and Max Graham—and for being one of Paris Hilton's favorite party stops. All ages and musical tastes will find something to like, though it's particularly strong on progressive electronic music. The City also draws international acts, such as the Black Eyed Peas, which can crowd the club to its 5,000-person capacity. Each night of the week has a different theme: Tuesdays, Moonlight Pool Party and Bikini Contest; Fridays, the famous Friday Party; and Saturdays, Flight Club, with roaming stewardesses and vintage aeronautical decor, command the higher open-bar prices. On other nights, you can enjoy the spectacle in relative calm. If you don't plan to down $35 or $45 worth of drinks, the standard cover is $15 every night. Get a table close to the center stage to see every twitch and ripple of muscle of the club's troupe of 40 performing acrobats. Fire jugglers, trapeze acts, and an eight-man bungee act also hold forth every night. And if you just can't bear to leave, The City Beach Club opens at 9am, featuring a pool with a wave machine and a towering waterslide.

Partiers who don't want to pay the cover or can't get in to Coco Bongo or The City gravitate to two open-air walk-up bars that function as little brothers to the two big clubs. The ground-level minishows at **Congo Bar** (Bl. Kukulcán Km 9.5; ☎ 998/883-0563 or -0564; www.congobar.com.mx; daily 9am–2am) and **Corona**

---

## Street Party

Barhopping along lively Avenida Yaxchilán, downtown's party central, is one of the best ways to cut loose with the people who live there. Just follow the sounds filtering onto the street and follow your whims; the varied choices include sports on big-screen TVs, karaoke, rock, and salsa. Many popular restaurants become serious party spots after the sun goes down; try **La Parrilla** (Av. Yaxchilán 51; ☎ 998/887-6141) or **Los Arcos** (Av. Yaxchilán 53–55 at Rosas; ☎ 998/887-6673). For a more refined evening, **Los Cuatro Elementos** (in Hotel Xbalamqué, p. 34; ☎ 998/884-9690), exudes an intellectual atmosphere where you can sip a drink and meet local artists playing rock, regional music, and ballads.

---

**Bar** (Bl. Kukulcán Km 9; ☎ 998/883-2145; www.cancunparty.net/restaurants/coronabar.html; daily 9am–2am) take their inspiration from the big guys. Both charge $15 for open bar some nights, while other nights have no cover; special events and shows cost $30 to $96.

Named for iconic Cuban salsa singer Celia Cruz's trademark slogan, **Azúcar** ★★ (Bl. Kukulcán Km 9 at Dreams Cancún Resort; ☎ 999/848-7000; $10 cover after 11pm; Mon–Sat 9:30pm–4am) is a sophisticated setting with intimate seating (maximum 215), a spacious dance floor, etched-glass railings, and soft glowing lights lining the bar and ceiling. The cool look belies the heat of the club's Latin music, from the Cuban house band to the best salsa and merengue groups from the Caribbean and South America. Get there early, not only for the free cover but to get a vantage point for seeing how it's done when the locals show up late and dance expertly long into the night. No T-shirts and flip-flops; style rules here. Drink prices (beer about $4.50–$5.50, cocktails $8–$10) are comparable to those in the United States; the music and dancing definitely are not.

When the evening starts, **Thai** ★ (La Isla Shopping Village, Bl. Kukulcán Km 12.5; ☎ 998/883-1401; www.interactivedolphins.com/restaurants.html; daily 6pm–1am) is all about the food (p. 37). But by 9:30 or 10pm—especially on weekends, when there's a live DJ—the lounge fills with a mix of young locals and tourists gathering for mojitos and other cocktails ($7–$9). If the signature Thai Fresh—coconut milk, Malibu liquor, Amaretto, vodka, grenadine, and frappé ice—doesn't mesmerize you, the backdrop of dolphins cavorting behind a glass wall shared with the Interactive Aquarium next door surely will.

## El Centro

For Cancún's best jazz, head downtown to **Roots** ★★★ (Calle Tulipanes 26; ☎ 998/884-2437; roots@cancun.com; $8 cover Fri–Sat; Tues–Sat 6pm–2am), where savvy locals gather to take in live jazz, flamenco, and blues. With its low lights, pony-tailed waiters, and Jimi Hendrix and Bob Marley posters sharing wall space with the work of local artists, it recalls an artsy college hangout where all the cool kids meet. Until the show starts, usually at 10 or 10:30pm, you can dine (p. 39) by candlelight. When the musicians take the small stage, you're in for

## Of Riverboats & Pirate Ships

They aren't bargains, but if a trip to Cancún just wouldn't be complete without a romantic dinner cruise, you can choose from several options. The romance quotient is highest on the couples-only **Lobster Dinner Cruise** (Aquatours Marina, Bl. Kukulcán 6.5; ☎ 866/393-5158 toll-free U.S., or 998/849-4748; www.thelobsterdinner.com), offering a three-course dinner, drinks, and dancing to live saxophone music during a 2½-hour cruise on Nichupté Lagoon in a Spanish-style galleon. The price is $79 with a lobster dinner, $74 for surf and turf. Daily departures are at 5pm (the sunset cruise) and 8pm. The **Cancún Queen** (Aquaworld pier, Bl. Kukulcán Km 15.2; ☎ 998/848-8327; www.aquaworld.com.mx) is a faux riverboat offering a similar but longer (by 30 min.) and more boisterous lagoon cruise, Wednesdays and Fridays at 5pm. For $43, including tax, you get a chicken, fish, or vegetarian pasta menu, live music, games and prizes, dancing, and open bar. A steak and lobster menu costs $65.

The 6-hour **Caribbean Carnaval** cruise (Playa Tortugas/Fat Tuesday marina, Bl. Kukulcán Km 4.1; ☎ 998/884-3760; www.caribbeancarnaval. com) is an unabashed party boat sailing to Isla Mujeres for a beachfront buffet, Caribbean show, calypso music, limbo contest, dancing, and open domestic bar. The price ($78 adults, $38 children) does not include the $4 port fee. The most raucous of the bunch, the **Captain Hook Pirate Cruise** 🧒 (Playa Linda, Bl. Kukulcán Km 4.5; ☎ 998/849-4451; www. captainhookcancun.com), is the best for families. Two replicas of 18th-century Spanish galleons—albeit equipped with modern air-conditioning, kitchen facilities, and light and sound systems—depart in different directions at 7pm daily. An open bar, steak or lobster dinner, pirate shenanigans, and games keep passengers distracted while sailing between Cancún and Isla Mujeres, until the other ship suddenly pulls up alongside and triggers a pirate sword fight. The price ($70 adults, $35 for children with steak dinner; $82 adults, $42 children for lobster) does not include a $7 pier tax.

hours of tunes that might include improvisation well into the early morning from such artists as Mexican jazz pianist Mario Patrón, Spanish flamenco guitarist Juan D'Anyelica, or U.S. folk/blues musician John Cooker. The club also hosts local art events; check the calendar inside.

Going strong for 3 decades, **Karamba** (Av. Tulum 9; ☎ 998/884-0032; www.karambabar.com; Tues–Sun 10:30pm–7am), is the city's favored gay dance club but is also straight-friendly. The high ceiling and ledge opening onto the street make it virtually an open-air venue. Karamba is known for stage performances that include lip-synching celebrity impersonators, drag shows, and strippers on different days of the week. Between shows, DJs keep the large dance floor heaving with salsa, American pop, rave, '70s disco, and current international hits. The big (capacity 450) club draws large numbers of foreign visitors, primarily from the United States, Canada, Europe, and recently Latin America, but the party really gets going when young and energetic locals start arriving after midnight.

**La Taberna** ★★★ (Av. Yaxchilán 23, btw. Sunyaxchen and Uxmal; ☎ 998/887-5433; www.la-taberna.com; daily 11am–6am) has a multiple personality. It's a cybercafe (12 pesos, or about $1, per hour), a restaurant, and a game room with pool tables, darts, dominoes, cards, backgammon, and chess . . . but most importantly, it's a sports bar flooded by fans when a game lights up the multiple satellite TV screens. The drink menu is extensive and reasonably priced, with two-for-one beers and cocktails. The balloon-festooned pub caters to locals ages 25 to 45 (though small children and baby boomers also are in evidence) but welcomes tourists.

**El Pabilo** ★ (Hotel Xbalamqué, p. 34; ☎ 998/892-4553; www.xbalamque. com; Mon–Sat 5–11pm) is about as far from the Hotel Zone as you can get. Describing itself as a "cafebrería," this bohemian combination of cafe, bookstore, and art gallery serves coffee and light meals in a bright, comfortable setting, surrounded by books and paintings on rotating exhibition. You can read while you sip wine or cappuccino or, after 9pm every night but Sunday, listen to live jazz, classical guitar, or other mellow music.

# The ABCs of Cancún

**American Express** The local office is at Av. Tulum 208 at Calle Agua (☎ **998/881-4000** or 881-4055), 1 block past Plaza México. It's open Monday through Friday 9am to 6pm, Saturday from 9am to 1pm.

**Area Code** The telephone area code is **998**.

**Business Hours** Most Hotel Zone stores are open 10am to 10pm daily. Downtown stores may close at 2pm for the traditional siesta and reopen from 4 until 9pm, though more are staying open throughout the day. Most downtown stores, except for the shopping malls, are closed on Sundays.

**Consulates** The **U.S. Consular Agent** is in the Plaza Caracol 2, Bl. Kukulcán Km 8.5, 3rd floor, Loc. 320–323 (☎ **998/883-0272**). Hours are 9am to 2pm Monday through Friday. The **Canadian Consulate**, on the same floor at Loc. 330 (☎ **998/883-3360**), is open 9am to 5pm Monday through Friday. The **United Kingdom's consular office** at the Royal Sands Resort, Bl. Kukulcán Km 13.5 (☎ **998/881-0100**, ext. 65898), is open 9am to 3pm Monday through Friday.

**Currency Exchange** Most banks sit downtown along Avenida Tulum and are usually open Monday through Friday from 9am to 4pm, though hours vary. Lines are shorter, service is faster, and cash is more likely to be available in the morning. There are also many *casas de cambio* (exchange houses). In the Hotel Zone, you'll find banks in Plaza Kukulcán and next to Cancún Center. Many banks and major grocery stores also have ATMs, and most merchants willingly change cash dollars. Exchange rates generally are better downtown. Avoid changing money at the airport as the exchange rate is the worst in the area.

**Emergencies** See also "ABCs of Cancún & the Yucatán," p. 288. **Total Assist,** Claveles 5, SM 22, at Avenida Tulum (☎ **998/884-8022;** totalassist@prodigy. net.mx), is a small (nine-room) emergency hospital with English-speaking doctors. It's open 24 hours and accepts American Express, MasterCard, and Visa. Some desk staff might have limited command of English.

**Hospitals** Try the **American Medical Care Center** (beside Plaza Quetzal in front of the Presidente Hotel, Blvd. Kukulcán Km 8; ☎ **998/883-0113**) and the 24-hour **American Hospital** (Calle Viento 15; ☎ **998/884-6068**).

**Internet Access** Free Wi-Fi (inalámbrico) is available in many hotels and some cafes. Many hotels also have Internet computers, sometimes for an extra charge. The Hotel Zone's limited number of Internet cafes are expensive. **Alienet,** in a kiosk on the second floor of Kukulcán Plaza (Bl. Kukulcán Km 13; ☎ **998/840-6099;** daily 10am–10pm), charges $7 per hour. **@Internet Cafe,** Bl. Kukulcán Km 3.5 across from El Embarcadero at Playa Linda (☎ **998/849-4193;** daily 8am–11pm), charges about $4 an hour. Downtown has dozens of Internet cafes that typically charge $1.50 an hour.

**Newspapers & Magazines** Most hotel gift shops and newsstands carry English-language magazines and English-language Mexican newspapers. **Librería Dalí** in Plaza Kukulcán (Bl. Kukulcán Km 13; ☎ **998/885-1404**) has an extensive selection of books, magazines, and newspapers in English. **Fama,** a department store with branches in Plaza Kukulcán and downtown at Av. Tulum 27 between Tulipanes and Claveles (☎ **998/884-6586**), also carries international books and magazines.

**Pharmacies** Across the street from Señor Frog's in the Hotel Zone, at Bl. Kukulcán Km 9.5, **Farmacias del Ahorro** (☎ **998/892-7291**) offers 24-hour service and free delivery. Major Hotel Zone shopping malls have plenty of drugstores that stay open until 10pm. Downtown, **Farmacia Cancún** is at Av. Tulum 17 (☎ **998/884-1283**). You can stock up on over-the-counter and many prescription drugs without a prescription.

**Police** Cancún has a fleet of English-speaking **tourist police** to help travelers; call ☎ **998/885-2277.** The **Procuraduría Federal del Consumidor (Consumer Protection Agency)** (Av. Cobá 9–11; ☎ **998/884-2634** or 884-2701), is opposite the Social Security Hospital and upstairs from the Fénix drugstore. It's open Monday through Friday 9am to 3pm.

**Post Office** The main correo is downtown at the intersection of avenidas Sunyaxchen and Xel-Ha (☎ **998/884-1418**). It's open Monday through Friday 9am to 4pm and, for stamp purchases only, Saturday 9am to noon.

**Safety** Cancún has very little crime aside from car break-ins, which happen most often around Hotel Zone shopping centers. VW Beetles and Golfs are frequent targets. People are generally safe late at night in tourist areas; just use ordinary common sense. As at any other beach resort, don't take money or valuables to the beach. Swimming on the Caribbean side of the island presents a danger because of the undertow. See "Water Safety" on p. 46.

**Tourist Information** The **Cancún Convention and Visitors Bureau** office is on the first floor of the Cancún Center (Bl. Kukulcán Km 9; ☎ **998/881-2745** or 881-2774). For information before you arrive, check its website, http://cancun. travel. The **State Tourism Office** (☎ **998/ 881-9000;** www.qroo.gob.mx; Mon–Fri 9am–8pm) is on the first floor of the same center. Cancún's **Municipal Tourism Office** is downtown on Avenida Cobá at Avenida Tulum (☎ **998/887-3379;** Mon–Fri 9am–7pm). Each office lists hotels and their rates, and ferry schedules. **Cancún Tips** (www.cancuntips.com), a free monthly guide handed out at the airport and other places throughout the city, has good info and some coupons. The same publisher's seasonal tabloid, available in most hotels, also has useful information, including some of the best maps you can find.

# Las Islas

IT'S EASY TO FORGET THAT CANCUN, WITH ITS CHEEK-BY-JOWL CONDO towers and easy land access, is an island. Not so the dabs of coral-based terra firma that surround it—and not only because you have to take a boat to get to them. Isla Mujeres, Cozumel, and Isla Holbox are anti-Cancúns, with their easygoing pace, populations reaching back for many generations, and dearth of chain hotels and restaurants.

The islands' proximity to Cancún has brought changes, of course. And that's not entirely a bad thing, even though longtime visitors may lament the time when their hideaways were cut off from the rest of the world in fact as well as in feel. All three islands are now easier than ever to get to and offer air-conditioning, a good selection of lodging and restaurants, and varied outdoor pursuits, while remaining bucolic Caribbean islands with provincial towns.

Isla Mujeres, 13km (8 miles) northeast of Cancún's Hotel Zone, is the easiest to reach and is a popular day trip for shoppers, snorkelers, and divers. Few buildings are taller than two stories and most hotels have fewer than 50 rooms; much of the island's wilderness has been left intact. The more remote Holbox, 10km (6 miles) off the northern tip of the Yucatán Peninsula, is the least known and is still more fishing village than resort, ideal for alternative tourism. About 19km (12 miles) from the mainland east of Playa del Carmen, Cozumel has hosted hordes of divers since Jacques Cousteau made his documentaries about its spectacular reefs in the 1960s. Cruise ships eventually followed, but its laid-back Caribbean vibe endures. Whether you make a quick day trip or stay over for a night or two to explore, you'll leave each of these islands planning to stay longer on your next visit.

## DON'T LEAVE LAS ISLAS WITHOUT . . .

**TOASTING THE SUN**   Become part of Isla Mujeres' most cherished tourist tradition by making your way to one of Playa Norte's *palapa* bars at sunset and nursing a margarita while the sky changes colors.

**CIRCLING ISLA MUJERES**   After bumping along the popular west coast beaches in a golf cart to take in the haunting landscape at the southern tip of the island, take your time coming back along the rugged eastern coast, with stops for beachcombing and exploring the residential *colonias*. See p. 70.

**VISITING ISLA CONTOY**   Take a boat to Mexico's largest uninhabited island, a federal sanctuary inhabited by hundreds of species of birds and sea life. You'll probably even be able to pet a wild sting ray. See p. 92.

**SWIMMING WITH WHALES**    At least 100 whale sharks, the world's largest fish, congregate off the shore of Isla Holbox every summer. If you time it right, you can don snorkel gear and swim right alongside them. See p. 101.

**SEEING THE BIG PICTURE**    Cozumel's stellar Museo de la Isla de Cozumel not only illustrates how the island came by its spectacular coral reefs but also sheds light on the long and often tragic history that shaped the character of the entire Yucatán Peninsula. See p. 120.

**KICKING UP YOUR HEELS**    Cozumel's main plaza on Sunday night is the best party in town, filling with local families who dress up to meet their friends and dance the night away to talented Caribbean bands. See p. 128.

**GOING UNDER**    Cozumel is cradled by the world-famous Great Maya Reef. If you're not a diver, you can get an eyeful in dozens of snorkeling spots where the underwater mountains of coral rise close to the surface. See p. 115.

# ISLA MUJERES

In Cancún, you'll inevitably be surrounded by people gazing longingly across the bay, either fondly recalling a visit to Isla Mujeres or planning one on the strength of other travelers' recommendations. And there's the irony: "Isla," as it is known, was one of the Mexican Caribbean's earliest tourist destinations, only to be quickly eclipsed by Cancún in the late 1970s. With its white-sand beaches and turquoise waters, its Caribbean-colored clapboard houses and languid tropical lifestyle, it is now a favorite refuge from the flashy upstart across the bay.

A party boat to Isla is one of Cancún's most popular excursions. It's a quick trip, allowing time to shop, sample some fresh seafood, lounge on tranquil Playa Norte, and have a drink at a waterfront bar. But to fully explore the village, appreciate the underwater landscape at El Garrafón Natural Reef Park, visit the natural wonder that is Isla Contoy National Park, and generally slip into the provincial, no-worries frame of mind, you have to stay awhile. Stories of tourists who came for a weekend and stayed for a month are legion.

The island is bordered by two reef systems that create a natural aquarium—the island's west coast is part of Mexico's Marine National Park system—so most of the adventure happens in the remarkably clear water that illuminates an array of coral and neon-colored tropical fish for snorkelers and divers. Isla Contoy, a federally protected bird sanctuary, draws flocks of nature lovers. For a balance between adventurous pursuits and blissful idleness, it's also easy to while away a day in Isla's casual open-air restaurants and cafes to the strains of reggae, salsa, and rock music, under *palapas* on the broad, tranquil beaches or in a golf cart, seeing the sights with no particular purpose in mind. Most businesses close at 9 or 10pm, but those requiring a nightcap will find bars open late on Playa Norte.

Isla is also one of the best bargains in the Caribbean, even though prices have risen. Its clean, comfortable hotels include the traditional places that still draw the type of Margaritaville seeker that fueled the island's pre-Cancún tourist boom; some of these attract regular gatherings of yoga devotees. But an expanding collection of boutique hotels and bed-and-breakfasts now lures midrange and

# Isla Mujeres

## Isla Mujeres Town

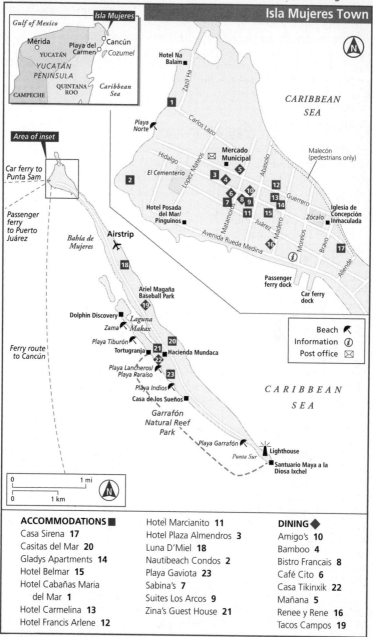

Gulf of Mexico

Isla Mujeres

Mérida
YUCATÁN
Playa del Carmen
Cancún
Cozumel
YUCATÁN PENINSULA
QUINTANA ROO
CAMPECHE
Caribbean Sea

Hotel Na Balam ■

**1**

Playa Norte

CARIBBEAN SEA

Malecón (pedestrians only)

Carlos Lazo

Zazil Ha

Hidalgo

Mercado Municipal ■

**5**

Abasolo

El Cementerio

**2**

**3** **4**

**10**

**12**

**6**

**8** **9**

**13**

**7**

Guerrero

Iglesia de Concepción Inmaculada ■

Lopez Mateos

**11**

**15**

Juárez

Madero

Zócalo ■

Hotel Posada del Mar/ Pinguinos ■

Matamoros

Avenida Rueda Medina

**16**

Morelos

Bravo

**17**

Allende

Bahía de Mujeres

Airstrip ✈

**18**

Ariel Magaña Baseball Park ■

**19**

Passenger ferry dock ■

Car ferry dock ■

ⓘ

Area of inset

Car ferry to Punta Sam

Passenger ferry to Puerto Juárez

Dolphin Discovery ►

Zama

Laguna Makax

Playa Tiburón ↖

Tortugranja

**21**

**20**

Hacienda Mundaca ■

Ferry route to Cancún

Playa Lancheros/ Playa Paraíso

**22**

**23**

Playa Indios ↖

Casa de los Sueños ■

Garrafón Natural Reef Park

Playa Garrafón ↖

Lighthouse ■

Santuario Maya a la Diosa Ixchel ■

Punta Sur

CARIBBEAN SEA

Beach ►
Information ⓘ
Post office ✉

0       1 mi
0       1 km

**ACCOMMODATIONS** ■
Casa Sirena **17**
Casitas del Mar **20**
Gladys Apartments **14**
Hotel Belmar **15**
Hotel Cabañas Maria del Mar **1**
Hotel Carmelina **13**
Hotel Francis Arlene **12**

Hotel Marcianito **11**
Hotel Plaza Almendros **3**
Luna D'Miel **18**
Nautibeach Condos **2**
Playa Gaviota **23**
Sabina's **7**
Suites Los Arcos **9**
Zina's Guest House **21**

**DINING** ◆
Amigo's **10**
Bamboo **4**
Bistro Francais **8**
Café Cito **6**
Casa Tikinxik **22**
Mañana **5**
Renee y Rene **16**
Tacos Campos **19**

upscale travelers, and the small island boasts a surprisingly good supply of apartments and villas for rent.

It's not only the hotel mix that has changed, of course. Zealous vendors beckon pedestrians into T-shirt shops, tour offices, and timeshare presentations, giving the town a midway feel during prime tour-boat hours. In the early morning and evening, though, Isla shows what it has always been at its core: a friendly tropical island with one foot in Mexico and the other in the Caribbean.

## A BRIEF HISTORY

Little is known about Isla Mujeres' ancient history, except that it was part of a commercial corridor and a pilgrimage route for the ancient Maya. As early as A.D. 565, it was the province of Ekab, one of four territories making up today's state of Quintana Roo. It was not a human settlement but a sanctuary to Ixchel, the Maya goddess of fertility and the moon. People journeyed from all over the Maya world to the small stone temple on the island's southern tip to pay her homage.

A Spanish expedition led by Francisco Hernández de Córdoba discovered the island in 1517, but it remained uninhabited for 3 centuries, visited only by fishermen and pirates. During the 17th and 18th centuries, many pirates used Isla Mujeres as a hideout and a supply station, picking up water and salt and, as legend has it, burying their booty under the white sands. Laguna Makax (Makax Lagoon), in the center of the island's west coast sheltered such sea dogs as Henry Morgan and Jean Lafitte. The last pirate to visit Isla Mujeres was slave trader Fermín Mundaca, who settled on the island when the British navy began routing slavers. He fell in love with a local beauty called La Trigueña ("The Brunette") and tried to woo her by building her a sprawling hacienda that covered 40% of the island's land surface. Unmoved, La Trigueña married an island man and Mundaca repaired to Mérida, where he reportedly died in a brothel.

After Mexico won its independence, a small village called Pueblo de Dolores grew on the tip of land where downtown stands today, populated by Maya people fleeing from the Caste Wars that ravaged the interior. The quiet fishing village became one of the Mexican Caribbean's first tourist destinations when Mexican vacationers discovered it in the 1950s, signaling from a makeshift dock on the mainland for a ride in a fishing launch. U.S. travelers soon followed, and Isla Mujeres was already a favorite haven for hippies and backpackers in the 1960s, when Cancún was merely a gleam in some computer programmer's eye.

As Cancún's growth brought more day-trippers, Isla's restaurants, shops, and hotels thrived. Today, tourism is the island's main source of income, though the fishing industry remains strong. The population of about 14,000 is primarily Mexican, with a sprinkling of expats who came for vacation and couldn't bear to leave.

## LAY OF THE LAND

Isla Mujeres is washed by the Caribbean Sea on one side and cradled by the turquoise Bahía de Mujeres on the other. It's not hard to get your bearings on the island, which is just 7km (4½ miles) long and less than a mile wide at its chubbiest. The island is shaped vaguely like a dolphin: The town, known as the *centro* (center), occupies the "tail" at the northern tip, while the remnants of Ixchel's temple stand on its pointy snout in the south. The *centro,* surrounded by sea on

## Island of Women

Several versions compete on how the island acquired its name, which means "Island of Women." A popular (though discredited) story is that Spanish buccaneers stashed female captives here while they were busy plundering. Another has it that Spanish explorers first arrived while local fishermen were out at sea, so they thought women were the only inhabitants. In another version, young virgins came to the island before marriage to seek Ixchel's blessings for fertility and successful pregnancies.

The story most widely accepted by archaeologists came from Francisco López de Gómara, the Spanish historian who chronicled the exploits of Hernán Cortés and other explorers. He reported that when Cortés's predecessor, Francisco Hernández de Córdoba, anchored at the island in 1517, his crew discovered a stone shrine with clay idols in the shape of Ixchel and her court, and they named the island after them.

three sides, is a very walkable 8 blocks long by 5 blocks deep, just behind the harbor and a short stroll from Playa Norte (also called Playa Cocos), the island's most beautiful beach.

The *zócalo* (central plaza) sits between the east-west avenidas Morelos and Bravo and the north-south avenidas Morelos and Hidalgo. Hidalgo, with its busy pedestrian strip and intersection with the plaza, lays the best claim to being the town's main street.

Isla Mujeres' hotels, restaurants, and sights dot the coasts; the interior has little beyond a few fishing villages and two salt marshes where Maya people harvested salt centuries ago. The island's widest road, Avenida Rueda Medina, runs from the *centro*'s western shore all the way to the southern tip of the island. Passenger ferry docks are near the center of town at Rueda Medina and Avenida Morelos, and the **Isla Mujeres Tourist Office** (Av. Rueda Medina 130; ☎ 998/877-0307; www.isla-mujeres.com.mx; Mon–Fri 8am–8pm, Sat–Sun 8am–noon) is just to the left as you exit the pier. The car ferry dock is less than ½-mile south.

Traveling south on Rueda Medina takes you past Laguna Makax, the remains of the lovelorn Mundaca's failed Taj Mahal (p. 85), and the island's best swimming beaches. A little more than halfway down the island a smaller road, Carretera Sac Bajo, forks off and loops back to the north along the western edge of the lagoon on a narrow spit of land separated from the rest of the island. Rueda Medina's name changes to Carretera Punta Sur at Parque Garrafón (the entire road is sometimes called Carretera Garrafón). Between El Garrafón and Ixchel's temple, the road curves east and becomes Avenida Martínez Ross, also called the Carretera Panorámica (Panoramic Highway), then hugs the eastern shore on its way back north to the *centro*. In contrast to the flat, sandy northern beaches, the eastern coastline is a landscape of steep, rocky bluffs that offer dramatic vistas but no safe swimming spots. The eastern highway enters town as Avenida Benito Juárez.

# GETTING TO & AROUND ISLA MUJERES
## By Boat

Isla Mujeres has a tiny airstrip, but you have to provide the plane. For the rest of us, the only way to get there is by ferry. Cancún's **Puerto Juárez** (☎ 998/877-0382) on Avenida Bonampak, about 15 minutes north of Cancún, consists of the original ferry dock and the newer Gran Puerto dock, 2 blocks south.

**Transportes Marítimos Magaña** (☎ 998/877-0065) runs ferries from Puerto Juárez daily every half-hour from 6:30am to 11:30pm, making the crossing in about 30 minutes. **Ultramar** (☎ 998/843-2011; www.granpuerto.com.mx) operates out of Gran Puerto, running fast, air-conditioned catamarans with cushy individual seats rather than benches, and TV screens that play promotional videos. They make the trip in about 15 minutes, departing daily every half-hour from 5:30am to midnight (returning 6am–12:30am). The fare with either company is 35 pesos (about $3.35) each way. You can buy a round-trip, but there's no discount, and you have to make sure you don't lose your ticket stub; the only advantage is avoiding the ticket booth on the return trip.

The ferries are infamous for leaving ahead of schedule if they are full. With departures every half-hour, that's not a major problem, but if you need to catch a particular ferry, arrive well ahead of time.

Several ferries also leave from the Hotel Zone, but they are more than twice as expensive, take longer, and run on more limited schedules. If you're staying in the Hotel Zone and just want a quick day trip, though, convenience might trump cost. Three choices all run between 9am and 4:15pm: five departures from El Embarcadero at Playa Linda (Bl. Kukulcán, Km 4) and four each from Playa Caracol (Km 9) and Playa Tortugas (Km 7.5). Round-trip fares start at $16.

There's little reason to take a car to Isla, unless you already have a rental that you don't want to leave on the Cancún side while you're on the island. Car ferries run by **Marítima Isla Mujeres** (☎ 998/877-0065) leave from Punta Sam, 8km (5 miles) north of Puerto Juárez on Avenida López Portillo. They also take walk-on passengers for just $1.50, but the schedules are more limited and the trip takes about 45 minutes, so the difference isn't worth it unless you're staying at Punta Sam. Departures generally are at 8 and 11am and 2:45, 5:30, and 8:15pm (returning at 6:30, 9:30am, 12:45, 4:15, and 7:15pm). The fare is about $19 for a car, $23 for a van, $8 for a moped, and $6 for a bike. Fares include the driver; additional passengers pay $1.50. Lines are long; arrive at least an hour early.

Schedules for any ferry can change with the season and the weather, so verify ahead of time with your hotel or the tourist office in Cancún.

A taxi to Puerto Juárez or Punta Sam will cost about $50 from Cancún's airport and almost as much from the Hotel Zone, but you can do better with a little advance planning. Private van shuttles from the airport cut the cost from the airport by more than half, if you don't mind a longer trip with stops for other passengers. One small and well-organized outfit, **Best Day Travel** (☎ 800/593-6259 toll-free in U.S. or Canada, or 998/287-3674; www.bestday.com) charges $9 per person and $17 round-trip (two-person minimum), and requires online reservations 2 days in advance. Taxis to Puerto Juárez cost less than $10 from downtown and take 10 to 15 minutes. If you're staying in the Hotel Zone, you can take the R1 bus for 6.50 pesos (65¢); just make sure it has PUERTO JUÁREZ or an obvious abbreviation on the window sign. A good compromise between cost and convenience is to take the bus downtown and catch a cab from there. If you're starting from downtown, you can also catch the R1 or R13 along Avenida Tulúm.

## Getting Around

Isla Mujeres is so small that a car is an unnecessary burden. Passenger ferries arrive at the docks on Avenida Rueda Medina in the center of town, within walking distance of most hotels, restaurants, and shops. Taxis line up to the right of the pier, but unless you're staying outside of town, just figure on walking a few blocks. Tricycle taxis will wheel your luggage—along with you, if there's room—to your hotel for a few dollars (some will quote a price; others just work for tips). Walking is by far the best way to get around town. To explore the rest of the island, there are several options.

**Taxis** (☎ 998/877-0066) swarm downtown and are fairly reasonable. Taxi stands are located at Parque Garrafón, Dolphin Discovery, and Playa Lancheros, but you won't have much of a wait to flag down a cab anywhere on the island. Typical rates from downtown are about $1.50 to Playa Norte, $2.50 to the Tortugranja turtle farm, and $4.50 to Parque Garrafón or Punta Sur. You can also rent a taxi for $15 an hour if you want to make your own private tour of the island.

The rates aren't carved in stone; I took a cab from Tortugranja down to the island's south end and all the way up the east coast back to town for $3.50—less than the cost of going just from downtown to Punta Sur. Rates are per trip, not per person, and taxis will pick up extra people if they have room. Taxis from the stand next to the passenger ferry pier charge an extra 10 pesos (about $1, which you can avoid by walking a block to hail one from the street). And rates are doubled between midnight and 6am.

The local **bus** system, which costs only 4 pesos (less than 40¢), is designed to serve residents of the *colonias* (suburban villages) beyond downtown. Because it doesn't cover the entire island and stops running at 10pm, it isn't an option for most tourist excursions. The route starts downtown behind the *mercado,* stops near the ferry docks, and continues to Hacienda Mundaca—the only tourist attraction on the route—a little more than halfway down the island before looping back to town. You can flag down a bus wherever you see one and get off wherever you please.

One of the most popular ways to get around town, among locals as well as tourists, is by **electric golf cart.** They are fun and stable, and can carry four people at a top speed of about 32kmph (20mph; the island is so small that you don't need to hurry). Rates are fixed at about $15 per hour, $45 per day (9am–5pm), and $50 for 24 hours, though you might be able to negotiate a lower rate for more than 1 day or for multiple carts. Rental agencies right at the ferry pier charge a bit more, so walk a couple of blocks into town and look for the carts lined up at curbs. In the center of town, **Ciro's** (Av. Guerrero, btw. López and Matamoros; ☎ 998/877-0568), **El Sol** (Av. Benito Juárez at Matamoros; ☎ 998/877-0791), and **Pepe's Carts & Mopeds** (Hidalgo 19; ☎ 998/977-0019) have well-maintained equipment and good reputations for service.

**Mopeds** (*motos*) are also hugely popular. Rental rates at the outlets that operate on virtually every downtown block depend on the motorbike's make and age, hovering around $8 per hour or up to $30 per day; agencies right at the ferry pier may charge slightly more. They come with helmets and seats for two, although adding a passenger makes the moped less stable. I've heard so many horror stories about accidents involving tourists that I'd stick with a golf cart instead; not only are they safer, but they also provide shade. Many moped places and some hotels also rent **bicycles** for about $4.50 an hour or $10 per day, usually including a basket and a lock.

*Note:* Rentals do not include insurance, so any damage to the vehicle (or yourself) is your responsibility.

## ACCOMMODATIONS, BOTH STANDARD & NOT

With its roots as a backpacker haven and its increasing popularity with more upscale travelers, Isla Mujeres is blessed with ample lodging in all price ranges, including rental apartments scattered all over the island. Most budget and midrange hotels are in the *centro*, while higher-end resorts claim secluded ocean perches around the northeastern end of the island and the on skinny Sac Bajo peninsula west of Laguna Makax.

### Apartment Rentals

Dozens of clean, cheerful, furnished apartments dot Isla Mujeres. While the *centro* has a few, most are at the edges of the *colonias* (suburban villages), offering a whole different view of island life along with your vistas of the Bahía de Mujeres stretching toward the Cancún skyline or the open Caribbean along the rugged eastern coast. They are ideal for weekly or longer-term rentals, but most will also rent by the night and beat the prices at many budget hotels in town. For insight into what's available and the pros and cons of various properties, check the lively forums at **MyIslaMujeres.com**, an indispensable website that also hosts many of the hotels' and vacation rentals' websites.

The island's three primary rental agencies represent a large percentage of Isla's apartments (and some of its hotels). All have been in business for years and have legions of satisfied customers. Their staffs, who know the properties intimately and make sure they're kept in top shape, will even e-mail you a list of available options if you send them your requirements. Some rentals appear on more than one site, but each agency has properties the others don't. The standard procedure is to send a 50% deposit (or, in some cases the full amount) to their U.S. bank and pay the balance in cash when you get there.

The two larger agencies represent apartments and villas across the price spectrum, but rates for more than half of their listings start at less than $100 for a double. Some of the budget gems at **Isla Beckons** (www.islabeckons.com) include two brand-new, one-bedroom, oceanview apartments with separate entrances on the top floor of a well-known local fisherman's family home for $45 a night in low season, $50 in high season; and a stylish modern studio decorated in bright Mexican colors, across the road from Caribbean beaches, for $330 to $390 a week. Among the lowest-priced properties at **Lost Oasis** (☎ 831/331-9106 U.S., 998/888-0429 Mexico; www.lostoasis.net) are an exuberantly landscaped, two-bedroom stone house on the Sac Bajo peninsula with views of the Cancún skyline for $100 to $140 a night (smaller *casitas* go for $50–$80), and cottagelike studios in a small apartment complex on a palm beach, for $65 to $75 a night.

**Mornings in Mexico** (www.morningsinmexico.com) specializes in unique, hand-picked budget and midrange properties. It was offering just 10 apartments the last time I checked, but none of the starting prices exceeded $105 a night. Examples include studio apartments on the beach for $50 to $55 a night, and a two-unit building in the *colonias* with a one-bedroom apartment for $60 per night and a two-bedroom for $70. Another great resource: **Kathryn's Travel** (☎ 952/447-4725; www.kathrynstravel.com), which specializes in the Yucatán and Isla Mujeres in particular. Kathryn Blume is based in Minnesota but lives on Isla part time and knows it intimately. She is the booking agent for nearly 30 inns, apartments, and homes and also handles numerous hotels. She scours for good deals, recommends properties for individual clients based on her personal experience, and stands by for any needed troubleshooting.

What follows is a sampling of Isla Mujeres apartments available for rent. In most cases, exact addresses are available only after booking.

**$** Probably not for the first-time visitor, **Zina's Guest House** ★★ (Colonia La Gloria; ☎ 998/888-0674 or 330/871-4772; www.zinahouse.com; PayPal or bank transfer only) is one of the island's best bargains at $300 a week (air-conditioning costs are expected to bump that higher for 2009). This modest but well-maintained house in the heart of Isla's main residential suburb, within walking distance of Hacienda Mundaca and Playa Lancheros, is best suited to travelers ready to immerse themselves in local life. The two air-conditioned one-bedroom apartments have roomy kitchenettes with a two-burner hot plate as well as a microwave. They are spare but comfortable, and the expat owner is tapped in to everything going on in the area.

**$–$$** Two downtown apartments are great values right in the heart of the action—which should tell you that their main drawback is going to be some street noise. A tiny entrance squeezed between storefronts leads upstairs to **Gladys Apartments** ★★ (Av. Madero, btw. Hidalgo and Guerrero; ☎ 998/888-0149; www.gladys-apartment.myislamujeres.com), three small, neat units furnished a lot like your first apartment out of college. Two one-bedroom units go for $35 a night in low season and $55 in high season, while a two-bedroom rents for $45 to $65. Optional air-conditioning will add $10 per night. The full kitchens are loaded with appliances; one even has a George Foreman grill. Weekly and monthly rates are generously discounted.

**$–$$** **Sabina's** ★ (Av. Benito Juárez; www.morningsinmexico.com), recognizable on the street by its turquoise window trim and peach balconies, is owned by a well-known local wedding planner who has decorated the three studios simply but with a modicum of Mexican style. The two upstairs apartments have balconies. All have queen-size beds, living and dining areas, and kitchenettes, and rent for $45 a night in low season, $55 in high season. One apartment has a fold-out sofa to accommodate an extra person ($5 extra per night).

**$$** **Playa Gaviota** (Carretera Garrafón; www.kathrynstravel.com) is a beach complex on the island's west side near Parque Garrafón, within walking distance of several popular restaurants. The main building has five spacious suites with private balconies, recently remodeled in clean modern style with bold color accents. A separate, more rustic beach cabana has two units opening directly onto the long, white beach. All units are air-conditioned and have kitchenettes, and all rent for $65 in low season, $75 high season. Daily maid service, unusual for apartment rentals, is provided.

**$$-$$$**   The four new studios at **Casitas del Mar** ✹ (Colonia La Gloria; ☎ 998/888-0034; www.joyceandbob.com/casitasdelmar) look like a Crate & Barrel photo shoot, and with their views of the peaceful Caribbean shore on the eastern side, you might never get around to going downtown. The on-site owners are longtime island residents and are generous with suggestions on nearby restaurants and activities. The apartments are in a safe, accessible section of the residential *colonia* and rent for $70 a night in low season, $85 high, jumping to $110 over the Christmas holidays. Each has cable TV, full kitchens with two-burner gas stoves, some of the most comfortable beds you'll find in Mexico, and a large patio for watching the sun rise. This is a nonsmoking, adults-only complex.

**$$-$$$**   Also new, and in the same price range, is **Luna D'Miel** ✹ (Av. Aeropuerto; ☎ 998/877-1667; luna-d-miel.islamujeres.info), with three studio apartments in the residential area just a few minutes from downtown. Their geometric minimalist exteriors and sleek, understated interiors are very Playa del Carmen, right down to the mosquito netting over the beds. With a back patio overlooking the waves crashing against the rocky eastern shore, and a front patio looking out on the calm bay waters, you can watch the sunrise and the sunset without ever leaving your room—just be aware that all three units share one large patio, and don't stumble out in your pajamas to greet the new day. The beds in two of the units are king size in width, but not in length: Tall people, take note. Kitchenettes have microwaves, coffeemakers, and small fridges but no stove. Low-season rent is $65 a night, high season $85, and Christmas holidays $120. Weekly rates are discounted in high season; renting for a month in low season cuts the nightly rate by half.

**$$$-$$$$**   **Nautibeach Condos** 🧒 (Playa Norte; ☎ 998/877-0606; www.nauti beach.com) is a longtime favorite for families, with its two-bedroom apartments, Playa Norte location, babysitting services, swimming pool, and tropical gardens just made for romping. The rent is $145 to $210 a night for a double, depending on season, $185 to $260 for three or four; add another $35 to $60 a night over the holidays. For just one or two people, there's one newer *"casita,"* which is basically a standard hotel room with no ocean view ($80–$115; $145 holidays) and a larger studio ($115–$145; $170 holidays). Two veranda condos, with a wraparound, bayview deck added to the basic layout, hardly seem worth the extra $40 a night. The style of each unit is determined by individual owners, but all units must meet minimum standards that include a well-equipped kitchen and no less than a queen-size bed in the master bedroom and a double and twin in the second. This large complex is one of Isla Mujeres' older buildings, and though well maintained, it was beginning to show its age.

## Hotels & a Bed & Breakfast

**$**   Bed-and-breakfast inns, a recent addition to Isla's lodging options, lean more toward boutique than homey. **Casa Sirena** (Av. Hidalgo, btw. Bravo and Allende;

## Highs & Lows

Isla Mujeres' high and low seasons aren't nearly as volatile as those in Cancún. Though they vary somewhat from one hotel to another, the low season is roughly from April to late December and high season from the second week in January through March or April. It's not unusual for prices to spike nearly 50% over Christmas and New Year's weeks, and minimum stays might be required.

☎ 998/877-1705; www.sirena.com.mx; PayPal) is one inn that's worth the price ($110–$150, depending on room, Christmas week $120–$150). The six rooms are in a 60-year-old house on the *centro*'s quiet Caribbean side, adroitly remodeled to meld modern elegance with colonial style. The traditional pasta tile floors are especially beautiful. All but two rooms have balconies overlooking the Caribbean or the Cancún skyline, but guests in the two less expensive rooms have ample compensation in the panoramic water views from the rooftop terrace (which also has a pool). Between the full Mexican breakfasts (special orders on request) and gregarious owner Steve Broin's free margarita-and-appetizer happy hours, you might find the *centro*'s nearby restaurants superfluous.

$ The venerable **Hotel Belmar** (Av. Hidalgo 110, btw. Madero and Abasolo; ☎ 998/877-0430; www.rolandi.com; AE, MC, V) has an elegant, if slightly worn, old-world feel, with lots of tile in the hacienda-style courtyard. It sits on top of the Pizza Rolandi (same owners), which can get noisy. Then again, they offer room service. There are no views to speak of, but the rooms are large and the beds are quite comfortable under the thinning spreads. It's one of the island's few hotels that includes TVs with U.S. channels. Doubles range from $35 in low season to $56 in high season, and shoot to $90 over Christmas.

$ The 14-room **Hotel Marcianito** ★ (Av. Abasolo 10, btw. Juárez and Hidalgo; ☎ 998/877-0111; www.isla-mujeres.net/hotels/marcianito; cash only) is clean and comfortable, though somewhat nondescript in a motel sort of way. It's in the center of the downtown action, so street noise can carry—but so can the soothing sound of ocean waves. It's a little newer and brighter than many budget hotels, and the owners go out of their way to make sure guests have everything they need. Rooms are not air-conditioned but have efficient ceiling fans. And the $35 room rate holds firm all year-round, including Christmas.

$ The large, clean rooms at the kid-friendly **Hotel Carmelina** (kids) (Av. Guerrero at Madero; ☎ 998/877-0006; cash only), are simple but comfortable, and the 25 rooms wrap around a cheery courtyard. Third-floor rooms have views of Playa Norte and downtown. Only one room has air-conditioning, but the open-air, purple-trimmed corridors pull in good breezes. With doubles costing about $37, this unassuming hotel is an ideal step up from a hostel.

$–$$$ The Magaña family regularly remodels the 24 rooms in the **Hotel Francis Arlene** ★★ (kids) (Av. Guerrero 7, btw. Abasolo and Madero; ☎ 998/877-0310;

www.francisarlene.com; MC, V), so no two look quite the same. I had a room with some furniture scuffs and intense blue walls that made me feel like we were underwater as daylight waned; others have brighter, more appealing palettes. Still, it was homey and comfortable; I especially liked the thigh-high second faucet in the shower, perfect for washing sand off your feet. The hotel wraps around a small, pretty courtyard, and some rooms have ocean views and balconies or patios. The hotel is wheelchair accessible, a rarity on Isla. Rooms overlooking the street get some noise, but the hotel is several blocks removed from the most raucous action. Rates start at $35 ($45 with air-conditioning) in low season and $55 in high season. Larger, top-floor rooms with air-conditioning and ocean views are $65 low season, $80 high.

**$$    Hotel Plaza Almendros** ★ 🄺 (Av. Hidalgo 14, btw. Mateos and Matamoros; ☎ 998/877-1217; www.hotelplazaalmendros.com; MC, V) is extravagantly white, from the exterior to the public spaces to the tile floors and kitchen cabinets in the spacious rooms. The effect is slightly sterile but soothing and comfortable, especially with rates ranging from $55 in low season to $75 high season. Most rooms are shielded from the busy street by a courtyard pool surrounded by grass and palm trees, which has more to offer kids than other hotels in the immediate area. The hotel is surrounded by discos and bars, though; you'll sleep better if you ask for a ground-floor room in the back.

**$$–$$$    Suites Los Arcos** (Av. Hidalgo 58, btw. Abasolo and Matamoros; ☎ 998/877-1343; www.suiteslosarcos.com; MC, V) looks bright and fresh the minute you enter the long, narrow lobby. Each of the 12 suites, decorated with warm colors and Mexican-style furnishings, has a kitchenette, a sitting area, and large, sunny balconies. Doubles are $65 to $75 for queen rooms, depending on season, and $75 to $85 for kings. Go for the odd-numbered rooms, which are in back of the hotel, away from the busy pedestrian stretch of Avenida Hidalgo. The popular Amigos restaurant across the street provides room service.

**$$$–$$$$    The Hotel Cabañas María del Mar** (Av. Carlos Lazo 1 at Playa Norte; ☎ 800/223-5695 toll-free U.S., or 998/877-0179; www.cabanasdelmar.com; MC, V) is the closest thing to a budget hotel that you'll find on Playa Norte. Low-season rates range from $75 to $99, depending on the room, but jump to $135 to $160 in high season; continental breakfast is included. The higher-priced Castle section rooms were recently remodeled in brash contemporary style and have balconies with partial ocean views. Rooms in the older Tower section look more generic but are just a few steps from the beach and come with terraces or balconies with partial ocean views. The 31 thatched-roof cabanas surround the hotel pool.

## DINING FOR ALL TASTES

Seafood is the specialty in Isla Mujeres, and since much of what Cancún serves up was caught here, you'll find it fresher and cheaper on this side of the bay. Many of the major restaurants line the pedestrian stretch of Avenida Hidalgo, while small, casual Mexican places can be found on many of the side streets. Artsy bistros and new-age eateries are also in good supply, courtesy of the island's historic popularity with backpackers and Europeans in general.

**$**  In a glaring fuchsia building with a yellow sun over the door, **Mañana** (Av. Guerrero 17 at Matamoros; ☎ 998/877-0555; Tues–Sat 9am–5pm; cash only) is also home to the Cosmic Cosas bookstore, but in morning hours, the focus is on the egg dishes, fresh baguettes, and Italian coffees ($2–$3). Later in the day, salads, burgers (meat or vegetarian), and fresh fruit shakes take over.

**$  Café Cito** (Matamoros 42 at Juárez; ☎ 998/877-1470; daily 8am–2pm, high season additional hours Fri–Wed 5:30–10:30 or 11:30pm; cash only) looks like a cross between a Cape Cod chow house (an intensely blue chow house) and a Caribbean bungalow. You can have breakfast until 2pm, if you've the mind to. The choices include croissants, rolls with coconut jam (strange but compellingly good), crepes, and egg dishes, all for less than $6. Even during high season, when the cafe reopens in the evening for dinner, everyone keeps coming back for the breakfast.

**$$–$$$**  True to its name, **Bamboo** (Plaza Los Almendros 4, on Hidalgo btw. Matamoros and Mateos; ☎ 998/877-1355; daily 8am–1am; AE, MC, V) serves such Thai specialties as chicken satay, curries, and pad Thai ($9–$12), as well as pineapple lobster (1 peso per gram). But that's only half the story. In the mornings, a different chef jump-starts the day with fresh French coffee and all kinds of Yankee-type breakfasts; a plate of mouthwatering crepes and orange juice comes to about $7. The place fills with locals on evenings when live salsa or Caribbean music is on the menu.

**$–$$$  Casa Tikinxik** ★★★ (Playa Lancheros at the Av. Rueda Medina–Sac Bajo fork; ☎ 998/877-0340; daily 11am–6pm; MC, V), a classic Mexican beach restaurant, has become an obligatory pilgrimage for seafood lovers. *Pescado tikin xic* is a fresh whole fish marinated in a spicy red sauce from ancient Maya recipes, wrapped in a banana leaf and cooked on a grill in the restaurant parking lot. Consensus has it that no one does it better. With fresh guacamole and salsa, and beer, expect to spend $10 to $15 per person. It takes a while to prepare this delicacy, so bring a swimsuit and pass the time playing in the waves.

**$–$$$$**  A handwritten sign on the door to **Renee y Rene** ★★★ (Av. Madero, btw. Juárez and Rueda Medina; daily 7am–7pm; cash only) proclaims BEST FOOD ON THE ISLAND. GREAT SERVICE TOO, signed by a family from Texas. An addendum from another customer reads, AND NICEST MAN ON THE ISLAND. I can't state empirically that those superlatives are accurate, but I can say this is the kind of place you discover by accident and keep coming back to, not only for Renee's cooking, but also for Rene's kindly-uncle ministrations. It's a versatile operation, serving breakfast, hamburgers, and snacks as well as Mexican dishes such as chicken fajitas, enchiladas, or steak for $6 and shrimp for $15. The last time I visited, my daughter and I shared a *pollo a la yucateca* and cheese enchiladas, plus drinks, for $14—not the cheapest food on the island, but just maybe the best.

**$–$$$$  Bistro Français** (Matamoros 29, btw. Juárez and Hidalgo; daily 8am–noon and 6–10pm; cash only) might appear to be an anomaly, until you stop to look around at the number of European tourists in Isla. The whimsical, Technicolor place, with the building sign and wall menu done up in comic-book

## Take Me Out to the Taco Game

The debate is far from over, but the current favorite in the taco derby is **Tacos Campos,** better known as "the baseball tacos." The stand is squirreled away under the bleachers on the south side of the ballpark in the *colonias* north of Salina Grande. Game night or not, the taco wizards start churning them out at about 8pm and keep them coming until 1am, or 2am, or . . . whenever. For about $1 apiece, you can sample a smorgasbord of fillings—give me the *al pastor* (spit-barbecued pork) every time—and embellish them with guacamole, grilled onions, fiery orange habanero sauce, pickled cactus with onions, and other Mexican condiments you've never heard of. There's no published game schedule, so you'll have to ask around if you want baseball with your baseball tacos. You'll also need to ask for directions, because tourist maps neglect to include street names for the residential areas beyond the *centro.* Go easy on the beer, though; you want to avoid the grotty *baños* at all cost.

font, packs them in for breakfast ($4–$5). The free coffee refills are only part of the story; the cook has a reputation for the best French toast on this side of the Atlantic and omelets cooked to perfection. After breakfast, the eclectic menu includes pasta rigatoni ($7.80), surf and turf ($22), and the *coc au vin* house specialty ($9.70).

**$–$$$$**    The good, classic Mexican food at **Amigo's** ✦ (Av. Hidalgo, btw. Matamoros and Abasolo; ☎ 998/877-0624; daily 7am–10pm; cash only) presents a dilemma: Go for the chicken *chilaquiles, huevos motuleños,* and other soul-satisfying breakfast dishes ($4–$6.50), or save yourself for the excellent and continually evolving dinner fare, from pasta and vegetarian dishes to Steak Roquefort and garlic shrimp (up to $20)? Either way, the killer *sopa de lima* (lime soup) and the puffy bread drizzled with oil and garlic are treats equal to the entrees.

## WHY YOU'RE HERE: THE BEACHES & TOP SIGHTS

Nature provides the means for both the relaxation and the adventure on Isla Mujeres that make lifelong devotees of locals and tourists alike. The broad white sands invite you to bask in the sun and cool off in sparkling turquoise waters as calm and warm as a bathtub, and offer many vantage points for watching sunsets flare and the Caribbean pound the shore. But don't be so dazzled that you overlook the island's man-made attractions. Remnants of an ancient temple, local gathering spots, and a lofty sightseeing tower are just a few of the ways to get a glimpse into island life both ancient and contemporary.

### The Beaches

The island's northern tip and southwestern coast boast some of the Mexican Caribbean's finest beaches. Bahía de Mujeres, the warm, placid bay between Isla and Cancún, offers beaches ideal for sunning, swimming, and snorkeling. Like

Robin Hood, Hurricane Wilma (and Gilbert before it) robbed Cancún of its white sand and gave it to Isla Mujeres, widening Playa Norte and other leeward beaches. But leave the tents and Coleman stoves behind; camping is prohibited on all island beaches. Isla Mujeres has no lifeguards and few safety warning flags; children 12 or younger are not allowed to swim unless supervised by an adult.

The east side of the island is washed by the open Caribbean, a turbulent sea with dangerous currents. Much of this wild coast is either privately owned, protected for turtle breeding, too rocky for beachgoers or accessible only through hotel properties or by boat. Enjoy its picturesque bluffs and dramatic vistas, but save your swimming for the beaches below.

**Playa Norte (Centro)** ✹✹✹ is the current name for two beaches once known as Nautibeach and Playa Cocos. The beach stretches from the ferry pier, around a point and along the northern edge of the island cradling the *centro*. With powdery white sand so soft you can sink to your ankles in it, and crystalline turquoise water, it's often ranked as one of the best beaches in the Caribbean. It certainly is Isla Mujeres' most beautiful beach, and the most popular among swimmers and sunbathers (some of them topless). It's also lined with hotels and worked by vendors, so it can get crowded, but the wide sands handle it without approaching Cancún-level frenzy. You can wade out 37m (120 ft.) on the gently sloping ocean floor and still be chest deep. The section of beach at the island's northwestern tip, known as **Playa Sol,** is usually a little less crowded and the drinks a little less expensive, though the water is deeper and not quite as clear as in the middle of Playa Norte.

The beach is easy to find; all the north-south streets in town end up there, and it's walking distance from the ferry and any downtown hotel. Watersports equipment and lessons are available along the beach. Umbrella and lounge chair rentals generally cost $5 to $15 for the day, but many restaurants let you use their patch of beach for free if you have a snack or a drink under their *palapas.*

The beaches about midway down the island's west coast, near Hacienda Mundaca, are more secluded. They offer open-air *palapa* restaurants, low-key souvenir stands run by local families, and bathrooms. Chairs and umbrellas, kayaks, and canoes are available for rent.

**Playa Lancheros** ✹, along with adjacent **Playa Paraíso** 〔kids〕, is widely considered Isla's second-best swimming beach. It is less manicured than Playa Norte and its sand somewhat coarser, but the abundance of palm trees give it that tropical hideaway feel, and its views over the bay to Cancún are among the finest. The calm water is perfect for children (though the ocean floor drops steeply farther out), and there is a small pen with sea turtles and harmless nurse sharks *(tiburones gatos)*. The casual, open-air Casa Tikinxik (p. 81) is a local favorite that's also popular with tourists for the specialty, fresh-grilled *tikin xic* fish. Beach clubs that flank the restaurant stage lively Cuban shows and traditional fiestas. This is the southernmost point served by local buses, and it's also a destination for tour boats from Cancún.

**Playa Tiburón,** north of Playa Lancheros near Villa Rolandi, also faces the Bahía de Mujeres and has exceptionally calm water. But it's more developed, with a big, popular restaurant and souvenir stands selling the usual T-shirts and jewelry. Sometimes there are women braiding hair and applying temporary henna tattoos. There are pens with soporific nurse sharks, too.

If you'd rather not jostle elbows with the Cancún party boat crowd, head south to **Playa Indios** ✸✸, a small, quiet beach club. The friendly owner lets you fish from his dock and will cook up what you catch. The quiet beach club has good swimming and snorkeling in clear, deep water, and the kayaks and lounge chairs are free if you buy food or drinks there. It also has a few golf carts for rent.

**Zama** (Carretera Sac Bajo; ☎ 998/877-0739; www.zamabeach.com) is still farther north, near the Hotel Villas Rolandi on the spit of land west of Laguna Makax. At this small, quite beautiful beach club and day spa, if you have lunch at its outdoor restaurant, you're invited to spend the day on its large, well-groomed beach. Relaxing in a comfy beach bed, swinging on a hammock in the leafy garden, getting some shade in the wooden pergola, and swimming from its dock or in its two connecting pools are all free.

## The *Centro*

Beyond the beaches, shops, and restaurants that draw most of the crowds, the island's history and character reveal themselves throughout town. By colonial Mexican standards, Isla's renovated *zócalo* ✸ (avs. Hidalgo and Madero) is modern and colorful but frankly a bit stark with its concrete benches and scraggly trees. Hurricane Wilma destroyed the lovely old traditional plaza, and the replacement lost something in the translation. But like everywhere in Mexico, it's a fulcrum of local life—which, for young people, seems to revolve around the basketball court. It's here that Isla feels most like a village, as you watch a hoops game, eavesdrop on local people sitting under the trees to catch up on the events of the day, and wait for the fountain's musical water show to begin in the evening.

The Catholic church, on the south side of the square, **Iglesia de Concepción Inmaculada** (avs. Morelos and Bravo; daily 10am–11:30am and 7–9pm), wouldn't be out of place in suburban Los Angeles, but it houses a highly prized artifact from centuries past: a wood-and-porcelain statue of the Virgin Mary brought to the island by Spaniards in 1790, the only one of three identical statues that remains on the island (see "The Three Sisters" on p. 85).

Isla Mujeres' only cemetery, **El Cementerio** ✸ (Av. López Mateos at Benito Juárez; daily until sunset), looks like a miniature city unto itself, with its jumble of engraved crosses and pink, yellow, and blue tombs shaped like temples. The pirate Fermín Mundaca has a tomb in the cemetery, marked with a skull and crossbones he carved himself, and a Latin epitaph that translates to "As you are, I once was; as I am, so shall you be." The scalawag himself, however, died and was buried in Mérida. To find the unidentified monument, walk straight in about 4m (12 ft.), turn right and walk about 3m (10 ft.) more, or ask a local to point it out.

At the brick-red **Mercado Municipal** ✸ (Av. Guerrero, btw. Matamoros and López Mateos; Sat–Sun 8am–sunset, restaurants daily 6am–sunset), merchants still sell a colorful array of fresh flowers, fruits and vegetables, aromatic fresh corn tortillas, and groceries from the stalls inside. But the market is better known for the inexpensive *loncherías* under its arches, where friendly proprietors serve authentic Yucatecan dishes.

From the market it's a short hop to the *malecón* ✸✸, the stone walkway that winds along Isla's dramatic Caribbean shoreline. The path, stretching about a mile south from Playa Media Luna (Half Moon Bay), is part of a long-term improvement project destined eventually to circle the island. From the *malecón*'s benches

## The Three Sisters

The site of today's *centro* was a deserted colonial settlement in 1890, when visiting fishermen discovered three wooden statues of the Virgin Mary with porcelain faces and hands. The statues are believed to have been brought to the island by the Spaniards more than 100 years earlier. Each of the fishermen carried a statue to his village, one to Izamal in Yucatán state, where it has been credited with numerous miracles, and another to Kantunilkin in northeastern Quintana Roo. Only one remained on Isla Mujeres, in a small chapel built of palm and wood. According to local legend, when the statue was moved into today's church, the little chapel inexplicably burst into flame. Some islanders still believe the virgin walks on the water around the island from dusk to dawn in search of her sisters.

and lookout points, you have views of Isla's wild side, from the thrashing sea to fishermen's shacks leaning willy-nilly next to creeping new construction. The *malecón* has been hit by hurricanes over the years and parts of it may still be under reconstruction when you visit. *Note:* The word *malecón,* which simply means "sea wall" and can describe any seafront path, is also used for Avenida Rueda Medina around the ferry piers on the bay side. With its vehicle traffic, constant activity, and hawkers peddling souvenirs and snorkeling tours, the western *malecón* is better suited to exploration on wheels.

## Exploring the Island

Although you can find an **island tour** if you look for one, especially from tour operators in Cancún, you'll see more, have the flexibility to explore at will, and pay a lot less by making your own tour. The local bus system (4 pesos/40¢ per person), while of limited use for getting to popular tourist attractions, can provide a great introductory tour to the local neighborhoods on the northern two-thirds of the island. Riding the route's entire loop will take you by the small airstrip, the naval base, Laguna Makax, the *salinas* (saltwater marshes), and through some of the streets and houses in neighborhoods where local people live. You might combine this with a stop at Hacienda Mundaca, the buses' turnaround point, which is also within walking distance of several beaches. To see the southern end of the island—and you should—rent a golf cart for a day (see "Getting Around" on p. 75).

If you do stop at **Hacienda Mundaca** (east of Av. Rueda Medina at end of Laguna Makax; $2.50; daily 9am–dusk), a red wall at an S-curved intersection marks the ruins of the lovelorn pirate's old estate. A disintegrating stone archway, a rusted cannon, a crumbling guardhouse, and a well are all that remain, though some of the gardens have been reconstructed and a zoo added to turn it into a park. The arch's stone pediment, ironically, is engraved, in Spanish, "Orchard of the Happy View Hacienda 1876." Mundaca's grand monument to his love was built of stone taken from Maya temples he found on the island and was constructed by some of the slaves he had captured during his worldwide forays. Its paltry remains are interesting, but hardly compelling in themselves. Only the romantic story, one suspects, keeps the place going. The hacienda's gardens look a little forlorn, and the animals in the small zoo seem tired (bring some bananas for the monkeys).

Far more worthwhile is **Tortugranja** ★★★ 🅺 (Carretera Sac Bajo 5; ☎ 998/877-0595; $2; daily 9am–5pm), a turtle hatchery founded to help replenish declining sea turtle populations. For millions of years, Isla's beaches have been nesting grounds for marine turtles that return every year from May to September to lay hundreds of eggs. Historically, fishermen would capture the exhausted turtles after they laid their eggs and kill them for the prized meat, shell, and eggs. About 20 years ago, one of those fishermen began persuading the others to spare the eggs, which he protected. In 1994, the government followed his lead and founded the center, which has released tens of thousands of hatchlings with local schoolchildren's participation. Visitors will see hundreds of turtles, from little flippers crawling all over one another to platter-size adolescents gliding lazily in indoor pens and outdoor pools. The indoor aquarium also displays moray eels, thorny lobsters, sea horses, anemones, rays, and fish. It takes about an hour to wander through the indoor pools, stop to feed the turtles in the outdoor pools (food $1 a bag), and stroll the pier over the Caribbean water where larger turtles swim in a fenced-off ocean pool. The center also has a small gift shop and snack bar.

After visiting Punta Sur (below), make your way back to town along the wind-buffeted **northeastern coast** ★★ where the road skirts crags pounded by high seas. You'll pass beaches perfect for beachcombing (but too dangerous for swimming), where the occasional vendor sells shells and other ocean treasures scoured from the rocky shores. You'll see the edges of numerous *colonias.* Keep your eyes peeled for the two-story, arcaded, and balconied "Crayola House," painted in every primary color plus a few others, just visible from the highway; the two *salinas;* and many large, beautiful houses built to take advantage of the wild ocean views. One of these is the landmark "Shell House," a remarkable work of architecture shaped like a conch shell. It was built by a local artist using a combination of concrete and recycled materials.

## Punta Sur

Because the island veers to the east as it stretches southward, **Punta Sur** ★★★ (daily 9am–5:30pm) is not only the southern tip of the island but the easternmost point in Mexico. A seaside path wends around the rocky cliffs offering stunning sunrises and views of Cancún, the Bahía de Mujeres, and the Caribbean Sea as it passes caves and dugouts. At 20m (66 ft.) above sea level, this is also the highest point on the island.

The park's rugged beauty is obscured somewhat by man-made attractions, including a 50m (165-ft.) sightseeing tower that was closed for renovations at press time. Nearby is the kitschy **Caribbean Village,** with narrow lanes lined by colorful clapboard buildings that house cafes, pricey souvenir shops, and folk-art displays. The lighthouse in the village is free to climb for yet more stunning Caribbean views. You'll have to pay a $3 admission fee to continue unless you've paid for entry to Parque Garrafón (see "Active Isla Mujeres," below), which now controls the tip of the point. Next comes the **Sculpture Park,** an extensive garden of large, multihued abstract sculptures donated by world-famous Mexican and international sculptors such as José Luis Cuevas, Sebastián, and Helen Escobedo, set against a backdrop of majestic cliffs and the turquoise sea.

## About Ixchel

The top woman of this "Island of Women" was Ixchel (*Ee*-shell), a multitasking goddess known as "Lady Rainbow"; "God Mother"; wife of Itzamná the Creator; "Madam of the Sea"; "Goddess of the Moon"; and patroness of weaving, childbirth, and the art of medicine. The temple dedicated to her on Isla Mujeres evidently was a mecca for women praying for fertility. The female figurines discovered by Spanish explorers are believed to have been left as offerings to Ixchel following a successful pregnancy.

Ixchel was married to the earth god Voltan but fell in love with the moon god Itzamná, who is credited with teaching Maya people to read, write, and grow corn. With him, Ixchel bore four powerful sons known as the Bacabs, who continue to hold up the sky in each of the four directions. Also called the "World-Weaver," she is portrayed as both a young, life-giving queen and a wise old crone, both a benign deity and a wrathful one. She is often depicted carrying a jug of water, symbolizing her continual gift of water to mankind as well as the floods she sent to cleanse the earth of the wicked. She is said to bestow special protection to those making the sacred pilgrimage to her sites on Cozumel and Isla Mujeres.

Beyond the sculpture garden, on a cliff overlooking the sea at the very tip of the island, lies the **Santuario Maya a la Diosa Ixchel** ★. This is a haunting vestige of the Maya shrine to the goddess Ixchel, where the bare-breasted clay idols believed to have given the island its name were discovered. Though historically one of Isla Mujeres' most important attractions, the temple fragment retains little to evoke the wonder of the ancient world or timeless deities. It was already in ruins before Hurricane Gilbert swept most of it away in 1988, and though it has been cleaned up, attempts at restoration have blasted open a natural rock arch beneath the ruin and repaired it with poorly disguised concrete. A lovely walkway around the area remains, and it is worth the hike if only for the lofty views of the open ocean on one side and the Bahía de Mujeres on the other. The rocky path continues a little way to the very tip of the island, called the Cliff of the Dawn. This is the first spot in Mexico to see the sun rise.

## THE OTHER ISLA MUJERES

Although Isla doesn't hide its "real" life to the extent Cancún does, it's not hard to spend an entire vacation hanging out with other tourists. Venture beyond the anointed tourist attractions, and you'll be surprised how much you can learn.

In the center of town, the publicly funded **Casa de la Cultura** ★★ (Av. Guerrero at Abasolo; ☎ 998/877-0639; Mon–Fri 9am–9pm) welcomes visitors and is a wonderful place for children and adolescents, with its frequent activities and classes in dance, drawing and painting, ceramics, and singing. (It's not a day-care center, though; parents are required to stay and supervise.) In the rather institutional-looking cement building, with its playground in front and the back overlooking the sea, the cultural center also holds frequent yoga classes and hosts art exhibitions, puppet shows, and a variety of special events: musical benefits for such organizations as the Little Yellow Schoolhouse (for local children with special educational needs), annual book fair programs, and Cancún Jazz Festival performances. Christmastime brings musical festivals, community theater productions, and children's games. The center's book exchange is Isla's closest thing to a public library; several shelves are devoted to English-language paperbacks. There is no admission fee, but a donation is requested.

Not far from Hacienda Mundaca in the Colonia La Gloria neighborhood, you can help Isla Mujeres' Maya residents just by sitting down to chat with them at **La Gloria English School** ★★★ 🄺 (Manzana 156, Lote 20, Colonia La Gloria; ☎ 998/888-0666; www.folges.org). The nonprofit school was started in 2004 by Maggie and Tom Washa of Wisconsin, who live half the year on Isla, to provide affordable English classes for some of the island's poorest residents. Volunteers spend time with children, teens, or adults to help them practice their new skills individually and in small groups. The school encourages volunteers to work in the same 1-hour class for 4 consecutive days, but also welcomes shorter commitments. You don't need to speak Spanish, and you'll get to know some friendly people in the heart of the island's Mexican community. Future plans also include an English-Spanish conversation partner program. Class schedules and volunteer procedures are on the website.

Travelers who are moved by the sight of sick and starving dogs in Isla Mujeres' streets can help do something about it by working with the **Amigos De Los Animales** 🄺 (www.islaanimals.org) clinic. Founded in 2000 by two expat women who were horrified by the government's regular roundups and extermination of strays, the nonprofit, volunteer-run organization has taken on the mission of rescuing homeless dogs and cats and reining in the local animal population. The nonprofit volunteer group picks up homeless animals and nurses them back to health, and it works with a local veterinarian to conduct a free weekly "Spay Day" for low-income pet owners. Animal lovers are welcome for as much or as little time as they can afford, whether it's as simple as taking a dog out for a walk or as involved as working with Dr. Pepe Vega in his Colonia La Gloria veterinary office. Allison Current, a driving force in the group who has provided foster care for as many as 40 homeless pups at a time in her home, started an adoption program in 2004 that finds homes in the United States for rehabilitated dogs. She always needs help walking, feeding, bathing, and playing with her foster babies. Details are on the website.

## ACTIVE ISLA MUJERES

Though Isla Mujeres is treasured as a place where you can slow down, nature has bestowed the island with an abundance of opportunities to pick up the pace for as long as you want. Much of the island's wilderness remains intact and ripe for exploration, while the numerous reefs in the warm, clear water between Isla and the mainland demand a closer look.

### Snorkeling

If you want to snorkel from **Playa Norte,** the best spot is the calm, shallow water at the northeastern tip, near the bridge to the Avalon Reef Club; equipment is available all along the beach for $10 to $15 a day. The protected waters along the entire western shore, mostly limited to depths of 8 to 11m (25–35 ft.), are ideal snorkeling grounds. It also has a few good shore spots, but you'll find the best snorkeling landscapes offshore. Tours can be booked at many hotels, on Playa Norte and at kiosks near the ferry pier, typically for about $25 per person (plus $5 if you need equipment) for about 2 hours. The personable **Captain Tony García** ★★ (Calle Matamoros 7A, btw. Rueda Medina and Juárez; ☎ 998/877-0229; www.isla-mujeres.net/capttony/home.htm), who has earned a fiercely loyal following, goes out at 10am every day that he isn't running a Contoy Island tour (see "Isla Contoy," below). Most groups go to **El Farolito,** a snorkeling park in the bay offshore from the ferry piers. Another excellent snorkeling spot is around **El Faro (the Lighthouse)** in the Bahía de Mujeres at the southern tip of the island, where the water is about 2m (6½ ft.) deep. For the best snorkel trips, go to a dive shop, which are more likely to take you to less visited areas.

**Garrafón Natural Reef Park** 🧒 (☎ 998/849-4748; www.garrafon.com; $50 adults, $38 children), unique in having part of the world's second-longest barrier reef just a few feet offshore, has long been Isla's favored snorkeling spot. Parque Garrafón, as it is usually called, was once was a public national underwater park but is now privately operated and is more akin to a theme park. Its ever-expanding lineup of attractions include a zipline over the water, a climbing tower, "snuba" (a tankless version of scuba diving that employs a helmet with compressed air) tours, diving platforms, and see-through canoes for viewing underwater life. Even as the facilities have been spiffed up, the coral reef has suffered from hurricanes, boats, and too many tourists. The steep all-inclusive entry fee includes breakfast and lunch, and snorkeling equipment, but towels, the zipline, bicycles, or a snorkeling tour will cost extra. The same basic package from Cancún costs $65 ($49 children) and includes a boat transfer. If you just want a day of snorkeling, you'll do better elsewhere, but if you have kids with short attention spans, the park has plenty to keep them happy.

You don't have to pay Parque Garrafón's fees just to get in some leisurely snorkeling; instead, go next door to **Garrafón de Castilla** ★★ 🧒 (Carretera Punta Sur Km 6; ☎ 998/877-0107; $4; daily 9am–5pm), a modest beach club where you can snorkel in the same soft ocean current among the colorful tropical fish. Once in the water, nearly 275m (900 ft.) of coral reef is your domain, including the section used by Parque Garrafón. Snorkel gear rents for $6, and lockers and towels are $2.50 apiece. Hour-long tours to nearby Manchones reef can also be arranged for $25 per person, including equipment.

## Diving

Beginning divers will appreciate the soft, almost imperceptible currents and vibrant sea life on Isla Mujeres' west side, while the east side offers advanced divers more challenges in up to 40m (130 ft.) of water with more varied terrain and even a couple of shipwrecks. Among the best dive sites:

- **Banderas Reef,** between Isla and Cancún, an elongated reef topped with elkhorn coral and home to barracuda, moray eels, langosta, and angel fish
- **Media Luna,** on the Caribbean side, a drift dive among unique coral arches, ridges, and ledges populated by sea anemones, spiny sea urchins, and lobster
- **Ultrafreeze,** a coral- and sponge-encrusted cargo ship under 30m (100 ft.) of notoriously chilly water 11km (7 miles) off the eastern shore, where turtles and rays are often seen

- **Manchones Reef,** off the southeastern coast opposite Punta Cancún, where the coral and sea life are in relatively good shape despite heavy traffic and the brass Cruz de la Bahía (Cross of the Bay, a sculpture) on the reef under the water just offshore
- **Navy Boat Wreck,** a World War II U.S. minesweeper later transferred to the Mexican navy, lying at a depth of 21m (70 ft.) among moray eels, nurse sharks, parrotfish, and lobsters
- **Tabos Reef,** an obscure site on the eastern shore, with unique limestone formations providing crevices and tunnels that attract gray and white-tip reef sharks
- **Punta Sur,** where the Gulf of Mexico's merger with the Caribbean provides a playground for dolphins and sea turtles and has the remains of an old wreck with a 400-year-old anchor

Most dive shops on the island offer similar one-tank reef dive trips for about $50 and two tanks for $70. Deep dives and adventure dives run as high as $95.

Six divers is the maximum group size at the highly recommended **Sea Hawk Divers** ★★ (Av. Carlos Lazo at López Mateos; ☎ 998/877-1233; www.isla-mujeres.net/seahawkdivers), whose owner, Ariel Barandica, is a PADI-certified instructor with more than 20 years of experience. He offers friendly, professional service and also rents out rooms above the shop; they usually fill up well in advance. **Mundaca Divers** (Av. Francisco Madero 10; ☎ 998/877-0607; www.mundacadivers.com) also has a good reputation for personalized service among professional divers and employs a PADI instructor. The PADI-affiliated **Coral Scuba Dive Center** (Av. Matamoros 13A at Rueda Medina; ☎ 998/877-0763; www.coralscubadivecenter.com) boasts many repeat customers for its wide variety of dive packages and its snorkeling trips. This is Isla's largest dive shop, and on busy days groups can grow to 12 or 14 divers, but the equipment is in top condition and its prices tend to be a little lower than other shops.

## Swimming with Dolphins

Most people reach **Dolphin Discovery** (Carretera Sac Bajo, just past Hotel Villas Rolandi; ☎ 866/393-5158 toll-free U.S., or 998/877-0207; www.dolphindiscovery.com) on a boat from Cancún; there isn't even an office or kiosk in downtown Isla. You can make reservations through most hotels, or try just showing up at its large facility at Treasure Island on the island's west side. The Dolphin Royal swim includes an educational video, an orientation session, and time to frolic with the dolphins. The price is $149; a 45-minute Dolphin Encounter for nonswimmers is $69 ($59 for children under 12) and a Dolphin Swim Adventure, also 45 minutes, is $99. Oddly, even if you show up under your own power, you pay the same price as the package from Cancún that includes round-trip boat transportation, which makes an already expensive proposition feel like a bit of a gouge. See the box on p. 57 for more on the ethics of swimming with dolphins; see p. 56 for information on making this trip from Cancún.

## Fishing

The **Sociedad Cooperativa Turística** (Av. Rueda Medina at Av. Madero pier; ☎ 998/877-1363), a cooperative made up of most of the local owners of snorkeling and

# Cave of the Sleeping Sharks

In 1969, an island fisherman named Carlos García Castilla was diving for lobster when he saw a cave about 21m (70 ft.) deep populated by sharks that showed a singular lack of interest in attacking—or even moving. Investigating further, he discovered several sharks sleeping with their eyes open inside the cave. Later explored by a cinematographer and Mexico's leading shark expert, the Cueva de Tiburones became Isla's most famous dive site.

No one knows why the sharks become so docile when they swim into the "cave," which is actually an undersea cenote where freshwater flows out of a subterranean river. Scientists have posed two theories: One, that the parasites that cling to the sharks lose their grip in the absence of salt-water, allowing the remora fish (the sharks' personal vacuum cleaners) to scrub them clean while they relax; the other, that the heightened oxygen levels in the fresh water induce a type of intoxication.

Sadly, after almost 40 years of overfishing and heavy diving, the sharks have started to wake up and get out of Dodge. These days, you have less than a 50% chance of seeing sharks slumbering in the caves.

fishing boats, rents boats for a maximum of 4 hours and six people for $120. (The cooperative also offers snorkeling trips and small boats for charter cruises.) **Captain Tony García** (p. 89) will take people bottom fishing or trolling for barracuda for $65 per person for 4 hours, and **Sea Hawk Divers** (see "Diving," above) runs fishing tours for barracuda, snapper, and smaller fish starting at $200 a day.

## Yoga

Isla Mujeres has developed into something of a mecca for yoga aficionados, and the place credited with starting it all is still one of the best values. **Na Balam** ✸✸✸ (Hotel Na Balaam, Calle Zazil-Ha 118; ☎ 998/877-0279; www.nabalam.com) on Playa Norte offers yoga instruction under its large poolside *palapa*, complete with yoga mats and props, at 9am Monday, Wednesday, and Friday. Classes are free for guests and $15 for the public (monthly rates available). The resort also hosts frequent yoga retreats.

The downtown yoga center, **Elements of the Island** ✸ (Av. Juárez 64, btw. López Mateos and Matamoros; ☎ 998/877-1715 8am–1pm, 998/877-1761 3–6pm; www.elementsoftheisland.com) offers classes from beginner to advanced levels on its *palapa*-shaded rooftop with a panoramic island view. Public classes are $12 (10 for $100) and private sessions are $60; all include mats, blankets, blocks, and straps. Down the island near Parque Garrafón, the boutique hotel **Casa de los Sueños** (☎ 998/877-0651; www.casadelossuenosresort.com) offers private yoga lessons for $40 per person (two-person minimum).

## Isla Contoy

When even Isla Mujeres feels too hectic, you're ready for **Isla Contoy National Park** ★★★ 🅺 (Av. Rueda Medina at Madero; ☎ 998/877-1513; www.conanp.gob.mx), a bird sanctuary and special biosphere reserve about 45 minutes north of Isla by boat (more if the water is choppy). Except for a scientific research station and about a dozen park rangers, the tiniest of Mexico's Caribbean islands is reserved for pelicans, egrets, ibis, strange brown boobies, and even stranger roseate spoonbills (best described as a platypus head on a flamingo body), among the more than 100 bird species. Less than 6km (4 miles) long and ½-mile wide, the island is covered by sand dunes, mangroves, shallow lagoons, and pristine beaches where iguanas, lizards, turtles, hermit crabs, and boa constrictors thrive.

Off the southern tip of the island, the Ixlaché coral marks the end of the Great Mesoamerican Reef system, which skirts the coast of Quintana Roo and continues to Honduras. Nutrients in the colliding currents of the Gulf of Mexico and Caribbean waters make the island an ideal nursery for a vast variety of wildlife. Flocks of flamingos arrive in April; from May to October, hawksbill and loggerhead turtles lay their eggs on shore. The only concessions to humans are some pathways and a visitor center with a small outdoor museum, cafeteria, and lookout tower.

Most excursions troll for fish (to be barbecued for lunch), anchor for about 45 minutes of the best snorkeling you're ever likely to experience, and quietly skirt the island for close-up but unobtrusive views of the birds before pulling ashore. While the captain prepares lunch, you can swim, explore nature trails, and browse museum displays on Contoy's animal life

## ATTENTION, SHOPPERS!

Beyond the tacky trinkets and cheap T-shirts proliferating around the ferry pier, Isla's narrow streets are studded with specialty shops selling clothing, handicrafts from all over Mexico, and the ever-present hammocks. The island is known especially for its duty-free prices on precious gems and locally crafted gold and silver jewelry. (If you can find basic underwear or a contact-lens case, though, you're a better shopper than I.)

Isla Mujeres' store hours are generally Monday to Saturday from 10am to 1pm and 4 to 7pm, though more shops now stay open during traditional siesta hours. Most are small family affairs that don't take credit cards, but dollars are welcome. Avenida Hidalgo is shopping central, and pitches from shop owners working the street are the most vigorous here. The side streets, though, usually yield better bargains. Merchandise mostly duplicates what you can find in Cancún, but prices are decidedly lower—and bargaining is expected. As a rule, start by offering half of the initial asking price, and expect to settle at about 75%. Don't get obsessed with haggling—this is the vendors' livelihood, after all—and keep it friendly.

and geology. Friendly park rangers will point you in the right direction and tell you all about the plants and animals, or you can use the map to explore on your own—be sure to stop at Sting Ray Beach on Contoy Bay, where amicable rays accept offerings of food and obligingly pose for photos.

*Important:* Please remember and obey the necessary restrictions on where you can go and what you can touch. Boat tours have been curtailed in the past and could be halted if tourism threatens the fragile environment.

The island is limited to 200 visitors per day, and only a few boats are authorized to run tours from Isla and Cancún. If at all possible, go with **Captain Tony García** (Calle Matamoros 7A; ☎ 998/877-0229; www.isla-mujeres.net/capttony/home.htm; $55; cash only), a gregarious and knowledgeable guide who many past visitors now consider a good friend. Stop by his house, ½-block from the Contoy dock on Isla Mujeres, a day ahead to book his 9am tour. Groups meet there a half-hour early to fit snorkeling gear and help load the boat. Plan the trip early in your vacation in case you need to reschedule; this safety-conscious captain won't go out unless the weather is perfect.

Other approved local operators include **Gaitan Tours** (Contoy Pier, Av. Rueda Medina; ☎ 998/877-0798) and **Contoy Express Tours** (Av. Rueda Medina, btw. Matamoros and Abasolo; ☎ 998/877-1367). You can buy tickets at the fishing cooperative (see "Fishing," below).

Tours from Cancún cost $75 for adults, $38 for children, and are available from **Kolumbus Tours** (☎ 998/884-5333; www.kolumbustours.com) and **Asterix Tours** (☎ 998/886-4847; www.contoytours.com).

The island's famous jewelry ranges from tasteful creations to flat-out fakes. You can find true bargains, but stay away from the street peddlers. The large branch of high-toned European jeweler **Van Cleef & Arpels** (Av. Juárez at Morelos; ☎ 998/877-0331), which has been on the island for more than 25 years, offers the highest quality on artistic designs of precious stones set in gold and silver. Prices are better than those in the United States, and there are some good values, but shoppers on a budget will do better across the way at its reduced-price sister store, **The Silver Factory** (Av. Juárez at Morelos; ☎ 998/877-0331).

For affordable quality jewelry from Taxco, Mexico's silver capital, try **Joyería Maritza** (Av. Hidalgo 14, btw. Morelos and Francisco Madero; ☎ 998/877-0526), which also has a selection of crafts from Oaxaca. For something different, **Opalo de Fuego** ★★★ (Av. Juárez at Nicolas Bravo; ☎ 998/877-1250), or Fire Opal, specializes in opals of many colors that were forged by the volcanoes near Mexico City. In addition to selecting from an array of loose stones and one-of-a-kind jewelry, you can choose your stone from amethysts, topaz, sapphires, rubies, and others, and have a piece made to your own design. The prices are fair and the owner scrupulously honest.

For impressive bargains on Mexican handicrafts, browse the stalls at the **Mercado Artesanías** ★★★ (Av. Matamoros at Carlos Lazo), where local artisans display their works, mostly *pareos* (sarongs), jewelry, hammocks, and T-shirts. In many of these little shops, if you don't see exactly what you want, you can have it made in a day or two. Isla regulars swear by **Hortencia** (the last stall on the left— look for her name painted on a planter); choose your fabric and pick a pattern for a dress, skirt, shirt, or shorts. At the **hammock stall** facing Matamoros, you can select your fiber and colors and watch it being made. You can also have one of **Carlo's** unique, silky *pareos* made with hand-sewn beads and shells.

Among the shops, **Artesanías Arcoíris** (Av. Hidalgo at Juárez; no phone) has good-quality silver, quartz, and alabaster stones, as well as pewter, carved boxes, Talavera ceramics, blankets, and other handicrafts. And if you want hassle-free hair throughout your vacation, the staff also does braiding. The store doesn't close until 9pm and is also open from 9am to 4pm Sundays. High-quality Talavera ceramics, Barra Negro pottery, silver serving pieces, Oaxacan hand-painted rugs, and other Mexican handicrafts from artists known throughout Mexico fill the tall, wooden shelves at **Galería del Arte Mexicano** (Av. Hidalgo 16; no phone), but the shop prides itself on the extensive selection of silver jewelry designed by local families. It's open until 9pm.

## NIGHTLIFE ON ISLA MUJERES

Isla Mujeres, once famous for rolling up the sidewalks at night, has developed a respectable club scene, though (appropriately) it doesn't approach the clamor or spectacle of Cancún's nightlife. Most clubs are restaurants by day, and the greatest density is along Avenida Hidalgo. *Palapa*-roofed hotel bars provide most of the action on Playa Norte.

### On the Beach

Known as the "Swing Bar" because it replaces bar stools with swings hanging over the sand, **Buho's** (end of Av. Carlos Lazo; no phone; daily 9am–1am) began dispensing food and drink before Cancún was built and remains the tourist favorite for schmoozing and relaxing with a beer as the sun sinks behind the Caribbean, even though prices have been creeping up. Locals don't come here much, but many long-time visitors consider a visit to Buho's the official beginning of their vacations. It certainly has all the trappings of a tropical idyll: hammocks under the palms, decor heavy on shells and buoys, and a front-row seat for sunset. It's often packed from the 2 to 5pm happy hour (two-for-one beers and cocktails) right on into the night.

Two other beach hotels on Playa Norte offer smashing ocean views and live music late into the night. The **Hotel Na Balam Beach Bar** ★ (Av. Zazil-Ha 118; ☎ 998/877-0279; www.nabalam.com) usually draws a crowd to its fresh breezes and stunning view of powdery white sand daily until about midnight; on weekends, live bands play late into the night. On the bay side, the Posada del Mar's restaurant, **Pingüinos** (Av. Rueda Medina 15A, btw. Matamoros and López Mateos; ☎ 998/877-0044)—Mexican slang for ice-cold beer—has a band playing every night during the high season from 9pm to midnight on its balcony.

The sunset views, reputed to be the best on the island, are the main thing that keeps pulling people back to the **Sunset Grill** (Av. Rueda Medina on Condominios Nautibeach grounds; ☎ 998/877-0785; daily 8am–10pm)—well, that and the 22-ounce goblets of frozen margaritas. The bar is also popular for its live music;

when the mics are quiet, the sound system pumps out an eclectic mix that has even been known to include the Moody Blues. Eat before you come for drinks, though; the food is pricey and the quality and service are hit or miss.

The Texans who own **Jax Bar and Grill** (Av. López Mateos at Rueda Medina; ☎ 998/877-1218; daily 8am–2am), dispense live country, blues, and classic rock beginning at 9pm most nights in the high season. The upstairs restaurant offers a more sedate atmosphere, but sports reign downstairs, where ESPN plays continuously on satellite TV and billiards or darts are usually in play. The bar can produce anything from buckets of ice-cold Corona to Dom Perignon. Located near the Lighthouse, it's popular with sunset-gazers and famous for its happy hour and its monumental grilled burgers.

## In Town

"Chill" is the operative word at **Om Bar and Chill Lounge** ★★★ (Av. Matamoros 30, btw. Juárez and Hidalgo; ☎ 998/820-4876; Mon–Sat 7:30am–1:30am), a very cool place where you can enjoy upbeat Latin jazz, reggae, and bossa nova while choosing from cocktails, 30 varieties of wine, or 20 types of organic tea. There's no lining up at the bar for your beer: you pull your own draft from a tap at your table, and they read the meter when it's time to pay the tab. Need a jolt? The house specialty, *La Viuda Express* (The Widow Express), is a concoction of espresso, tequila, Baileys, Kahlúa, and sugar. Imagine post-Impressionist paintings with Moroccan and Thai influences and you've got an idea of what covers the walls of this romantic, dimly lit cave.

Connoisseurs, aficionados, and novices alike will find a home at **La Adelita** ★★★ (Av. Hidalgo 12A; ☎ 998/877-0528; daily 6pm–3am), the island's only tequila bar. And its all-the-time two-for-one shots should make you think twice about drinking tequila anywhere else. You can sample reggae, salsa, and Caribbean music, and a variety of cigars, along with 150 kinds of Mexico's national beverage. And you can't get much more Mexican than La Adelita's tile roof, brick arches, woven leather sidewalk chairs, and photos of Pancho Villa. Inside, you can buy a bottle of your favorite tequila from the glass shelves surrounding the small bar. Cocktails and margaritas are available, too.

## Dance Clubs

Don't confuse **Bamboo Too** ★★ (Av. Nicolas Bravo; ☎ 998/845-7384; daily 7:30pm–3am) with the restaurant on Avenida Hidalgo (p. 81), though it is run by the same owner. This savvy, rambling disco, sits right on the *malecón*. One of its myriad spaces is bound to suit your style: chat on the upstairs patio, swing 3m (10 ft.) from Caribbean waves on the downstairs back porch, shoot some pool, play the high-tech video jukebox. A long corridor separates the front and back bars, and seating is on heavy chairs imported from Thailand, carved of tree stumps whose nooks and crannies serve as arm rests and bottle holders. A DJ plays techno, salsa, reggae, and dance music, but things are pretty quiet until midnight, when the crowds show up and rock until dawn.

Locals and tourists also crowd together on the tiny dance floor at **Nitrox** (Av. Guerrero 11 near Matamoros; ☎ 998/877-0568; Wed–Sun 9pm–3am). The music is mostly techno, disco, and reggae. Ladies' Night is held on Wednesdays, Latin Night on Fridays, and two-for-one beer always.

# ISLA HOLBOX

Quintana Roo's northernmost island is a secret even to most Mexicans living outside the Yucatán. Isla Holbox (Ohl-*bosh*) is still populated by descendants of the families who settled the island in the 19th century. Most are fishermen who pull lobster, octopus, grouper, conch, and variety of other fish from the rich waters where the Caribbean and the Gulf of Mexico mingle. The island is part of the Yum Balam protected area, established in 1994 to safeguard the dolphins, flamingos, pelicans, and other wildlife that flourishes there.

Life goes on pretty much as it always has for the island's 2,000 residents. Their village has packed-sand streets lined with palm-thatched huts and brightly painted houses. There's no ATM, cellphone service, hospital, or post office. You can spend days without seeing a car; adults and children alike scoot around in golf carts.

The biggest draw for tourists is the annual congregation of more than 100 whale sharks, the world's largest fish. Tour operators in Cancún and Playa del Carmen offer day trips, rousting visitors long before sun-up and delivering them back to their hotel that night, but such marathon jaunts defy the very nature of Holbox. A far better plan is to spend a couple of days to stroll the beach, walk around town, and explore the wildlife on uninhabited islands nearby.

Whale shark tours have brought a measure of prosperity to Holbox, and visitors will now find air-conditioning, a couple of Internet cafes, and satellite TV. Thatched *cabañas* (bungalows), a few of them quite luxurious, stand along the northern beach, and several small restaurants serve just-caught seafood. While the nutrient-rich water is greener and less crystalline than Cancún's pure Caribbean, the broad, pristine beach's fine white sands yield a galaxy of shells. Whale shark season is the only time Holbox gets anything resembling a crowd, and the island is one of Mexico's best refuges for relaxing and clearing your head.

## A BRIEF HISTORY

The Maya people abandoned Holbox at least 300 years before the first Europeans arrived in 1856 to harvest the many varieties of hardwood for export. Those who stayed on settled near the middle of the island and married local people—refugees from the inland Caste Wars who began arriving at about the same time. When a hurricane swept their small village away around 1900, killing 100 people, the survivors moved east to the island's highest point, about 30m (100 ft.) above sea level, where the town of Holbox remains today.

The island's name comes from the Mayan *xol-box,* meaning "black hole." The local explanation is it was named for the color of the water in the lagoon on the south side of the island, where the white sandy bottom is interrupted by a deep cenote that makes the water appear black.

Beachcombing hippies and dedicated fishermen were the only foreigners who happened upon Isla Holbox until 2002, when local fishermen began taking people out in their boats to see the gargantuan but benign whale sharks that spend their summers feeding off the island's shore. The island's efforts to develop a low-impact tourism industry have already produced more tourist comforts. But perhaps because Holbox takes some determination to get to, growth has been cautious and slow. It's still a long way from being swamped by foreigners (most of those it does see are nature-loving Europeans). And if jobs in hotels and tour services have

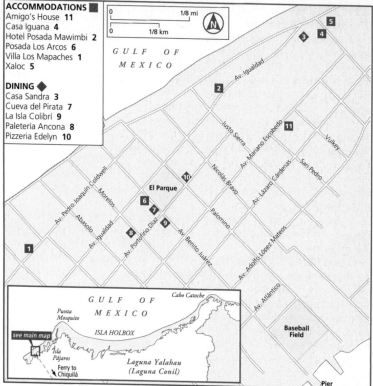

**ACCOMMODATIONS ■**
Amigo's House **11**
Casa Iguana **4**
Hotel Posada Mawimbi **2**
Posada Los Arcos **6**
Villa Los Mapaches **1**
Xaloc **5**

**DINING ◆**
Casa Sandra **3**
Cueva del Pirata **7**
La Isla Colibrí **9**
Paletería Ancona **8**
Pizzeria Edelyn **10**

made life easier, tourism is incidental to daily life; fishermen still get out on the water by sunrise and carry their catch through town later in the day.

## LAY OF THE LAND

Isla Holbox, 64km (40 miles) northwest of Cancún, is a narrow spit of land separated from the northwestern tip of the Yucatán Peninsula by 11km (7 miles) of water—the shallow Laguna Yalahau, domain of flamingos, pelicans, wild dolphins, and other exotic creatures. The island is about 11km (7 miles) long and about 3km (2 miles) at its widest point. The northern shore is all beach, while the southern shores along the lagoon are mostly mangrove marshes.

Cabo Catoche, the cape at the northeastern tip of the island (and the Yucatán Peninsula), is where Gulf and Caribbean waters meet in a kaleidoscope of shifting turquoise, emerald, and aquamarine hues. The island's entire population lives in the village at the southeastern end. Its tidy grid is simple to navigate: The main street, Avenida Benito Juárez, runs from the lagoon-side ferry dock straight through town to the north-facing beach, where bungalow hotels line up to the left and right. El Parque, the central square, is 2 blocks from the beach at Benito Juárez between Igualdad and Porfirio Díaz. ***Note:*** All the streets were renamed in 2005, so if you have a map, make sure it's a recent one.

# GETTING TO & AROUND HOLBOX

The **Marítimo 9 Hermanos** ferry ($4) to Holbox makes the half-hour crossing from the mainland village of Chiquilá, departing daily roughly every other hour from 6am until 7pm. There is no phone number or website, so ask at your hotel or a local tourist office to confirm schedules for you. Ferries sometimes leave ahead of schedule, so arrive a half-hour early. If you miss the last boat, water taxis will gladly take you across the lagoon for about $25. Some of the hotels will also send a private launch by advance arrangement.

The quickest way to get to Chiquilá is by car, about 2½ hours from Cancún or 3½ hours from Mérida. Take the *libre* (free) Hwy. 180 (not the toll road, called the *autopista* or *cuota* on road signs) to El Ideal, about 100km (62 miles) west of Cancún. Turn north on Hwy. 5 and continue about 140km (87 miles) to Chiquilá, staying right where the road forks. Families living near the ferry dock rent out safe parking spaces for about $4 to $7, depending on your negotiating skills; look for signs along the street.

If you aren't traveling by rental car, it's not worth renting one just to get from Cancún to Chiquilá. Second-class buses make the trip in about 3 hours ($7) from the main bus terminal two or three times a day; check with your hotel or call **Ticketbus** (☎ 800/702-8000 toll-free Mexico) for current schedules.

When you land in Holbox, a golf-cart taxi to the beach hotels will cost about $3. The town is only about a dozen square blocks, and even the farthest hotels are no more than a half-hour's walk from town. But if you want to join the locals zipping around town, numerous *rentadoras* will rent you a golf cart, including **Rentadora Glendy** (Av. Porfirio Díaz at Morelos; ☎ 984/875-2093) and **Rentadora El Brother** (Av. Benito Juárez at Igualdad; ☎ 998/875-2018). You can also book a cart in advance through **Holbox Island** (www.holboxisland.com), the closest thing Holbox has to an official tourist site, for $11 an hour, $50 for 12 hours, or $60 for 24 hours; the rental company is not specified.

# ACCOMMODATIONS, BOTH STANDARD & NOT

Isla Holbox isn't overendowed with vacation rentals, but the owners of the popular Amigo's bed-and-breakfast inns on Cozumel and in Bacalar have built **Amigo's House** ★★★ 🧒 (Jerónomo de Aguilar, btw. calles Vulkey and San Pedro; ☎ 987/872-3868 Cozumel office; www.isla-holbox.net), a couple of blocks from the town center and the beach. "House" might not be the right word—it's actually three separate buildings. One contains two huge, air-conditioned bedrooms that sleep four people and have private bathrooms; another has a living room (with TV, VCR, and DVD player) and full kitchen; and another is a staff residence. The rooms are bright and the decor simple, with colorful touches. At $100 a night, it's an incredible bargain for a family or group. Four guests or fewer have the option of renting just one bedroom and the kitchen for $70.

## Hotels

The small bungalow hotels that line the beach have traditionally been cooled only by ceiling fans, but more recent arrivals also offer air-conditioning. They vary in style, amenities, and price but all focus on peace and relaxation. The lowest-priced lodging is in town, offering basic comforts a short walk from the beach. Unlike most of the Yucatán, high season here often includes summer months, when the whale sharks are in residence.

**$** The island's longtime budget favorite is **Posada Los Arcos** (Av. Benito Juárez at El Parque; ☎ 984/875-2043; www.isla-holboxhotelarcos.com; cash only), on the central square. The five rather stark rooms, each with a full and a twin bed, are beginning to look a little tattered, but they are large and clean, come with air-conditioning and TV, and surround a quiet, bougainvillea-filled courtyard. Some have a separate kitchen/dining area with a fridge but no stove. Doubles start at $35 with air-conditioning ($25 fan only) and go up to $45 ($35 fan only) in high season. The location puts you right in the middle of things, which is convenient but might subject you to noise from nearby clubs and restaurants at night.

**$–$$$** One of the best deals on the beach, **Casa Iguana** ★★ 🄺🄸🄳🅂 (Av. Damero at the beach; ☎ 305/396-6987 U.S., or 984/875-2173; www.casa-iguana.net; AE, MC, V) offers six varied rooms and suites shaded by dense tropical foliage. The front opens onto the beach and the garden is equipped with hammocks and chairs. The rooms' breezy, tropical style includes red-tile floors, white walls, and wood trim and furniture. High-speed ceiling fans do the job most of the year, but ground-floor rooms in back can be stifling in summer; try to get an upstairs room in front for maximum benefit from ocean breezes. Basic rooms are $45 a night in low season, $55 high; larger rooms, which can sleep four and have an upstairs terrace or a garden patio, are $65 to $75. Spacious oceanfront suites with beds for four go for $80 to $120; a two-bedroom house, ideal for families, rents for $800 to $1,000 a week. Easter week and late December are 20% more.

**$–$$$** If you crave privacy, you won't do better than **Villa Los Mapaches** ★★★ (Av. Pedro Joaquín Coldwell at the beach; ☎ 984/875-2090; www.losmapaches.com; AE, DISC, MC, V, PayPal), one of Holbox's first bungalow hotels. With an attentive multilingual staff, its five homey bungalows come in assorted sizes, shapes, and colors, all well separated and tucked into a bower of mature palms and tropical plants. The Blue House, which sits next to the road and in front of the maintenance storage, does get some noise. Even when the hotel is full, you'll rarely share the beach with more than three or four other people. Some bungalows, with their tall A-line thatched roofs, resemble Indonesian stilt houses; others look like traditional Maya huts. Interiors are simple, colorful, and artsy, and most have large bedrooms and bathrooms, kitchenettes, and a patio. Rates range from $50 to $90 a night in low season, $55 to $100 midseason, and $60 to $110 high season. Use of the hotel's bicycles is included in the rate.

**$$–$$$$** You might never leave the front garden, with its hammock-strung palm trees, at Italian-owned **Hotel Posada Mawimbi** 🄺🄸🄳🅂 (Av. Igualdad at beach; ☎ 984/875-2003; www.mawimbi.net; MC, V with 5% surcharge). Even the cheapest standard doubles ($60 low season, $70 high; $70–$90 with balcony) are airy and brightly decorated. Rooms with two beds range from $80 to $100; a huge, two-story bungalow with two beds and a kitchenette (ceiling fan only) is $95 to $105; and an oceanfront junior suite with king bed is $110 to $130. The varied decor blends European and Mexican style, with such touches as wood-post beds with colorful woven spreads, area rugs, tile counters, and mosquito netting. You can use hotel kayaks for free or book wildlife and fishing tours. Four-night minimum stays are required July to August; it's a 2-night minimum if you also book a whale shark tour.

**$$$–$$$$**    Offering luxury at tolerable rates, **Xaloc** ★★★ (Calle Chacchi at the beach; ☎ 800/728-9098 toll-free U.S./Canada, or 984/875-2160; www.holbox-xalocresort.com; AE, MC, V), is owned by a Spanish architect who built the 18 round bungalows in rustic style with pointy thatched roofs. The stylish, molded-concrete interiors are quite romantic, with yards of mosquito netting over the beds (two doubles or a king—in length as well as width, a rarity), shuttered windows and terra-cotta tile floors; and large divided bathrooms with double sinks. Though a little close together, the bungalows are situated so you feel like the place is yours alone, even when swinging from a hammock on the wooden porches. Rooms facing the two white limestone swimming pools start at $90 in low season and go up to $143 over Christmas; gardenview rooms are $110 to $171. Oceanview rooms, though, cost $144 to $196. Local booking sites such as **Best Day Travel** (www.bestdaytravel.com) can shave $6 to $12 off the nightly rate. Optional full- and half-board plans ($16–$26 per person, per night) are a decent value; the hotel's Maja'che restaurant is quite good, serving mainly fish and lots of fresh seasonal fruits. The upstairs lounge serves some of the best cocktails on Holbox.

## DINING FOR ALL TASTES

**$**    First and foremost, ice cream: Holbox is famous for **Helados Maresa**'s ★★★ natural coconut confection and homemade waffle cones (about $2), served every night from a stand in El Parque and also available around town—including the family home 2 blocks south of the square (look for the ice cream "truck," a converted golf cart, in front). You can also choose *piña* (pineapple) or a wide variety of other tropical flavors. Another possibility is **Paletería Ancona** (Morelos, btw. Díaz and Igualdad), which sells not just ice cream but juices and popsicles flavored with peanuts, tamarind, rice, and corn.

**$–$$**    Nearly every square inch of the funky clapboard, tin-roofed interior of **La Isla Colibrí** ★★ 🧒 (Benito Juárez at Av. Porfirio Díaz; daily 8am–1pm and 6–11pm; cash only) is covered with posters, photos, and artwork. This is my choice for breakfast, with yogurt, granola, and huge fruit juices along with even heartier offerings for $3.50 to $8. The fish dishes served in the evening are good, too, but not as much of a deal.

**$$**    You can pick other toppings for the thin-crust pizzas at **Pizzería Edelyn** ★★ 🧒 (Av. Palomino at Porfirio Díaz; ☎ 984/875-2024; daily 11am–midnight; cash only), but the one everyone raves about is the lobster, loaded with garlicky chunks of the precious shellfish ($13; serves two). Other options include fish, pasta, and Mexican finger foods. Take a table on the porch to keep your cool.

**$$–$$$**    Owned by Italians and frequented by lots of foreigners, **Cueva del Pirata** ★★ (Av. Benito Juárez at Porfirio Díaz; ☎ 984/875-2183; Mon–Sat 8am–11pm; cash only) is an elegant dinner place with candlelit tables on a porch facing the plaza and soft jazz playing in the dining room. The menu offers seafood, meat, and poultry dishes, but the specialty is homemade pastas from about $8 to $18—lobster marinara commands the top price.

**$$–$$$$**  Some of the appetizers at **Casa Sandra** ★★★ (Calle Igualdad at the beach; ☎ 984/875-2431; daily 7–10pm; MC, V) easily make a meal and that's a good thing, because this isn't budget dining. I especially like the $10 eggplant parmesan. But the restaurant in Holbox's island's most luxurious hotel, created by an artist from Cuba, serves the best food on the island, and it's worth saving up for. The menu, which changes daily, is a mix of Mexican and international dishes, with an emphasis on Cuban preparations. For about $15 to $25, you might choose from pork filet in tamarind sauce, Thai chicken satay, Provençal-style herbed chicken and fish cooked in everything from simple garlic and parsley to curry and coconut sauce.

## WHY YOU'RE HERE: THE TOP SIGHTS & ACTIVITIES

For a lot of Holbox's visitors, doing nothing is activity enough. But if you get restless, you've got plenty of options. The **main beach,** which has no name, extends a little bit west from Avenida Benito Juárez and miles and miles to the east. The perpetual winds and ample dune grass make it less than ideal for sunbathing, but it's perfect for walking, beachcombing, and gathering shells. If you swim, dry off quickly: The horseflies have radar for skin moistened with saltwater.

### Swimming with Whale Sharks

A shark the size of a whale sounds like a science-fiction nightmare, but Holbox's whale sharks, which can reach 15m (50 ft.), are peaceable creatures unperturbed by all the human attention. They swim around at a leisurely pace, gulping thousands of gallons of water in their cavernous mouths to filter out microscopic organisms. More than 100 of the polka-dotted behemoths muster in shallow waters about 16km (10 miles) east of the village from May to September, feasting on the plankton and krill churned up by the meeting of Gulf and Caribbean waters. The white spots covering their bodies inspired the local nickname, "Domino."

Swimming with these giant fish is a unique and awe-inspiring experience. Holbox is the best place in the world to do it, partly because the sharks feed in shallow waters and stay close to the surface. Only a few arrive in May or stick around through September, but sightings from mid-June to early September are virtually guaranteed. Tour boats pull alongside a shark and let two guests at a time slip into the water, accompanied by a guide. The smaller the group, the more time each pair has to swim with the sharks. On the way to or from the sharks' feeding grounds, you might be treated to guest appearances from curious dolphins or manta rays (which can measure 6m/20 ft. from wingtip to wingtip). Guides readily anchor for impromptu swims or, if there is time, for snorkeling at Cabo Catoche.

Tours cost about $90 per person, last 4 to 6 hours, and typically include snorkel gear, a life preserver, a box lunch, and nonalcoholic drinks. Most hotels in town can arrange a whale shark tour, but habitual Holbox visitors prefer to deal directly with their favorite operators, which include **Willy's** (Mini-Super Besa, just off El Parque; babyshark6977@hotmail.com), **Monkey's** (Av. Benito Juárez, a block south of El Parque; ☎ 984/875-2029; www.holboxmonkeys.com.mx), and **Holbox Tours & Travel** (end of Calle Bravo; ☎ 305/396-6987 in U.S., or 984/875-2173; www.holboxwhalesharktours.com).

## Look but Don't Touch

Mexico's whale sharks were classified as endangered species in 2002, and the government and environmental groups monitor the tours closely. Captains and guides, most of whom are commercial fishermen, must be licensed by the government and pay large fines if they allow illegal activities. Restrictions limit the size and number of boats, their speed, and how closely they approach the animals. Tourists must stay 1.8m (6 ft.) from the animals and use only biodegradable sunscreen; scuba diving and flash photography are not allowed. For more information about whale sharks, see the Mexico conservation commission's Domino website (www.domino.conanp.gob.mx/rules.htm).

## Nature Tours

A whole different landscape awaits in **Laguna Yalahau,** the shallow lagoon separating Isla Holbox from the mainland. The water is bordered by mangrove forests and populated by wild dolphins and all manner of fish, while tens of thousands of nesting flamingoes visit from April to October. A 20-minute boat trip will take birders and nature lovers to **Isla Pájaros (Bird Island),** a wildlife sanctuary in the middle of the lagoon that harbors more than 150 species of birds. Visitors can spot cranes, white ibis, brown and white pelicans, roseate spoonbills, and herons from the island's walkways and two observation towers; iguanas, horseshoe crabs, and other creatures scuttle around on the ground. Most boat trips also stop at **Ojo de Agua (Eye of Water),** a crystal-clear cenote in the mangroves that provided fresh water for ancient Maya people and pirates through the centuries. Today, the spring is a gorgeous swimming hole equipped with a large *palapa,* picnic area, and pier.

If Holbox hasn't gotten you far enough away from it all, tiny **Isla de la Pasión (Passion Island)** is just 15 minutes away. The barren island, just 50m (164 ft.) wide, is known for its white-sand beach and emerald-green water, perfect for would-be Robinson Crusoes. Trees and a large *palapa* provide some shade, but you'll need to bring your own water and snacks.

**Turística Holbox** (El Parque; ☎ 984/875-2028; holboxislandtours.com) is a local tour operator that will take you on a trip to all three islands for $25 per person, or $80 for a private boat carrying up to five people. You can also ask about tours or from the whale shark operators above or at your hotel, or try negotiating a better price from fishermen at the beach.

## Scuba Diving & Snorkeling

Cabo Catoche, at the northeastern tip of the island, is Holbox's best snorkeling site. Though the water is cloudier than in Isla Mujeres or Cancún, the coral reef is more intact and populated by great numbers of stingrays, moray eels, nurse sharks, conch, and other fish. It's a long and tiring trip from town, though, and usually combined with whale shark or full island tours. Whale shark tour operators and hotels can sometimes arrange snorkeling trips to Cabo Catoche, which will take 4 to 5 hours and cost about $60.

## Sportfishing

Holbox is still a relatively unknown fishing haven. The star of the show is the gigantic tarpon, available April through August, but snook and jack crevalle are also pulled from these waters, along with limited numbers of permit and bonefish. Hotels can arrange tours; deep-sea fishing costs $250 to $450, depending on how long you go out, while fly-fishing runs $250 to $375 for 4 to 8 hours. Local fishermen charge about $100 for 4- to 5-hour excursions in search of smaller fish. Two highly regarded locals are **Willy's** (see "Swimming with Whale Sharks," above), who leads bottom-fishing trips using the traditional method of fishing with just your line and your hands; and Alejandro Vega, aka **"Mr. Sandflea"** (☎ 984/875-2144; www.holboxtarponclub.com), a renowned fly-fishing guide who runs a guide service employing men who've been fishing here their entire lives.

## THE OTHER HOLBOX

Holbox itself is the "other" Yucatán, and the townspeople are famously gregarious. If you have just a bit of rudimentary Spanish, you only need to spend some unstructured time wandering the town and you'll soon be exchanging life stories with any number of local people. Be sure to stop at the **Hammock House** (Igualdad at El Parque), the oldest house on the island, where women still carry on the island's oldest industry, weaving hammocks in all colors of the rainbow. If you stop by on a weekday, you might get an informal tour. The recently remodeled **El Parque,** which is deserted in the heat of the day, bursts with life in the evening with children lighting firecrackers, couples flirting, and tourists filling the patios and rooftops at restaurants around the square.

If you hear a roar rising from the direction of the ferry pier, make your way to the baseball field behind the port office between avenidas Benito Juárez and Palomino. **Baseball** is an important social event on Holbox and rooting for the local amateur team, Selección Holbox (Team Holbox), will forever endear you to its residents. Sometimes a fiesta follows the game, with fans cheering and children and grandmothers alike dancing between the bleachers to blaring salsa. It's only good manners to join in. The season lasts all summer; ask about game schedules in your hotel. Admission is about $2.

## ATTENTION, SHOPPERS!

Shopping isn't much of an activity on Holbox, though it will fit the bill if you're moved to seek out locally crafted souvenirs. All shops are cash only. The few stores are generally open Monday to Saturday, from 10am to 2pm and 4 to 8pm.

The largest handicraft store on Holbox is **Lalo.com** (Abasolo 139, btw. Pedro Joaquín and Igualdad; ☎ 984/875-2118), which strangely enough doesn't actually have a working website. The brightly painted shelves display a variety of handmade hats, picture frames, carved figures, and other crafts made by island people. The shop is known for its large collection of polished shells from the island and all over the world.

Silver jewelry, bohemian clothes, bags, and handmade tchotchkes adorn **La Bambina** (Calle Morelos at Av. Pedro Joaquín Coldwell; ☎ 984/875-2420), a tiny shop behind the Hotel Faro Viejo. It's run by a Swiss expatriate who sells the work of locals and artists passing through.

# NIGHTLIFE ON HOLBOX

Nightlife on the island consists primarily of going for a walk and meeting friends at El Parque, or lingering over a drink at one of the restaurants and bars that surround it. But on Saturday nights, it seems that everyone on the island—young and old, gay and straight, entire families—makes at least a brief appearance at **Disco Cariocas** (on the beach just east of Av. Benito Juárez). The simple beach place has an open-air section, an indoor section where a DJ runs things, and a huge video screen playing popular music videos. Some nights, a beauty pageant or other local event may be going on.

# COZUMEL

Mexico's largest island, 53km (33 miles) long by 14km (9 miles) wide, lying 19km (12 miles) from the mainland, is also its most multifaceted. Cozumel's pristine coral reefs are the number-one draw, making it one of the world's top diving and snorkeling destinations. It's also Mexico's busiest cruise port, with more than six ships a day docking during the high season. At the same time, the island's interior and its entire eastern coast remain undeveloped, without even electricity or telephone service.

The waterfront of San Miguel, the island's only town, presents a phalanx of franchise jewelry stores, duty-free and souvenir shops, and overpriced open-air restaurants and bars to reel in passengers disgorged by the ferries and cruise ships. You have only to walk a few blocks inland beyond that little sliver of Cancún to find the small Mexican town where family-run restaurants, *papelerías* (stationery stores), *farmacias* (pharmacies), and neighborhood markets line the streets. Even the pleasant central plaza, command central for day-trippers, reverts to a traditional *zócalo* at night, especially on Sundays, when locals congregate to dance to live music, eat, and visit with friends.

The northern and southern hotel zones are dominated by private beachfront villas, high-rise hotels, and expensive, all-inclusive resorts. Staying in San Miguel, therefore, is not only convenient but gives your budget a fighting chance and puts you in the middle of the agreeable, easy-going people who give Cozumel its charm. The town itself has much to offer, including comfortable small hotels, an excellent museum, some fine restaurants, and unique shops. Its rocky waterfront doesn't have the good beaches, but many free snorkeling and sunbathing beaches are a short ride away. Look at it this way: If you stayed in the hotel zones, you'd have to make the trip in reverse, to get to San Miguel's dive shops, restaurants, nightlife, banks, and other services.

Beyond the town, you'll want to explore the rest of the island's beaches, Maya ruins, and family-friendly eco-parks. Meander along the 32km (20-mile) stretch of unpopulated east coast, with its Margaritaville-style watering holes, rocky shores, and small, sandy coves that will be yours alone. You'll forget all about those 8,000 day-trippers on the other side of the island.

Enjoying all Cozumel has to offer is partly a matter of timing. Follow the locals' lead: Have a leisurely breakfast and do some errands in the morning, then spend the day at the beach, under the water, or exploring the east coast. Return after the ships sound their departure blasts, around 5 or 6pm, when San Miguel is once again the domain of *cozumeleños* and laid-back visitors.

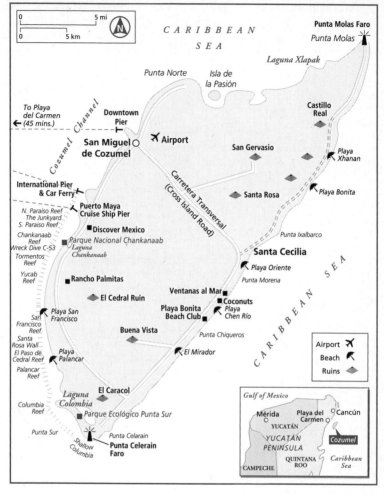

## A BRIEF HISTORY

The Maya people called Cozumel Ah-Cuzamil-Petén (Land of the Swallows). It was not only a center of navigation and trade—its salt and honey were more valuable than gold—but a sacred pilgrimage site, bringing pilgrims from all over Mexico and Central America to honor Ixchel, goddess of fertility, the moon, and healing. First inhabited as early as 300 B.C., Cozumel reached its height between A.D. 1250 and 1500, when the Putún people, also known as the Chontol or Itzáes (builders of Chichén Itzá), dominated the region as seafaring merchants.

Spanish explorer Juan de Grijalva claimed the island for Spain during a slaving foray in 1518, inspiring Hernán Cortez to visit the following year. Cortés encountered two Spanish men, Geronimo de Aguilar and Gonzalo Guerrero, who had been shipwrecked on Cozumel years earlier and eventually accepted by the Maya. Aguilar joined Cortez in establishing a military base and used his knowledge of the Maya against them in what was to be the first strike in the conquest of Mexico. Guerrero, who died defending his adopted people, is still a hero to today's Maya.

By 1570 most native islanders had died of violence or disease, and the island was soon abandoned. Pirates, including the notorious Jean Laffite and Henry Morgan, took over in the 17th and 18th centuries, sheltering in its harbors and secreting treasure in Maya catacombs and tunnels. By 1843, the island was deserted once again. Twenty families fleeing the inland's brutal War of the Castes arrived 5 years later; their descendants still live on Cozumel. The mestizos founded San Miguel on the west coast, and the Maya settled inland at El Cedral.

Cozumel slowly rebounded, aided by world demand for its *henequén* (sisal used for making rope) in the late 19th century, *chicle* (for chewing gum) in the early 20th century, and later its coconut oil. During World War II, a U.S. air base boosted the local economy, and military divers' reports of the splendid coral reefs lying beneath Cozumel's clear waters reached famous undersea explorer Jacques Cousteau. Cousteau's television show revealed Cozumel's underwater landscape to the world in 1960s, turning it into one of the world's most popular diving destinations. With Cancún's rise on the mainland in the 1970s, Cozumel, too, found its fortune in tourism, which provides jobs for the majority of today's population of more than 75,000.

## LAY OF THE LAND

Passenger ferries arrive at the Muelle Fiscal, the municipal pier at the town's main square. The main waterfront street is Avenida Rafael Melgar. Running parallel to Rafael Melgar are other north-south *avenidas* numbered in multiples of five, beginning with Avenida 5. Avenida Benito Juárez runs east from the ferry dock, dividing the town into northern and southern halves. Even-numbered *calles* (streets) run parallel to Juárez to the north in multiples of two, while odd-numbered calles run east and west south of Juárez. Calle Rosado Salas, the one exception, runs east and west between calles 1 and 3.

Avenida Juárez leads to the Plaza del Sol, the town square, across from the ferry pier. The **Isla Cozumel Tourism Office** (Calle 2 Norte 299-B; ☎ 987/872-7585; www.islacozumel.com.mx; Mon–Sat 8am–9pm) has its main information booth at the corner of the plaza as you leave the ferry (others are at the International Pier, the Puerta Maya pier, and the airport).

Avenida Rafael Melgar becomes Carretera Costera Sur (also called Carretera a Chankanaab) as it follows the coastline south along the island's western coast, which faces the mainland. Its extension into the northern hotel zone is called Carretera Santa Pilar (or San Juan); hotels stretch along this road north and south of town. The road runs to the southern tip of the island (Punta Sur), passing Chankanaab National Park.

Avenida Juárez runs all the way through town and becomes the Carretera Transversal, the cross-island road that continues east across the island, passing the airport and the turnoff to the ruins of San Gervasio before reaching the undeveloped coast on the open ocean. It then turns south and follows the coast to the southern tip of the island, where it meets the Costera Sur.

# San Miguel de Cozumel

**ACCOMMODATIONS** ■
Amaranto Bed & Breakfast **14**
Amigo's Cozumel **15**
Coral Reef Inn **16**
Hotelito **9**
Hotel Flamingo **3**
Hotel Pepita **12**
Mary Carmen **11**
Suites Vima **5**
Tamarindo **6**

**DINING** ◆
Casa Denis **10**
Guido's **2**
Kinta Mexican Bistro **8**
La Choza **13**
Pancho's Backyard **1**
Parrilla Mission **7**
Restaurante del Museo **4**

# GETTING TO & AROUND COZUMEL

## By Air

Cozumel's small international airport, **Aeropuerto Internacional de Cozumel** (☎ 987/872-1995 or 872-0485) is 3km (2 miles) north of San Miguel on Avenida 65 and Bulevar Aeropuerto. **Mexicana, American, Continental, United, Northwest, Delta,** and **Frontier** airlines fly to Cozumel from U.S. destinations, making at least one stop. During winter and spring, the lowest rates into Cozumel are only about $30 higher than flights to Cancún, but in low season, when substantially fewer flights into Cozumel are available, the gap increases to about $140. Unless you're also planning spending time in Cancún, it's worth flying directly into Cozumel in high season; the airport isn't as busy, and immigration will go more quickly. But during low season, the money you'll save by flying into Cancún (see p. 272 for tips on finding the lowest fares) and taking the bus and ferry to Cozumel (see below) compensates for the extra 2 to 3 hours of travel.

### GETTING TO & FROM THE AIRPORT

**Flying into Cozumel:** If you're picking up a rental car, the counters are along a short hallway to the left of the airport exit. Otherwise, go to the Transportes Terrestres counter. Their air-conditioned Suburbans can be hired as *colectivos* (about $4 per person to downtown, $8 to the northern hotel zone, and $8–$15 to hotels along the south shore), which wait for the van to fill up and stop along the way to drop off other passengers, or private *especiales* (about $11 to town, $21 to the hotel zones, and up to $38 to the all-inclusive hotels at the south end of the island). Regular city taxis are not allowed to pick passengers up, but you can beat the system by walking across the parking lot to the road outside the airport, where you'll have a good chance of flagging one down. For about the same cost as a *colectivo,* you'll have a quicker trip and a cab all to yourself (although cabs may stop for additional passengers if there's room.) For the return trip, taxis to the airport cost about $5 from downtown and $10 to $30 from the hotels.

**Flying into Cancún:** Comfy, air-conditioned ADO buses leave Terminal 2 of Cancún's airport nine times a day, from 8am to 6:15pm, for Playa del Carmen; buy a ticket at the taxi counter, turn right as you exit the terminal and walk to the buses at the end of the sidewalk. They take you straight to Playa's bus station on Avenida 5, 2 blocks from the ferry terminal, in less than an hour for about $8. You can also book a shared airport shuttle to Playa del Carmen for $23 per person, which will take at least as long because of stops for other passengers; a private taxi for two costs $72, and a private van carrying 3 to 10 passengers $77 to $81.

## By Boat

**Cruceros Marítimos** (☎ 987/872-1588; www.cruccerosmaritimos.com.mx), also called Mexico Waterjets, and **Ultramar** (☎ 998/843-2011; www.granpuerto.com. mx/cozumel.htm) both run fast ferries (35 min.) and charge about $12 each way. Ferries depart Playa del Carmen for Cozumel daily almost every hour from 6am to 11pm and make the return trip from 5am to midnight. Except for the early morning and late night, if one ferry isn't running, the other is, and you can readily exchange tickets between the two. The **Marítima Chankanaab** (☎ 984/ 872-1507) car ferry runs daily several times a day between Calica pier, about 8km (5 miles) south of Playa del Carmen just beyond Playacar, to Cozumel's

International Pier in the southern hotel zone. It is expensive ($55–$80 plus $5 per passenger) and more trouble than it's worth, in my opinion, with an unreliable schedule, interminable lines, and a crossing time of about 2 hours—if you are lucky enough to avoid one of the frequent long delays. And many car-rental agencies (including all of those on Cozumel) don't allow you to take their vehicles on ferries.

## Getting Around

In town, you can easily walk wherever you want to go. You'll need a car, moped, or bike to explore the far reaches of town or the rest of the island; the powerful taxi union has squelched efforts to start a public bus service.

Taxis cluster around the major hotels, near the main passenger pier on Avenida Rafael Melgar and around the plaza, and they are easy to flag down on San Miguel's major streets. Calling the central number (☎ 987/872-0236) usually produces a cab within in 5 or 10 minutes; call the night before for one earlier than 7am. Fares are set by a complicated zone system, costing about $2 to $4 within town, $6 to $8 to the northern or southern hotel zones, $12 to $25 to the far southern hotels, and $14 to $32 for destinations on the east side of the island. Rates are for up to two; additional passengers cost $1 or $2 extra, varying by destination.

You can also rent a taxi for a half-day to explore the island for $60. I prefer this to renting a car, because the drivers are often bilingual and thrilled to tell you as much as they can about their island. They will stop as long as you like anywhere you want to go, and seem to have a gaggle of friends at every stop that they are happy to visit with as you explore, making for a much more relaxed excursion than you'll have as you try to suss out the driving customs and figure out how to get to where you want to go on your own.

If you decide to rent a car, go to the agency yourself rather than letting one of the friendly guys at the pier lead you to one (they are working on commission). Rental cars typically start at $40 or $50 a day for a VW bug, including insurance (most plans don't cover driving on unpaved roads). The popular scooters—which I don't recommend for safety reasons—are also are rented by most car agencies and typically rent for $20 to $25 a day.

The friendly, family-owned **Rentadora Isis** (Av. 5a Norte 1811 btw. calles 2 and 4; ☎ 987/872-3367; www.islacozumel.net/services/isis) consistently has the best prices on the island, offering well-maintained VW bugs and compact Chevys (some convertible) for $30 to $45 with Internet specials. **Rentadora Isleña** (Calle 7 Sur, ½-block from the beach; ☎ 987/872-0788; www.cozumelhomes.com/buggy/buggy.htm) has VW bugs for $35 (3 days or more) to $45 (less than 3 days), and Jeeps for $50 to $65 per day. Its master mechanic, who has Volkswagen factory training and 12 years' experience, also has built some of the coolest dune buggies on the island, which are used for popular island tours; they are available for rent first come, first served. **Hertz, Avis,** and **E-Z Rent-A-Car** have rental facilities on the island. You can get a standard economy car (no VW bugs or jeeps) for a few dollars less than at the local agencies by reserving online in advance— keep in mind, though, the prices quoted don't include the mandatory Mexican insurance that can double or even triple the daily rate. See p. 277 for more information about Mexican car insurance.

# ACCOMMODATIONS, BOTH STANDARD & NOT

Cozumel is blessed with a variety of small, unique (and sometimes quirky) accommodations, many of them well within budget range. The best values are in or near San Miguel, but some affordable beach properties are available, too.

The two hotel zones stretching along the beach north and south of town are dominated by high-priced all-inclusive resorts, high-rise hotels, and private villas. The end of the southern hotel zone closest to town and to the cruise-ship piers does have some midrange hotels, mostly catering to divers (many instructors work out of the area). The traffic-choked area isn't particularly appealing to nondivers. As you continue south, the coastline becomes quieter and accommodations become fewer and more expensive; a rental car is virtually a necessity.

Though many air/hotel packages to Cozumel are available, most deal only with high-end all-inclusive resorts (see p. 18 for a discussion of packages). Among the exceptions, Funjet and Bookit.com offer only a couple of affordable properties; Best Day Travel and DoCancun, both Mexican companies, have a slightly larger selection. But because Cozumel has so many interesting independent budget lodgings, this is one case where packages don't measure up.

## Condos & Vacation Rentals

Vacation rentals are a different story. Cozumel's gradual but steady building binge has produced so many condos and villas that it's hard to know where to start. Again, the best values are in San Miguel. Most vacation rentals are not downtown but in two adjacent neighborhoods. In Midtown San Miguel, a safe residential area beginning at Avenida 30 and extending to Avenida 65, you can find bargains on smaller vacation villas (usually renovated older homes), B&Bs, and some monthly and weekly rental apartment complexes, but you'll probably want to rent a car. More rentals are in Corpus Christi, an upscale 14-square-block residential area of large, new homes abutting downtown at Calle 11 Sur. Many rentals here are only 2 or 3 blocks from the ocean, but you might not be able to see the water because of high-rise construction along the waterfront.

Many condo and villa owners advertise their properties on the Internet. Because vacation time is a finite resource, I recommend using an agency that will help you find a rental you'll be happy with and take care of the details.

**Cozumel Insider** (☎ 866/732-8375 toll-free U.S., or 987/869-0504; www.cozumelinsider.com), run by Texas native Sherri Davis, who has lived on the island for more than 15 years, manages vacation rentals in Corpus Christi, Midtown, and the northern hotel zone. These include a remodeled two-bedroom, one-bathroom Corpus Christi home, decorated with light colors and bamboo furniture, among tropical gardens, for $650 a week. A larger two-bedroom, two-bathroom home with red-tile floors and vaulted ceilings, also in Corpus Christi, is $875 a week or $125 a day. An upstairs bedroom suite with a private entrance can be rented separately ($65 a day, $455 a week) or as a third bedroom. Midtown rentals include several one-bedroom units at IslaMar Vacation Villas, a small complex of airy, Caribbean-style apartments, for $55 a day or $385 a week; and a four-bedroom, two-story home for $135 a day or $895 a week. Three- and four-bedroom oceanfront town homes and condominiums range from $1,500 to $2,800 a week. Davis, who owns the IslaMar condos, knows the owners of the other properties she lists and is familiar with every unit. She oversees cleaning and maintenance and greets guests when they arrive at the airport.

**Cozumel Vacation Rentals** (☎ 713/523-1013 U.S.; www.cozumel-vacation-rentals.com), also based on the island, has San Miguel apartments and homes starting at $300 a week in low season to $375 in high season. The least expensive, a small, simply but brightly decorated one-bedroom apartment, is the farthest from downtown. A cheery, modern one-bedroom house with a private garden in Corpus Christi rents for $476 to $595 a week. Two-bedroom homes for four to six guests rent for $850 to $855 in low season, $1,075 to $1,086 in high season; three-, four- and five-bedroom homes in San Miguel are also available, along with four- and five-bedroom oceanfront villas ($3,150–$4,592 a week). This is a professional management company that keeps tabs on each property to make sure its meets standards of cleanliness, maintenance, and furnishing. Representatives meet guests at the airport and are on call 24 hours.

If you still don't know where to start, start with Kelly Mattheis, aka the **Cozumel Concierge** (☎ 987/878-4323; www.cozumelconcierge.com). If you can describe what you want, she will find it for you. Part gadabout and part bloodhound, Mattheis uses her personal contacts and research skills to keep on top of everything that happens on the island. She knows about houses and condos before they are advertised; when I was there, she told me about a pretty two-bedroom house near the plaza renting for $600 a week and a one-bedroom at the edge of downtown for $440 a week. Taking the hotel concierge as her model, Mattheis started her business in 2004 after working in the U.S. tourism industry and later as manager of the Hotel Flamingo in downtown Cozumel. (She can also find you just the right dive trip, rental car, cooking class, or anything else you can think of.) And like a hotel concierge, she doesn't charge for her services, operating purely on gratuities.

## Bed & Breakfasts

**$–$$**   With three colorful rooms and a large, hacienda-style communal *palapa* where breakfast is served, **Amigo's Cozumel** 🧒 (Calle 7 Sur; ☎ 987/872-3868; www.cozumelbedandbreakfast.net; PayPal) is a thatch-roof compound set in an Eden-like garden with fruit trees and a big pool. Each spacious, simply furnished room comes with a kitchenette and all the necessities, right down to dish soap. The quiet street on the edge of town looks a little run-down (though Amigo's is not), but it's just 5 blocks from the beach and a 7-minute walk to the main plaza. Doubles cost $40 in low season, $50 in midseason, and $65 in high season.

**$–$$**   Calling **Tamarindo** ★★★ 🧒 (Calle 4 Norte 421, btw. calles 20 and 25; ☎ 987/872-6190; www.tamarindocozumel.com; PayPal) a bed-and-breakfast is underselling the place. There are four bed-and-breakfast rooms ($45–$48 a night fan only, $54 a night with air-conditioning), plus two suites with room for four ($10 extra). Rates for the suites, which have kitchenettes, don't include breakfast. The location—a 5-minute walk from the plaza or the oceanfront, but safely away from the hubbub—couldn't be better. The owner, a gregarious French expatriate with boundless energy, lives in a house at the front of the shady garden and is generous with her knowledge of the area and with her companionship, if you want it. A simple but elegantly decorated two-bedroom bungalow in Corpus Christi (still a work in progress with air-conditioning and cable TV yet to come when I was there) is also available for $55 to $59, depending on the number of people (expect rates to go up when the TV and A/C go in).

**$–$$    Amaranto Bed & Breakfast** ★★ (Calle 5 btw. avs. 15 and 20 Sur; ☎ 987/872-3219; www.cozumel.net/bb/amaranto; cash only) is hard to miss: The unique, Gaudí-meets-Rivera tower rises from a quiet street within sight of the sea, containing two round suites next to three separate Maya-style bungalows. The bungalows are air-conditioned and cost $49 (discount at owner's discretion in low season) or two spacious suites ($61) in the three-story circular tower ($61). The suites have king-size beds, separate sitting areas, and windows making a nearly 360-degree circle around the room; the upper suite has great views and a shower with an open-air ceiling. The first floor of the tower houses a large kitchen and dining room with a TV and VCR. I might quibble with calling this a bed-and-breakfast, since the breakfast costs $5 extra . . . but at these rates, we'll let it go.

## A Hostel

**$**    Cozumel's lone hostel, **Hostelito** (Av. 10, btw. Juárez and Calle 2 Norte; ☎ 987/869-8157; hostelitocozumelmx@gmail.com; cash only), is a block from the central plaza (easy backpacking distance from the ferry). It's brighter, more modern, and more spacious than your average hostel. Dorm rooms cost $12 per person; people traveling in a group can ask for the air-conditioned dorm with six beds and private bathroom. There's also a spacious, air-conditioned studio with two beds, a larger bathroom, and a full kitchen ($35 per person). An outdoor communal kitchen was completed this year, and a one-bedroom apartment for a minimum of 15-day stays was in the works when I was there.

## Hotels

Even the least expensive hotels tend to be clean and comfortable, if not always in the most convenient locations. If you stay near the plaza, especially on the party-bar side, ask for a room away from the street.

**$**    For 50-plus, **Hotel Pepita** (15 Av. Sur 120, btw. calles 1 and Rosado Salas; ☎ 987/872-0098; cash only) doesn't look a day over 30. Frequent paint jobs and handsome wooden window shutters keep this longtime downtown budget favorite from showing its age, and the motel-courtyard layout is softened by ample foliage and white wrought-iron patio furniture. The solicitous owners keep the rooms in good shape, and cable TV, air-conditioning, and refrigerators are almost shocking perks when you're paying $35 for a double ($5 per person extra).

**$**    Old rectangular cement hotels can be depressing, but the **Mary Carmen** (Av. 5 Sur 132, btw. calles 1 and Rosada Salas; ☎ 987/872-0581; www.cozumelisla.com.mx/hotelmarycarmen/index.html; cash only), with plants, fountains, and fresh paint in pastel-mint hues, is downright cheery. The smallish rooms ($37 a night low season, $47 high) aren't bad either, with their mosaic-tile headboards, efficient air conditioners, and cable TV. Bathrooms sport the occasional mismatched tiles, but they are spotless. The hotel is ½-block from the central plaza, so ask for the quieter rooms toward the back.

**$** There's nothing remarkable about **Suites Vima** (Av. 10 Norte, btw. calles 4 and 6; ☎ 987/872-5118; suitesvima@hotmail.com; cash only), but its 12 large, plainly furnished rooms (two doubles or one king) have adequate lighting, fridges, cable TV, and good showers. That's a deal at $50 for a double, year-round, and the quiet location is just 3 blocks from the central plaza's activity and two from the waterfront. There's also a pool and lounge area. The staff speaks almost no English, which is pretty typical for small hotels.

**$$** Friendly, down-to-earth innkeepers and large, beautiful rooms (each with an accent wall in a different bold color) keep people coming back to the **Coral Reef Inn** ★★★ (Calle 15 Sur 363, btw. calles 20 and 15; ☎ 888/843-5717 toll-free in the U.S. or Canada, or 987/872-7390; www.cozumelcoralreefinn.com; AE, DISC, MC, V). The three king rooms and one queen cost $55 in low season, $75 in high; one room with double queen beds costs $10 more. The inn is 4 blocks from the waterfront in Corpus Christi. A popular choice for divers, it provides rinse tanks and dry gear storage. The supremely comfortable pillow-top mattresses and large bathrooms with two-person showers are a couple of the reasons everyone else loves it, too. Next to the shared rooftop kitchen is a sheltered patio perfect for catching ocean breezes and watching the sun set. This is an adults-only hotel.

**$$–$$$** Run by a couple from British Colombia, **Summer Place Inn** ★★ 🄺 (Av. 10 Sur, btw. avs. 17 and 19; ☎ 987/872-6300; www.cozumelinn.com; MC, V, PayPal) rents four tidy private units with fully equipped kitchens ($65 a night or $450 a week in low season, $90/$630 high), as well as a two-bedroom condo for $1,200 a week in low season ($1,600 high). One of the more unusual amenities: telephones with free calls to the United States and Canada. The building is 3 blocks from the beach in Corpus Christi, about a 10-minute walk to the center of town. A quiet pool area and garden with banana trees and coconut palms make a restful retreat.

**$$–$$$** Since its thorough post-Wilma renovation, the **Hotel Flamingo** ★ (Calle 6 Norte 81, btw. avs. 5 and 10; ☎ 800/806-1601 toll-free Mexico, or 987/872-1264; www.hotelflamingo.com; MC, V) isn't quite the budget bargain it used to be, but it's still a good deal for what has turned into a rather chic property for the heart of downtown. A courtyard room costs $65 to $79, depending on season. Larger superior rooms with a balcony, mosquito netting, robes, and a minifridge are $85 to $92; though their luxury touches are appealing, these rooms get more noise. The hotel bar hosts live music on weekend nights.

**$$$** The only hotel on Cozumel's pristine east coast is **Hotel Ventanas al Mar** ★ (Carretera Costera Oriente Km 43.5; www.ventanasalmar.com.mx; cash only), set on a long beach where turtles nest in summer. Somehow the long, narrow rooms and designer chic leave me a little cold, but with its incomparable view of the thrashing Caribbean, this small, eco-friendly hotel could put you up in cardboard boxes and you wouldn't complain. And you can't fault its ecological credentials: wind- and solar-powered, no phones or computers. The rooms certainly are comfortable, and private decks and patios take full advantage of the unique seaside perch. First-floor rooms are $94 a night and top floor are $104; there are also two-story suites for $164 to $184. Rates include full breakfast.

## DINING FOR ALL TASTES

Cozumel isn't a culinary powerhouse, but you can eat well at reasonable if not dirt-cheap prices. Like the island itself, restaurants tend to be amiable and unpretentious. Seafood and Yucatecan recipes are staples on most menus, which tend to emphasize fresh ingredients and straightforward presentation.

**$** After **El Mercado** 🧒 (corner of Av. 25 and Rosada Salas; no phone; Mon–Sat 7am–1pm; cash only), the municipal market, closes at 1pm, the restaurant stalls hold down the nearly empty fort, serving the cheapest bites in town. The voluminous menu at Lonchería Chelly, for example, features lots of soup (seafood, chicken), mole enchiladas, and quesadillas, all for $2.50. The *comida corrida,* or fixed-price menu with a wide selection of soups and main courses to choose from, is $3 to $3.50. Meat dishes are all $5 or less, and fresh fish is $7. None of it tastes cheap—but they might start running out of ingredients as the day wears on.

**$-$$** A couple of blocks beyond the landscaped brick sidewalks of the tourist zone, **Parrilla Mission** ⭐ 🧒 (Av. Pedro Coldwell, btw. calles 2 and 4; ☎ 987/ 872-6340; www.missioncoz.com; daily 8am–10pm; cash only), you can choose anything from tacos to filet mignon and you won't be able to spend more than $10 per person, even for seafood ($7–$10). The Mexican dishes are especially good—the chiles rellenos ($6) are a revelation with their crispy batter and sauce thick with chunks of tomato. The cement walls and orange plastic tablecloths are pure, working-class Mexico, and so is the spicy *arrachera* beef.

**$-$$** It's hard to say whether **Restaurante del Museo** ⭐⭐ (Av. Rafael Melgar, btw. calles 4 and 6; ☎ 987/872-0838; daily 7am–2pm; cash only), the breezy rooftop restaurant of the island museum, is such a good breakfast and lunch place because of the food or the view. The latter takes in a huge swath of waterfront and some of Carnival's or Royal Caribbean's big white ships; the former includes fluffy omelets ($6.50–$7.20) and fruit, pancake, or breakfast sandwich specials ($3.90–$7.50). You easily can nurse a killer fruit shake ($3.20) and the pile of croissants and pastries that replaces the classic basket of chips until lunchtime; one of the best entrees is the chimichanga, a fried burrito ($8.60).

**$-$$$** Cozumel's oldest restaurant, **Casa Denis** ⭐⭐⭐ 🧒 (Calle 1 Sur 132, btw. avs. 5 and 10; ☎ 987/872-0067; Mon–Sat 7am–11pm, Sun 6–11pm; cash only) is crowded now by the tourist commerce from the plaza, but the classic Caribbean-style clapboard building exudes tradition all the same. There's no hustle and no chatter—just hearty breakfasts ($2.80–$4.50), bargain *tortas* (sandwiches, $1.80–$5), and Yucatecan specialties such as *sopa de lima* ($4.50) and *pollo pibil* (spiced chicken baked in banana leaves, $12).

**$-$$$** Everyone finds the way to **La Choza** ⭐ 🧒 (Calle Adolfo Rosado Salas 198 at Av. 10; ☎ 987/872-0958; www.lachozarestaurant.com; daily 7am–10:30pm; AE, MC, V) sooner or later, but this family-run, purely Mexican restaurant turns tables over quickly even when deluged with cruise-ship passengers. A full Mexican breakfast averages about $4.50. Among the main courses, the platters of poblano chilies stuffed with shrimp are a standout at $17—and that's as much as you'll pay for anything here. The table sauces, such as thick guacamole and a creamy chili sauce, are different from the usual spread and especially good.

**$–$$$$** "Awesome margaritas" are the claim to fame at **Pancho's Backyard** (Rafael Melgar at Calle 8; ☎ 987/872-2141; www.panchosbackyard.com; Mon–Sat 10am–11pm, Sun 5–11pm; MC, V), but I recommend the Cafe Maya, dosed with Xtabentún liqueur ($3.95). This dress-for-dinner favorite is colonial elegance personified in gurgling fountains, dueling arches, and marimba music, but the prices aren't burdensome. Light fare ranges from $4.95 to $7.95, and lunch is $11 to $13. Dinners are mostly $9.95 to $18, including *sopa de frijoles* (black-bean soup), steak fajitas, and grilled shrimp house specialties.

**$$–$$$$** Pizzas baked in a wood-fired oven, with traditional Italian toppings, are **Guido's** ✸ (Av. Rafael Melgar, btw. calles 6 and 8 Norte; ☎ 987/872-0946; www. guidoscozumel.com; Mon–Sat 11am–11pm; AE, MC, V) stock in trade and the best deals at $12 to $13. But don't overlook the homemade pasta ($13 for traditional Italian sauces; $20 for shrimp, garlic, and olive oil) and seasonal fresh fish ($20) main courses, which go especially well with the house-made *pan de ajo,* a puffy garlic bread flavored with rosemary. The breezy interior, with director's chairs and wood tables, takes on a romantic glow at night.

**$$–$$$** One of Cozumel's newest restaurants, **Kinta Mexican Bistro** ✸✸✸ (Av. 5, btw. calles 2 and 4; ☎ 987/869-0544; Tues–Sun 5:30–11pm; cash only) was opened in early 2008 by the former chef at Guido's. The mellow Latin jazz and lighted white-rock pathways between tables on raised platforms in a palm-filled courtyard are Playa del Carmen cool. Service falls short of lightning fast, but prices are quite reasonable for the sophisticated food, which I'd describe as regional cooking with a nouvelle cuisine twist. The menu changes every 2 months, but when I was there, a $10 *pollo colorado* was cooked in an *achiote*–pumpkin seed sauce and served with a brochette of cilantro and cheese. For the same price, I could have had a *chile poblano relleno,* stuffed with vegetable ratatouille and cheese, in a red-chipotle-cream sauce. The top price was $15, for sautéed shrimp in tamarind-chipotle sauce.

## WHY YOU'RE HERE: COZUMEL'S CORAL REEFS

Cozumel has been one of the world's top dive sites ever since the 1960s. The island is fringed by a complex coral reef ecosystem, part of the massive Great Mesoamerican Reef chain (also called the Great Maya Reef) stretching from the Gulf of Mexico to Honduras, the second-largest reef system in the world after Australia's Great Barrier Reef. Mountains of coral run for 32km (20 miles) along Cozumel's southwest coast from the international pier to Punta Celarain at the tip of the island, creating an underwater wonderland of towering coral walls, peaks, valleys, arches, and tunnels inhabited by more than 4,000 species of fish and thousands of other plants and animals.

Cozumel is famous for its drift diving. The currents that pull nutrients into the reef also allow divers to glide effortlessly among coral formations as the Gulf Stream flows north to south. Its force depends on weather, season, and phase of the moon, and generally is strongest along the deep walls at the edge of the reef shelf.

## Anatomy of the Coral Reef

Corals are polyps, tiny animals with hollow, cylindrical bodies that attach by the thousands to hard surfaces of the sea floor. The polyps extract calcium carbonate from the seawater to create hard, cup-shaped skeletons that assume an endless variety of shapes and sizes. These massive limestone structures shelter nearly one-fourth of all marine life. The soft, delicate polyps retreat into their skeletons during the day, but their protruding tentacles can be seen when they feed at night.

Two distinct types of coral formations dominate Cozumel's waters. Bases of the less developed platform reefs, such as Colombia Shallows, Paradise, and Yucab, are rarely more than 9 to 15m (30–50 ft.) in depth. Edge reefs are more complex structures built up over many millennia, and their layered structures peak high above the edge of the drop-off, extending as much as 55m (180 ft.) below the surface. These are found mostly in the south; examples include Palancar, Colombia Deep, Punta Sur, and Maracaibo.

---

Cozumel's fragile reef system, which hosts about 60,000 divers a year, is now protected in a national marine park, **Parque Marino Nacional Arrecifes de Cozumel.** Hurricane Wilma battered the reefs in 2005, mostly in shallower areas close to shore, but they are still very much alive and teeming with life. More than 30 individual charted reefs offer dozens of dive sites. Dangerous conditions limit sites along the wilder east coast to expert divers; most visitors should stick with the more predictable sites off the southwest shores. Here are some of the most popular, from north to south:

**Paraíso** (beginner; snorkelers): Three long coral ridges running parallel to shore, offering both boat and shore access. Paraíso hosts more divers per day than any other site and is a popular night dive. The main section of the reef has abundant angelfish, blue tangs, parrotfish, and hamlets around the coral heads, with lobsters and king crabs in crevices near the sandy bottom.

**The Junkyard** (beginner; snorkelers): A flat, sandy site formerly called Airplane Flats; the bulk of the litter is the remains of an old twin-engine plane sunk in 1977 for a Mexican disaster movie. A wing, engine pods, and landing gear lie upside down in 10m (32 ft.). Fortunately, that hasn't deterred parrotfish, damselfish, sea fans, small coral heads, and octopus from calling it home.

**Chankanaab Reef** (beginner; snorkelers): A long band of colorful coral reefs just off Parque Chankanaab. Crevices and channels are filled with sand rays, scorpion fish, moray eels, big spiny lobsters, and king crab. To the south are the Balones, a series of balloon-shaped coral heads where eagle rays can be spotted, and some freshwater cenotes, where cold, fresh water flows out. Nocturnal reef squid and octopus make the shallows a popular night dive.

**Wreck Dive C-53** (intermediate; snorkelers): An artificial reef formed by a Mexican navy minesweeper, deliberately sunk in 2000 (also called the Felipe Xicotencatl Wreck). The coral-encrusted ship rises 24m (80 ft.) from a sandy sea bed (the tip of its mast is about 8m/25 ft. below the surface) and has become a condominium for grouper, jewfish, barracuda, and swarms of glassy sweepers and sardines.

**Tormentos** (beginner): Flourishing conch, moray eels, brain sponges, and the occasional large lobster make for a terrifically colorful edge dive with several over-hangs and holes. Light coming in from the opposite end casts a glow on the "bar-racuda swim-through" near the end.

**Yucab** (beginner): A dense ribbon of low-profile corals and sponges in sand dunes sculpted by the currents. The reef is inhabited by octopus, scorpion fish, and splendid toadfish; curious lobsters greet divers at the southernmost end.

**Paso del Cedral** (intermediate): A wide, flat ridge hosting a collage of finger coral, fans, and sponges, named after the ancient Maya settlement inland from the beach. Residents include great barracudas, large grouper, green moray eels, and nurse sharks. The ridge rises just 3m (10 ft.) from the sandy bottom on the inland side, while the wall on the ocean side drops sharply into the abyss. This is where experienced divers find a stunning coral garden often visited by eagle rays.

**Santa Rosa Wall** (intermediate): A classic wall dive renowned for deep dives and drift dives among towering columns of coral separated by sand. Its canyons slope to a vertical drop-off at about 15m (50 ft.). The current carries ascending divers along tunnels and caves in the dramatic overhangs full of elephant-ear sponges, lobster, black grouper, horse-eyed jacks, and angelfish.

**Palancar Reef** (beginner–intermediate; snorkelers): The island's most famous reef, a long stretch of house-size coral columns anchored on the edge of a vertical drop-off to 30m (100 ft.). Four distinct formations include Palancar Bricks, named after red bricks dropped by a capsized barge in the 1960s, where grouper, hogfish, and hawksbill turtles swim along the sandy slopes. Novices and snorkelers can explore the shallower Palancar Gardens, where hundreds of species of multicol-ored coral are jammed together and rise to within 3 to 5m (10–15 ft.) of the sur-face. Crevices harbor shrimp, horse-eyed jacks, blue chromis, barracudas, and sometimes sea turtles.

**Devil's Throat at Punta Sur** (advanced): A deep wall dive that has become a rite of passage for advanced divers. The opening is a dark, narrow tunnel, lined with red sponges, that leads to a sunlit opening at a depth of 40m (130 ft.) on the wall overlooking the abyss. Eagle rays, sharks, and some turtles are spotted here.

**Colombia Reef** (advanced; snorkelers): An enormous coral buttress rising from the sea floor 9m (30 ft.) below on the shore side and plunging straight into the abyss on the other, in a succession of terraces, canyons, and ravines. Narrow chan-nels open onto the nearly vertical seaward wall of 18 to 21m (60- to 70-ft.) coral pinnacles covered with huge sponges, anemones, and swaying sea fans. The favored entry is "the Keyhole," an arch leading to open ocean and a welcoming committee of eagle rays, nurse sharks, barracuda, and the occasional sea turtle. On the reef's shallow shore side, snorkelers can see coral heads rising to within 5 or 6m (15–20 ft.) of the surface, surrounded by huge parrotfish, tame French angels, and some small sea turtles.

## Scuba Diving & Snorkeling

With more than 100 dive shops, healthy competition keeps the operators on their toes. Check around for the best price, but be aware that the lowest prices usually are for the dreaded "cattle boats," which pile as many as 24 divers in. One-tank dives range from $35 to $50, two-tank dives $60 to $95; advanced dives cost more. Full PADI open-water certification courses, which last 3 to 5 days and allow you to dive without a divemaster, generally range from $335 to $450. Most shops also offer night dives ($35–$60) and cenote dives ($60–$180, depending location and number of dives). Except for instruction courses, equipment rental usually costs an extra $20 to $25. Many shops offer multiday dive packages and dive-hotel package for a reduced price, and some offer snorkeling trips.

Reef sites are usually chosen by the group, but the divemaster has final say. Dive operators are required to charge a $2 Marine Park fee for each diver, but some include it in the price. What follows is a selection of trustworthy shops that emphasize safety and offer well-maintained equipment and knowledgeable, conservation-minded guides.

One of the island's oldest and most highly regarded shops, **Aqua Safari** 🅚 (Av. Rafael E. Melgar 492, btw. calles 5 and 7 Sur; ☎ 987/872-0101; www.aqua safari.com) offers two-tank dives for $60 and 4-day full PADI certification courses for $350; they will work with students needing extra help for a reasonable extended period. Owner Bill Horn has a long history of involvement with efforts to protect the reefs. Prices here are among the island's lowest, but some boats carry up to 16 divers, which is beyond most people's comfort level. The friendly, well-informed staff still manages to treat every diver warmly. Try to book the fast boat, which leaves early in the morning and carries just eight divers.

Small groups, reasonable prices, and fast boats make **Scuba Staff Divers** ✪✪ (Calle 4 Norte 71, btw. avs. Rafael Melgar and 5; ☎ 866/712-6161 toll-free U.S. or Canada, or 987/872-7734; www.scubastaffdivers.net) a local favorite. Two-tank dives are $60, a 3-day full PADI course is $385. Most groups are 6 to 10 divers, but one boat can carry as many as 14. Owners Martin and Adriana Perez Duran are certified PADI instructors, and Martin is also a certified paramedic; their experienced guides are patient and accommodating. Advanced deep dives, night dives, and cenote dives are available.

Another mom-and-pop shop, **Scuba Gamma** ✪✪ (Calle 5 at Av. 5 Sur; ☎ 987/878-4257; www.scubagamma.net), is one of the few with specialized training in working with disabled divers. The personable French owners promise personalized service with no more than six people per boat. Two-tank dives cost $70 (including tanks, belts, and snacks) and a 3-day PADI course is $380. They also offer snorkeling trips and cenote dives.

**Scuba Du** 🅚 (Carretera A Chankanaab Km 6.5; ☎ 310/684-5556 U.S., or 987/782-9505; www.scubadu.com), in the InterContinental Hotel, regularly gets international dive magazines' top ratings for its knowledgeable, bilingual dive-masters

## Keeping the Reef Healthy

The **Cozumel National Reefs Park** manages and protects the reef system through ecological monitoring, surveillance by park rangers, regulation of activities, environmental education, turtle rescue, and beach and underwater clean-ups. But one of the biggest threats to this fragile ecosystem is the 1,500 visitors that descend upon the island each day, and conservation depends on them as well. Here's what divers and snorkelers can do to promote a healthy reef:

**Be selective:** Choose "coral-friendly" dive operations that give thorough orientations, hold buoyancy control checks, and participate in conservation programs. Also ask what your boating store, tour operator, and other businesses are doing to protect the reefs.

**Keep your distance:** Don't touch, feed, or chase marine life; never stand on or rest against corals; and secure all equipment close to your body. Novices and rusty divers with limited buoyancy control should allow more than the required 1m (3 ft.) of distance to avoid damaging the reef.

**Don't pollute:** Don't wear gloves, and use only biodegradable sunblock.

**Vote with your wallet:** Don't buy souvenirs made from coral or other marine life. Eat at restaurants that keep reef species such as conch and grouper off their menus, and request proof that their lobster was caught legally.

---

and instructors. Two-tank dives cost $78, including equipment rental, and the four-day PADI course is $458, including a one-tank boat dive after completion. Night dives, advanced dives, and a snorkeling trip visiting three different reefs are also available. Special scuba lessons are offered for children 8 or under.

**Scuba Tony** ✰✰✰ (☎ 626/593-7122 from U.S. or 987/869-8628; www.scuba tony.com), one of a growing number of operations with no physical storefront, is Tony Anschutz, a former Los Angeles policeman who leads all his own dives and courses. His service is highly personalized, meeting with divers the evening before a dive and providing a cellphone for clients' use on the island. His boats carry a maximum of six divers. A two-tank dive costs $80, while a full PADI course (3–4 days) is $400. He also offers night and cave dives.

Anyone who can swim can snorkel, and equipment is available for about $10 a day at nearly all hotels and beach clubs. Some dive sites are also popular snorkeling spots, and many shops, including some of those listed above, offer snorkeling tours for $25 to $45, depending on the number of reefs visited. Paraíso, the Junkyard, Chankanaab, La Quebrada (or Beachcomber Cavern), and Dzul-ha (the beach is now called Money Bar) can be accessed from shore as well as boat.

Booths on the central passenger pier may sell less expensive tours, but they pack their boats with large groups. Unless you're desperately short on time, you'll have much better snorkeling with a dive shop. For a neat twist, glass-bottom boat snorkeling tours maximize your sea-life spotting time and provide a glimpse even for passengers who don't go into the water. The **Cha Cha Cha Dive Shop** (Calle 7 no. 9, btw. avs. Rafael Melgar and 5 Sur; ☎ 987/872-2331; www.chachacha diveshop.com) visits several popular snorkeling sites in its 3-hour glass-bottom boat trips ($30 per person, including equipment).

# THE TOP SIGHTS & ATTRACTIONS
## San Miguel

Housed in a former luxury hotel, Cozumel's small but well-designed **Museo de la Isla de Cozumel** ✿✿✿ 🄺 (Av. Rafael E. Melgar, btw. calles 4 and 6 Norte; ☎ 987/872-1434; $3; daily 8am–5pm) begins with an exhibit on the island's endangered species and a plea for preservation, moving on to displays on the island's origins, development of the coral reefs, and its human and natural history. History exhibits on the Maya civilization and the colonial era offer insight into the culture of the entire Yucatán Peninsula and include a re-creation of a typical Maya home. Especially intriguing in the second-floor galleries are photos of Carnaval princesses from the 1930s and 1940s, along with photos of settler families who created social links and traditions through events like Carnaval. You don't have to pay admission to eat in the rooftop restaurant (p. 114).

## Archaeological Sites

Archaeologists have identified between 30 and 40 sites with evidence of Maya settlement on Cozumel. The only one that offers much to see is **San Gervasio** (Carretera Transversal Km 7; www.cozumelparks.com; $6; daily 7am–4pm), the hub of Maya life on the island from about A.D. 200 until well after the Spanish conquest (50 skeletons found in a crypt are thought to be those of 15th-c. Maya who died from European diseases). The conquerors tore down much of the city's temple and the U.S. Army dismantled the rest during World War II when building its air base here. The site's significance outshines its aesthetics; all that remains is one small structure with an arch, some *palapas* sheltering recovered stelae, and some small, squat buildings. Perhaps the most fascinating feature is a network of ancient *sacbeob,* the raised, white limestone roads the Maya built to connect their cities.

Other vestigial Maya sites include **El Caracol** at Punta Sur (see below) and **El Cedral,** a popular destination for horseback rides (p. 125).

## Western Beaches & Beach Clubs

Cozumel's beaches take a back seat to its coral reefs, but it has its share of beautiful white sand. Beach clubs on the placid western side, facing the protected, bathlike Caribbean between Cozumel and the mainland, are the best to enjoy the sun and sand, but they can get crowded; east-side beaches are windy and picturesque, but the surf is too rough for swimming, except in a couple of spots.

A "beach club" can mean just a *palapa* hut that serves soft drinks and fried fish to the public, or it can mean a beach with locker rooms, a pool, a restaurant, and a full gamut of watersports. The biggest, **Mr. Sancho's** (Carretera Costera Sur, Km 15; ☎ 987/879-0021; www.mrsanchos.com; free admission) and **Playa Mía** (Km 15; ☎ 987/872-9030; www.playamia.com; $12 admission or $42 all-inclusive), are

## The Far North

A sandy road beside Mezcalito's leads to the wildest, northernmost tip of Cozumel. A favorite destination for ATV and jeep adventure tours, the road was chewed up by Hurricane Wilma in 2005 and later closed for environmental and land-use studies. It remained closed at press time, but presumably it will reopen so that visitors will again be able to explore the island's most isolated landscape. When it does, the best (and perhaps only) way to get there is by guided ATV and jeep tour (see "Uncommon Tours," below).

The awe-inspiring scenery of jagged shoreline is home to two particular points of interest. About halfway to the point, **Castillo Real** is a scattering of partially excavated Maya ruins. This "royal castle," evidently a lookout site to guard against approaching enemies, consists of a lookout tower and a temple with two chambers capped by an arch. Several shipwrecks, and fish who haven't encountered enough humans to be afraid, also make this a fine snorkeling spot when the surf isn't too rough.

The road ends at **Punta Molas Faro,** a lighthouse at the island's isolated tip. This serene spot, with its panoramic view, is a bird-watcher's paradise. Though swimming is dangerous, the sands turn up sea glass, bottles, seedpods, and other treasures to delight beachcombers.

---

full-gamut places heavily visited by the cruise-ship crowd. On **Playa San Francisco** (Km 10), on one of Cozumel's longest and finest stretches of beach, the **Nachi-Cocom** beach club (Km 16.5; ☎ 987/872-1811; www.cozumelnachicocom. net; $69 all-inclusive) gets packed with the cruise crowd, too. Locals prefer the adjacent **Paradise Beach** (Km 14.5; ☎ 987/871-9010; www.paradise-beach-cozumel.net), whose $5 flat fee covers lounge chairs, kayaks, snorkel gear, a trampoline, and an iceberg-shaped climbing wall in the water. Both clubs have huge open-air restaurants and snorkel trips ($35 per person, 2 hr.), and other watersports.

To truly get away from the hubbub, try **Playa Palancar** (Km 19.5; $10 minimum food or drinks), well south of the resorts, ½-mile off the highway along a rutted ½-mile road. It rarely gets crowded and caters to visitors who just want some quiet time in a hammock under the coconut palms or snorkeling in the famous Palancar reef ($30 for 1½ hr.; two-tank dives $80). A *palapa* restaurant serves classic Mexican seafood ($5–$12) and a wide range of drinks.

### The East Side

Cozumel's east coast presents a splendid succession of mostly deserted rocky coves and narrow powdery beaches on the thrashing Caribbean, and several casual restaurants (without any electricity on the "other side" of the island, they truck their ice in and close at sunset) where a snack or a drink earns you the right to hang out as long as you like. If you take the cross-island highway from San Miguel, you first encounter two low-key restaurants where the road hits the coast. **Mezcalito's** (☎ 987/872-1616; www.mezcalitos.com) and **Señor Iguana's** both serve beer, margaritas, and tequila shots and have similar menus (ceviche, fried fish, hamburgers, $6–$14). Hammocks and *palapas* are free if you buy something from the restaurant. About 6km (4 miles) south, **Coconuts Bar and Grill** sits on a bluff over broad, beautiful Playa Tortugas and serves good beach grub for $5 to $13.

The beaches are perfect for solitary sunbathing, but only a couple offer safe swimming. The best is **Chen Río** 🐟, ½-mile south of Coconuts, on a wide, protected bay usually manned by lifeguards. The restaurant, however, is expensive; if you're hungry, press on another 2km (1½ miles) to **Playa Bonita** 🐟, where homemade gorditas, fish, ceviche, and fajitas cost $7 to $10 and you get a complimentary shot of tequila. The heavy surf nixes swimming, but the beach is great for families, with a playhouse for kids and a massage concession for all.

## Parks

Cozumel's famous **Parque Nacional Chankanaab** ★★ 🧒 (Carretera Costera Sur Km 14; ☎ 987/872-2940; www.cozumelparks.com; $18; daily 7am–5pm), about 9km (5½ miles) south of San Miguel, is a beautiful, fascinating place, but the entry fee has escalated steadily until it now seems overpriced. Its archaeological park, with reproductions of a Maya village and numerous stone carvings, feel a bit too neat and . . . well, parklike, though the garden with more than 30 plant species is truly idyllic. The park has a branch of the popular **Dolphin Discovery** (☎ 800/713-8862; www.dolphindiscovery.com; $69–$125 per person) program with the standard menu of dolphin encounters and swims, and a small museum with exhibits on coral, shells, and park history. It also doubles as a beach club on steroids and is popular with families who spend the day sunbathing, swimming in the ocean, snorkeling, kayaking, and scuba diving in waters that harbor underwater caverns, a sunken ship, and a sculpture of *La Virgen del Mar (Virgin of the Sea)*. I met several local residents who love to shop for unique craft items at the park's gift shops.

More to my taste is **Parque Ecológico Punta Sur** ★★★ 🧒 (Carretera Costera Sur Km 27; ☎ 987/872-0914; www.cozumelparks.com; $10, free for kids under 8; daily 9am–4pm), encompassing more than 1,000 hectares (2,500 acres) of coastal dunes, mangroves, lagoons, reefs, and beaches at the southern tip of the island. Among the dozens of protected animal species are crocodiles, flamingos, egrets, herons, sea turtles, and 30 types of sea birds. You can spot crocodiles from an observation tower and visit a small Maya ruin, **El Caracol (The Snail),** whose snail figures in the cupola amplified the wind and sounded a hurricane warning. At the island's very tip, you can climb to incredible views at the top of the lighthouse, **Punta Celerain Faro,** or stay below and visit the maritime museum, which includes a replica of the keepers' quarters. Cars aren't allowed past this point, but park trucks take you to the beach, where you can take a boat tour (for an extra charge) or just sunbathe, swim, and snorkel along more than a mile of deserted beach (look for sea turtles in the sea grass). From the main beach, you can walk west toward the point and find your own private patch.

**Discover Mexico** ★★ 🐟 (Carretera Costera Sur Km 5.5; ☎ 987/857-2820; www.discovermexico.org; $15; Mon–Sat 8am–6pm), which opened in 2007, is kind of a CliffsNotes version of Mexican history and culture, but it's a blast. The hybrid museum/theme park promises to deliver "the whole of Mexico" in 90 minutes, and for the most part, it does, immersing you in the country's traditions through art exhibits and continuous films reeling out luminous images in a state-of-the-art theater as you take a whirlwind guided tour through the pre-Hispanic, colonial, and modern eras. In the rainforest setting outside, you can inspect replicas of Chichén Itzá and other archaeological sites, as well as colonial buildings, monasteries, and Mexico City's *zócalo*. After the tour, you can snack on local fare in a Mexican market before browsing authentic wares in the gift shop.

## Uncommon Tours

Among all the pirate cruises, sunset sails, and glass-bottom boat tours that every travel agency will be glad to sell you, the **Atlantis Submarines** ★ (kids) (☎ 987/872-5671; www.atlantisadventures.com; $79 adults, $45 children 4–12) is a novel, if pricey, experience. Unlike Aqua World's Sub See Explorer, which is little more than a glass-bottom boat, Atlantis is truly a submarine. You'll dive to the ocean floor to get a gander at 9m (30-ft.) coral heads and other reef formations in the company of parrotfish, grunts, groupers, and other tropical fish. The underwater part of the voyage only lasts 40 minutes, but it's one way to find out what all those divers are addicted to without laying out $400 for a PADI course.

**Wild Tours** ★★★ (kids) (☎ 800/202-4990 toll-free Mexico, or 987/872-56747; www.wild-tours.com; $86 on single bike, $70 per person on double, $46 kids) ran Cozumel's most popular ATV excursions along the undeveloped eastern shore, including Castillo Real and the Punta Molas lighthouse. While the road is closed, its 2-hour "Beach and Jungle Adventure" visits the native Maya town of El Cedral, caverns, a cenote, and a small Maya ruin, ending with snorkeling Chankanaab reef. A shorter jungle tour costs $66 ($55 per person on a double bike).

For about the same price, **Dune Buggy Tours** (Calle 7 Sur, ½-block from the beach; ☎ 987/872-0788; www.cozumelhomes.com/tours/tour1.htm) offers full-day island tours in converted VW bugs its mechanic designed especially for Cozumel's terrain. The tour follows the coast to the southern tip of the island, stopping for snorkeling, beach exploration, and a visit to a butterfly farm. Beer, soft drinks, water, and a full lunch on the beach are included. The cost is $89 for adults, $45 for children; all drivers must have a valid driver's license.

# THE OTHER COZUMEL

If you're in the throes of an addiction to *cochinita pibil, sopa de lima,* or *tikin xic* fish, maybe it's time to learn the secrets of creating those mysteriously piquant dishes from a master. Josefina Gonzales Luigi, a teacher at Cozumel's Spanish English Academy, learned to cook all of Mexico's great cuisines from her grandfather, a renowned chef. She opens her home for **Josefina's Kitchen** (www.cozumel sea.com/gpage7.html) classes to one-time vacationers as well as longer-term students. The *maestra* takes a hands-on approach, ushering students through the *mercado* for fresh ingredients (and perhaps a little Spanish practice) before returning to her home to demonstrate exactly the right way to roast and peel a poblano chili or grind up ingredients for a special *poc chuc* garnish in a *molcajete* (a large Mexican version of a mortar and pestle). The basics (guacamole, *frijoles,* tacos, quesadillas, cactus salad) are mandatory; the choice of which main course to cook is yours. *Chiles en nogada, pollo abodabo, poc chuc,* tamales—the list is approximately the length of the Magna Carta. If your favorite isn't on the list, ask. Classes cost $79 per person for two to three people ($69 for four to six).

Volunteer-minded travelers can join the efforts to aid and protect Cozumel's animals in two quite different ways. The local **Humane Society** (☎ 987/800-1897; www.humanecozumel.org; humane@cozumelinsider.com for volunteer info), which operates a clinic and shelter 6 days a week, has a cadre of regular volunteers, but visitors who can put in a half-day at the shelter are always welcome. San Miguel residents are familiar with volunteers in Humane Society T-shirts who march dogs through town to inspire adoptive parents to step forward. One of them could be you, or you might simply provide care and attention to cats and dogs in the shelter or assist Humane Society staff. Whatever you do, you'll be working with local people dedicated to making animals' lives easier.

Cozumel Insider (p. 110) is also the liaison for the **Turtle Salvation Program Volunteer Brigade** (☎ 987/872-2940 for Punta Sur only; www.cozumelinsider.com/turtles), which patrols at Parque Punta Sur and the east coast beaches during the evenings when females are nesting and babies hatching. Punta Sur is closed in the evenings, and the east coast beaches are restricted to all but park biologists, interns, and volunteers in the evenings during turtle season. You won't be able to see the phenomenon on your own, and you certainly wouldn't be able to walk the beaches, tag nesting females, search for their nests and hatchlings, and get them to a safe place. However, depending on the time of month, you might be releasing hatchlings out to the sea. Since cruise-ship traffic increased in 2003 and raised widespread environmental alarm among Cozumel's population, the volunteer brigade is not hurting for volunteers. The government decided in 2006 to allow untrained observers to participate in the rescue operation for a night or two in the interest of education. To request a slot on the brigade, request your dates and send details to turtles@cozumelinsider.com.

## ACTIVE COZUMEL

### Sportfishing

Cozumel's waters, with more than 230 species of fish, offers world-class fishing year-round. Prime time is billfish season, from late April through June, when anglers chase the grand slam: hooking a blue marlin, a white marlin, a sailfish, and a swordfish all in one day. Tuna, barracuda, dorado, wahoo, grouper, and snapper are among the others found nearly all the time.

Some dive shops offer fishing trips, and hotels can arrange charters, while some offer special deals, with boats leaving from their own docks. But most visitors book directly with their favorites. Fishing charters include captains and crew, gear and bait, and snacks, beer, and water (full lunch with 8-hr. charters). Most restaurants in town will be happy to cook your catch for you.

**Luis Erosa** ★★★ 🧒 (www.cozumelmycozumel.com/Pages/CozumelDeepSeaFishing.htm) operates just two boats, but they are among the best on the island: a 31-foot Bertram that can be chartered for up to four people ($375 for 4½ hr., $475, 6 hr., $600, 8 hr.) and a 40-foot Viking that can hold six ($600/$750/$900 for same lengths). Erosa and his brother have been in business for 40 years and have numerous fishing trophies between them. Their schedules are flexible, and they have a secret snorkeling stop that will appeal to nonfishing family members.

Another small operation, **Go Fish** ★★ (www.cozumelinsider.com/Gofish), runs just one 23-foot boat for four people and charges some of the lowest rates on the island: $270 for 4 hours, $320 for 6 hours. Captain Roger and his mate, Megel, are experienced, hard-working *cozumeleños* who regularly turn up trophy-size prizes in short order and handle the fish well.

One of the best of the larger operations is **Albatross Charters** (☎ 888/333-4643 toll-free U.S., or 987/872-7904; www.cozumel-fishing.net). Known for its accommodating owners, it has a fleet of five comfortable boats, carrying a maximum of six, with experienced captains and crew. Charters cost $420 to $450 for 4 hours, $500 to $575 for 6 hours, and $575 to $650 for 8 hours, and include hotel pickup and drop-off.

## Golf

Cozumel's new 18-hole, par-72 Jack Nicklaus championship golf course is at the **Cozumel Country Club** (Carretera Costera Norte Km 5.8; ☎ 987/872-9570; www.cozumelcountryclub.com.mx), at the end of the hotel zone north of San Miguel. The gorgeous fairways among mangroves on a lagoon are within an Audubon nature reserve and offer a moderately challenging course. If you tee off after 1:30pm, you'll pay $105; regular fee is $169, including a shared golf cart.

The challenging 18-hole **Cozumel Mini-Golf** (kids) (Calle 1 Sur 20 at Av. 15 Sur; ☎ 987/872-6570; www.czmgolf.com) has appeal even if you're not a fan of miniature golf. Just 3 blocks from the ferry pier, the parklike setting has hundreds of banana trees, birds, fountains, and a waterfall. You can choose your own music from a selection of more than 800 CDs and order sodas, beer, or sangria from a walkie-talkie; they'll be delivered to you on the green. Admission is $7 for adults, $5 for kids.

## Horseback Riding

A few ranches on the inland side of the southwestern coastal highway offer horseback tours; the best of the bunch is **Rancho Palmitas** (Carretera Costera Sur Km 15; ☎ 987/871-3060) across the highway from the Nachi Cocom beach club. The friendly guides speak functional English, and the horses are healthy and cooperative. A 2½- to 3-hour tour ($35 per person) includes stops at a cavern and cenote, the small, overgrown El Cedral archaeological site, and a few unexcavated ruins. You can opt for a 1½-hour tour ($25) just to the cave. The sights are unremarkable but interesting stopping points on what is basically a trail ride through beautiful canopied woods. Consider the weather when choosing which trip to take—3 hours can be a long time on a horse on a hot, humid day.

## ATTENTION, SHOPPERS!

Don't be totally put off by the lineup of jewelry, perfume, and souvenir shops jammed along the waterfront. Cozumel does have some unique and reasonably priced shops, and many of them are on the much-maligned waterfront.

## Pax Be with You

**Pax** (Av. Juárez at Av. 15 Norte; ☎ 987/872-5269; Mon–Sat 9am–5pm; www.islacozumel.net/services/pax) is less a music store than an extension of a life devoted to studying indigenous cultures and the role music has played throughout the centuries. Even a short visit with owner Alejandro Alcocer Alvirde, a big bear of a man whose broad range of knowledge encompasses 2,000 years and 37 countries, is sure to contain surprises; he shared lore with me about my own hometown that I'd never heard before.

His Casa de Música sells musical instruments. The shop has dozens of guitars (from $69 for beginners, $139 for better quality and on up to professional quality made of mahogany) and other stringed instruments, some of them from Paracho, Michoacán's famous craft town. He has Maya flutes, drums from Oaxaca, and many other traditional instruments, as well as CDs of music recorded in Mexico's jungles and villages. The shop also carries beautiful masks and woodcarvings. But the best reason to seek it out is to shoot the breeze with the owner, a well-traveled anthropologist, musicology professor, concert artist, collector, and poet. If you're hooked, you can visit his home in the evening to see the extensive museum he maintains there (☎ 987/872-0514; Mon–Sat 6–8pm), with more than 700 instruments from indigenous cultures all over the world—including Appalachia.

Most downtown shops accept U.S. dollars, and quote their prices in dollars. Paying in pesos usually saves a little money, and paying in cash avoids the surcharges many shops add to credit-card purchases. Traditionally, stores are open Monday to Saturday, from 9am to 1pm and 5pm to 9pm; virtually the whole town closes on Sunday. Stores near the piers tend to stay open all day, particularly during high season. To avoid the pandemonium, shop first thing in the morning or in the evening, after the cruise ships set sail.

The **Mercado Municipal** (Av. 25 at Adolfo Rosado Salas; cash only), where Cancún residents buy fresh meat, fish, fruit, and vegetables, is a good place to find local spices. Some clothing and sandal vendors work the market, and you might also find Mexican pottery, Cuban cigars (which you cannot legally take back to the United States), and flowers. It opens daily at 7am and closes at 1pm, so the only crowds you'll have to fight are the locals.

One of Cozumel's first luxury stores, **Los Cinco Soles** (Av. Rafael Melgar at Calle 8 Norte; ☎ 987/872-0132), offers the island's best shopping for crafts from every part of Mexico. A few blocks removed from the main shopping arena, its warren of display rooms meander through a renovated warehouse covering the entire block. The shelves are full of handmade pottery, clothing, and jewelry, as well as furniture and artwork; a lot of vanilla extract and silver bracelets from here are packed into suitcases returning to the United States. Unfortunately, the extensive selection of premium tequilas carry some of the highest prices on the island (so hold off on buying those). A sister store, **Mi Casa** (Av. Rafael Melgar, btw. Adolfo Rosado Salas and Calle 3 Sur; ☎ 987/872-2040), is right in the thick of things on Avenida Melgar, and specializes in gifts and items for the home, culled from the main store's vast selection.

Cozumel's best bookstore, **Librería del Parque** (Av. 5 on main plaza; ☎ 987/ 872-0031) carries the Miami Herald, USA Today, and English- and Spanish-language magazines and books. If you can focus despite the loud, piped-in music, browse the remarkably good selection of international magazines and books on Mexican history and archaeology. It also sells phone cards.

Tourists pack their suitcases with coffee from **Café Chiapas** (Calle 2, btw. avs. 5 and 10 Norte; ☎ 987/872-1384), and local residents recycle the rustic coffee-leaf containers for home decor. The tiny shop specializes in Mexican Altura (high-grown) coffee, either freshly ground or whole beans. It has a one-stool coffee bar for tasting, but this is essentially a take-out place.

## NIGHTLIFE ON COZUMEL

Maybe it's because all those divers need to get up early to catch their boats, or because hard-working *cozumeleños* only have 1 day off, but nightlife just isn't the cornerstone of Cozumel's appeal. Beyond such chains as the Hard Rock Café and Señor Frog's, the island has a sprinkling of lively but sane night spots, some of them quite sophisticated in the 1950s Tropicana sense. **The Havana Club** (Av. Rafael E. Melgar, btw. calles 6 and 8; ☎ 987/872-2098), certainly falls into that category, with urbane jazz and men sipping cognac or whisky (imported and expensive) rather than two-for-one Coronas. You've got to love cigars to spend any time here, as the authentic Cuban variety is the club's trademark (the manager might give you a tour of his humidor, if you ask nicely).

The refined **1.5 Tequila Lounge** ✪ (Av. Rafael Melgar at Calle 11 Sur; ☎ 987/ 872-4421; $5 cover), with its South Beach decor and view of the Cancún skyline from a deck over the water, inspires locals to dress up with some degree of glamour, though the effect is watered down a bit by tourists in shorts and flip-flops. Guests can take the stairs to the beach and savor their cocktails on a lounge sofa or a table on the sand while listening to the DJ-powered rock from a distance.

**Ambar Lounge** (Av. 5 no. 141, btw. Calle 1 and Rosado Salas; ☎ 987/869-1955), brings cosmopolitan Art Deco flair to the main plaza. The modern, white indoor area, which features a martini bar and a DJ playing jazz and funk, feels a little cramped; the courtyard in back is the saving grace. The small restaurant in front serves creditable Italian food.

Compared with **Neptuno** ✪✪✪ (Rafael Melgar at Calle 11 Sur; ☎ 987/872-1537; cover varies), Cozumel's other clubs are just restaurants with bars. The only real disco is a little slice of Cancún, calling upon the power of multimedia with three projection screens, state-of-the-art sound, a large dance floor, and a dazzling light-and-laser show. With its waterfront location and mix of Latin, dance, and Top 40 tunes, this is one of Cozumel's best parties, and it goes until the early-morning hours. The cover charge depends on the theme of the night but averages about $5, and women usually pay less than men.

The **main plaza** ★★★ 🧒 is the only place to be on Sunday night, when families cut loose on their only day off with stunningly good local Caribbean bands that make the thumping from Fat Tuesday and Hard Rock across the square sound monotonous and lame. Little girls in lacy dresses and patent-leather shoes run full-tilt after their brothers while mom in her little black dress and dad in his *guayabera* sway and dip to the reggae beat. Around the periphery, women and girls sell homemade tacos, enchiladas, spaghetti, and cake to raise money for church; the aroma of roasted corn on the cob and deep-fried churros wafts in from the sidewalks, where freakishly talented street painters create seascapes out of a spray can. Some nights, clowns and hair braiders appear. Multimedia, indeed.

# 4 The Riviera Maya

## Caribbean coasting

As little as 10 years ago, travelers could feel smug about discovering the achingly beautiful white-sand beaches and turquoise waves on the unspoiled Caribbean coast south of Cancún. With its idyllic fishing villages, abandoned Maya cities, and mysterious cenotes hidden at the ends of small roads shooting off the coastal highway, this was the secret alternative to high-rise glitz, known only to those with some unfettered time and an adventurous spirit.

International resort developers discovered this stretch of coast and its magnificent offshore reefs before most tourists did; the past 10 years have turned the once-forgotten frontier into a destination in its own right as the Cancún building frenzy spilled south. The Riviera Maya, as the northern half of Quintana Roo's coast was officially branded in 1999, now has as many hotel rooms as Cancún does; Playa del Carmen, once a hideout for beachcombers and dropouts, is Mexico's fastest-growing city. Today, the coastlines north and south of Playa and from Puerto Aventuras to Akumal are lined with sprawling all-inclusive and ultra-luxury resorts and condominium developments. Dozens of dive and snorkel shops line the 97km (60 miles) of beach waiting to show you the Great Mesoamerican Reef or inland cenotes, and eco-parks up and down the coast introduce you to the area's natural wonders. Development uprooted some small Maya communities, which had to relocate to the inland jungle.

But even though the Riviera Maya is no longer a secret, it still remains a more relaxed, and more Mexican, alternative to Cancún. You can turn off the highway and follow narrow (though paved) roads to age-old fishing villages that have somehow managed to retain their tranquil character despite being surrounded by resorts. The tourist industry, steered by government mandate, has trodden lightly on the wildlife-rich mangroves, offshore reef, inland jungle, and remnants of ancient Maya cities. Inland Maya villages keep Yucatecan food, music, and holiday traditions alive. Even Playa del Carmen, the Riviera Maya's unofficial capital, offers a more relaxed, informal version of urban comforts, including an ample supply of small budget hotels among the sprawling resorts. Right now, the Riviera Maya enjoys a rare and almost perfect balance of tourist comforts and simple authenticity. As the wave of luxury development builds to tidal proportions, though, fans of this idyllic patch of Caribbean splendor can only watch and hope.

## DON'T LEAVE THE RIVIERA MAYA WITHOUT . . .

BEING MAYA FOR A DAY   Deep in the tropical forest, families living much as the ancient Maya did will show you their jungle paths and hidden cenotes, bestow ancient blessings, and serve you lunch in an open-air *palapa*. See p. 144.

# The Costa Maya

The recently dubbed **Costa Maya,** tucked under the Sian Ka'an Biospehere Reserve on a wide peninsula jutting out from the mainland, remained largely unnoticed—except by fly-fishing enthusiasts—while Cancún, Cozumel, and the Riviera Maya grew into world-famous resort areas over the last few decades. Lying 354km (220 miles) from Cancún's airport and more than 48km (30 miles) from the highway, the Costa Maya's beaches might never see Riviera Maya–scale growth, but tourism development efforts have already brought changes. Carnival Cruise Line and the government's tourism arm, seeking to siphon off some of the Riviera Maya's lucrative tourism, brought a huge cruise port to the tiny fishing village of Mahahual in 2001. On port days, the laid-back town's packed-sand main street bustles with tipsy, sunburned cruise-ship passengers, only to empty at night and return to being a sleepy seaside town. The port has a small tourist zone with a beach club, shopping mall, and tour companies offering at least two dozen adventure excursions, while a minicity with its own suburb of homes and apartments has sprouted nearby. New roads built to smooth the way for cruise passenger day trips have cut the trip to the even smaller and more remote village of Xcalak—the southernmost settlement on the Mexican Caribbean—from 4 hours to less than 1. Spanish luxury giants Sol Meliá and Iberostar are rumored to be on the way, but tourism officials vow to break with the Cancún/Riviera Maya model, integrating the local population in limited development of small, eco-friendly hotels and nature tours.

For now, the Costa Maya remains a landscape of mangrove marshes, low jungle, and long stretches of palm-fringed, white-sand beaches. Affordable inns and bungalows and small restaurants serving fresh-caught fish await travelers drawn to the region's cenotes, centuries-old villages, Maya ruins, and incomparable snorkeling and diving along one of the most intact sections of the entire Great Mesoamerican Reef . . . you might think you've been time-warped to the Riviera Maya of 20 years ago.

Coverage of the far southern reaches of Quintana Roo's coast is beyond the scope of this guide, although we do suggest a couple of side trips (p. 179). If you want to explore beyond the Riviera Maya, it's still an inexpensive and pretty uncomplicated part of the world. Travel information sites maintained by the **Port of Costa Maya** (www.puertocostamaya.com) and the **Xcalak and Mahahual Support Association** (www.xcalak.info) can get you started. **Mahahual.com** is a real estate-oriented site that has a decent lineup of hotel and vacation rental listings.

**GOING UNDERGROUND**    Thousands of cenotes—openings to underground rivers—pock the jungle between Playa del Carmen and Tulum. Many are popular swimming holes, but you can get a taste of how early cave divers felt when they discovered one of the ancient Maya's sacred passages to the underworld by heading to one of dozens that tourists rarely see. See "Notes from the Underground" on p. 156.

**MOVING AT A TURTLE'S PACE**    There's a reason quiet Akumal is named "Place of the Turtles": Its central beach is one of the only places where people regularly encounter the endangered reptiles with little effort. During nesting season, you can join evening expeditions to protect the hard-working mothers or usher hatchlings safely back to the sea. See p. 165.

**PONDERING THE MYSTERY**    Just 64km (40 miles) inland from Tulum, whose bluff-top site is the most beautiful of any Maya ruin, the grander city of Cobá keeps its secrets hidden beneath a shroud of jungle growth. Visit both. See p. 166 and 174, respectively.

**GETTING WILD**    A trek through jungle paths and a boat ride through the canals of the Sian Ka'an Biosphere Reserve is a brief glimpse into a vast world of undisturbed beaches, unrestored ruins, and resident howler monkeys, crocodiles, jaguars, sea turtles, and hundreds of species of birds. See p. 176.

**GOING SOUTH**    Kayaking on the freakishly beautiful "Lake of the Seven Colors" and snorkeling in the cool waters of Mexico's deepest cenote are a taste of the vast and mostly empty expanses of southern Quintana Roo. See "Southern Forays" on p. 179.

# A BRIEF HISTORY

Quintana Roo's Caribbean coast is dotted with Maya archaeological sites, many still unexplored. The Maya civilization, centered in its early days around Guatemala's lowland Petén region, spread north in the late **Preclassic period** (300 B.C.–A.D. 250). Archaeologists believe the migrants were hunter-gatherers who founded villages throughout the Yucatán and turned to corn cultivation. The earliest inscriptions were dated A.D. 564 in Tulum—the only city the Maya built right on the water.

Cobá, Kohunlich, Dzibanché, and Muyil in present-day Quintana Roo grew into important ceremonial cities during the **Classic period** (250–900), the peak of the Maya empire of independent city-states. This era produced the Maya's greatest intellectual and artistic achievements, such as development of an accurate calendar, the mathematical concept of zero, hieroglyphic writing, and grand architecture.

The Classic period ended with the collapse of the southern lowland cities, the cause of which is still being debated. Tikal was abandoned in 899, though northern cities flourished during the **Postclassic period** (900–1521). Quintana Roo's coastal cities of Tulum, Xcaret, Xaman-Há (now Playa del Carmen), and Xel-Há were important commercial and religious centers along an extensive Maya trade route, and Cobá became the most powerful Maya city in the northeastern Yucatán.

It took the Spanish Conquest to deal the final blow to the ancient Maya civilization. Overcoming decades of fierce resistance, the *conquistadores* founded the city of Mérida in 1540. Maya natives became slaves, first on Franciscan missions and, after Mexico's independence, on lucrative *henequén* plantations. After nearly 300 years of subjugation, the Maya rose in a massive revolt in 1848, touching off the longest and most brutal war in Mexican history. During 60 years of intermittent but often intense fighting that almost extinguished the Maya population, many fled the slaughter and settled on the coast.

Descendants of the early Maya fugitives built a capital city called Chan Santa Cruz ("Small Holy Cross") on the site of today's Felipe Carrillo Puerto. The Mexicans didn't know about it for decades—none who ventured into the Quintana Roo jungle ever lived to tell about it. Inspired by a miraculous talking cross (later discovered to be a ventriloquist), the city was the last rebel holdout, finally destroyed by a huge Mexican force in 1901. The war was officially declared over, though sporadic fighting continued until 1915.

Quintana Roo remained an isolated and sparsely populated territory with few paved roads for most of the 20th century. It became a state only in 1974, the year Cancún's first resorts opened. Tourists seeking an alternative to phalanxes of megaresorts began finding their way down the coast in the 1980s, but it remained jungle backcountry until 1995. The Mexican government, faced with expensive repairs and sinking land prices in the wake of Hurricane Roxanne, opened up the coastline to international resort development. Today, the Riviera Maya rivals Cancún as a tourist destination.

The largely inaccessible Costa Maya remained an enclave of fishing collectives and traditional Maya communities until the cruise port came to Mahahual. By 2005, Puerto Costa Maya was drawing more port calls than Puerto Vallarta or Mazatlán, on Mexico's Pacific Coast. The expanding port gave the region its name when officials declared the region a bona fide destination in early 2007, with a plan to expand the port's small tourism zone and excavate and open more of the southern coast's dozens of little-known Maya sites to tourism.

## LAY OF THE LAND

The "Riviera Maya" and the "Costa Maya" are promotional terms for the northern and southern halves of Quintana Roo's roughly 378km (235 miles) of Caribbean coastline south of Cancún.

The first town you come to heading south is **Puerto Morelos,** about 35km (22 miles) from Cancún. Despite being rapidly surrounded by some of Mexico's most exclusive resorts, the Riviera Maya's gateway town remains a tranquil fishing village. The 32km (20-mile) stretch of beach from Puerto Morelos to **Playa del Carmen** is rapidly filling with luxury resorts, most of them all-inclusives. They're secreted less than a kilometer (about ½-mile) off the road in such beach areas as Playa Paraiso, Maroma, Mayakoba, and Punta Bete. Playa is the region's only real city.

**Hwy. 307** (also called Carretera Cancún-Tulum) runs the length of the coast from Cancún to Chetumal, the state capital on the Belize border. The 51km (32 miles) between Cancún's airport and Playa del Carmen is a fast (up to 110kmph/68 mph) four-lane road with a few traffic lights and speed zones along

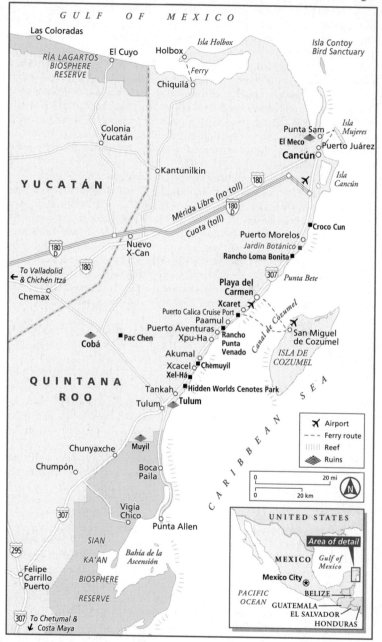

GULF OF MEXICO

Las Coloradas

El Cuyo

Holbox

Isla Holbox

Isla Contoy
Bird Sanctuary

RÍA LAGARTOS
BIOSPHERE
RESERVE

Ferry

Chiquilá

Colonia
Yucatán

Punta Sam

Isla
Mujeres

El Meco

Puerto Juárez

Cancún

YUCATÁN

Kantunilkin

Isla
Cancún

Mérida Libre (no toll)

180

180 D

Cuota (toll)

Croco Cun

Puerto Morelos

Jardín Botánico

Rancho Loma Bonita

Nuevo
X-Can

180 D

180

180

307

Punta Bete

To Valladolid
& Chichén Itzá

Playa del
Carmen

Chemax

Xcaret

Canal de Cozumel

Puerto Calica Cruise Port

Paamul

Pac Chen

Puerto Aventuras

Cobá

Xpu-Ha

Rancho
Punta
Venado

San Miguel
de Cozumel

Akumal

ISLA DE
COZUMEL

QUINTANA
ROO

Xcacel

Chemuyil

Xel-Há

Tankah

Hidden Worlds Cenotes Park

Tulum

Tulum

C A R I B B E A N   S E A

Chunyaxche

Muyil

✈ Airport

Chumpón

Boca
Paila

- - - Ferry route

|||||| Reef

Ruins

0           20 mi

Vigía
Chico

0           20 km

N

Punta Allen

295

SIAN

KA'AN

Bahía de la
Ascensión

UNITED STATES

Area of detail

Felipe
Carrillo
Puerto

BIOSPHERE

RESERVE

MEXICO

Gulf of
Mexico

307

To Chetumal &
Costa Maya

Mexico City

PACIFIC
OCEAN

BELIZE

GUATEMALA
EL SALVADOR

HONDURAS

the way. A construction project to widen the road south of Playa from two to four lanes had reached Akumal at press time and was working its way toward Tulum. The trip from Cancún's airport to Tulum takes about 1½ hours; it's another 3 hours to Chetumal.

A colossal entry gate 29km (18 miles) south of Playa leads to **Puerto Aventuras,** basically a golf resort and marina on steroids that lures tourists with the Dolphin Discovery park and numerous dive, fishing, and watersports. Condos, villas, and sprawling all-inclusive resorts claim hidden beaches in the areas known as Xpu-Há and Kantenah on the way to **Akumal,** 3km (2 miles) farther south. Nesting sea turtles share the beaches with divers, snorkelers, and kayakers, and lodging consists primarily of condos, private homes and a few all-inclusive resorts.

Development thins out south of Akumal, with pockets at the beach areas of South Akumal, Aventuras Akumal, Xel-Há, and Tankah. **Tulum**'s famous ocean-view Maya ruins lie 29km (18 miles) from Akumal; its nearly-as-famous *palapa* hotels end their march down the beach road, east of the highway, about 8km (5 miles) south of the ruins at the entrance to the **Sian Ka'an Biosphere Reserve.**

Hwy. 307 narrows as it veers inland south of Tulum to skirt the edges of Sian Ka'an. By the time you get to **Felipe Carrillo Puerto,** a town of little tourist interest but great historical significance, you're more than 48km (30 miles) from the sea. Just past Limones, 77km (48 miles) south, you can turn east to Mahahual on the **Costa Maya,** or continue another 82km (51 miles) to **Chetumal.**

# PLANNING YOUR TRIP TO THE RIVIERA MAYA

Travel packagers, which bundle airfare and lodging with the option of adding rental cars, tours, activities, and travel insurance for less than the price of purchasing them separately, are following the stream of tourists down the Caribbean coast. Though Cancún is still the major companies' prime target (see "Air/Hotel Packages" on p. 16), many also offer Riviera Maya packages—the majority in or near Playa del Carmen, with a sprinkling around Puerto Morelos, Puerto Aventuras, and Akumal. Budget travelers, though, will do best with smaller companies based in Mexico.

Here's why: Big U.S. companies focus almost exclusively on all-inclusive resorts and a few big-name luxury hotels that, even with the most generous discounts, won't likely make it onto the budget traveler's itinerary (it hardly matters that you can save $150 a night if the regular rate is $450). All-inclusives (where rates include lodging, meals, tips, activities, and often children's programs—they're very popular with families) sometimes dip into the lower end of the price range, offering some excellent values. Their convenience and lack of "gotchas" are appealing, but you have to decide whether you really want to eat most of your meals in one place. Food quality generally ascends with the price scale; the less you pay, the more you'll be tempted to eat out—and eat into the savings. A bigger drawback, in my opinion, is that by trying to meet all your needs, all-inclusives cosset you away from the place you presumably came to visit.

Mexican packagers (see below), by comparison, not only provide a wider range of options—they're the only ones that will put you in a beach *palapa* in Tulum, for example—but they include a greater percentage of lower-priced, independent hotels. Now, these are *not* rock-bottom cheap hotels, but you might find a nicer room or a better location for about the same price. The Mexican sites don't always yield the greatest per-night savings over separate airline and hotel bookings, because the most expensive properties give the biggest discounts. But the high nightly savings from packagers that focus on high-end resorts are deceptive; your vacation will ultimately cost less with a more modest discount at one of the lower-priced hotels or resorts in packages from such Mexican companies as Cancun.com, Best Day Travel, and Mexicana Airlines.

Playa del Carmen is the most fertile ground for affordable, locally owned lodging. Puerto Morelos, Puerto Aventuras, and Akumal packages are mostly limited to big, expensive all-inclusives, while Tulum packages barely exist at all. Mexican packagers do have a smattering of more affordable properties in these areas with discounts that bring them within budget range.

The following companies offer the best choice of Riviera Maya packages and appear roughly in order of preference. Numbers are based on a search for air/hotel packages booked 2 weeks in advance (you'll get even more options by booking farther ahead). Savings compared with the cost of booking two flights and a double room separately are based on the property's published lodging rates, although some are available on discount booking sites for $5 to $30 per night less.

**Cancun.com** (☎ 998/287-3671; www.cancun.com) has a wide range of choices (67 in this search) and beats other package prices almost every time, particularly in its ample selection of budget properties. Per-night savings on a sample of low- to midpriced properties ranged from $19 to $59. Plenty of all-inclusive and luxury properties are included, if that's what you're looking for. Using the site is a snap, and you can search specifically for Riviera Maya (sorting by location) or Cozumel packages without getting Cancún deals mixed in.

**Best Day Travel** (☎ 800/593-6259; www.bestday.com) has the most extensive selection of packages at budget properties—including the only Tulum beach cabanas under $100 a night that I've found among package deals. Nightly savings on these lower-priced lodgings are modest, ranging from $0 to $22 a night in this search, but the package prices are low. The website is smooth and speedy, though Riviera Maya packages are mixed in with Cancún deals, and you can't sort results by location. About half of the 160 listings were in the Riviera Maya. Competitor **DoCancun** (☎ 998/881-7206; www.docancun.com) offers a nearly identical lineup to Best Day Travel, both in terms of properties and prices, but its less user-friendly site makes it the second choice.

**Expedia** (☎ 800/397-3342; www.expedia.com) is one U.S. company that excels at Riviera Maya packages. It displays Riviera Maya choices without Cancún listings, offering 91 in this search; you can further sort the results by specific locations. Expedia turned up savings of $19 to $188 a night (though the latter was for the Ceiba del Mar, whose lowest regular nightly rate was $456). All-inclusives and luxury resorts dominate here, but Expedia offers a better selection of lower-priced, locally owned hotels than other big packagers do.

**Orbitz** (☎ 800/504-3248; www.orbitz.com) has fewer Riviera Maya packages than Expedia does—59 in this case—but offers some properties Expedia doesn't, including less expensive options in Akumal and Tulum. Nightly savings for this search ranged from $3.50 to $137 (again, at a luxury resort). It also displays a matrix with a choice of airlines (or "multiple carriers," which is usually the cheapest option) and prices.

Mexicana Vacations (☎ 800/380-8781; www.mexicanavacations.com) would have been closer to the top of the list if its Riviera Maya packages weren't limited to Playa del Carmen. It does a good job with Playa, though, offering 41 choices in this case, including a decent selection of smaller hotels in town, and produced nightly savings of $19 to $135.

# PLAYA DEL CARMEN

There's no getting around it: "sleepy fishing village" no longer applies. The deserted beach that attracted refugees from Cancún's high-rise glitz is now full of lounge chairs and tanned, scantily garbed bodies. The sandy seafront road has turned into a paved pedestrian mall brimming with beach clubs and hotels, restaurants and shops, chic lounges, and raucous bars. And yet . . .

Playa, as it is affectionately called, still has the heart of a beach town and something of a counterculture attitude. There's glitz enough, but it's of the low-rise variety, and with a European tilt that comes off as cosmopolitan and serene rather than frenetic. Playa's prices have risen along with its popularity but rarely approach Cancún heights, and the handful of huge condo and resort projects is largely confined to pockets north and south of the main tourist zone.

For tourists, this means a welcome blend of comfort and informality. Budget travelers are treated as well here as the big spenders. Accommodations are a jumble of slick modernist creations and local architecture adopting native stucco, wood, and thatch-roof details. Cuisine ranges from simple to ultra-sophisticated, and nightlife is lively but relatively sane. If Playa is no longer the antithesis of Cancún, it is still a relaxed and savvy alternative.

## GETTING TO & AROUND PLAYA DEL CARMEN

Most people fly to Cancún's airport (p. 14) and rent a car or take a bus or shuttle to Playa. If you're coming from Cozumel, **Cruceros Marítimos** (☎ 987/872-1588; www.crucerosmaritimos.com.mx), also called Mexico Waterjets, and **Ultramar** (☎ 998/843-2011; www.granpuerto.com.mx/cozumel.htm) run fast ferries (35–45 min.) daily to Playa and charge about $12 each way. Ferries depart from the Playa del Carmen dock, 2 blocks south of the bus station, daily almost every hour between 5am and midnight. Except for early morning and late night, when one ferry isn't running the other is, and you can readily exchange tickets between the two. Schedules change constantly, so check ahead of time.

### Getting to & from the Airport

**BY CAR**    Playa del Carmen is less than an hour from Cancún's airport on Hwy. 307. The highway divides as you approach Playa; keep to the inside lanes to allow left turns at any of the traffic lights. The two main arteries into Playa are Avenida Constituyentes, leading to northern Playa, and Avenida Benito Juárez, a straight shot to the main square. Playacar has its own entrance to the south.

**BY BUS**    Buses coming from Cancún and the Riviera Maya arrive at Playa's **main bus station** (Av. 5 at Av. Benito Juárez), also called the Riviera Terminal, next to the town square. Buses coming from inland or out of state arrive at the **ADO station** (Av. 20, btw. calles 12 and 14).

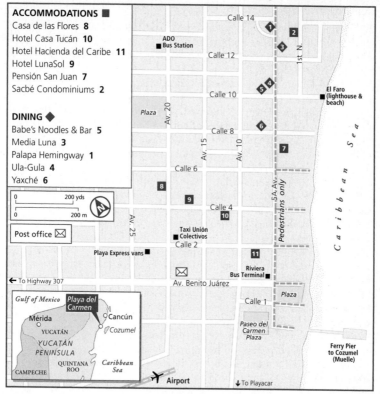

**ACCOMMODATIONS** ■
Casa de las Flores **8**
Hotel Casa Tucán **10**
Hotel Hacienda del Caribe **11**
Hotel LunaSol **9**
Pensión San Juan **7**
Sacbé Condominiums **2**

**DINING** ◆
Babe's Noodles & Bar **5**
Media Luna **3**
Palapa Hemingway **1**
Ula-Gula **4**
Yaxché **6**

Post office ✉

← To Highway 307

*Gulf of Mexico* — Playa del Carmen — Cancún
Mérida — Cozumel
YUCATÁN
YUCATÁN PENINSULA
QUINTANA ROO — *Caribbean Sea*
CAMPECHE
✈ Airport

ADO Bus Station ■
Calle 14
Calle 12
Calle 10
Plaza
Calle 8
Av. 20
Av. 15
Av. 10
Calle 6
Calle 4
Av. 25
Taxi Unión Colectivos ■
Calle 2
Playa Express vans ■
✉
Av. Benito Juárez
Riviera Bus Terminal ■
Calle 1
Plaza
Paseo del Carmen Plaza
1st N.
El Faro (lighthouse & beach) ■
*Caribbean Sea*
5A. Av.
Pedestrians only
Ferry Pier to Cozumel (Muelle)
↓ To Playacar

Comfy, air-conditioned ADO buses leave Terminal 2 of Cancún's airport nine times a day from 8am to 6:15pm; buy a ticket ($8) at the taxi counter, turn right as you exit the terminal and walk past the taxi stand to the buses at the end of the sidewalk. They take you straight to Playa's main bus station in less than an hour. (You can also book a shared airport shuttle to Playa del Carmen for $23 per person, which will take at least as long because of stops for other passengers.)

Cancún's downtown station has buses to Playa about every half-hour. They take about 80 minutes and cost $3 to $3.75. You can also catch a *colectivo* van ($3.50) at the bus station. They depart every 10 to 15 minutes and stop wherever passengers want to get off along the way. Playa Express vans are clean and comfortable and take you to their stop at Calle 2 between avenidas 25 and 30. Taxi Union vans have less comfortable seats and are often overcrowded, but they stop at the main bus station as well as at their downtown location.

**BY TAXI** A private taxi from the airport costs $72 for one or two passengers or $77 for three or four. Larger groups can get private shuttles costing $77 for up to seven passengers and $81 for eight to ten.

## Getting Around

The main street, Avenida Juárez, leads east from Hwy. 307 to the town plaza at Avenida 5 (called "Quinta Avenida," or simply "La Quinta"). This is the closest to the beach of the north-south avenues, which are numbered in multiples of five; east-west cross streets are multiples of two. Quinta Avenida, the spine of the tourist zone, is closed to vehicle traffic from the plaza to Calle 6, and often beyond in the evenings.

Most of the town lies north and west of the square. Playacar, the huge resort development, has its own highway exit but can also be reached by turning south on Avenida 10 from Avenida Juárez (but not from streets north of Juárez).

Playa's tourist center is compact, running along the beach from the ferry dock to Avenida Constituyentes. You'll be able to walk everywhere you want to go. **Taxis** are fine for occasional longer forays. The official rate for short trips around town is $2 to $5, but tourists rarely get the government-approved fares. Negotiate the price before you get into the taxi, and if you think you're being played, ask to see the *tarifario,* the official fare schedule drivers are required to carry.

Much of what you'll want to do while staying in Playa is outside of town. If you're not driving, the cheapest way to visit the nearby villages is by *colectivo* vans, which run up and down the coast from 5am until 10 or 11pm, stopping wherever passengers want to get off. For trips north, Taxi Union *colectivos* leave every 15 minutes from Calle 2 Norte between avenidas 15 and 20, and Playa Express vans leave from Calle 2 between avenidas 25 and 30. Both charge about $3 and make their final stop at the Cancún bus station. Taxi Union goes south to Tulum every 15 minutes for about $2.50. *Colectivos* drop passengers along the highway; but you'll have to walk or take a taxi from there to your final destination.

The **bus** is a great way to get between the coast's major cities. It doesn't run as frequently as a *colectivo,* but it's comfortable and it takes you into the center of town. You can get to Akumal or Tulum from the main bus station for about $4.

**Taxis** can also take you anywhere along the coast. They are more expensive than *colectivos* or buses, but they're cheaper than taking a tour, even if you have to pay for waiting time. Taxi fares to Xcaret are about $10, Puerto Aventuras, $15, Akumal, $25, and Tulum, $41. Remember that fares are variable and negotiable; don't get in until you agree on a price.

## ACCOMMODATIONS, BOTH STANDARD & NOT

Playa's building boom means a huge selection of lodging, including plenty of appealing small hotels. The price scale has been skewing upward, but Playa still has a respectable supply of affordable rooms. The vacation rental market is also a big force here, vastly expanding your chance of finding a rate you can live with.

### Condos & Vacation Rentals

A squadron of property management companies and vacation rental booking sites stand ready to help you find a condo or home to rent. The good news is that you are almost sure to find an attractive place in a good location for around $75 a night for a couple (which in larger rental homes means $150 a night for two bedrooms, $225 for three, or $400 for four). The bad news is that you might have to take a week's vacation just to sift through all the possibilities.

The largest single source of rental listings is not from a travel booking agency but from **VacationRentals.com** (www.vacationrentals.com), which simply serves as a link between private owners and potential renters. Many great matches are made this way, but there are more risks involved than with renting through an established agency. I'm not suggesting that you should avoid these rentals, only that you need to educate yourself about the pitfalls (see "Condos & Vacation Rentals" on p. 21).

Playa del Carmen is the most fertile ground for vacation rentals in all the Yucatán. Most are fairly new, well-maintained houses and condominiums whose contemporary designs range from sleek, simple lines to elaborate flourishes. The best incorporate some traditional details into the design or folk art in the decor; the least appealing rely on leftover 1970s furniture. In either case, you can usually expect an ocean view.

Most vacation rental companies in the Riviera Maya specialize in one or two areas. One exception is **LocoGringo.com** (www.locogringo.com), which (despite the name) is a trustworthy travel information and rental site started in 1996 by two obsessed cave divers as a means of living near the objects of their obsession. My main complaint about the site is that it provides no easy way to quickly compare prices: You have to click each one individually, open it up, scroll to the bottom of a long page and write the number down, and go back and do the same again for each property. (To be fair, that's true of many similar sites.) I would also feel better if the website provided a phone number.

**PlayaBeachRentals.com** (www.playabeachrentals.com) is the biggest, in terms of properties available, of the sites focusing solely or primarily on Playa del Carmen. The numbers are a little misleading, though, because the site is run by a property management company in Playacar, and 62 of the 97 listings were in that upscale gated golf and residential development south of town. There were some interesting other rentals, though, such as a three-bedroom unit in the Sacbé Condominiums, right on the beach at the north end of downtown, for $1,750 a week. Another long-established real estate agency devoted to Playacar is **MM Rentals and Realty** (www.rentalsplayadelcarmen.com), which has a full staff devoted just to rentals so that clients can call any time if they have a problem.

Even though many of the properties handled by **Villas Playa** (www.villasplaya delcarmen.com) are beyond budget range, it's worth checking for the odd gem. For example, I saw a one-bedroom apartment for $500 to $750 a week. The unit itself was nothing special, but it was pleasant enough—and the North Playa location is hot. This is a one-woman operation, and she had 27 properties that came up on this search. Two other sites to try are **Playa Paradise Luxury Rentals** (www.playacondos.net), which has a wider range of prices than the name implies; and **Sea Monkey Business** (www.seamonkeybusiness.com).

## Hotels

**$–$$$** If you can get around the noise issue, **Pensión San Juan** (Av. 5, btw. calles 6 and 8; ☎ 984/873-0647; www.pensionsanjuan.com; MC, V), will serve you well. The small inn, right in the heart of Quinta Avenida's action, offers basic, colorfully decorated rooms with obvious affection for Mexican tradition (an anomaly in Eurocentric Playa). This is one of the few places left where an air-conditioned double room goes for less than $50 a night (in low season, at least). And guests have run of the third-floor terrace kitchen. Being steps away from dozens of restaurants, shops, bars, and the beach is both the inn's best feature and its worst, since rooms overlooking the avenue are bombarded by construction noise during the day and revelry at night. Insist on a room at the back. Standard rooms ($49 low season, $59 high, and $69 holidays) are small but manageable; superior rooms ($59–$79) are larger and have some neat features like a domed, painted ceiling. Note that there's a 5% surcharge if you pay by credit card.

**$–$$$**    The lazy atmosphere at **Hotel Casa Tucán** (Calle 4, btw. avs. 10 and 15; ☎ 984/873-0283; www.casatucan.de; MC, V) breeds sociability. The Playa institution, still one of its best bargains, fills its overgrown courtyard with lounge chairs and hammocks that invite hanging out around the 5m-deep (16-ft.) pool (used by the on-site dive school for training). Other common areas include a yoga *palapa,* a TV bar, a language school, and a book exchange. The warren of rooms includes thatched cabanas with shared bathrooms ($50 a night), basic doubles ($55), and two-room apartments with kitchenettes ($87). They are quite plain and a little dark, though murals and Mexican textiles help to banish the gloom. None of the rooms have TVs, and not all have A/C. An on-site restaurant has reasonable breakfasts.

**$$–$$$**    New Canadian owners have turned small budget-priced Hotel Ziranda into the **Hotel LunaSol** ✿✿ (Calle 4, btw. avs. 15 and 20; ☎ 984/873-3933; www.lunasolhotel.com; cash only). Prices have nudged up ($60 low season, $93 high, $100 holidays) but are still a solid value for the 16 spacious, spotless rooms, each with its own sherbet-color scheme, one or two modern platform beds, and a private balcony or terrace. (The rates above are for advance online bookings; walk-in prices fluctuate up or down with the hotel's occupancy.) At press time, the new owners were busy painting, changing curtains and lamps, installing air-conditioning, and adding a communal kitchen for guests and a swimming pool and whirlpool to the large property's parklike rear garden.

**$$–$$$**    The best thing about **Hotel Las Golondrinas** ✿ (Av. Constituyentes 178 at Calle 20; ☎ 984/873-2805; MC, V) is that it's far enough off La Quinta to charge lower prices but not far enough to keep you from joining the party whenever you like. The rooms wrap around a peaceful courtyard dominated by a pool and fountain. It's a tight fit, and the building shades the pool most of the day— whether that's good or bad depends on your point of view. Rooms are far from fancy but a step above basic, with comfortable beds, plenty of color, and sturdy, tile-accented wooden furniture. Standard rooms have two double beds and standard plus rooms have a king and a double. A twin configuration puts double beds in two separate rooms. All rent for $67 in low season, $90 high, and $121 holidays, but summer specials can shave off about $10. Large two-bedroom suites are also available, for $117 to $135. Constituyentes is a busy street, so avoid the rooms at the very front. Rates include a decent buffet breakfast.

**$$–$$$**    It's neither the trendiest nor the cheapest hotel along Quinta Avenida, but **Hotel Hacienda del Caribe** ✿✿ (Calle 2, btw. avs. 5 and 10; ☎ 984/873-3130; AE, DISC, MC, V) strikes the right balance. Its pleasing design resembles an old hacienda painted in crayon colors, and it's set ½-block off the avenue, just enough to be safe from the fray. Published rates start at $75 for a room with one king in low season and $82 for two double beds, going up to $90 to $97 in high season and $112 and $119 over the holidays. But its website is often papered with special rates and you can get as much as $30 off the posted rate just by walking in. Rooms have interesting details like painted tile sinks and chairs with painted birds carved into them. The one downside: Rooms don't get much natural light, and the supplemental light provided isn't up to the task.

**$$–$$$$** Painted in mix-and-match pastels and designed with hacienda-style details, **Casa de las Flores** ★★★ (Av. 20, btw. calles 4 and 6; ☎ 984/873-2898; www.hotelcasadelasflores.com; cash only) is a bright spot on a somewhat unappealing downtown street. Two levels of rooms extend behind a leafy courtyard with a small, stone-paved pool (big enough for cooling off but not for serious swimming). Standard rooms with one queen or two double beds rent for $60 low season, $75 high, and $130 holidays; "standard plus" rooms ($70–$85; $145 holidays) have kings, queens, or double beds and minifridges; some also have private terraces. Abundant foliage keeps wings shaded and cool (they're air-conditioned, too); decor in the spacious rooms is simple but classy. The few cushy touches, such as cable TV and hair dryers, don't usually show up at these prices.

## DINING FOR ALL TASTES

Avenida 5 bristles with restaurants, many of which defy categorization. The quality tends to be high, and so do prices. The good news is that portions generally are more than generous, so sharing a meal and perhaps an appetizer is almost always an option. For a cheap meal, try the taco carts on Juárez close to the beach, or the inexpensive *comida corrida* and grilled chicken places around Avenida 5.

**$–$$$** The location 10 blocks from the main tourist zone is probably the only reason there's ever an empty seat at **La Cueva del Chango** ★ (Calle 38 at Av. 5; ☎ 984/116-3179; Mon–Sat 8am–11pm, Sun 8am–2pm; cash only). Its relaxed hippie vibe melds perfectly with *mañana* attitude. It lives up to its name ("The Monkey's Cave") with a couple of spider monkeys that hang around in back. Breakfast ($4–$7) is the big favorite here, with standards such as crepes and innovative concoctions like eggs with polenta and *chaya* (a Yucatecan spinachlike plant). They also make their tortillas by hand. Dinners are original and tasty, with fresh fish and Mexican standards ($14) prepared with healthful natural ingredients.

**$–$$$$** Typifying Playa's international mélange, **Babe's Noodles & Bar** ★★ (Calle 10, btw. avs. 5 and 10; ☎ 984/120-2592; Mon–Sat noon–11pm, Sun 5–11pm; cash only) is a Swedish-owned Thai noodle house that is decorated with pinup girls and Barbie dolls and serves a fine Cuban mojito. It's one of the least expensive restaurants in the trendy heart of La Quinta, and with lots of tofu concoctions, ordering is a cinch for vegetarians. Babe's also lets you order half portions, a practice I wish high-priced restaurants would adopt. Simple dishes like pad Thai or green, red or yellow curry start at $6. Yes, they do have Swedish meatballs, and they are quite popular, thank you. This place is small, so you might have trouble getting a seat when it's busy (you could also try its second location on Av. 5, btw. calles 28 and 30).

**$–$$$$**    Just off Avenida 5, **Yaxché** ★★★ (Calle 8, btw. calles 5 and 10; ☎ 984/873-2502; www.mayacuisine.com; daily noon–midnight; AE, MC, V) is Playa's most intriguing restaurant, full of unpronounceable Maya dishes redolent with *achiote*, pumpkin seeds, sour orange, and *xcatic* peppers. Many hew to ancient methods handed down by the owner's mother, while others are updated: cream of *xcatic* pepper–and-potato soup ($5), or grilled shrimp fajitas marinated in *achiote* ($12). All are prepared with fresh local produce and Maya condiments, as are the traditional *poc chuc* and *cochinita pibil* ($11–$13). Fish entrees, including *tikin xic*, range from $14 to $23. Your surroundings are reproduction stelae from local ruins and murals of Maya gods and kings. A shaman bestows blessings on couples during a special Valentine's Day dinner and during Hanal Pixan, the Maya Day of the Dead. For a seductive finale, order a Café Maya, an elixir of Kahlúa, Xtabentún, brandy, and vanilla, set aflame at your table.

**$–$$$$**    The inventive menu at **Media Luna** ★ (Av. 5, btw. calles 12 and 14; ☎ 984/873-0526; daily 8am–11:30pm; cash only) mixes Mexican flavors with international styles, producing an array of popular vegetarian dishes, fresh fish, great pastas, and huge salads. Lunchtime offerings include huge sandwiches or black-bean quesadillas and crepes for $6 to $8, while dinner entrees such as pan-fried fish cakes with mango and honeyed hoisin sauce will run $17 to $18. The prices are a bit steep for this type of menu, but portions are enormous. Several meatless dishes make this another good place for vegetarians.

**$$–$$$$**    Though **Ula-Gula** (Av. 5 at Calle 10, 2nd floor; ☎ 984/879-3727; daily 5:30–11:30pm; MC, V) is Argentine-owned and operated, you wouldn't know it from the menu. Artsy presentations notwithstanding, it's a friendly, unassuming place where you'll find international fare in an appealing upstairs dining room overlooking the street corner. Salads ($8–$9) full of seared tuna or grilled vegetables are meals in themselves, and pasta and meat dishes ($9–$16) are excellent. But seafood is the star; you can't go wrong ordering the fish of the day ($17–$25) and choosing how you want it prepared—I recommend the Marley style, in smooth tomato broth with sweet-potato croquette, prosciutto, and red bell pepper spiked with zesty spices.

**$$–$$$$**    With its huge *palapa* roof and wicker lamps hanging from tree branches, **Palapa Hemingway** ★★ (Av. 5, btw. calle 12 and 14; ☎ 984/803-0003; www.palapahemingway.com; daily 8am–midnight; MC, V) is one of the avenue's prettiest restaurants. Dinnerware is the work of Cuban and Mexican artists, and the cuisine playfully adds Caribbean zing to an international lineup of seafood, pasta, salads, and traditional Mexican dishes served with handmade tortillas and hot sauces. Entrees like shrimp in curry-coconut sauce are high on the list, but a humble appetizer, *plátanos caribeños*, also gets repeated raves: plantains coated with goat cheese, rolled in coconut, and then baked. The varied menu includes Mexican and Maya favorites such as chicken mole, *chile en nogada*, and *tikin xic* grilled fish. With a taco plate costing $8 and some other entrees topping $20, be glad they also serve a good, all-you-can eat Mexican lunch buffet where you can sample some of these treats for about $10.

# WHY YOU'RE HERE: THE TOP SIGHTS & ATTRACTIONS

Quinta Avenida's beaches, shops, and restaurants are all that many visitors to Playa del Carmen care to see. But more waits just beyond Playa's boundaries.

## Around Town

**Quinta Avenida** begins at the ferry pier, near a small plaza. It stretches almost 20 blocks to the north, moving farther from the beach after it crosses Constituyentes. The whole avenue bustles from morning until, well, early the next morning with strollers, shoppers, diners, drinkers, and people-watchers. Around the ferry pier, La Quinta's first few blocks are rife with the souvenir shops, hawkers, and chain restaurants. The atmosphere calms down by calles 10 and 12, where bistros, cool bars, and funky clothing stores rule; the farther north you go, the more mellow and upscale the avenue feels.

The first **beach** that greets ferry passengers at the south end of town is a lovely stretch of sand between the dock and **La Ruinas Beach Club** (Calle 2). Much of the beach from La Ruinas north to Avenida Constituyente has areas of sharp limestone, both in the sand and in the water. **Playa El Faro,** between calles 8 and 10, is an exception. Named for the large lighthouse (*faro*) at one end, it has plenty of room to spread out your towel without interference from encroaching hotels.

Playa del Carmen's best beaches are north of Avenida Constituyentes. The most beautiful (and unfortunately the most crowded) extends north to about Calle 28 (most streets stop running all the way to the beach after Constituyentes, making it more difficult to judge distance). Possibly the finest of all is the area known as **Playa Tukán** ✦✦✦, extending from Constituyentes north to **Mamita's Beach Club** (access at Av. 1 Sur, btw. calles 28 and 30). Just to the south, the **Kool Beach by Playa Tukán** beach club also rents chairs and umbrellas and has a bar, restaurant, and swimming pool. This is the best swimming beach, with shallow waters that deepen gradually, while breaking waves farther out provide ample fodder for water play. For obvious reasons, this area is crowded more often than not. Playa Tukán, unfortunately, is being squeezed by condo developments, and future public access is far from assured.

At the northern reaches of Playa Del Carmen, the **Zubul Reef Beach Club** (Calle 42) sits on a sublime stretch of thick, silky sand with almost no exposed limestone. Snorkeling boats tied near the shore, though, sometimes intrude on the tranquility. North of Zubul Reef are secluded areas with no services, large waves, and a gradually sloping ocean floor. One of Playa's northernmost roads leads down to the farthest beach, which is popular with locals on weekends.

## Just Beyond Town

It's worth a detour to Puerto Aventuras just to see the **Museo Sub-Acuático CEDAM** ✦✦ (Puerto Aventuras Marina, Bldg. F; ☎ 984/873-5000; www.puerto aventuras.com/services.html; by donation; Mon–Sat 9am–1pm and 2:30–5:30pm). CEDAM translates to "Explorations and Water Sports Club of Mexico." This is no musty maritime museum but a compelling array of coins, weapons, gold dentures, clay dishes, and other items from colonial-era shipwrecks. All were recovered by the club's founding members, a group of former World War II frogmen determined to promote ocean conservation. Most of the shipwreck artifacts came

## The Other Riviera Maya

Deep in the tropical forest, not far from the ancient Maya city of Cobá, is a village of 27 families who exist much as their long-ago ancestors did, living in round thatch huts with no electricity, indoor plumbing, or paved roads, gathering plants in the jungle for medicinal and other uses on their way to dip into a hidden cenote, appealing to the gods for successful crops. But the people of Pac Chen are very much of today's world. Every day they open their homes to as many as 80 tourists who hope to learn what Maya village life is in the 21st century.

The only way to visit Pac Chen is on trips organized by **Alltournative** (Hwy. 307 Km 287, Playa del Carmen; ☎ 800/507-1092 in U.S., or 984/803-9999; www.alltournative.com; $115 adults, $105 children) an ecotour company that has worked with villagers for 10 years to help them become self-sustaining without depleting their land. Today, all 100-plus residents work on the tourism project, and their income has doubled. They still farm pineapple, beans, and plantains but no longer depend on it for their livelihood; they can survive now without burning the land to squeeze out the last remaining nutrients.

It's a brilliant arrangement that benefits the villagers, the environment, and the tourists who visit Pac Chen. Local men take you through the jungle, explaining what various plants and land formations meant to their ancestors and how they are used. They send you gliding over a surface cenote on a zipline (not a traditional Maya practice, to be sure), help you rappel into the underground Jaguar Cenote, and then install you in kayaks to explore a lagoon guarded by howler and spider monkeys. After an elder bestows a copal-incense visitors' blessing, village women serve a robust lunch of such traditional dishes as grilled *achiote* chicken.

Before I took the trip, I thought it was overambitious to pair a visit to Pac Chen with a visit to Cobá, as Alltournative's full-day tour does. In retrospect, it was perfect: Two glimpses of a fascinating yet mysterious civilization at opposite ends of an era, each one illuminating the other.

from *El Matancero,* a ship that foundered close to Akumal in 1741. Other displays include Maya offerings dredged from the peninsula's cenotes, artifacts from local archaeological sites, and early photos of cenote explorations. Together, they paint a vivid picture of coastal life in past eras. The museum is located on the second floor of a pink building near the main entrance.

If you're in need of a crash course in all of the Yucatán's natural wonders and cultural riches, **Xcaret** kids (Hwy. 307, 10km/6½ miles south of Playa del Carmen; ☎ 800/292-2738 or 998/881-2451; www.xcaret.com; daily 8:30am–9pm, until 10pm in summer) will hand it to you all wrapped up in a bow. Once a sacred Maya city and port, Xcaret is now the Riviera Maya's most heavily advertised attraction that tries to be authentic but comes off as the tourist magnet it is. The megapark offers water activities such as a boat ride through a jungle river, snorkeling in short underground rivers, and swimming with dolphins (some of these at extra cost). It provides close-up wildlife views on jaguar and puma islands, a butterfly pavilion, and an aquarium. You can explore a replica Maya village and ride a horse through the jungle to see Maya ruins. Cultural shows include the Voladores de Papantla (flying maypole dance) and a reenactment of the ceremonial pok-ta-pok ball game played in the ball courts found in every Maya ruin. The park also maintains scarlet macaw- and turtle-breeding areas and an orchid greenhouse, all with educational exhibits. Everything in the park is fun, interesting, or just plain beautiful, but taking a family of four will put a serious dent in the budget. Admission is $70 for adults ($35 children 1.3–1.4m/50–55 in. tall), $110 with hotel transportation or $99 with food and snorkel gear. One way to ease the pain is to come in the evening, when tickets drop to $49 ($24 children).

## ACTIVE PLAYA DEL CARMEN
### Scuba Diving

The stretch of reef off Playa del Carmen's shore is almost as spectacular as the coral in Cozumel, and many inland cenotes as are easily accessible as well. Playa has scores of dive shops, and prices are pretty reasonable. Reef dives cost about $40 to $50 for one tank and $70 for two tanks, while Cozumel and two-tank cenote trips are around $110 to $120. For Cozumel dives, almost all the shops require you to take the ferry over on your own and board the dive boat there. Multidive packages, offered by most shops, will save about 10% to 15%; the operations below also offer dive/hotel packages, which reduce the cost of both diving and lodging.

One of the first dive shops in town, and still among the best, **Tank-Ha Dive Center** (Av. 5, btw. calles 8 and 10; ☎ 984/873-0302; www.tankha.com) has PADI-certified teachers and is the only operator that takes divers from Playa to Cozumel instead of sending them over on the ferry. PADI-affiliated **Yucatek Divers** (Av. 15 Norte, btw. calles 2 and 4; ☎ 984/873-1363; www.yucatek-divers.com) specializes in cenote diving and in dives for people with disabilities. Also recommended: **Abyss** (Av. 1 north of Calle 12; ☎ 984/873-2164; www.abyssdiveshop.com), with a long-standing reputation for emphasizing safety and fun, and **Dive Mike** (Calle 8, btw. Av. 5 and beach; ☎ 984/803-1228; www.divemike.com), a friendly, professional shop.

### Snorkeling

Snorkeling isn't very rewarding along Playa's shore, and though the reef isn't very far, it's not a good idea to try to swim there because of boat traffic and sometimes dangerous currents. The best snorkeling spots are not right in front of town but at Moché reef to the north (about 10 min. by boat) and Inna reef to the south (20 min.). Dive shops will take you to these spots on guided snorkeling tours costing $30 to $40 and snorkeling in cenotes for $50 to $60, including gear. Find out how many people will be on your trip, how long it will last, and how many reefs you'll visit (for ocean trips) before you book.

In addition to the dive shops, small boats docked up and down the beach offer snorkeling tours. They'll go whenever you show up, and usually it will be just your group, even if there are only two of you. They are a little less expensive than the dive shops: around $20 to $25 per person for a reef in front of Playa or $30 for Moché or Inna reefs. Beachfront guides recommended by regulars for their friendly service and safe boats include **Hawaii Watersports,** just north of Calle 14; **Dani Sailing,** at Calle 28; and **Wahoo Watersports,** just north of Calle 4.

Jaime's Marina (Playa El Faro, end of Calle 10; ☎ 984/130-2034; www. jaimesmarina.bravehost.com), operating out of a beach kiosk next to El Faro (the lighthouse), offers friendly service and good snorkeling tours (among a number of water activities). Two-hour snorkeling trips ($35) include an hour of sailing to and from the reef in a Hobie Cat. You can also rent a kayak and snorkel gear and create your own tour ($15 single, $20 double for 3 hr.).

## Dolphin Swims

About 8km (5 miles) south of Playa del Carmen, **Delphinus** (Hwy. 307 Km 282, Playa del Carmen; ☎ 800/335-3461 toll-free Mexico, or 998/206-3304; www. delphinus.com.mx) offers swimming with dolphins in a facility that attempts to duplicate their living conditions in the wild. (It also operates the dolphin swim programs at Xcaret and Xel-Há parks). For $149 ($134 if booked online; children must be 1m/43 in. tall), participants get 50 minutes with the dolphins, including a foot push and a dolphin kiss, and remain with them while they execute a series of jumps. You also get time for free swimming with the pod. Admission includes a wetsuit, goggles, and round-trip transportation from many hotels.

## Golf

Playa's showcase championship course, the **Golf Club at Playacar** (Paseo Xaman-Há opposite Hotel Viva Azteca; ☎ 998/881-6088; www.palaceresorts.com), in the upscale development south of the tourist zone, charges a championship price: $260, or $165 after 2pm. To get in some tee time without busting the budget, head south to **Puerto Aventuras Club de Golf** (across from Building B, Puerto Aventuras Marina; ☎ 984/873-5109; www.puertoaventuras.com; daily 7:30am–dark). The greens fee at the 9-hole, par 36 course start at $79, dropping to $65 after 1pm and $55 for the last tee time at 3pm. The course, designed around palm trees, bougainvillea, and tropical foliage, is across the road from the north edge of the marina. Two tennis courts are also available for $20 an hour.

## Horseback Riding

Of several places along Hwy. 307 that offer horseback rides, **Rancho Punta Venado** (Hwy. 307 Km 279; ☎ 984/803-5224; www.puntavenado.com) feels the most authentic, and the horses are well cared for. The ranch, just south of Playa, 2km (1¼ miles) past the Calica overpass, has 4km (2½ miles) of beach with a sheltered bay. The 1½-hour ride, in groups of no more than 20, follows the shore and returns to the ranch through lush vegetation. If you don't choose another activity, you can spend the rest of the day at the beach. The ranch also offers kayaking, snorkeling, and ATV and jeep jungle tours. Less than 20% of its 810 hectares (2,000 acres) of jungle has been explored.

## And Manatees, Oh My

Puerto Aventuras's branch of **Dolphin Discovery** ✹✹✹ (Puerto Aventuras Marina, 29km/18 miles south of Playa del Carmen; ☎ 800/417-1736 in U.S., or 984/873-5078; www.dolphindiscovery.com; daily 8am–5pm) is a unique treat as its special Sea Life Discovery Plus program ($199) also includes romping with three resident manatees, beginning with feeding them a back 40's worth of lettuce and ending with kisses. The vegetarian behemoths were rescued from starvation in 2001 and have thrived on a steady supply of lettuce and adoring humans. I have kissed sea lions and I have kissed dolphins, and I can now state definitively that manatees deliver the best smooch. Dolphin-only programs range from $69 to $149 depending on the type of interaction; participants under 12 are $59 to $149 (minimum age 1 year).

### Body Work

Tucked into a bower of tropical foliage off of La Quinta, **Spa Itzá** (Calle Corazón at Av. 5; ☎ 984/803-2588; www.spaitza.com; daily 10am–9pm) is as relaxing outside the building as it is in the massage room. You can simply stop in to work out some kinks in the sauna, steam room, and sun deck for $15 an hour, or take advantage of its full range of services. The spa offers 30- to 80-minute massage therapies ($45–$110), Maya healing baths ($55), body treatments ($55–$95) and hydrotub bath remedies ($70), along with the usual lineup of facials and salon treatments. Treatments specially geared for men and brides also available.

## ATTENTION, SHOPPERS!

Shopping is the main event for a large percentage of visitors here, and Playa earns the honor with some of the best shopping on the coast. Avenida 5 is shoppers' central, with high-end clothing, Cuban cigars, specialty tequila, handicrafts, jewelry—pretty much anything you can think of to spend money on. The best folk art and boutiques are concentrated between calles 4 and 10; a shady pedestrian area called Calle Corazón, between calles 12 and 14, has art galleries, restaurants, and boutiques. Most stores stay open daily to 10pm; credit cards are widely accepted.

One of my favorite shops is the **Colors Collection Boutique** (Calle 2, btw. avs. 5 and 10; ☎ 984/879-3272; modabeatriz@yahoo.com), an unassuming little side-street shop with 100% cotton dresses, halter tops, flippy skirts, *guayaberas,* and shorts and shirts designed and manufactured by the owner and her sister, the attentive but unobtrusive manager. Most cost between $20 and $40—less than half the tab for similar items on the avenue. Sizes are sometimes inconsistent, but the fabric is sublime and the clothes well made. (The owner also has a larger shop, D'Beatriz, on Calle 4 at the beach.)

Other Avenida 5 picks include **La Sirena** (Av. 5 at Calle 26; ☎ 984/803-3422), an Italian-owned boutique selling beautiful art from around Mexico; **Blue Planet** (Av. 5, btw. calles 10 and 12; ☎ 984/803-1504), with retro '70s-style fashions ranging from funky to romantic; and **Casa Tequila** (Av. 5 near Calle 14; ☎ 984/873-0195), which sells a good selection of silver jewelry in addition to more than 100 types of fine tequila—and you sample before you purchase.

At the north end of the tourist zone, **Ah Cacao** (avs. 5 and Constituyentes; ☎ 984/803-5748; www.ahcacao.com) is an obligatory pilgrimage for chocoholics. This cafe and gift shop produces rare *criollo* chocolate, the Maya's "food of the gods." It's chocolate for grown-ups: intense, complex, with secondary notes like fine wine. Choose your form, either chocolate bars (more than 70% cacao, compared with less than 15% in most store brands), unsweetened cocoa, or roasted beans, not to mention body bars and moisturizers. The shop also sells gift bags of coffee—Starbucks will never seem the same after sampling Ah Cacao's fudgy brownies, mochas, frappes, and chocolate shots.

Away from the main tourist center, **Mundo-Librería-Bookstore** (Calle 1 Sur, btw. avs. 20 and 25; ☎ 984/879-3004; www.smallworldbooks.org) has several cases of new and used books in English, from beach reads to serious novels, non-fiction, and many titles on Maya culture. You can bring your used books for 50% in cash or trade, and profits from English-language books are donated to Mexican schools.

Playa has a plethora of shopping malls, most of little interest. The exception is **Paseo del Carmen** (southern end of Av. 5), an outdoor center housing small boutiques, jewelry stores, art galleries, and restaurants. With its shade trees and fountains, it's a pleasant place to window-shop and worth a stop in the evening for a mojito or an upscale dinner.

## NIGHTLIFE IN PLAYA DEL CARMEN

When the sun goes down, the street party revs up along La Quinta. Though you can find any type of music in the varied mix of bars every night, most people have gravitated in the past few years to the intersection with Calle 12, which has accumulated the highest concentration of cool clubs and lounges.

Playa's longstanding hot spot, at least for tourists, is the **Blue Parrot** (Calle 12 at the beach; ☎ 984/206-3350; www.blueparrot.com; $10 cover after 11pm), planted right on the beach. Sand floors, swing bar seats, a candlelit *palapa* lounge, and a small dance floor with DJs dispensing popular tunes that appeal to most age groups add up to a party air that keeps customers loyal over the years. An additional covered lounge features techno and dance music. Wherever you're hanging out, head to the beach at 11pm to see the fire dancing.

Stone steps echoing a Maya temple lead to **Deseo Lounge** (in Hotel Deseo, Av. 5 at Calle 12; ☎ 984/879-3620; www.hoteldeseo.com; no cover), on a Christo-meets-pool-party roof patio. At night, sheer white drapes wafting in the aqua-and-purple glow evoke an underwater dream. Guests lounge on large blue daybeds to watch movies projected on the wall or listen to the pulsing music. The martini menu is the big draw here, ranging from cucumber to *chamoy* (a Mexican candy). The signature Cubano Royale is an alchemic brew of mojito and champagne.

Locals and tourists mix with the pretty people from Mexico City at the eclectic **La Santanera** (Calle 12, btw. avs. 5 and 10; ☎ 984/803-2856; cover varies). Known for anything-goes music (mostly Latin-tinged international) and strong drinks, its main club has an air-conditioned dance floor, a light show, and disco balls. The breezy open-air lounge upstairs is decorated with kitschy *lucha libre*

(Mexican wrestling) posters, *calaveras* (skulls), and *santería* (an Afro-Caribbean religion) masks, making a fine place to relax with DJ-generated tunes (except on weekends, which get terribly crowded). The cover charge changes with the door-man's whim: Sometimes it's $10, sometimes $30 per couple, sometimes only after 11pm, or sometimes none at all.

# PUERTO MORELOS

Before you get to Playa del Carmen on your way south from Cancún, you come first to the small, colorful town Puerto Morelos. It was the Mexican Caribbean's boomtown 100 years ago, when its port, with its trademark leaning lighthouse, shipped the region's hardwoods and *chicle* (for chewing gum) to U.S. and European markets. Today, its biggest attraction is its idyllic atmosphere. It's still the kind of place where you can watch fishermen unload the day's catch that will be on your plate within hours at one of the waterfront restaurants, and where a plaza lined with craft shops and restaurants is central to local life, coming alive with a small fair every Sunday. Offshore from its wide, uncrowded beaches, Puerto Morelos's section of the Great Maya Reef, recently declared a national park, is renowned as one of the Caribbean coast's best snorkeling spots.

More and more people—especially those looking for the Playa del Carmen of old—are discovering that this is an ideal base for exploring the Riviera Maya and even Cancún. Despite being gradually surrounded by large all-inclusive resorts and condominiums, its relaxed village atmosphere has endured, offering small hotels and budget inns among the large hotels and condominiums. Puerto brims with foreign tourists at times during in the high season, but low season is low in the extreme; many businesses close in May, September, and October.

## GETTING TO & AROUND PUERTO MORELOS

Puerto Morelos is 35km (22 miles) south of Cancún on coastal Hwy. 307, halfway to Playa del Carmen; after you pass Croco Cun on the east side of the highway, turn left at the next exit and drive about 2km (1½ miles) into town.

Playa Express and ADO buses traveling between Cancún's **Terminal de Autobuses** (avs. Tulum and Uxmal; ☎ 998/884-5542; $1.80) and Playa del Carmen run daily about every 10 to 15 minutes between 5am and 9pm, every 20 minutes until midnight, and less frequently throughout the night. They will drop you at the bus stop on the highway 1 block south of the turnoff (northbound buses stop on the other side of the highway right at the intersection), where taxis line up to shuttle people into town for about $1.50.

If you're going directly to Puerto Morelos from the Cancún airport, the same ADO bus that goes to Playa del Carmen (p. 136) will take you to the Puerto Morelos stop for $4. You can also book airport transfers to Puerto Morelos; a shared shuttle costs $23 per person ($45 round-trip), a taxi $54 for up to two passengers or $59 for three or four. Private vans for larger groups charge the same rate as a taxi for up to seven passengers, or $63 for eight to ten.

Unless you're staying at one of the resorts at the far end of Puerto Morelos, you'll do most of your sightseeing on foot. For the occasional foray farther afield, **taxi** stands are located on the central plaza and at the highway intersection. A trip within town costs about $1.50; the resorts north and south of town are a $6 to $7 ride. A trip to Playa del Carmen will cost $24; to Cancún, $25.

# ACCOMMODATIONS, BOTH STANDARD & NOT

## Condos & Vacation Rentals

Despite the luxury resorts closing in around Puerto Morelos, the cost of renting condos, apartments, or even houses around town remains modest by Riviera Maya standards. Even better, there are a surprising number located right in the heart of town rather than segregated into tourist zones. You don't have to look far to find a cozy, contemporary, one-bedroom apartment on a quiet residential street 2 blocks from the plaza and ½-block from the beach, for as little as $450 a week or $900 a month. Of course, you get more—space, proximity to the beach, decor—if you pay more, but $650 or $700 a week can rent a centrally located one-bedroom apartment or condo with plenty of space and a bit of style. If you want to be right on the beach, you'll probably have cough up about $1,000 or more.

In addition to vacation rental companies that handle properties throughout the region (p. 21), the owners of **Alma Libre Bookstore** (☎ 994/871-0713; www.almalibrebooks.com) are a great source of Puerto Morelos rentals. Their website has about 20 listings at any given time, and they personally know each property and owner. Rentals range from stylish one-bedrooms in town (from $500) to a five-bedroom beach mansion that sleeps 10. Two other agencies specializing in local rentals operate solely online: **Puertomorelosmexico.com** (the better organized and easier to use of the two) and **www.visitpuertomorelos.com**. Both have some good deals on appealing properties, and they are recommended by repeat customers. Still, one word of warning bears repeating: Don't sign anything or give out a credit card number unless you're provided with a way to contact a breathing human being if you need immediate help.

## Hotels

**$–$$**   One of the town's most captivating hotels happens to be one of its best bargains. **Posada El Moro** ★★★ (kids) (Av. Javier Rojo Gómez north of José Morelos; ☎ 998/871-0159; www.posadaelmoro.com; cash only) rents 10 spacious, brightly painted rooms for $40 a night in low season, $50 high, and $60 over Christmas. An additional suite with two double beds, a futon, and a kitchenette ($65–$85) is ideal for families. Choosing a room here is a little like ordering dim sum: Add $5 a night to get air-conditioning, $5 more for TV, and another $5 for a fully equipped kitchenette. French-paned sliding doors and windows flood the rooms with light, and each has an outdoor table and chairs. The simple, cheery furnishings include queen-size beds with nearly perfect mattresses. Rates include an ample continental breakfast, and you have free rein of the kitchen with its electric juicer so you can squeeze your own from a selection of fresh fruit. The pretty garden has a small pool perfect for kids, and the homey atmosphere is enhanced by the amiable, English-speaking family who runs the place.

**$$–$$$**   The vantage point on Puerto Morelos' best stretch of beach, in front of the cenote for which it is named, would be enough to recommend **Hotel Ojo de Agua** ★★ (kids) (Av. Javier Rojo Gómez 16; ☎ 998/871-0027; www.ojo-de-agua.com; AE, MC, V), especially since it has a good dive shop, watersports facilities, and a popular restaurant jutting out onto the sand. But this friendly, family-run hotel, 2 blocks from the main square, is a good deal to boot. Simple but colorful air-conditioned rooms have rattan furniture and telephones, though not all have TVs.

**ACCOMMODATIONS** ■
Club Marviya **1**
Hotel Ojo de Agua **2**
Posada El Moro **4**

**DINING** ◆
Doña Triny's **5**
Hola Asia **7**
John Gray's Kitchen **3**
Pelicanos **8**
Posada Amor **6**

0                    1/8 mi
0          1/8 km

← to Highway 307

Ejercito Mexicano

Niños Héroes

Javier Rojo Gómez

■ Wet Set Diving

Almost Heaven Divers ■

Casa de la
Cultura ■

■ Dive Puerto Morales

*CARIBBEAN
SEA*

Jose Morelos

■ Fishing Cooperative

Tulum

Plaza

Alma Libre Bookstore ■

■ Main pier &
leaning lighthouse

Rafael Melgar

Hunab Kú market ■

*Gulf of Mexico*

Cancún

**Puerto Morelos**

Mérida

YUCATÁN

YUCATÁN
PENINSULA

QUINTANA
ROO

CAMPECHE

Doubles ($60–$70 a night, depending on season) with one queen bed are roomy, and deluxe rooms with two doubles ($70–$80) are quite spacious. Studios with kitchenettes and small yards ($80–$90) come with one king bed or a double and two twins. Even at $10 per extra person, they are well suited for families (except in summer, since they have ceiling fans but no air-conditioning).

**$$–$$$   Club Marviya** ★ (Av. Rojo Gómez at Ejército; ☎ 998/871-0049; www. marviya.com; MC, V) is actually two properties. Rooms in the original Hotelito Marviya occupy the second floor of a converted mansion, where small terraces offer terrific views and refreshing breezes. The airy contemporary rooms, with firm king-size beds and ceramic-tile floors, ooze Mexican style. Room rates swing from $60 in low season to $95 in high, then to $110 during Christmas and spring holidays. All but the low-season rate include breakfast in the covered courtyard, where the personable Canadian and Mexican owners often visit with guests. Hammocks on the terrace and a large communal kitchen and lounge contribute to the relaxed atmosphere. Marviya's Studios recently opened down the street with nine newly renovated units ($60–$125 a night; no breakfast). Neither property has A/C (sea breezes suffice through most of the year), and they are 3 long blocks from the town center, but only 1 block from the best beach in town.

## If You Only Splurge Once

After chef John Gray left the Ritz-Carlton Cancún, he cooked his way around the world awhile and finally resurfaced in Puerto Morelos in 2002. Gray, who elevated the Ritz's Club Grill to iconic status, has since opened restaurants in Playa del Carmen and Cancún, but **John Gray's Kitchen** ★★★ (Av. Niños Héroes north of José Morelos; ☎ 998/871-0665; daily 6–10pm; MC, V) is where it all began, and where he still lives.

Tucked into a bower of palms and other tropical trees, the restaurant's exterior resembles an urban apartment building dressed in grass skirts; inside, the dining room has a chic Manhattan aura. What comes out of the kitchen each day changes with the chef's mood and what's fresh on the market. The first time I ate there, Gray added swordfish and fresh clams to the menu while I was still deciding between pork loin with Roquefort crust ($18) and grilled chicken breast with cilantro pesto ($14). Clearly, this isn't a budget place, but prices aren't beyond the pale—the most I could have spent was $29. It's worth saving up for, but a couple of the intriguing sides, such as crab cakes with a Mexican twist or Gray's ambrosial baked red-chili cauliflower ($5–$8), can make a satisfying meal in themselves. If you arrive at opening time, you'll probably get a table; otherwise, make reservations. This is one restaurant you shouldn't miss.

## DINING FOR ALL TASTES

Puerto Morelos has a supply of good restaurants, blending local flavors with those contributed by expats from all over the world, all out of proportion for a village of this size. Most are on the plaza, where the entire town seems to end up in the evening.

**$-$$   Doña Triny's** (avs. Javier Rojo Gómez and José Morelos; Thurs–Tues 8am–1am; cash only), a raucously painted hole in the wall on the plaza's northwest corner, makes no concession to wimpy gringo palates. The salsa is fiery and the tacos are cheap (about 60¢), but don't miss out on the *salbutes* (fried tortillas stuffed with beans and topped with chicken or turkey), quesadillas, chiles rellenos, and other Mexican and Yucatecan standards. The savory *arrachera* steak ($8.25) is especially good.

**$-$$**   For 4 years running, the top spot in the annual survey of locals' favorite restaurants has belonged to **Hola Asia** ★ (Av. Tulum 1; ☎ 998/871-0679; www.holaasia.com; Mon and Wed–Sat 1–10pm, Sun 3–10pm; AE, MC, V). The small, open-air restaurant on the south side of the plaza serves healthy portions of fine Chinese, Japanese, and Thai food. The big favorite, a spicy sweet-and-sour chicken, is $6.25; chicken teriyaki, shrimp, and Thai fish with tamarind run $9 to $11. Upstairs tables have views of the ocean and plaza, and the rooftop tiki bar is an expat gathering place.

**$–$$$**  Puerto Morelos' oldest restaurant, **Posada Amor** ✷✷ (avs. Javier Rojo Gómez and Tulum; ☎ 998/871-0033; daily 7am–10pm; AE, MC, V) is run by the founder's son and has patrons who have been eating here for nearly 30 years. The *palapa*-roofed dining room, ½-block south of the plaza, is a great place for a complete breakfast ($4.50–$7), and the Sunday breakfast buffet ($5.50) is an unconscionable bargain. Whole-fish plates and stellar ceviche are standouts on the lunch and dinner menus, which focus on fresh seafood and Mexican Yucatecan-influenced dishes that top out at less than $20.

**$–$$$$**  Masterfully prepared seafood is one good reason to head to **Pelicanos** (Av. Rafael E. Melgar; ☎ 998/871-0014; daily 8am–10:30pm; MC, V), a family-owned stalwart across from the plaza's southeast corner. The L-shaped patio, one side looking out over the ocean and the other over the plaza—is another. The large fish filet *al ajo* (in garlic butter, $8.25) is pretty hard to beat, but shrimp, octopus, and lobster (up to $36) also come in fresh off the boat.

## WHY YOU'RE HERE: THE TOP SIGHTS & ATTRACTIONS

You can walk the compact town from end to end in about 20 minutes. The beach runs the length of town and beyond.

### Town Center

As is typical of small-town Mexico, the central **plaza** is the fulcrum of local life; to see it in full bloom, browse the produce market on Wednesdays, go to the *tianguis* (flea market) and fair on Sundays, or attend the open-air musical performances every second Thursday night (Jan–Apr).

Behind the plaza lies the **main pier** (end of José Morelos), home to Puerto Morelos's famous leaning lighthouse. Nearly toppled by Hurricane Beulah in 1967, the old beacon has become the town's defining landmark, though the big concern is that another hurricane will one day set it right again. For the best view of the tippy beacon, whose duties have been taken over by a new lighthouse nearby, walk out to the end of the dock and look back.

The **beach** in the center of town is rocky in many places and strewn with seaweed; the best beaches are north of the main pier, especially at the Ojo de Agua hotel (Av. Ejército Mexicano at the beach). Buying a beer or a soda entitles you to you use the beach chairs, umbrellas, and pool. The farther north you go, the more secluded the beaches become, and you can walk seemingly endless white sands dotted with natural sea grass, seashells, and skittering sandpipers. You'll need transportation to get to the resort area at the south end of town, which also has some lovely, isolated beaches.

### Beyond Town

About 5km (3 miles) north of the Puerto Morelos turnoff on Hwy. 307, **Croco Cun** ✷✷✷ 🧒 (p. 47), a wonderful little tropical zoo where you can get touchy-feely with not only crocodiles but iguanas, boa constrictors, spider monkeys, and tropical birds, among other denizens of the surrounding jungles.

Once acquainted with the local fauna, head south just past the Puerto Morelos turnoff for an introduction to the Yucatán's jungle and marshland flora at the

## Dive Packages

If you're planning a diving vacation, check dive operators' websites for package deals that include daily dives and, in some cases, airport transfers, jungle tours, or other excursions, with a wide variety of lodging choices. These can save $100 to $200 over the price of booking dive trips and lodging separately.

**Jardín Botanico Dr. Alfredo Barrera Marín** (Carretera 307 Km 33; ☎ 998/206-9233; $7; Mon–Sat 9am–5pm). Also called Yaax-Ché, the peaceful botanical garden (named for a local botanist) has plants labeled in English, Spanish, and Latin. A nature walk in the mangroves (bring bug spray) leads through 3km (nearly 2 miles) of medicinal plants, ferns, palms, Postclassic Maya ruins, and a replica *chiclero* camp where you can see how the sap of the *zapote* (sapodilla) tree is tapped for its *chicle*, used to produce natural chewing gum. Caretakers will let bird-watchers in at dawn to spot members of more than 220 species, as well as the occasional spider monkey. A treehouse lookout on-site will reward plucky climbers with spectacular views.

## THE OTHER PUERTO MORELOS

If you're in Puerto Morelos during the winter tourist season, you don't have to sit back and idly enjoy the music that fills the plaza on the second Thursday evening of each month—you can be part of the show. For the past 3 years, the **Casa de la Cultura** (Niños Héroes, just north of José Morelos) has staged a music festival to promote local amateur and professional music and art while giving the town a cultural night out. You can simply enjoy an evening of music under the stars, or take the stage if you're so moved. The cultural center is looking for musicians to perform and artists to display their work during the festival, and the stage is open to everyone. If you're interested (or just want more information), contact the Alma Libre Bookstore (see "Attention, Shoppers!" below).

Casa de la Cultura also has a regular schedule of dance and art classes, yoga, Pilates, aikido, and Capoeira (a highly athletic Brazilian dance) that welcomes tourists as well; for a schedule, check www.almalibrebooks.com/casa_cultura.pdf.

## ACTIVE PUERTO MORELOS

The Great Mesoamerican Reef (or Great Maya Reef) runs just 183 to 550m (300–900 ft.) off the Puerto Morelos' coast, blessing the shore with calm, safe waters. Seaweed and turtle grass make the beaches more popular for strolling than swimming, but you won't find better snorkeling and scuba diving anywhere. Declared a National Marine Park in 1998, efforts to keep this stretch of reef healthy are funded by a $2.50 per person, per day usage fee.

### Snorkeling

The reef's gargantuan proportions and convoluted formations right in front of town provide an abundance of colorful sea life within less than 1m (3 ft.) of the surface in some places, making Puerto Morelos ideal for novice snorkelers. The best way to see the reefs is with a boat and guide. Snorkeling tours generally cost $25 per person for a 1½- to 2-hour excursion. Prices include gear, but the park fee is usually additional. Try to go in late morning, when the sun is high enough for good visibility but the afternoon winds haven't started up.

The local **Fishing Cooperative** (main pier; Mon–Sat 8am–3pm), a group of boat owners and guides, offers excellent snorkeling tours ($25 per person) in boats with sun shades, visiting two sites for about 45 minutes apiece. The price includes the park fee, and boats leave every 30 minutes from the municipal pier. Sign up at the kiosk at the northeast corner of the plaza; if you have fewer than three people, captains may wait up to 30 minutes to see if more passengers arrive.

The dive shops in town (see below) also offer snorkeling tours. **Almost Heaven Divers** (see below) offers a night snorkeling tour that lifts the curtain on a whole different cast of characters for $40. **Wet Set Diving** (see below) has some lower-priced basic tours, including a 45-minute one-site trip for $12 per person, a 45-minute two-site trip for $18, and a night snorkel tour for $25 per person.

## Scuba Diving

Dive shops in town offer one-tank dives for $45 to $50, and two-tank dives for $65 to $70. Open-water certification courses run 3 to 4 days and cost $300 to $350; "Discover Scuba," equivalent to "resort courses" offered by many hotels, are $85 to $100.

The dean of dive shops is **Dive Puerto Morelos** (Av. Javier Rojo Gómez 14, ½-block north of the plaza; ☎ 998/206-9084; www.divepuertomorelos.com), with small groups and experienced English-speaking guides that operate efficiently but without rushing. It also offers dive tours to two cenotes on private property near town as well as to others farther afield. One-tank dives cost $85; two tank/two cenote dives are $125.

Some of the best prices in town come from **Wet Set Diving** (Hotel Ojo de Agua Hotel, Av. Javier Rojo Gómez, 2 blocks north of plaza; ☎ 281/224-2026 in the U.S., or 998/871-0198; www.wetset.com): One-tank dives are $45; two tanks, $60; and a one-tank night dive, $65. A one-tank cenote dive is $95; a two-tank, two-cenote dive with lunch is $130. Divemaster Paul Hensley and his crew, who have been in the area for more than 20 years, have discovered several dive sites on their own. Unlike most shops, Wet Set doesn't charge extra if you need buoyancy control devices, regulators, or a flashlight. Groups are limited to six or eight divers, depending on the boat. The shop offers dive/lodging packages at local hotels, starting at $98 per person per night; at Ojo de Agua, the shop's landlord, a special singles package costs the same as the double-occupancy per-person rate ($440 for five dives and 4 nights' lodging).

## Reef Safety

Do not swim to the reef from anywhere along the beach. Although it's close enough for strong swimmers to reach, boats use the channel between the reef and the shore, and tourists have been struck and killed in the past.

# Notes from the Underground

The Maya called them *dzonots* (sacred wells). The Spanish mangled the Mayan name and called them cenotes. Today, we call them unsurpassable swimming holes.

The Yucatán peninsula is a geological oddity, a flat limestone shelf too porous to hold water on the surface. The terrain is devoid of rivers, but rainwater seeping through the stone carves subterranean channels in the peninsula's foundation. Breaches in the tunnel ceilings create sinkholes that reveal subterranean waters to the world above. Precious stones, ancient ceramics and bones unearthed in cenotes suggest the ancient Maya used these gateways to the underworld as ceremonial sites.

The area west of the Playa del Carmen–Tulum corridor has one of the largest concentrations of cenotes on the Yucatán Peninsula, numbering in the thousands. Countless others remain hidden by jungle. Some are at least partially underground, while others are open wells. Still other cenotes open to the surface like a lake. Many cenotes have been penned up in nature parks along the Caribbean coast, such as Xcaret near Playa del Carmen and Hidden Worlds near Akumal (site of the IMAX movie *Amazing Caves*). Below are five cenotes where you can at least imagine what they might have been like during the height of the Maya empire. All are accessible from Hwy. 307. Most have bathrooms, are open daily from about 8 or 9am until 5 or 6pm, and charge about $3 for entry.

**Cristalino** (just south of Puerto Aventuras, east of the highway across from Barceló Maya Resort, and 2km/1¼ miles north of Xpu-Há). Though it's close to the hugely popular Cenote Azul, not many tourists find their way to this local favorite, which has a great jump-off point and a cave to explore. It overflows on Sundays with people beating the heat, but the rest of the week you might have it to yourself. Take a cue from the locals: Bring a cooler and blanket, and make an afternoon of it.

The highly recommended **Almost Heaven Divers** (Rojo Gómez, a block north of plaza; ☎ 998/871-0230; www.almostheavenadventures.com) specializes in night dives (one tank $55, two tanks $70). The moonlight show stars octopus, squid, lobster, and cuttlefish. The gregarious owner, Enrique Juárez, holds groups to five divers and has been in business for more than 13 years. His shop is known for good briefings and attentive boat crews. Almost Heaven offers packages with local hotels and vacation properties, starting at $275 for 3 nights and 4 days. The company also runs jungle tours and excursions to Maya ruins and the botanical gardens, starting at $35 per person.

## Fishing

Most local dive shops will help anglers nab that marlin, sailfish, mahi mahi, or other exotic catch. The average rate for a 4- or 5-hour expedition for four people

**Jardín del Edén** (1.6km/1 mile north of Xpu-Há, just south of Cenote Azul). "El Edén," looking like a big swimming pool in the middle of the jungle, tempts snorkelers with a wide variety of freshwater tropical fish and eels drawn by the big, moss-covered rocks and plants on the bottom. In addition to a high jump-off point, a conveniently placed tree provides daredevils a launch point. As a main entrance point into the underground cave system, it also attracts divers.

**Xunaan Ha** (outside of Chemuyil, 12km/7½ miles south of Akumal). Perhaps the least known of the Riviera Maya's accessible cenotes, this one is reached by winding through a small Maya village. Signs point to the small cenote nearly hidden in the jungle, where you can swim or snorkel with schools of fish and the occasional freshwater turtle. Be prepared: no bathrooms here.

**Manatí** (Tankhah, east of the highway 10km/6 miles north of Tulum). The large, open lagoon near Casa Cenote restaurant is the last cenote in one of the world's longest underwater cave systems before it empties into the sea. Fresh water bubbling up into ocean waters create significant but not dangerous currents that attract a great variety of saltwater and freshwater fish. Swim upstream toward the caves, then wind your way back down through the mangroves toward the beach.

**Cenote Escondido** (4km/2½ miles south of Tulum). Highway signs mark the dirt road leading east to this crisp, cool pool, fringed with fan palms on a rocky bluff. Because it requires a short jungle trek, it draws fewer visitors than Cristal, its roadside neighbor. Swimmers can see hundreds of fish in the clear water, but it takes snorkeling equipment to make out the stunning stone formations less than 6m (20 ft.) below.

is $275, going up to $425 to $450 for eight. The **Fishing Cooperative** charges $250 for as many as five people, and **Wet Set Divers** offers the option of taking just two people out for $195 ($25 more for each additional person).

## ATTENTION, SHOPPERS!

The **Hunab Kú market** (Javier Rojo Gómez, south of plaza; daily 9am–8pm) is a collection of *palapa*-style stands, about a block from the plaza, where the local artisans' cooperative sells hammocks, hand-embroidered clothes, masks, jewelry, colorful blankets, ceramics, and other handicrafts. There's nothing you can't find elsewhere in the Riviera Maya, but it has some good bargains.

The affable Canadians who run **Alma Libre Bookstore** ✸✸✸ (Av. Tulum, btw. Javier Rojo Gómez and Rafael Melgar; ☎ 994/871-0713; www.almalibre books.com; Oct–June Tues–Sat 10am–3pm and 6–9pm, Sun 4–9pm) on the south

## Puerto Aventuras

You won't likely get far into a Riviera Maya vacation without seeing promotions for Puerto Aventuras, 29km (18 miles) south of Playa del Carmen. Don't fall for the hype. The self-contained, color-coordinated golf resort and marina don't exactly add up to a town, even with the restaurants and shops ringing the marina and the surrounding upscale condos and summer homes. Passing through the monumental entry gate feels like being locked away from Mexico. It's hard to find a vacation rental for less than $200 a night, and the few hotels start at more than $300. I haven't found lodging interesting enough to recommend at those prices. And while the faux-cobblestone roads and luxuriant landscaping are lovely, they are no more so than any other country-club development in the world.

That is not to say you won't have reason to go to Puerto Aventuras. Its Dolphin Discovery park (p. 147), the region's only maritime museum (p. 143), and the Riviera Maya's most affordable golf course (p. 146) are all worth a detour. Puerto Aventuras is 20 minutes from Playa or Tulum by car. *Colectivo* vans from Cancún, Playa del Carmen, or Tulum ($2–$3) will drop you off at the entrance gate, leaving you about a .5km (⅓-mile) walk to the marina. Taxis to or from Playa del Carmen cost about $15.

side of the plaza has the largest selection of English-language books (mostly used) in the Yucatán—more than 20,000 beach reads, classics, tomes on Maya culture, and local guidebooks and maps. The store also serves as a book exchange, unofficial tourist information center, vacation rental agency, and travel consultancy. They'll even copy your digital photos onto a CD to free up space on your camera's storage card. Note that they're closed during summer months.

# AKUMAL

Akumal, the coast's senior resort area, is a curious mix of unbridled development and ecological dedication. Like Puerto Aventuras (see above), it's basically a small business district with a lot of upscale homes and condos. Unlike its neighbor, Akumal has a relaxed, uncommercial feel. A major draw is the chance to see rare loggerhead and green sea turtles who have been laying their eggs on these beaches for hundreds of years (Akumal means "Place of the Turtles" in Mayan). Its calm bays and barrier reef make it a major diving and snorkeling destination.

The town snakes along four consecutive bays. Akumal Bay, in the center of town, is sea turtle central. The vast majority of rooms for rent are in private homes and condos on Half Moon Bay to the north. Developments to the south are purely residential (although Aventuras Akumal has some dive centers and a convenience store) and aren't connected to the rest of town, or each other, except by the beach.

# GETTING TO & AROUND AKUMAL

Akumal is 3km (2 miles) beyond Puerto Aventuras on Hwy. 370 (just past the Km 255 marker), 101km (63 miles) from Cancún, and 34km (21 miles) from Playa del Carmen. Driving is your best option; though *colectivos* (about $2 to or from Playa del Carmen or Tulum) and second-class buses stop at the Akumal turnoff, that leaves almost a kilometer (about ½-mile) walk into town.

You can easily navigate the little town center on foot, but getting to Half Moon Bay would be a hot, and potentially treacherous, walk on a narrow road that climbs and twists for more than a mile. Plan to drive or take a taxi (about $3) from the stand just outside the entrance arch. Another option is renting a bicycle (if you aren't staying somewhere that provides them), available for about $10 a day from **Akumal Travel** (☎ 984/875-9030), near the Akumal Dive Shop and Centro Ecológico Akumal, or **Akumal Tours** (☎ 984/875-9115) just inside the arch.

You could walk south along the beach as far as Aventuras Akumal in about 45 minutes; practically speaking, you'll need to go back to the highway and drive south to separate access roads for Jade Beach, South Akumal, or Aventuras (about 2.5km/1½ miles).

# ACCOMMODATIONS, BOTH STANDARD & NOT

Akumal has far more condominiums and villas than hotel rooms for rent. Although many are aimed at the luxury traveler, there are some affordable options; large villas, especially, can be reasonable options for families or large groups.

## Condos & Vacation Rentals

The majority of rooms for rent are along Half Moon Bay, and that is where most of the more affordable rentals are. Akumal Bay's few rentals tend to be more expensive, and those on Jade Beach to the south are highest of all. Aventuras Akumal, the southernmost residential development, has a mix of reasonable and high-priced rentals.

Akumal rentals are generally well kept and relatively new, and boast stylish, contemporary furnishings. Though they don't exude local character, they are on the water (if not necessarily a swimming beach) and usually have great views. Villas, which are detached homes and typically have three or more bedrooms, far outnumber condos. With multiple bathrooms, full kitchens, maid service, and usually an on-site caretaker, they cost more than condos but can be economical when fully occupied. Most condos occupy buildings of no more than eight units and have one or two bedrooms, partial or full kitchens, and patios or balconies with ocean or jungle views. Villas rent by the week, usually Saturday to Saturday, while condos are available by the night.

Akumal is well covered by rental agencies. Many villas and condos list with several or even all of the agencies, and at the same prices. The least expensive—and scarcest—condos, studios, and *casitas* start at $60 a night. A few one-bedroom units are available for as little as $80 a night, but $100 is the lowest rate you're likely to find. Likewise, a few two-bedrooms start at $120, but in general, the low point is $140. It's possible to find a three-bedroom villa for as little as $1,800 a week, but $2,200 (equivalent to about $105 a night for a couple in a full house) is a more realistic starting point.

Since prices for any property are the same no matter where it appears, agencies with the greatest number of listings give you the best chance of finding an affordable deal. In this case, that's **Akumal Vacations** (☎ 800/448-7137 toll-free U.S.; www.akumalvacations.com), an online-only agency listing 55 houses and 28 condos, including a few in nearby Soliman and Tankah bays. About 25% of its properties start at around $100 a night per couple. **Akumal Travel** (☎ 984/875-9030; www.akumaltravel.com) has fewer listings (33 villas, 14 condos, and a few hotels), but a couple of its studios and *casitas* start at $60 a night, and condos here have some of the lowest starting prices available ($80 for one bedroom, $135 for two). Villas generally exceed the $100 a night per couple threshold, but several come close to the budget end, especially for houses in Aventuras Akumal or Punta Soliman to the south.

**Akumal Rentals** (☎ 998/185-6222; fax 815/642-4580 U.S.; www.akumalrentals.com), a local company run by two longtime Akumal residents, offers just three condos, which work out to $96 to $143 per couple per night. The majority of its 33 villas are large houses for eight or more guests; seven of these charge the equivalent of about $100 per night per couple when the house is full. **Riviera Maya Villas** (☎ 678/528-1775 U.S.; www.rivieramayavillas.com) is a U.S. company with all its staff living in the Akumal area. They know every villa and work with property managers who visit arriving guests to answer any questions. Of its 49 villas, 8 work out to about $100 per couple per night.

**Caribbean Fantasy** (☎ 800/523-6618 toll-free U.S.; www.caribbfan.com) has a good stock of condos (25) as well as 60 villas, but its website doesn't divulge actual rates. It provides a broad range, requiring a call or e-mail for exact prices. Five of its listings, which include a few in Soliman Bay and Tankah, fall into the $40 to $140 range and 28 into the $75 to $300 range. The sales office is in the United States, but the company has representatives in Akumal.

Keep in mind that "from" or "starting at" in front of the price means low season, generally from late August until about Thanksgiving. Mid- and high-season prices will be higher—whether a little or a lot varies with individual properties—and the exorbitant holiday season will be at least twice as much.

**$$$–$$$$**    Some of the vacation properties that rental agencies handle also rent directly to guests. I particularly like the houses at the **Hotel Club Akumal Caribe** ★★ (kids) (inside town entrance arches; ☎ 800/351-1622 toll-free U.S., 800/343-1440 toll-free Canada, or 915/584-3552; www.hotelakumalcaribe.com; AE, MC, V), which also has a hotel and bungalows. Its spacious, modern Cannon House studio, with plenty of sliding glass doors opening onto a grassy garden overlooking the ocean, rents for $119 to $139 a night (excluding Christmas weeks). On higher ground, the truly expansive and quite beautiful two-bedroom Cannon House ranges from $139 to $224. The hotel also acts as booking agent for two-bedroom ($160–$300) and four-bedroom ($420–$600) condos on Half Moon Bay. Unlike most rental properties, these have a long low season, from the last week in April through the last week before Christmas.

## Hotels

**$$–$$$**    A short walk from Yal-Ku lagoon at the north end of Akumal, **Que Onda** ★★★ (Caleta Yal-Ku; ☎ 984/875-9101; www.queondaakumal.com; MC, V) is a happy blend of contemporary European and traditional Caribbean style. Each of the seven spacious rooms ($60 low season, $80 high, $100 holidays) is a little different, but all have a queen- or king-size bed, tile floors, streamlined wood-accented furniture, and striking art on whitewashed walls. Upstairs rooms have high thatched roofs and shaded balconies. Two additional suites are a substantial jump in price. All rooms face a meandering tropical garden with a beautiful small pool. The building doesn't have A/C, so upstairs rooms with their high ceilings and sea breezes are the best choice. The hotel provides bicycles and snorkel gear, and its Italian restaurant is terrific (see below).

**$$–$$$$** You have a choice at **Vista del Mar Hotel and Condos** (south end of Half Moon Bay; ☎ 877/425-8625 U.S., or 984/875-9060; www.akumalinfo.com; AE, DISC, MC, V). Rooms in the three-story hotel ($75–$95 low season, $90–$100 high, $130–$150 holidays) are one of Akumal's best beachside values. Small but not cramped, they have oceanview terraces or balconies, and colorful accents. Higher-priced rooms have two double beds; the others have one queen. Next door, spacious condos with Spanish colonial touches, large full kitchens, and oceanfront balconies can be rented by the night: $110 to $280, depending on season, for studios; $110 to $320 for two bedrooms (lower-priced units have air-conditioning only in bedrooms; the most expensive have two baths); and $175 to $375 for three bedrooms with three baths. The property sits on a beautiful beach and includes a dive shop, watersports equipment rental, and a popular restaurant.

**$$$–$$$$** The only hotel on Akumal Bay is **Hotel Club Akumal Caribe** ★★ [kids] (inside town entrance arches; ☎ 800/351-1622 toll-free U.S., 800/343-1440 toll-free Canada, or 915/584-3552; www.hotelakumalcaribe.com; AE, MC, V). Renovated one-story bungalows—Akumal's first accommodations, built in the 1960s for the CEDAM dive club (p. 143)—are the best deal here, with doubles renting for $89 to $119, depending on season. They have acres of space and are simply but comfortably furnished with one queen or two double beds, a table and chairs, and a refrigerator. The bungalows are set in a parklike garden and don't have ocean views, but they're just steps from the beach where, at the right time of year, you can pretty much count on having sea turtles for playmates. I liked their space and privacy better than the rooms in the three-story hotel (doubles $109–$139), which have more elaborate furnishings and decor, as well as balconies or terraces; some rooms have kitchenettes. The property also has a good restaurant, a bar, a spa, and a kids' club (daily 9am–2pm and 6–9pm; 2–6pm on request; $6 per hr.).

## DINING FOR ALL TASTES

**$–$$** Tucked beside the Super Chomak grocery is the best deal in town, whether for breakfast, lunch, or dinner. **Lonchería Akumalita** ★★ (near entrance arch; daily 7am–9pm; cash only) is just a funky outdoor counter wrapped around the kitchen. I never saw other vacationers there; instead, a steady stream of locals appreciates the consistently good Mexican and Yucatecan dishes. I loved the smooth, rich enchiladas mole and the sloppy *chilaquiles* (sauce-smothered tortilla chips topped with cheese and onions; $5). Breakfast starts at $3.50.

$–$$$$   Breakfast, served under the palms in an outdoor dining room, is where **Turtle Bay Cafe & Bakery** ★ (kids) (northeast corner of Plaza Ukana; ☎ 949/226-8082 U.S., or 984/875-9138; www.turtlebaycafe.com; daily 7am–3pm, Thurs–Sat 6–9pm low season, Mon–Sat 6–9pm high; MC, V) shines. The menu reads like a Mother's Day brunch, but with tasty Mexican twists such as eggs Florentine and goat cheese, made with *chaya* instead of spinach ($5.40) and steak and eggs using grilled *arrachera* beef ($9.50). Smoothies and fresh sticky buns or other baked goods will satisfy lighter appetites. The restaurant is on the northeast corner of Plaza Ukana, the shopping quadrangle that passes for a downtown. It's open for dinner only during the high season. Homemade fettuccini primavera ($9.50) is a tasty and frugal choice on a somewhat pricey menu of international meat and fish dishes. The short children's menu is just $3 to $4.

$–$$$$   Your first choice at **La Buena Vida** ★★ (Half Moon Bay beach, btw. Akumal and Yalku Lagoon; ☎ 984/875-9061; www.akumalinfo.com/restaurant.htm; daily 11am–1am; AE, MC, V) is whether to wiggle your bare toes in the sand at *palapa* tables, have your dinner in the upstairs dining room, or dine in a *mirador*, a lookout tower. The menu, emphasizing seafood, is varied and the fare excellent—especially the Maya chicken, *tikin xic* fish (marinated in *achiote* and sour orange, then grilled), and other regional specialties ($13–$16)—and the staff takes a personal interest in every diner. The two lookout towers claim the coast's best view of Half Moon Bay. Plus-size swings are your seats at the sand-floored bar, which serves its own unique cocktails as well as a barrage of special tequilas. *Note:* If you opt for a *mirador*, order a bottle of wine at the bar and take it with you up to your perch so you don't have to wait longer than you'd like for waiters to scale the ladder for refills.

$–$$$$   Northern Italian staples are served under a giant *palapa* or in the garden at **Que Onda** ★★ (Caleta Yalku; ☎ 984/875-9101; www.queondaakumal.com; Wed–Mon 7:30–11am, noon–4pm, and 5–10pm; MC, V). The Swiss-Italian couple who runs the hotel whip up fresh pasta and serve it with all kinds of sauces, from gorgonzola to curry shrimp to Thai chili, for $7 to $12. Different types of lasagna run $9 to $15. Just for variety, they also offer items like shrimp flambéed in cognac (a splurge at $20).

## WHY YOU'RE HERE: THE TOP SIGHTS & ATTRACTIONS

Akumal sits in the midst of one of nature's splashiest shows, with water in the starring role and geological formations playing an important supporting role.

The slow-curving crescent of **Akumal Bay** laps a wide swath of soft white sand where you'll hardly need a beach umbrella for all the shady coconut palms, the living legacy of a large coconut plantation that once operated here. Not only is the beach in the center of town a top contender for the title of the Riviera Maya's most ravishing beach, it's one of the few places where you can regularly see sea turtles without even trying. The water is a bit rocky on the bottom, and you need to watch for boat traffic when you're in the water. **Half Moon Bay,** to the north, is also good for swimming and snorkeling, but the beach is narrower and interrupted in places by rocky shore.

Snorkeling in **Laguna Yal-Kú** ★★★ (kids) ($7 adult, $4 child; daily 8am–5:30pm) is like nowhere else. Turtles, rays, barracudas, parrotfish, and a host of other interesting creatures revel in the dog-legged lagoon where underground river water streams up to meet the flow of the sea. The water is about 2 to 5m (6–15 ft.) deep, ensuring good views of the convoluted underwater landscape and making it a good spot for children and beginning snorkelers. Once a secret known only to devoted snorkelers, the lagoon is now a park (entrance fees fund conservation efforts) with a parking lot and a tour schedule, but it's still a refreshing and inexpensive alternative to the commercial bustle of Xel-Há (see below). Even when the seas get rough, the lagoon remains calm. Come before 10am or after 3pm to avoid crowds. Snorkeling gear ($10) and lockers ($2) are available for rent. The lagoon is at the northern end of Akumal, at the end of the road that leads from the highway into Akumal and winds north at the beach. If you don't have a car, take a taxi rather than trying to walk.

Guided tours of the **Atkun Chen** ★ (Hwy. 307, 4km/2½ miles south of Akumal turnoff; ☎ 998/892-0662; www.aktunchen.com; $24 adults, $13 children under 11; daily 9am–5pm, until 7pm Jun–Aug) cave system introduce you to a stunning underground world of dramatic stalactites and stalagmites that the Maya called "cave with an underground river." An informative 75-minute, 1km (½-mile) guided tour (in English and Spanish) leads to a giant domed chamber with sunlight seeping through a hole where a tree has grown through the roof, and a 12m-deep (40-ft.) cenote filled with crystal-clear water crossed by a wooden bridge. You'll get a brief nature walk through part of the park's nearly 405 hectares (1,000 acres) of forest and stop at a small zoo ruled by mischievous spider monkeys and other local fauna. Most area hotels offer trips here that include transportation; otherwise, look for the turnoff just across from Aventuras Akumal and continue about 3km (2 miles) to the entrance. Mosquito repellent and a bottle of water are recommended. The last tour starts at 4:30pm (6pm in summer). The website has 20% discount coupons.

## North of Akumal

Among a cluster of cenotes just off the highway north of Xpu-Há, **Ecopark Kantun Chi** ★ 🄺 (Hwy. 307, approx. 2km/1 mile south of Puerto Aventuras; ☎ 984/873-0021; www.kantunchi.com; $23 adults, $13 kids 12 and under; including cave tour $38 adults, $30 kids; daily 9am–5pm winter, until 6pm summer) is Maya owned and operated, and its simplicity is a peaceful alternative to the Riviera Maya's big, commercialized nature parks. Four of its cenotes, along light jungle trails, are open for swimming and snorkeling, including the strangely shaped Uchil Ha, which wraps around what was once the roof of the cavern. You can also kayak through an underground cavern formed by two connecting cenotes, see some small Maya ruins, and tour a botanical garden inhabited by strange and interesting creatures (*dzereque, tejón,* and *mapaches*). Note that the minimum age for cave tour is 8 years old.

The southernmost of these cenotes, **Cenote Azul** ($5; daily 9am–6pm), is the best known, probably because it's closest to the road (which may be why it's the priciest in the area). It has several large pools, a fun jump-off point on a section of overhanging rock, and a wooden lounging deck jutting over the water. Walkways along the edge make it easier to get in and swim with the abundant catfish. Sundays can be crowded and entrance is cut off when the area gets too full.

## Forest Sprites

Around cenotes and ancient Maya sites throughout the Yucatán, you may see or hear references to the *aluxes* (ah-*loo*-shehs). These mythical beings were small, humanlike creatures who remained hidden until nighttime, when they emerged to walk through the forests. The Maya believed that if they were treated well, the *aluxes* would take care of the forest's plants, protect the animals, and ward off illness and negative energy. They often included supplications to the *aluxes* in their ceremonies, asking the gods' permission to drink from or bathe in the cenotes that provided the Maya's only source of water.

## South of Akumal

There are no beach clubs or even restrooms, and therefore few visitors, on the soft white sands at **X'cacel** ★★ (6km/4 miles south of Akumal just beyond Chemuyil). That's part of what makes this quiet beach Mexico's most important nesting ground for endangered Atlantic green and loggerhead turtles. Rescued by ardent environmentalists from development plans in 1998, its deep powder sands, minimal outer reef, and lack of people are perfect for turtles. The only structure is a small thatched-roof building where ecologists monitor the turtle-nesting season from May to October. The guard at the gate might charge an entry fee (about $2), but collection has been sporadic. Once on the beach, you'll find a path to the south that leads into the jungle (about a 5-min. walk) to a freshwater cenote where you can swim and snorkel among tropical fish. When you go in spring or summer, be careful not to tramp on any mounds of sand—those are turtle nests—or disturb any turtles you might see laying their eggs.

After Xcaret (p. 144), **Xel-Há** (Hwy. 307, 16km/10 miles south of Akumal and 10km/6 miles north of Tulum; ☎ 984/875-6000; www.xelha.com; $75 adults, $50 children; daily 8:30am–6pm summer) is the busiest park in the Riviera Maya. Before it went to an all-inclusive price, it was an affordable opportunity to snorkel in a pristine natural aquarium made up of coves, inlets, and lagoons cut from the limestone shoreline. It was brimming with iridescent fish and a perfect introduction to snorkeling. Now it costs a family of four $250 just to walk in, and there are more people and fewer fish each year. Hidden Worlds and Cenote Dos Ojos are better options nearby. Laguna Yal-Kú, only a little farther afield, will yield ample rewards for the extra travel time.

The American-owned **Hidden Worlds Cenotes Park** ★★ 🄺🄸🄳🅂 (Hwy. 307, btw. Tulum and Akumal; ☎ 984/877-8535; www.hiddenworlds.com; $10–$90 depending on activities; daily 9am–5pm) can get pretty crowded, too, but you have a choice as to how much you want to spend, and it comes by its popularity with terrific tours and professional service. The park, which earned a measure of fame as the star of the 2002 IMAX film *Journey into Amazing Caves,* offers guided diving and snorkeling tours through some of the Yucatán's most spectacular cenotes, full of fantastic rock formations. Prices are all over the map, depending on what you want to do; unlimited access to all activities costs $90 ($60 for children under

12). Kids less than 1m (40 in.) tall get in free. In addition to snorkeling tours ($40 for 2½ hr., $25 for 1½ hr., including gear) and cavern diving ($50 for one tank, $90 for two), you can take a zipline over the jungle for $10 or the Skycycle (an inverted bicycle suspended over the jungle on a cable) for $75 (children $50). Book online to get $10 (sometimes more in summer) off the all-inclusive package or the Skycycle tour.

For something a little more low key, **Dos Ojos** (☎ 984/877-8535; $8; daily 8am–5pm) is a more modest operation just north of Hidden Worlds. Its guided tours ($30, including gear and underwater lights) lead through an underground cavern system—twin caverns (hence the name) with several cenotes.

## THE OTHER AKUMAL

The guardian of Akumal's turtle population is the **Centro Ecológico Akumal** ✰✰✰ (☎ 984/875-9095; www.ceakumal.org; $10; Mon 2–6pm, Tues–Fri 8am–2pm and 4–6pm, Sat 10am–2pm), a nonprofit scientific organization just past the Hotel Club Akumal Caribe on the road to Half Moon Bay. Akumal would be a charmed place if all it offered was an usually high chance of finding a sea turtle swimming alongside you in the bay, but during nesting season (May–July) you can witness a sight few tourists see. In the evenings, you can volunteer to join CEA workers who walk the beach in search of new turtle nests and help to protect the exhausted mothers as they make their way back to sea. You'll also help retrieve eggs from dangerous places and move them to hatcheries where they can incubate safely. From August to October, you'll usher the tiny hatchlings safely back down the beach to begin their lives in the sea. Think of it as a way of saying "thank you" to your finny swimming companions.

The turtle walks take place Monday through Friday at 9pm, and are limited to 10 people; sign up at the center during the day. You can stop by any time of year to see the free displays, join beach clean-up crews (Mon 7am), or attend presentations on ocean ecology.

## ACTIVE AKUMAL

Akumal is where scuba diving got its start on the Mexican Caribbean, and it still holds a special place in divers' and snorkelers' hearts. Its protected bays make reef diving easy and fun, while the abundance of cenotes make this one of the biggest areas for cavern diving.

### Scuba Diving & Snorkeling

Two-tank reef dives generally cost $60 to $70. Cenote dives cost $65 to $75, and night diving ranges from $45 to $65. PADI open-water certification courses, which may last from 3 to 5 days, run $420 to $485. The three major dive shops in town all have similar names, so be sure to check the location to make sure you've got the one you want.

After more than 30 years in business, the **Akumal Dive Shop** (☎ 984/875-9032; www.akumal.com) is practically a historic landmark. It's located in the center of town next to the Centro Ecológico Akumal. The shop offers 10 dive packages ($70–$290) and will customize packages combining a variety of activities. The **Akumal Dive Center** (☎ 984/875-9025; www.akumaldivecenter.com)

has been around almost as long and offers a similar lineup at comparable prices. It's between the Lol-Ha restaurant and the Hotel Akumal Caribe. Less famous but equally reputable is **Akumal Dive Adventures** (☎ 888/425-8625 toll-free U.S., or 984/875-9157; www.akumaldiveadventures.com) on Half Moon Bay, just north of La Buena Vida restaurant. This area is generally more affordable than central Akumal, and the shop's prices are slightly lower than the shops in town. All three shops also offer lodging/diving packages. Akumal Dive Adventures, for example, offers 3 nights at the Vista del Mar Hotel and four open-water reef dives for $290 per person ($260 in low season), saving 10% on accommodations and 15% off the dives.

The large, calm **Laguna Yal-Kú** (see above) at the north end of Half Moon Bay, with its unique mix of fresh- and saltwater ecosystems, is Akumal's top snorkeling spot. Snorkeling equipment rents for $14 for use only at the lagoon.

The shallow north end of **Akumal Bay,** which is out of the way of boat traffic and has a labyrinth of rocks and boulder coral teeming with tropical fish and plant life, offers good snorkeling from shore. Dive shops offer 1- to 3-hour guided snorkeling tours, depending on the number of sites visited. A typical 1½-hour tour costs between $18 and $25 and includes gear. For snorkeling on your own, dive shops rent gear for $10 to $12 a day or $50 a week.

## Sportfishing & Sailing

Although fishing is excellent year-round, April through July are the best months to catch sailfish, marlin, dorado, barracuda, yellow fin tuna, and many other prized species. All three dive shops offer fishing tours; a typical 2-hour outing for one to four people will cost about $90 to $115 per boat, and $30 to $55 for each additional hour.

**Akumal Dive Shop**'s popular 5-hour "Robinson Crusoe Cruise" sails a 36-foot catamaran up the coast to Playa X'cacel or Chemuyil (depending on weather conditions) for fishing, with time for swimming, snorkeling, sunbathing, and beachcombing, while the crew prepares a lunch of fresh fish and ceviche. Cost is $85 per person. The 2-hour "Sunset Cruise" ($40, including refreshments) dispenses with the fishing and focuses on the tropical sunset views from the bay.

# TULUM

In all the Maya world, reaching from Chiapas state in the north to Honduras in the south, Tulum is the only city the ancient Maya built directly on the ocean. It's not hard to imagine why the ancient Maya built their city on this 15m (50-ft.) bluff overlooking the aquamarine Caribbean waters. What's hard to imagine is why no one else did the same.

In discovering the most beautiful setting of any Maya site, tourists also discovered one of the Caribbean's most beautiful swaths of beach. A longtime backpacker haven, this beach is now Tulum's hotel zone, attracting an increasingly well-to-do crowd seeking respite from big resorts and packaged natural attractions. The collection of 30 or so solar-powered *palapa* hotels has become nearly as famous an attraction as the splendid ruins, but unassuming Tulum Pueblo, straddling the highway, offers its own modest pleasures (not the least of which is a supply of decent, inexpensive hotels with A/C).

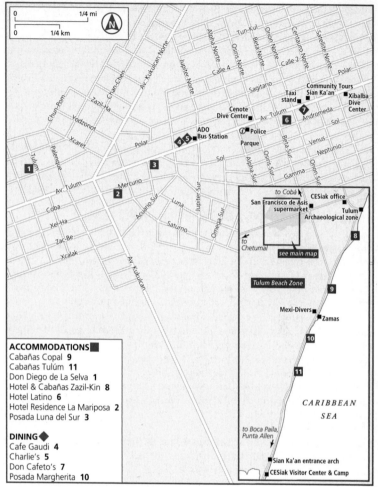

**ACCOMMODATIONS** ■
Cabañas Copal **9**
Cabañas Tulúm **11**
Don Diego de La Selva **1**
Hotel & Cabañas Zazil-Kin **8**
Hotel Latino **6**
Hotel Residence La Mariposa **2**
Posada Luna del Sur **3**

**DINING** ◆
Cafe Gaudi **4**
Charlie's **5**
Don Cafeto's **7**
Posada Margherita **10**

## GETTING TO & AROUND TULUM

Tulum is 130km (81 miles) south of Cancún. You pass the entrance to the ruins before reaching the traffic light in town; turn right at the intersection to get to the ruins of Cobá, to the left is the road to the beach hotels. Past the light, the highway widens and becomes Avenida Tulum, the pueblo's main street, crossed by streets with celestial names (Centauro, Orión, Osiris, Júpiter).

To get to the beach, turn left at the light, following the sign toward Boca Paila–Punta Allen. This access road dead-ends after about 3km (1¾ miles) at the beach road. To the left are some of the cheaper cabana hotels and, a little over a mile beyond, the back entrance to the ruins. Upscale hotels, mixed in with their more modest siblings, line the beach road to the right, becoming ever sparser before ending altogether at the Sian Ka'an Biosphere Reserve 7km (4½ miles) later. Most hotels' addresses mark their location on the Carreterra Tulum–Punta Allen (also called the Carretera Boca Paila), marked in kilometers from 1 to 7.

Renting a car is the best way to explore this area, but you can also cover much of it by bus. Buses make the 2-hour trip from Cancún ($5.40–$7.60, depending on class) roughly every half-hour around the clock, though more frequently in the middle of the day and less often from midnight to 7am. Departures from Playa del Carmen (1 hr., $2.20–$4.40) are even more frequent. From Tulum's bus station south of the town center, you're best off taking a taxi to the ruins ($2.50) or the hotel zone ($4–$5.50). *Colectivo* vans ($2) run every 10 to 15 minutes between Tulum and Playa del Carmen and will stop along the highway on the way. If you're day-tripping from Playa, though, be aware that catching a van back north might be a challenge, as they often fill up in Tulum Pueblo. Tulum's station also has buses to Cobá ($3.25), Valladolid ($6.50), and Chichén Itzá ($11).

## ACCOMMODATIONS, BOTH STANDARD & NOT

Beach cabanas are Tulum's hot thing—quite literally, since air-conditioning is almost nonexistent—but it's not the cheap hippie haven it used to be. When well-heeled travelers showed up looking for a piece of that relaxed beach vibe, they brought demands for clean floors and good food. Upscale eco-hotels with fine linens and massage services weren't far behind, pushing up prices of even humble huts with little more than four walls around a sand floor.

The unspoiled beaches are indeed beautiful enough to inspire dreams of never leaving, but after a couple of days it's frankly a relief to head to an air-conditioned hotel in town to cool off and sleep without sand in your sheets. In the pueblo, rustic lodgings charge rustic prices, and a growing number of attractive hotels make staying in town a more appealing option.

Rates given below are for low and high seasons; Christmas and New Year's week prices may jump by 10% or more over high season, especially at the beach.

### Beach Zone

**$-$$$$**    You have a choice at **Cabañas Copal** ★ (Carretera Tulum-Boca Paila Km 5; ☎ 888/898-9922 toll-free U.S./Canada, or 800/514-3066 toll-free Mexico; www.cabanascopal.com; cash only), which packs 47 cabanas into a small forest clearing. You can recapture the hippie hut experience in two sand-floor cabanas with thatch roofs, mosquito nets, and shared bathrooms for $30 a night low season, $35 high. Or you can go upscale via a larger cabana with king-size bed, cement or natural stone floors, and hand-carved furniture ($70–$110, depending on season, size, and location). Family quads with two queens cost $95 to $130. Seaview units get the ocean breezes and have wrap-around windows to take advantage; they are well worth the higher price. In all you'll have access to the hotel's wellness programs, exercise classes, and spa treatments. None of the cabanas have electricity, though bathrooms have plenty of hot water. The reception area and restaurant-bar runs on a small generator at night, and torch-lit pathways make a romantic sight. The hotel has one of Tulum's few clothing-optional beaches.

**$–$$$$**   The longtime backpacker favorite, **Hotel & Cabañas Zazil-Kin** 🧒
(Carretera Tulum-Boca Paila Km .47; ☎ 984/124-0082; www.hotelstulum.com/
zazilkin; cash only), the closest hotel to the ruins, has added an air-conditioned,
motel-type extension to its motley collection of rustic cabanas. A palm-roofed
cabana with cement floors, mosquito netting, simple furniture, and shared (but
quite clean) bathroom rents for $35 a night year-round. Cabanas with such "frills"
as multiple beds, private terraces, and cold-water bathrooms, however, seem over-
priced ($48–$72) for very basic accommodations. A generator provides electric-
ity 7pm to 6am. The new rooms are considerably more comfortable, with
louvered windows, hot water in the bathrooms, 24-hour electricity, and air-con-
ditioning from 7pm. At $121 low season and $132 high for a double, they aren't
cheap; electricity and cool air are precious commodities you don't usually find
here without paying well over $200 a night. The hotel is planted on the dunes of
one of Tulum's finest beaches and has a dive center on-site; its bar is a lively gath-
ering place for international travelers.

**$$**   You'll find the best price for a modicum of comfort at **Cabañas Tulum** ★★ 🧒
(Carretera Tulum-Punta Allen Km 7; ☎ 984/879-7395; www.hotelstulum.com; cash
only), a row of cement bungalows tucked between two luxury hotels. The simple
rooms are a notch above rustic, with two comfy double beds, a table, and one electric light (which works only during the hours that electricity is provided, 7–10am
and 6–10:30pm—bring your reading light). Small tiled bathrooms have hot, if salty,
water. Standard rooms have sea views and rent for $60 year-round; ocean-side
rooms ($70) open directly onto a beautiful stretch of quiet, palm-shaded beach. The
front desk rents hammocks ($4) to hang on your private patio. Housekeeping is
adequate, though not impeccable. The staff dotes on children, and the hotel has a
little play structure for kids who aren't too busy burying coconuts in the fine, white
sand. Ping-Pong, billiard tables, and other games are also available for guests' use.
The restaurant serves good, basic food, or you can indulge in fine dining at neighboring Ana y José or Los Lirios.

## Pueblo

**$–$$**   A block off of downtown Tulum's main drag, **Hotel Latino** ★★★ (Calle
Andromeda L-20, btw. Orión and Beta Sur; ☎ 984/871-2674; www.hotel-latino.
com; cash only; no children) is a little slice of Playa del Carmen, mixing minimalist with vaguely hacienda-style architecture. The whitewashed, air-conditioned
rooms are small but appealing, with designer linens, mood lighting, river-stone
showers, and small flat-screen TVs. There's no view or garden here, but the cool
blue pool has a pleasant lounge area. The rates are as soothing as the rooms: $50
to $70, depending on season, for one or two beds, including use of a bicycle. An
attractive dorm room can sleep six at $16 to $20 per person, and three upstairs
terrace suites rent for $70 to $90 in low season, $90 to $110 high. Check the website for specials, which occasionally offer great weekly rates.

**$$**   An intimate and nearly perfect B&B, **Posada Luna del Sur** ★★★ (Calle
Luna Sur 5; ☎ 984/871-2984; www.posadalunadelsur.com; cash only; no children
under 16) is ensconced in a two-story Mediterranean-style building ¹/₂-block off

Avenida Tulum. The stylishly decorated rooms rent for $58 a night in low season ($75 high), including a breakfast of fresh fruit, Mexican *pan dulce,* and fresh-ground coffee. All have efficient air-conditioning, sitting areas, good-quality linens, refrigerators, and 5-gallon jugs of purified water. Sliding glass doors open onto a peaceful garden (upstairs rooms have balconies). The innkeepers have earned legions of repeat guests with their unflagging personal attention. A night here will have you wondering why anyone would consider paying more than $100 a night for fewer comforts on the beach—which is less than 10 minutes away.

**$$–$$$**    At the southern end of town but within an easy walk of shops and restaurants, **Hotel Residence La Mariposa** ✸ (Calle Mercurio Poniente 23, btw. Kukulcán y Saturno Sur; ☎ 984/745-7583; AE, MC, V) is a homey place with solicitous, multilingual hosts and a variety of rooms, apartments, and suites. All are large and simply but cheerfully decorated, and upstairs units have large, shaded corridors furnished with tables and chairs. Double rooms cost $50 in low season, $80 high; suites with two double beds are $80 to $120. Spacious apartments with a king and a double sofa bed, full kitchen, dining area, and small back yard with a hammock (or a balcony in upstairs units) rent for $60 to $100. All have private baths, and most are air-conditioned.

**$$$**    With its huge *palapa* restaurant and jungle garden full of colorful flowers and fruit, **Don Diego de La Selva** ✸✸ (Calle Tulum, 1km/½-mile past ADO bus station; ☎ 984/114-9744; www.dtulum.com; MC, V) could have been lifted from the beach—except for the 24/7 electricity, immaculate rooms, and courtyard around a large, clear swimming pool. The gregarious French owners serve drinks and visit each night with guests, and the concierge dotes on guests like a loving nanny. The eight spacious, air-conditioned rooms ($85 a night) open onto garden patios with chairs and hammocks. Rooms have one king or two double beds with orthopedic mattresses, hot showers with skylights, thick towels, and simple, elegant furnishings. Two large bungalows ($75) come with queen-size beds and are cooled by ceiling fans. Room rates include a filling breakfast with fresh fruit and a different cake baked every morning. The excellent restaurant serves dinner every night but Wednesday. The hotel is down a dirt track at the south end of the pueblo, about a 5-minute walk to town and a $5 taxi ride to the beach.

## DINING FOR ALL TASTES

Most restaurants at the beach are in hotels that serve international cuisine. Many are good, but none are kind to the budget. Tulum Pueblo, whose restaurant scene has burgeoned in the past couple of years, is the place to go for Mexican food that hasn't been toned down, or priced up, for foreign taste buds.

**$**    **Café Gaudí** (Av. Tulum, btw. calles Alfa and Júpiter; daily 7am–10pm; cash only) is at its best in the morning, when its breakfast specials include fruit and yogurt, eggs cooked to order, and authentic Spanish tortillas ($3–$6). The cozy little cafe also serves strong coffee and espresso; Spanish sandwiches built with salami or roasted vegetables make a good, inexpensive lunch (up to $7).

**$–$$**    With its oversize *palapa* roof and famous broken-bottle wall murals, **Charlie's** ✸ (Av. Tulum, btw. calles Alfa and Júpiter; ☎ 984/871-2573; Tues–Sun

7:30am–11pm; MC, V) has all the earmarks of a tourist trap but is in fact a family-owned restaurant serving robustly seasoned Mexican fare, from classic fish tacos and *pollo con mole* to perfectly blended black-bean soup, all under $10. Grilled fish is $12, and that's as high as it goes. Past customers make a point of stopping in town just for Charlie's flan. During the high season, come on Saturday night, when local talent takes the stage with an unpredictable mix of music that might range from flamenco to Caribbean tribal music. The service is not as prompt as it is friendly, but what the heck—use the time to join the conga line for a spell.

**$–$$** The irregularly shaped and sized tortilla chips are a sure indication that you're getting real home-style cooking at **Don Cafeto's** (Av. Tulum, btw. calles Centauro and Orión; ☎ 984/871-2207; www.doncafeto.com; daily 7am–11pm; MC, V). One of Tulum's oldest restaurants, it serves traditional, and fearlessly spicy, Mexican staples (don't lick your lips after eating the salsa). Entrees such as mole, enchiladas, fajitas, grilled meat, and seafood platters range from $8 to $12. Most days, a guitarist or pianist provides background music.

**$–$$$$** Perhaps because of its popularity with Europeans, Tulum is awash in Italian food. The restaurant at **Posada Margherita** ★★ (Carretera Tulum–Punta Allen Km 4.5; ☎ 984/801-8493; daily 7am–10pm; cash only), owned by two men from Genoa, does it best. Fresh pasta and savory sauces are made every day with organic produce and served with fish, fresh vegetables, and homemade bread ($6–$20). It also has one of the coast's most extensive wine lists. You can watch the cooks work behind the counter on the deck, or step down to the upholstered sofas and chairs on the fine white sand. Hearty international breakfast standards ($5–$8) make a good start to the day.

## WHY YOU'RE HERE: TULUM ARCHAEOLOGICAL ZONE

One of Mexico's three most-visited archaeological sites (after Teotihuacán, near Mexico City, and Chichén Itzá, in Yucatán state) **Tulum** ★★ ($5, parking $3, video permit $4; daily 8am–5pm) is more famous for its beauty than for its architecture or historical significance. It certainly is the most scrubbed and manicured of Quintana Roo's archaeological sites. Archaeologists believe the city was occupied during the late Postclassic period (A.D. 1200–1521) at the convergence of land and maritime trade routes to Central America and the Aztec empire, and that it was an important link in a string of coastal forts, lookout towers, and ports built from Chetumal to Cancún.

Tulum, whose original name was Zama (Sunrise), was one of the few Maya cities still occupied when the Spanish arrived. Today's gray, weather-beaten stones give little clue to the sight that greeted Juan de Grijalva in 1518. Its buildings gleaming with red, blue, and yellow paint, and a ceremonial fire burning atop its main temple, Tulum appeared to him fully as grand and as beautiful as Seville. This was one of the last ancient cities to be abandoned, about 75 years later.

Visitors enter the site through a breach in the 5m (16-ft.) wall that surrounded the city on its three land sides (*tulum* means "wall" in the Mayan language). The walls protected the city during a period of strife between Maya city-states, though most of the population lived outside them. The civic and ceremonial buildings and palaces within—the ones we see today—most likely housed Tulum's ruling class.

The first major structure you come to is the two-story, colonnaded **Templo de los Frescoes (Temple of the Frescoes).** Faint traces of blue-green paintings—the main attraction before the temple was closed, hiding the clearest frescoes from view—depict the three worlds of the Maya and their major dieties in one of the most elaborate decorations found at Tulum. One amazing scene, painted later than the others, portrays the rain god Chaac astride a four-legged animal, clearly inspired by the Spaniards on their horses.

Tulum's tallest and most famous building, **El Castillo (The Castle),** rises at the edge of a 15m (50-ft.) limestone cliff just beyond the Temple of the Frescoes. The fortresslike pyramid likely served as a watchtower as well as a temple. Its broad stairway has been roped off to preserve the worn steps, so you can't see the temple at the top. Its Toltec-style columns depict the plumed serpent god Kukulcán, echoing those at Chichén Itzá.

To the left of the Castillo is the **Templo del Dios Descendente (Temple of the Descending God),** named for the relief above the narrow door showing a winged god diving to earth. It's one of Tulum's curiosities that this upside-down figure, believed to be the Maya god Itzamná, appears all over the city but rarely elsewhere in the Maya world. Experts can only speculate as to whether he represents the setting sun, or rain, or even bees, since honey was one of the Mayas' most important exports.

In the small cove to the north of the castle and the temple, Maya traders once came ashore in their canoes far below the city; today it is dotted with swimming and sunbathing tourists. If you plan to join them, wear your suit under your clothing, since the site has no changing rooms.

Tulum can easily be explored in 2 hours (unless you plan to swim or stroll on the beach). Tour buses start arriving around 9:30am, so get there when the site opens to miss the crowds. Late afternoon is the next best time. The entrance to the ruins is about 1km (½-mile) from the site entrance, where you buy your ticket among vendors' booths, a museum, a restaurant, and bathrooms. A shuttle from the visitor center costs another $2.50 (kids under 10 ride free). Informational signs are translated into English, but you can hire a licensed bilingual guide at a stand next to the path to the ruins for about $25. They will point out architectural details you might otherwise miss, but be skeptical about tales of virgin sacrifice or other outrageous stories—some of their delivery is more entertainment than history.

## ACTIVE TULUM

If you're staying in town, you're going to need to find a beach that isn't claimed by one of the beach hotels. The two easiest areas to reach are north of the junction of the highway access and beach road. One tack is to pay about $6 a day to use the beach chairs and umbrellas at **El Paraíso Beach Club** (Carretera Tulum-Boca Paila Km 1; ☎ 984/801-0315; www.elparaisotulum.com.mx), standing on the broad Playa Paraíso, between La Vita Bella restaurant and Cabañas Mar Caribe. You can also eat in the popular restaurant or take advantage of its snorkeling, diving, and kiteboarding services, or beachfront spa if you are so moved. If that's too busy for you, or you just object to paying, head to the next beach north, another broad, unspoiled patch of sand in front of the Mar Caribe.

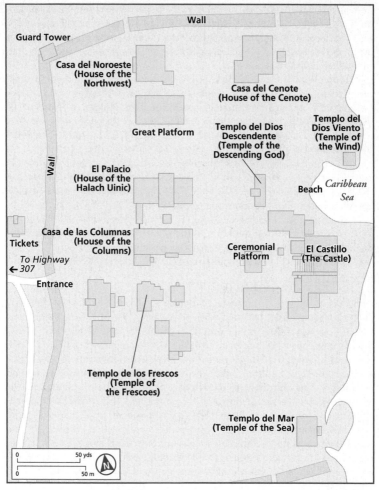

Tulum's finest beaches, boasting nearly empty white sands, are at the southern end of the hotel zone. That's also the province of the most exclusive hotels, which presents a challenge for nonguests. While hotels are allowed to restrict use of their chairs and umbrellas, the beach itself is public. Just south of the hotel zone's minivillage, near Cabañas Copal at Km 5, is a public beach. Though rocky and not very appealing, it abuts the beginning of the sublime southern beaches. Just walk down the shore and pick your spot.

## Diving & Snorkeling

Tulum's reef is as spectacular as any in the Riviera Maya, but the main attraction here is the abundance of nearby cenotes and caves. Divers with open-water certification may make "cavern" dives (no more than 9m/30 ft. deep or 40m/130 ft.

from an air pocket); full-cave diving requires special certification. Prices for cenote dives at Tulum's dive shops are generally $70 to $80 for one tank and $110 to $130 for two, including equipment, transportation, and entrance fees. Tulum's shops also offer multidive packages and full-cave certification courses, as well as reef diving and snorkeling.

**Hidden Worlds Cenotes Park** (p. 164), with its daily cavern diving and snorkeling trips, make the easiest introduction to cenotes. Otherwise, you can choose from an array of local dive shops. The **Cenote Dive Center** (Av. Tulum at Calle Osiris; ☎ 984/871-2232; www.cenotedive.com) is affiliated with the highly regarded Abyss Dive Center near the turnoff to the Tulum ruins. The **Xibalba Dive Center** (Av. Tulum, btw. Av. Satelite and the Cobá-to-Tulum beach road; ☎ 984/871-2953; www.xibalbadivecenter.com) specializes in cavern and cave diving and gets rave reviews from an international clientele. **Mexi-Divers** (Zamas Hotel, Carretera Tulum-Boca Paila Km 7; ☎ 998/185-9656; www.mexidivers.com) is a reliable shop known for outstanding service.

Snorkeling gear is widely available for rent, but the reef is far enough from shore to make a boat tour the better option. Operators have booths up and down the beach, and dive shops offer snorkeling as well. A 2½-hour ocean snorkeling tour should cost $20 to $30; cenote snorkeling tours average $20 to $30.

## SIDE TRIP TO COBA

Lying 64km (40 miles) northwest of Tulum, the Maya city of **Cobá** ★★★ ($4, children under 12 free; parking $1.50, video permit $4; daily 8am–5pm), sprawls over 174 sq. km (67 sq. miles) with 95% of the site still unexcavated. The least reconstructed of all Maya cities, its enormous crumbling temples swaddled in jungle growth present a dramatic contrast to the extensively restored buildings and wide-open setting of Tulum. Cobá's shady depths, particularly in the hush of early morning or late afternoon, are an effective time machine to the ancient Maya world. And travelers disappointed by the closing of Chichén Itzá's El Castillo to climbers will be happy to know they can ascend a pyramid here that tops El Castillo by 18m (60 ft.).

Though Cobá's mysterious beauty has begun to draw more visitors, its building clusters are spread out over a couple of miles, so it never feels crowded. You'll often have the hushed, shaded pathways to yourself, allowing for sightings of toucans, coatis, and spectacular tropical butterflies. Allow at least a couple of hours here; rent a bike at the entrance ($3) to cover more ground, or hire a *triciclo* (a three-wheeled Maya bike, from $10) to pedal you between sites.

Archaeologists believe Cobá, whose name means "water stirred by wind," was settled around A.D. 100, much earlier than Chichén Itzá or Tulum. It grew up around a cluster of five lakes—among the very few lakes in the Yucatán. The fresh water supply enabled the Maya to cultivate enough corn to feed themselves and have a surplus to market. Cobá became an important trade center and grew into one of the largest cities in the northern lowlands, with as many as 40,000 people. Cobá dominated lowland Maya culture from 400 until Chichén Itzá rose to power in the 9th century.

Most of Cobá's major structures were built between 500 and 800. Its architecture is a curiosity, showing influences both from the Petén region, typified by Guatemala's Tikal, and from coastal styles similar to those at Tulum. Its extensive

# Cobá

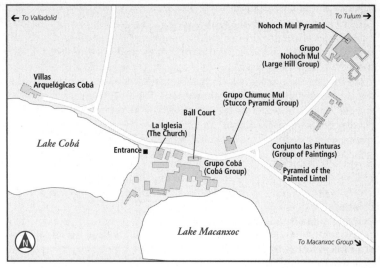

network of the raised limestone causeways known as *sacbeob* (plural of *sacbé*), built sometime between 600 and 800, are evidence of its expansion. At least 40 of these roads radiated out to other cities, including one reaching more than 96km (60 miles), the longest *sacbé* known in the Maya world.

The city's earliest surviving buildings are those in the **Grupo Cobá (Cobá Group),** to your right as you enter the ruins. Among the pyramids surrounding a sunken patio, the most impressive is **La Iglesia (The Church),** a 24m (79-ft.) high structure topped by a temple dedicated to the rain god, Chaac. Maya people still come with offerings to improve their harvests. Its steep rise from a low platform is clearly a version of the Petén style of architecture, bearing no resemblance to the long palaces and ornate facades of the nearby Puuc cities. It's tempting to climb La Iglesia, which is as tall as El Castillo at Chichén Itzá, but you might want to save your energy for even greater things to come.

Behind the pyramid is a restored ball court, that staple of Maya cities. Games were not a sport but a religious ceremony representing the Maya creation myth. Farther along the main path on your left is the **Grupo Chumuc Mul (Stucco Pyramid Group).** Little has been restored here, but you can make out the remnants of colorful stucco motifs on the main pyramid.

Continuing on the main path leads along the edge of Laguna Macanxoc, through jungle-covered pyramids and weathered stelae protected by thatched shelters, to a fork in the road. If you take the left fork, it's a 1km (½-mile) trek to the **Grupo Nohoch Mul (Large Hill Group),** home to the second-largest pyramid in the Yucatán (topped only by Calakmul's Structure 2). Its 120 steps, equivalent to 12 stories, has a rope running top to bottom to help you climb to the temple on top; even so, be prepared for sore muscles the next day. The temple's facade bears a decently preserved carving of the Descending God, also seen at Tulum. But the most compelling sight is the lofty view of vegetation-shrouded pyramids piercing the forest canopy for miles around.

## Keep Your Bearings

Cobá is spread out, with its main attractions as much as a kilometer (½-mile) apart. Main paths are labeled, and it's easy enough to keep track of where you are if you pay attention. Branching off from the labeled paths are numerous trails into the jungle, used by local people as shortcuts. These paths are tempting to birders, but it's easy to get turned around in the maze of dirt roads. If you can't resist plowing deeper into the jungle, be careful to remember your way back—drop breadcrumbs if you have to. Better yet, go with a local guide.

The right fork leads straight ahead to the **Conjunto Las Pinturas (Group of Paintings),** named for the multicolored friezes on the inner and outer walls of the **Pyramid of the Painted Lintel.** Climb the stairs to see traces of its original bright colors above the door. Another kilometer (½-mile) beyond the Las Pinturas group is the **Macanxoc Group,** with another pyramid accessible by a stairway and a collection of stelae bearing reliefs of royal woman thought to have come from Tikal.

The drive from Hwy. 307 at Tulum to Cobá, 64km (40 miles) inland, takes about 45 minutes. Close to the village of Cobá, you come to a triangle offering three choices. Be sure to follow the sign to Cobá and not Nuevo Xcan or Valladolid. The entrance to the ruins is a short way past a large lake and some small restaurants.

Buses run daily from Tulum's station to the Cobá ruins five times a day from 7am to 6pm and charge less than $4. A taxi from Tulum costs about $20. Guided tours, including transportation and lunch, are available through most hotels and travel agencies and average about $75.

## SIAN KA'AN BIOSPHERE RESERVE

Much about the Maya remains a mystery today, but once you pass through the entrance arch at the end of Tulum's hotel zone, there's no wondering why they named this land Sian Ka'an (Syan Ca-*an*), Mayan for "where the sky is born." Nowhere is sunrise more like witnessing the birth of a day than in this inexpressibly beautiful tract of wild landscape, the domain of howler monkeys, ocelots, crocodiles, eagles, tapirs, jaguars, sea turtles, hundreds of bird species, and miles of undisturbed beaches.

The Mexican government created the 526,000-hectare (1.3-million acre) **Reserva de la Biosfera Sian Ka'an (Sian Ka'an Biosphere Reserve)** in 1986. The following year, the United Nations declared it a World Heritage Site—an irreplaceable natural treasure. The reserve protects 10% of Quintana Roo's land from development; its 100km (62 miles) of coastline constitute almost one-third of Mexico's Caribbean shore.

As part of UNESCO's Man and the Biosphere Program, Sian Ka'an's challenge is to integrate human activity that won't threaten the more than 100 mammal species, 346 bird species, and thousands species of plants that flourish here. The reserve encompasses almost every ecosystem that exists in the Yucatán: medium and low-growth jungles, beaches, savannas, marshes, freshwater and brackish lagoons, cenotes, underground rivers, and virtually untouched coral reef. A unique canal system links 23 known archeological sites dating back 2,300 years.

More than 2,000 people, most of them Maya, live in Sian Ka'an. All are original residents of the area, or their descendants. Part of the long-term protection plan is enlisting residents in conservation and education efforts. When my family took a canal tour through the reserve, our guide was a young marine biologist who had grown up nearby on land his family had occupied for countless generations. He had no field guide, and no need for one. Everything he told us about the birds, the plants, the water, and the ruins had been part of his life since childhood.

## Getting There

To enter the park on your own, follow the beach road until you run out of hotels and reach a Maya-style arch (about 7km/4½ miles). You'll need to stop at the guard station on the other side and get a bracelet ($2). No trails lead into the jungle, so you'll be limited to swimming or snorkeling on the beaches. Guided tours are the only way to see the most of the reserve's sights. Otherwise, there is no good way visit Sian Ka'an except by car, and if you plan to go beyond the visitor center (several miles into the reserve) it had better be four-wheel drive. You can follow the narrow, rutted dirt road all the way down the narrow peninsula, which separates the Boca Paila Lagoon from the sea, to its end in Punta Allen. This small fishing village, which has adopted sustainable fishing practices with the help of CESiaK (Centro Ecológico Sian Ka'an), is where most Sian Ka'an residents live. It's only 60km (37 miles), but can be up to 3 bone-rattling hours, from the entrance. You'll pass several fishing lodges and go through the even smaller village of Boca Paila about halfway down the peninsula.

## Tours

When booking a tour to Sian Ka'an, be sure to ask about group size. Traipsing through the reserve in a group of 20 people or more can feel decidedly not eco-friendly and actually counter-productive for the biosphere (see "What Is a Biosphere Reserve?" below). The two organizations I've listed keep their groups small and work only through the local people.

Tours from the Centro Ecológico Sian Ka'an, or **CESiaK** (Hwy. 307 just south of Tulum ruins turnoff; ☎ 984/104-0522; www.cesiak.org) help to fund the non-profit conservation organization's education and community development programs (CESiaK also runs the Sian Ka'an Visitor Center). An all-day canal tour ($70 per person, including lunch), the most popular, begins with an orientation at the visitor center and a guided walk along coastal dunes and through the jungle, and continues with a boat trip across two brackish lagoons where a cold, fresh water from cenotes well up in places, creating the strange optical illusion of a black oil slick. The trip continues into a narrow channel leading through mangroves and grass savanna to a small temple where Maya traders stopped to make offerings and ask for successful negotiations. By the time the tour wraps up with a float in the currents of a freshwater lagoon and snorkeling in a cenote, you understand just how much Maya life was at the mercy of nature's whims.

Other choices include a sunset bird-watching tour ($70 per person) that visits nesting sites by boat and a guided bird-watching tour in kayaks ($45). You can rent kayaks ($20 single, $30 double for 3 hr.) and explore on your own, armed

# What Is a Biosphere Reserve?

"Biosphere" might conjure images of beleaguered, white-coated scientists locked in a dome in the Arizona desert, but Mexico's biosphere reserves are something else entirely. These redoubts of the world's last remaining natural habitats, along with their wild inhabitants, offer glimpses of some of the country's most exotic terrain and its resident whales, monkeys, big cats, and extravagantly plumed birds.

While Mexico's national parks (think volcanoes and Mayan ruins) focus on historical, scientific, or aesthetic virtues, ecology isn't always part of the equation. Internationally recognized biosphere reserves, though, are protected pockets of biological diversity designated by UNESCO (United Nations Educational, Scientific, and Cultural Organization). They must have at least 10,000 hectares (about 39 sq. miles), at least one pristine ecosystem, and threatened or endangered endemic species.

Mexico's first reserves were Mapimí, created in 1977 to preserve 20,000 hectares (50,000 acres) of Durango state's desert plains, home to North America's largest desert tortoise; and Monte Azules in Chiapas, a 335,000-hectare (828,000-acre) swatch of tropical vegetation teeming with quetzal birds, jaguars, tapirs, and toucans, designated in 1979. Creation of 18 new reserves in October 2006 brought Mexico's total to 34, surpassed only by the United States (with 47), the Russian Federation (38), and Spain (37). Almost a dozen, including Sian Ka'an, have special status with UNESCO's Man and the Biosphere Program, which links national and international research, conservation, and training.

Mexico pioneered a zoning system that allows some carefully managed tourism. The heart of a biosphere reserve is limited to scientific research, and this core area is surrounded by a buffer zone that allows only conservation-related activity. On the periphery, a transition zone permits sustainable use of natural resources to benefit local communities—such as the tours mentioned above. Unlike national parks, biosphere reserves allow original residents to remain while banning new population centers. Local people, in fact, are recruited to conduct research, monitor, and manage the flora and fauna while developing sustainable activities such as ecotourism.

with tips from a guide. Fishing, mountain biking, and archaeological tours can also be arranged; most tours include hotel pickup, lunch, and a bilingual guide.

**Community Tours Sian Ka'an** (Av. Tulum, btw. calles Centauro and Orión; ☎ 984/114-0750; www.siankaantours.org) is a cooperative of local Maya guides from the reserve who run similar conservation-minded tours at comparable prices, but their "Forest and Float" ($95 adult, $75 child) canal tours begin with a visit to the Muyil archaeological site south of Tulum and enters the reserve from that side. They also offer a 10-hour "Punta Allen Eco-Adventure" ($110 adult, $90 child) that combines wildlife viewing in a mangrove lagoon and snorkeling at the coral reef with a visit to the town at the end of the Boca Paila Peninsula and lunch. Like CESiaK, Community Tours Sian Ka'an plows all the proceeds from their tours right back into the communities that live in the reserve.

## Accommodation

If you want to be there to see that sunrise, you can stay in CESiaK's **Boca Paila Camps** ✖✖ (see above; MC, V) near the visitor center. The eco-lodge consists of tent cabins hidden at the edge of the jungle on a clean, white beach; doubles with a double and single bed rent for $70 ($100 over the year-end holidays), while deluxe cabins with one queen and ocean or lagoon views are $80 to $90 ($120 holidays). Meals are extra. They have no electricity, and guests share bathrooms with composting toilets, but wind and solar power provide hot water. While the staff doesn't seem very well organized—there were room mix-ups and confusion about which menu items actually were available during my visit—they are well informed about the area's plants, animals, and local culture. The reasonably priced restaurant turns out better meals than it has any right to in such a remote location. Tent cabins are on raised platforms to avoid interfering with the sand's natural processes; they can be quite cozy with their many screened windows zipped up or completely airy when open. The good linens and solid wood furniture make it feel less like camping, but when night falls and you're stumbling around by candlelight, it definitely feels rustic. The bathrooms are kept clean, though at night I wished they were just a little closer to the cabins. The bathroom building's view of the sea is so far-reaching that you can see the curvature of the earth.

# SOUTHERN FORAYS

The long roads and vast empty spaces of Quintana Roo's remote southern reaches require more time than most vacationers in the Riviera Maya have, but a couple of destinations are both within reach and worth making time for.

## LAGUNA BACALAR

An easy 2½-hour drive (217km/135 miles) from Tulum on Hwy. 307 takes you to the otherworldly, multihued Laguna Bacalar. Considered Mexico's second-largest lake, it's actually a lagoon, with a series of waterways leading eventually to the ocean. On a sunny day, you'll see why it's nicknamed Lago de los Siete Colores (Lake of the Seven Colors): The white sandy bottom makes the crystalline water pale turquoise in shallow areas, morphing to brilliant vivid turquoise and through a spectrum to deep indigo in the center. Colors shift with the passing of the day, making a mesmerizing backdrop for a day or two of exploring.

The lagoon, fed not by surface runoff but by underground cenotes, is almost 50km (31 miles) long. You'll glimpse the jewel-toned water long before you reach the town of Bacalar, about two-thirds of the way down, where you must go for swimming or kayaking. Get kayaks from your hotel or rent them from **Club de Vela Bacalar** (Av. Costera at Calle 20; ☎ 983/834-2478; $10 per hr.), and head for the wetland channels at the south end, where you can swim in the fast current of the small outlet called Río Chaak.

The swimming is just as good, or even better, in **Cenote Azul** ✖✖ (Hwy. Bacalar Km 15; ☎ 983/834-2038; free admission; daily 8am–6pm, until 8pm high season), about a mile south of town. Measuring 185m (607 ft.) across, this is

Mexico's biggest and deepest cenote, surrounded by lush flowers and trees, and filled with water so clear that you can see 60m (200 ft.) down into its nearly 92m (300-ft.) depth. Ladders provide easy access, and a rope stretched all the way across helps even weak swimmers to make it safely across. Its abundance of underwater caves attracts divers as well as swimmers and snorkelers. The town is nothing special, but you shouldn't miss the **Fuerte San Felipe Bacalar** (Av. 3 at Calle 29; $5; Tues–Thurs 9am–7pm, Fri–Sat 8am–8pm, Sun 9am–7pm), on the eastern edge of the central plaza. Built to protect the Spanish from the pirates and Maya rebels who regularly raided the area, it also houses the excellent Museo de la Piratería, devoted to regional history with a focus on the pirates who regularly attacked the shores. Bacalar also has some lovely inns dotting the lagoon's western shore that make ideal bases for exploration.

Bacalar is worth at least a night or two, and Chetumal's Museum of Maya Culture (see below) is less than 48km (30 miles) away. Skip the well-known but charmless Hotel Laguna Bacalar; instead, try **Casita Carolina** (Av. Costera, btw. calles 16 and 18; ☎ 983/834-2334; www.casitacarolina.com; cash only), with six units in a converted family home near the central plaza for $25 to $55, or **Amigos B&B Laguna Bacalar** (Av. Costera; ☎ 987/872-3868; www.bacalar.net; PayPal), with five rooms of various sizes and configurations overlooking the water about a mile south of the plaza for $50 to $60.

## CHETUMAL

Quintana Roo's state capital, 14km (9 miles) from the Belize border, is better known to travelers heading to or from Central America than to Riviera Maya vacationers. Rebuilt in modern concrete after being leveled by Hurricane Janet in 1955, Chetumal holds little appeal for tourists, with one huge exception: The **Museo de la Cultura Maya** ★★☆ (Av. de los Héroes, btw. avs. Mahatma Gandhi and Cristóbal Colón; ☎ 983/832-6838; $6; Tues–Thurs 9am–7pm, Fri–Sat 9am–8pm, Sun 9am–7pm), which qualifies as a genuine must-see.

This sophisticated museum is the best place in the Yucatán to sort out the Maya's intricate spiritual and temporal worlds, in a tasteful setting with marble floors and soft classical music. Exhibits are designed around three floors representing a *ceiba,* the sacred tree that symbolized earth's relationship to the cosmos. The upper level, devoted to the world of the gods, corresponds to the tree's leaves and branches, which held the 13 heavens. The middle floor is the tree trunk, the world of humans; the lower level is the tree's roots and the Maya underworld, or Xibalba.

The well-designed interactive exhibits (in English as well as Spanish) illuminate Maya architecture, class system, politics, and customs. Push a button and indigenous plants appear, with Mayan and scientific names and an illustration of how they were used; push another to see how different social classes dressed. Especially fascinating are the ancient notions of beauty that led people to deform their craniums and induce cross-eyed vision. Dramatic video screens fly you over the great Maya cities from Mexico to Honduras and show how the various pyramids probably were built before you walk on a glass floor over models of many of the sites.

A striking sculpture outside the museum's entrance takes on added meaning after you've viewed the museum. The *Alegoria del Mestizaje (Allegory of Mestizo/ Mixed Race)* symbolizes the joining of the Spanish and Maya cultures in a depiction of shipwrecked Spanish sailor Gonzalo Guerrero's union with his Maya wife and the birth of the first of Mexico's mestizo race.

Chetumal is 251km (156 miles) south of Tulum, about a 3-hour drive. I wouldn't stay here but in Bacalar, about 45km (28 miles) away. When Hwy. 307 ends at Hwy. 186, turn east and continue 20km (13 miles) to Chetumal. The road becomes Avenida Alvarado Obregón as you enter town; continue to Avenida de los Héroes and turn left; the museum is 5 blocks farther.

# Mérida

MÉRIDA, CAPITAL OF THE STATE OF YUCATAN, HAS BEEN THE PENINSULA'S leading city since the Spanish Conquest, and it should be a required stop for the legions of ruins-chasers tromping from pyramid to temple. La Ciudad Blanca ("The White City," named after its limestone buildings) is not just an extraordinarily beautiful city filled with gentle, dignified people, it is the coda to the story of a lost civilization that wasn't lost after all. Mérida is the place where the Maya civilization's glorious past and vital future come together.

A busy city of one million people, Mérida is not without its urban frustrations, traffic and noise primary among them. It is 466 years old, and gritty in parts. But the city's historic heart has a calm, small-town geniality. That, combined with its dazzling colonial architecture, parks and plazas at every turn, and cobblestone streets (which make walking not only a pleasure but the most efficient mode of transportation in that part of town), make it one of the most comfortable cities to settle in to and get to know.

Treated for too long as a hub in which to arrive, grab a rental car or a bus schedule, and depart for more famous destinations, Mérida has experienced a rush of expat investment in the past decade (the city's unusual bounty of bed-and-breakfasts is almost entirely foreign owned). Prices have been creeping up, but it's still a budget traveler's dream, in the very center of some of the most culture-rich landscape in Mexico.

Méridians know how to have fun, and it's impossible for visitors not to get pulled in. The best part: The nonstop festivities are not manufactured for visitors' entertainment. They are Méridians' own celebrations, reflecting their heritage and determination to keep it alive. When you're in Mérida, you're a part of Mérida.

## DON'T LEAVE MERIDA WITHOUT . . .

**KICKING UP YOUR HEELS**   Every night of the week, the city sponsors free concerts, dances, and fiestas that keep traditional Yucatecan culture a vital part of Mérida's contemporary life. Whether they are mamboing to a Cuban big band, sighing to a romantic *trova,* or clapping along with *vaquero* dancers, Méridians are happy to have you join them—and you'll be happy, too. See "Una Semana Yucateca" on p. 203.

**GOING TO A HOUSEWARMING**   The Museo de la Ciudad recently moved into palatial quarters in the beautiful and painstakingly renovated Post Office building. When you visit the museum in its new home, you'll have elegant architectural details and perfectly preserved tile floors to ogle along with an expanded array of items from Mérida's past and present. See p. 197.

**BEDDING & BREAKFASTING**   Mérida is bursting with B&Bs that occupy graceful colonial buildings of all shapes and sizes. Whether they are simple spruced-up family homes, formal showplaces or thoroughly renovated experiments in modern design, they come with hosts who take you under their wing and give you an entree to the best of Mérida. See "Bed & Breakfasts" on p. 190.

**GETTING YOUR HANDS DIRTY**   Sotuta de Peón isn't just a restored hacienda; it's an entire *henequén* (sisal) plantation and processing plant that produces 10 to 15 tons a month of the "green gold" that made Mérida fabulously wealthy a century ago. You can witness the whole procedure and try your hand at combing the fiber and spinning it into twine—then cool off after your labors in an underground cenote. See p. 199.

**FEELING THE CHILL**   Local muralist Fernando Castro Pacheco's boldly colored, aggressively modernist murals are the best reason to visit the Palacio de Gobierno. The larger-than-life images depicting the bloody conquest of the Yucatán from the losing side's point of view will stay with you. See p. 196.

**TIME TRAVELING**   In the Palacio Cantón, perhaps Mérida's most sumptuous colonial mansion, the fine Museo Regional de Antropología exhibits the ancient Maya's limestone jaguars, deformed skulls, and sacrificial offerings, surrounded by European Beaux Arts architectural flourishes. See p. 198.

# A BRIEF HISTORY

After Columbus first encountered the Maya off the coast of Honduras in 1502, the Spanish officially "discovered" Mexico when Fernando Hernández de Córdoba landed to fierce resistance on Yucatán's shores in 1517. Two years later, Cortés landed on Cozumel and busied himself conquering the Aztecs while one of his captains, Francisco de Montejo, set about subjugating the Maya. After 20 years of bitter struggle, Montejo passed the bloody chore on to his son of the same name.

Montejo the Younger founded Mérida in 1542 at the holy Maya city of T'ho, dismantling its five white temples and using the stones to build churches, cathedrals, and even his family home. Despite a bloody 5-month rebellion beginning on November 8, 1546, the Spanish prevailed. But the Yucatán remained a colonial backwater; Spanish control was tenuous and sporadic warfare continued for centuries.

Commercial production of *henequén,* the thorny agave that yields a natural rope fiber called sisal, began in 1830. Despite the interruption of the Caste Wars (p. 211), demand soared, becoming almost insatiable during World War I. With a virtual monopoly on the "green gold," Yucatán went from one of Mexico's poorest states to one of its richest, though the wealth went mostly to families who had received land grants generations before. *Henequén* is still produced commercially, but it became far less profitable after World War II, when nylon became the rope material of choice.

At the peak of its wealth, Mérida's plantation owners built baronial homes, paved its streets, and installed electric street lights, long before Mexico City had them. They traveled to Europe rather than Mexico City, sent their children to

European schools, and imported European fashions, Italian tile, Carrara marble and, especially, architects. Lebanese merchants poured into the Yucatán to get in on the boom, adding another cultural layer.

Not until the 1930s, when Quintana Roo finally made peace with the government, did the Maya begin to become a part of Mexico. Most still see themselves as Yucatecans first, Mexicans second. As in the rest of Mexico, most Yucatecans are mestizos, of mixed Spanish and Maya blood. But a large percentage is Maya, descended from the rich, complex society that built the temples and pyramids travelers flock to today.

Today, though the *henequén* trade is all but dead, Mérida remains elegant, prosperous, and sophisticated. The streets are filled with a vibrant mix of Maya, mestizos, Lebanese, and more recent transplants from Mexico City and abroad, all drawn by the city's mellow yet cosmopolitan feel.

## LAY OF THE LAND

Downtown Mérida is laid out on the grid system typical in the Yucatán. Even-numbered streets run north and south, with the low numbers starting on the east side of town and increasing as you go west. Odd-numbered streets run east to west, ascending from north to south. Most streets are one-way. The central square, variously called **Plaza Grande,** Plaza Principal, or Plaza Mayor—and sometimes simply El Centro—is between calles 61 and 63 to the north and south, calles 60 and 62 to the east and west.

**Calle 60,** which runs in front of the cathedral, connects the plaza with several smaller plazas and has the city's greatest concentration of handicraft shops, restaurants, and hotels. The large, busy public market, **Mercado Lucas de Gálvez,** is 4 blocks southeast of the plaza at calles 65 and 56, surrounded by several blocks of smaller markets and commercial activity.

Mérida's broad, tree-lined **Paseo de Montejo,** modeled after Paris' Champs d'Elysées and known for its grand, European-style mansions, starts 6 blocks north of Plaza Grande, at Calle 49, and runs north between calles 56 and 58.

Calle 60 and Paseo de Montejo both lead north to meet Hwy. 261, the road to Puerto Progreso on the Gulf coast. Other major streets leading out of town are Avenida Itzáes (best reached from downtown by driving east on Calle 65), running south to the airport and Hwy. 180's southward route to Campeche as well as Hwy. 261 to Uxmal; and Calle 59, which leads to Hwy. 180 east to Chichén

## The Numbers Game

Address numbers in Mérida don't follow any logical sequence; no. 564 might be next door to no. 872, and no. 736 a block or two away. Fortunately, addresses are usually given with the cross streets, often leaving out the building number altogether. What you'll usually see is "Calle 70 no. 549 X 69 y 71," which means Calle 70 no. 549, between Calle 69 and Calle 71. Streets are not so neatly organized outside of downtown, so make sure you get the name of the neighborhood where you want to go, and take a taxi.

Itzá and Cancún (follow the signs, which will direct you back to Calle 65—the street you came in on if you arrived from Cancún). A beltway called the *periférico* circles the city, with exits into different city neighborhoods and to highways leading out of town.

# GETTING TO & AROUND MERIDA

## BY AIR

Most major U.S. airlines, as well as **Mexicana** (☎ 800/531-7921 toll-free U.S., or 800/502-2000; www.mexicana.com) and **Aeromexico** (☎ 800/237-6639 toll-free U.S., or 800/021-4000; www.aeromexico.com) fly from U.S. destinations to Mérida. Mexicana's fares are usually among the lowest. Flying to Mérida costs anywhere from $5 to $140 more than flying to Cancún. If your travel plans include both cities, it makes sense to fly into Cancún and drive or bus to Mérida, but for vacations focusing on Mérida and Yucatán state, the $30 highway toll and 4-hour drive (or the bus fare) from Cancún usually cancel out the savings.

Most international flights require at least one connection. **Continental** (☎ 800/523-3273 toll-free U.S., 999/927-9277 Mérida; www.continental.com) has nonstop flights from Houston costing about $20 to $135 more than the least expensive connecting flight. Aeromexico flies nonstop from Miami and charges even higher premium (and I've never met anyone who has flown the airline without encountering multiple problems).

If you are headed to Mérida from somewhere else in Mexico, or you can get a low fare to one of their hub cities, Mexico's relatively new contingent of discount airlines presents another avenue to explore (for more details, see p. 272).

### Getting to & from the Airport

Mérida's small, modern **Manuel Crecencio Rejón Airport** (Carretera Mérida-Uman Km 4.5; ☎ 999/946-1372; www.asur.com.mx) is on the outskirts of town about 13km (8 miles) southwest of the city center. Buy a ticket at the transport desk outside the airport doors for an authorized taxi, costing about $17 for up four people and taking 20 to 30 minutes. Vans for up to seven people are available for about $24. The public bus that serves the airport, no. 79 ("Aviación"), costs only about 50¢ but is difficult to negotiate with luggage, and the stop is a long walk from the terminal.

If you rented a car (see "By Car," below), airport signs will direct you to Avenida Itzáes. Turn right (north) and follow Itzáes to Calle 59; turn right to get to the center of town.

## BY CAR

If you drive to Mérida from Cancún, you have two choices, and both of them are Hwy. 180. The old *carretera federal* (federal highway), or Hwy. 180 *libre* (free) is narrow but well maintained. This is definitely the scenic route, requiring you to slow down for so many villages that the trip takes 6 hours. The four-lane divided Hwy. 180 *cuota*, or *autopista*, is a toll road extending to Kantunil, 56km (35 miles) east of Mérida. You'll pay $30 and endure some monotony, but you'll avoid 43 villages and 83 *topes* (speed bumps on steroids), cutting the trip to 4 hours or less.

Hwy. 180 enters Mérida from the east on Calle 27, which soon feeds into Calle 65, a major downtown street that passes 1 block south of the Plaza Grande. From the south (Campeche or Uxmal), you'll enter the city on Avenida Itzáes; turn right on Calle 59 (the first street after the zoo) to get to the town center. The *periférico*, or beltway, makes it possible to avoid city traffic if you're going to other neighborhoods or to highways radiating in different directions to surrounding towns, but you need to keep a sharp eye on the proliferation of signs.

## BY BUS

Mérida is the Yucatán's transportation hub, and it has a profusion of bus stations. If you come by long-distance bus, you will most likely arrive at the main first-class station, **Terminal CAME** (Calle 70, btw. calles 69 and 71; ☎ 999/924-8391; www. ticketbus.com.mx). The ADO bus line and its luxury affiliates, ADO GL and UNO, operate out of this station, along with long-distance lines from other parts of Mexico. ADO GL is only slightly better than first class, but UNO has extra-wide seats that can make a long trip more tolerable; otherwise, departure times are usually more important than the difference in buses.

Around the corner from the first-class CAME station is the main second-class station, **Terminal Segunda Clase** (Calle 69, btw. calles 68 and 70; ☎ 999/923-2287), with ATS, TPR, Oriente, and Del Mayab lines. The **Terminal Noroeste** (Calle 50, btw. calles 65 and 67; ☎ 999/924-7868) is another second-class station, used by the Occidente and Oriente lines.

Bus stations are far enough from the city center that you'll probably want to take a taxi (about $3–$5) to your hotel.

## GETTING AROUND

Big as Mérida is, most of what you'll want to see and do is within walking distance of the Plaza Grande—and you'll move faster than the traffic creeping along the city streets, especially in market areas. You can easily spend a week in Mérida with only an occasional taxi or bus ride. You're actually better off without a car in the city; driving is no fun, and if your hotel doesn't provide free parking, you'll need to find a space on city streets or resort to the *estacionamentos* (parking garages), which charge double if you leave your car overnight. Here's the dilemma: Driving is by far the best way to explore the surrounding villages, ruins, and haciendas that you'll probably want to see (see chapter 6). A reasonable compromise is to group your day trips and rent a car for just a couple of days.

### By Car

Rental cars cost a little less in Mérida than in Cancún, but more than in the United States, once you add taxes, fees, and Mexico's mandatory insurance (see "Getting Around the Yucatán: By Car" on p. 274). All the major international companies have desks at the airport and either downtown (many on Calle 60, btw. calles 57 and 55) or in the hotels on Paseo de Montejo. Reserving before you leave the United States generally produces the best rates; expect to pay $50 to $75 a day by the time you add in tax and insurance. (Major booking engines such as Orbitz or Travelocity display rates including taxes and fees, but not insurance, which can double or triple the initial rate).

## First-Class Bus Service to & from Mérida's CAME Station

| From Mérida to: | Fare | Duration | Lines & Frequency |
| --- | --- | --- | --- |
| Campeche | $12–$15 | 2½–3 hr. | ADO, ADO GL; about every half-hour |
| Cancún | $20–$38 | 4–4½ hr. | ADO, ADO GL, UNO, MTS; about every half-hour |
| Chetumal | $26 | 5½ hr. | ADO; 5 from 7:30am–11:30pm |
| Chichén Itzá | $9 | 1¾ hr. | ADO; 6:30 and 9:15am, 12:40pm |
| Mexico City | $97–$115 | 19–21 hr. | ADO, ADO GL; 7 from 10am–9:15pm |
| Palenque | $33 | 7½–8 hr. | ADO, OCC; 4 from 8:30am–11:55pm |
| Playa del Carmen | $28–$33 | 4½–5½ hr. | ADO, ADO GL; 17 from 2:15am–midnight |
| Tulum | $19 | 4–4½ hr. | ADO; 5 from 6:30am–11:30pm |
| Villahermosa | $37–$46 | 7½–9 hr. | ADO, ADO GL, UNO; about every hour |

Second-class buses serving these destinations cost about 25% less and make local stops, so trip times are longer. Second-class buses also go to and from Celestún ($4, 2 hr.), Felipe Carrillo Puerto ($15–$28, 5½–6 hr.); Izamal ($2.50, 1½ hr.) Mayapán ($2.50, 1½ hr.), Progreso ($2, 1 hr.), Río Lagartos ($7–$9, 3–4 hr.), Ticul ($4.50–$5.50, 1¾ hr.), Tizimín ($8–$10, 2½–4 hr.), and Valladolid ($9–$13, 2½–3 hr.).

Mérida is full of local rental companies that often beat the international chains' prices, especially in low season. Walk-ins get the best deals; many have special promotions or discounts for paying cash, and their rates usually include at least basic insurance, which are reasonable compensations for not having a reservation when you land. In low season you might be able to get a car for as little as $35 or $40. Two recommended companies are **Mexico Rent A Car** (Calle 57A no. 491, btw. calles 58 and 60; ☎ 999/923-3637; mexicorentacar@hotmail.com) and **Kimbila Car Rental** (Paseo Montejo 486, btw. calles 41 and 49; ☎ 999/923-9316; www.kimbila.com).

## By Bus

Mérida's bus system is convoluted and tricky to figure out, and you won't often be tempted to use it. One exception is getting from the Plaza Grande to Paseo de Montejo, which is a bit of a hike on a hot day. Most buses heading north on Calle 60 will get you within a couple of blocks of Montejo. You can flag them down at any corner; fares are posted on the doors. Bus 52, Norte, Ruta 2, which departs from Calle 59 between calles 58 and 56, will take you to all the points of interest on Paseo de Montejo.

Mérida's many second-class buses serve all the surrounding towns of interest (see chapter 6). In addition to the major stations, the **AutoProgreso Terminal** (Calle 62 no. 524, btw. calles 65 and 67; ☎ 999/928-3965), has buses to Progreso and Dzibilchaltún. Buses to Celestún and other villages east of Mérida operate out of a small station on Calle 71 between calles 64 and 66, and you can catch buses to Izamal at the station on the corner of calles 69 and 68.

*Colectivos,* also called *combis,* are a bit more expensive than regular buses—about $3 or $4 for towns about 48km (30 miles) away—but much faster. The white minivans can usually be found lined up along the side streets, or you can go to the Sitio de Combis at Parque San de Juan on Calle 69 at Calle 64. Traveling by *colectivo* is a lot easier if you speak a little Spanish.

### By Taxi

Mérida is crawling with taxis. The regular taxis have fixed rates, with a minimum fare of $3. That should get you anywhere within downtown, and a ride to the city's outskirts shouldn't be more than $8. Most hotels have a list of fares. These taxis are usually white, and you can hail them all around town or from *sitios* (stands) at Parque Hidalgo (Calle 60 at Calle 59, a block from the plaza), Parque de San Juan, and other locations. Call **Taxi Sitio 14** (☎ 999/924-5918) for a pickup. As always, agree on the price before you get in.

A newer fleet of metered taxis, usually painted in bright colors, has been roving Mérida's streets for several years now—look for a TAXI METRO or RADIO TAXI sign. Their rates are usually lower than the regular taxis, but watch to be sure the driver starts the meter at zero. You can flag these down in the street or call **TaxiMetro** (☎ 999/928-3030, 924-5427, or 168-0510).

# ACCOMMODATIONS, BOTH STANDARD & NOT

Mérida, more than most cities, is kind to the budget. Though winter is the most popular time to visit, tourism fluctuates less here than in the resort cities and many hotels charge the same rates year-round. Most of the rest stick to one high and one low season, though exceptions can be found, especially for Christmas and New Year's weeks. Most hotels offer at least a few air-conditioned rooms, and some have swimming pools. Some offer free parking, and those that don't have arrangements with nearby garages, usually with a discounted fee.

**Best Day Travel** (www.bestday.com) has the best air/hotel packages to Mérida and is the only one that has a selection of smaller, less expensive downtown hotels. Unfortunately, the prices are about the same as booking airfare and hotels separately. The number of bed-and-breakfast inns in Mérida is unusual for the Yucatán, reflecting the growing number of expats moving to the city and buying handsome colonial buildings for renovation. The same phenomenon has produced a small but growing supply of vacation rental homes.

## VACATION RENTALS

The supply of vacation rentals in Mérida is relatively small but exceptionally attractive and affordable, and is certain to grow. These are mostly colonial renovations that have preserved the architectural detail but added all the comforts you would find in a hotel. The interiors are quite tastefully updated with good-quality but simple furniture that blends well with the colonial architecture and makes good use of the sometimes quirky spaces.

One-bedroom houses are in shortest supply but start at $450 to $700 a week, going up to about $800 in high season, when you can find them. Don't worry if you can't, because two-bedroom houses start at $500 a week ($800 in high season). Three and four bedrooms will cost from $1,000 to $2,500 in low season,

# Where to Stay & Dine in Mérida

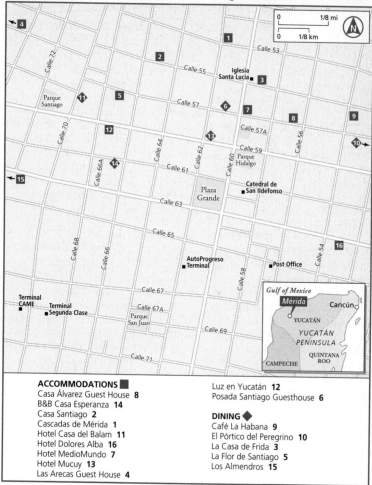

**ACCOMMODATIONS**
Casa Álvarez Guest House **8**
B&B Casa Esperanza **14**
Casa Santiago **2**
Cascadas de Mérida **1**
Hotel Casa del Balam **11**
Hotel Dolores Alba **16**
Hotel MedioMundo **7**
Hotel Mucuy **13**
Las Arecas Guest House **4**

Luz en Yucatán **12**
Posada Santiago Guesthouse **6**

**DINING**
Café La Habana **9**
El Pórtico del Peregrino **10**
La Casa de Frida **3**
La Flor de Santiago **5**
Los Almendros **15**

$1,100 to $3,000 high. The greatest concentration appears in the Santa Ana and Santiago neighborhoods, both within walking distance of the Plaza Grande but removed enough to be peaceful.

The excellent **Yucatán Living** (www.yucatanliving.com), produced by a former California couple for other expats in Mérida, provides rental listings on its website. So does the old standby, **Vacation Rentals** (www.vacationrentals.com), but I prefer Yucatán Living because they are personally familiar with the properties they list, and they have a track record of reliable information and responsiveness to questions. Neither of these sites acts as agents; you'll be directed to the owners to make a transaction. Some homes appear on both sites, but each has properties the other doesn't.

# BED & BREAKFASTS

$   Home away from home is no cliché at **Las Arecas Guest House** ✪✪ (Calle 59 no. 541, btw. calles 66 and 68; ☎ 999/928-3626; www.lasarecas.com; cash only). Owner Mauro Ruiz, who was born here on the kitchen table, spruced up the family homestead to create this modest B&B, which he runs with help from a day manager and his son. Each of the five simple rooms has its own style, but they share the typical Yucatecan tile *mosaico* floors and brightly painted walls and doors. Some rooms have kitchenettes; one has a private garden; another has a rooftop view. Decor is far from fancy and includes some random '50s-era furniture and '60s-style lava lamps, but bathrooms have new tile, everything works, and all is immaculate. The two least expensive rooms ($31–$33) have no air-conditioning; the others range from $36 to $46 a night. A light breakfast is served in the tropical inner courtyard in the mornings. This is one of the few B&Bs run by Yucatecans, and getting the real scoop on Mérida, past and present, is a treat. The location, 3 blocks from the plaza, couldn't be better.

$$   **Casa Santiago** ✪✪✪ (Calle 63 no. 562, btw. calles 70 and 72; ☎ 314/266-0378 U.S., or 999/928-9418; www.mexicanbedandbreakfast.com; PayPal), one of Mérida's new kids on the block, is a real pleasure. With a long, open common area running through the middle of the house and the owners, Vince and Frank, living in their own house next door, it offers an ideal blend of comfort and privacy, traditional detail and modern style. Vince, the innkeeper most in evidence, is a burly, gregarious sort who gives reliable advice and often accompanies guests on day trips and even errands. Each of the four rooms ($59) is different; go for the one with private patio enclosed by unrestored stone walls. All have the original *mosaico* tile floors (made in Mérida for centuries with a technology brought over from Spain) and some of the most comfortable mattresses in Mexico or anywhere else. The inn is in the Parque Santiago neighborhood, 5 easy blocks from the plaza. A hearty breakfast is laid out each morning in the big central dining room, but guests can also use the modern house kitchen. The garden has a small pool and several distinct lounging areas.

$$   The riot of purple, pink, and pumpkin-colored walls give the **Posada Santiago Guesthouse** (Calle 57 no. 552, btw. calles 66 and 68; ☎ 999/928-4258; www.posadasantiagomx.com; PayPal) a bright, contemporary look, but it's actually a thoroughly renovated 19th-century colonial built around a courtyard dominated by a spotless pool. Colors are toned down a bit in the four guest rooms, each of which has great beds, spick-and-span kitchenettes, flat-screen cable TV, and new tiled bathrooms. Breakfast is just toast and fruit, so you might want to make use of your kitchenette. Most rooms have queen, double, or twin beds and rent for $75; a single is available for $65. It's also in the quiet Parque Santiago neighborhood. The congenial bilingual host is also available for hire for trips to nearby ruins, the Celestún flamingo reserve, or beaches.

$$–$$$   **B&B Casa Esperanza** ✪✪✪ (Calle 54 no. 476, btw. calles 55 and 57; ☎ 999/923-4711 or 155-6049; www.casaesperanza.com; AE, MC, V for advance online deposits; cash only on-site), is as romantic as can be, built by the architect who designed the mansion that now houses the city's Anthropology Museum. The French-inspired colonial residence has 5m (18-ft.) ceilings, columns, arches,

hand-painted tiles, and the original stained-glass windows; unique art and antiques fill the house. The three spacious rooms, $75 to $95, have private entrances and are painted in floral pastels that echo the extravagantly landscaped gardens with several peaceful patios, fountains, and a large, sparkling pool. The innkeepers have mastered the art of being available when you need them and making themselves scarce the rest of the time. Their famous breakfasts, made with ingredients fresh from the market and garden, will fuel the entire day.

$$$   The *cascadas* (waterfalls) at **Cascadas de Mérida** ★★☆ (Calle 57 no. 593C, btw. calles 74A and 76; ☎ 305/978-5855 U.S., or 999/923-8484; www.cascadas demerida.com; PayPal) don't stop at the waterfall spilling into the pool but include individual waterfalls in each shower and a channel under glass running beneath the nightstands. The quirky and delightful inn is the creation of Ellyne and Chucho Basto, a teacher from New York and a carpenter from Mérida. Chucho's ingenious design for transforming his ancestral home uses recycled native stone, and decor includes Mexican hand-crafted furniture. The four free-standing rooms ($83–$96, depending on season), set around a pool and garden, are deliciously private; the owners are friendly and talkative but know when to leave you alone. Breakfast is fresh fruit, coconut yogurt, and an egg dish that changes daily.

## HOTELS

$   The longtime budget standby, family-operated **Hotel Mucuy** (Calle 57 no. 481, btw. calles 56 and 58; ☎ 999/928-5193; www.mucuy.com; cash only), still charges just $24 for a double with ceiling fan and $29 with A/C. One-and-a-half blocks from busy Calle 60, the hotel has a pleasant courtyard bursting with flowers and a small pool. The clean rooms, which have shared balconies and desks, have simple but beautiful wooden furniture and iron headboards that give them some colonial atmosphere. Most have two twin beds or a queen, with good mattresses. Bathrooms are a bit dated, with well-used green porcelain and tile, but in good shape. The staff doesn't speak a lot of English but are friendly and kind.

$–$$   Many guests come to **Casa Alvarez Guest House** ★★★ kids (Calle 62 no. 448 at Calle 53; ☎ 999/924-3060; www.casaalvarezguesthouse.com; cash only), 4 blocks from the plaza, for extended stays with the hospitable Enrique and Miriam Alvarez. Enrique is a student of history and antiques who restores vintage clocks and Victrolas. The eight spacious rooms ($40–$60) all look different, though all feature vivid colors and a variety of wooden, iron, and painted headboards. Each has a private bathroom, small refrigerator, and cable TV. Larger rooms have air-conditioning and command the higher prices. The eat-in kitchen where guests may prepare their own meals is stocked with breakfast food and invariably becomes a social center. The Alvarezes go out of their way to keep children happy, sometimes even inviting them on outings with members of their extended family.

$   The **Hotel Dolores Alba** ★★ kids (Calle 63 no. 464, btw. calles 52 and 54; ☎ 999/928-5650; www.doloresalba.com; MC, V) is a true respite from a busy and not very pleasant street, offering cheerful, comfortable rooms for just $46 double. A family of four gets a break, paying the $51 triple rate instead of $58 for a quadruple. The newer three-story section (with elevator) wrapping around the pool courtyard in back has larger, more stylish rooms with two comfortable double beds or a double and a twin; other amenities include marble-tile floors, large TVs, balconies, and whisper-quiet A/C. Older rooms have small bathrooms but are decorated with local crafts, and have ceiling fans in addition to air-conditioning. The property has a decent restaurant and bar, and the front courtyard is shaded by an old mango tree. The hotel is 3½ blocks from the central plaza and is managed by the family that owns the Hotel Dolores Alba outside of Chichén Itzá.

**$–$$$**    Located next to Santa Lucia Church in what is rumored to have been its convent, **Luz en Yucatán** ★★★ (Calle 55 no. 99, btw. calles 60 and 58; ☎ 503/336-4082 U.S., or 999/924-0035; www.luzenyucatan.com; cash only) has a dizzying variety of rooms, suites, studios, and apartments in the main building and tucked into the garden around the pool. Its unique sliding scale system sets your rate by asking, "How Successful Are You?" (Click "not at all," "moderately," or "exceedingly" to see your price: $35–$45 for *casitas* with no air-conditioning, $50–$60 for doubles, $60–$70 for studios with kitchenettes, $70–$90 for apartments.) A liquor cart (gratis) greets you in the hallway. Guests who remember Luz when it was a cult favorite—run by an eccentric and somewhat ambivalent artist who really wanted to start a wellness center—will be surprised by the new owners' renovations and gratified that they haven't tampered with its freewheeling charm. A big kitchen is available for guests' use (though some units have their own), and a large dining area offers a beautiful table that seats 12.

**$$–$$$**    Bright colors and lush gardens distinguish **Hotel MedioMundo** (Calle 55 no. 533, btw. calles 64 and 66; ☎ 999/924-5472; www.hotelmediomundo.com; MC, V), a renovated, two-story colonial in a downtown residential area 3 blocks north of the main plaza. The 12 spacious rooms are simple and beautiful, with custom-made hardwood furniture, original tile floors, high-quality mattresses, good lighting, quiet air conditioners, and large bathrooms with separate dressing areas. Each is uniquely decorated in its own vivid but not overpowering color scheme. A generous breakfast is served in one of two courtyards: in addition to a large patio with a small swimming pool, there's a pond and fountain surrounded by trees laden by fruit or flowers. The lack of TVs adds to the feeling of serenity. Rooms with one queen bed and no air-conditioning are $60 in low season, $75 high season; kings with air-conditioning are $75 to $85. Rooms with two beds are also available for $80 to $90.

**$$$**    If I could, I would spend all my nights in Mérida at **Hotel Casa del Balam** ★★★ (Calle 60 no. 488 at Calle 57; ☎ 800/624-8451 toll-free U.S./Canada, or 999/924-8844; www.casadelbalam.com; AE, DISC, DC, MC, V), a colonial mansion converted to a hotel in 1968. Even with a king-size bed and massive wooden furniture, rooms have space enough to do cartwheels across the marble floor. Rooms overlooking Calle 60 have heavy cedar doors, which I prefer to open to the heavenly breeze bringing in the clip-clop of horse-drawn buggies on the cobblestone streets (ditto the windows over the lush courtyard dining room, which catch the strains of piano wafting up). With the rich decor and details like hand-painted plates, it still feels more like a mansion than a hotel, with luxury touches of a bygone era tempered by modern air-conditioning and double-paned windows to keep unwanted noise out. It's just 2 blocks from the plaza, in the middle of the best shopping, and the concierge staff treats you like their favorite niece or nephew. This is luxury at a palatable price: rates May to October are $75 for standard rooms and $85 for junior suites; rates November through December are $85 and $95. However, expect rates for the next year to go up $5 a night. The hotel also has sumptuous suites going up to $160 a night.

# DINING FOR ALL TASTES

Downtown Mérida has a limited number of fine dining restaurants but a good supply of midrange and budget places. To really cut corners, you can always head to one of the *mercados* (Parque Santa Ana is the local favorite) and tuck into a cardboard boat full of *panuchos* ($1 apiece), the fried, stuffed tortillas that Yucatecans eat for breakfast, lunch, and dinner.

**$** The older couple who own **Wayan'e** ★★★ (Felipe Carrillo Puerto 11A no. 57C at Calle 4, Col. Itzimná; ☎ 999/938-0676; Mon–Sat 8am–2 or 3pm; cash only) are always behind the counter of their little storefront taco stand. Some 20-odd fillings, from eggs (preferably scrambled with chaya) to cactus to tripe, as well as stellar *pollo poblano, poc chuc,* pork loin in smoky chipotle sauce, and other meats, can stuff tacos or *tortas* (sandwiches on a French roll with cheese). The tab won't top $7 unless you have a huge appetite and order a lot of fruit juice. Locals are crowded in by 9am, but gringos unaccustomed to heavy carnivorous breakfasts might want to wait for lunch—but not too long. Food is cooked fresh every morning, and doors close when the food runs out, usually around 2pm.

**$–$$** Lazy ceiling fans, a polished wood bar, white-jacketed waiters, and cigarette smoke give **Café La Habana** (Calle 59 no. 511A at Calle 62; ☎ 999/928-6502; daily 24 hr.; MC, V) an old-world, Europe-meets-Caribbean ambience perfect for sipping its array of specialty coffees. It's always open, so you might end up there more than you mean to. In the morning, stick with the eggs and Mexican breakfasts ($2.20–$5.40); the cereal and yogurt are standard Denny's issue and cost just as much. A decent lineup of reasonably priced dinner entrees includes meat dishes (Yucatecan and other Mexican recipes) from $7.50 to $10 and seafood for $8.50 to $12. The real deal, though is the $4.50 *executivo* set lunch, different each day of the week.

**$** Across from Parque Santiago, **La Flor de Santiago** ★★ (Calle 70 no. 478, btw. calles 57 and 59; ☎ 999/928-5591; daily 7am–11pm; cash only), has the feel of a Buenos Aires coffeehouse, with fans spinning under hangar-high ceilings, varnished wood shutter doors, and portly gentlemen undertaking serious conversation over coffee. A generous plate of *poc chuc* or *pollo ticuleño* will set you back only $4, and *chamorro* (lamb) *pibil* is $5. The most you can spend here is $5.50 on the *pierna de pavo a la Yucateca* (Yucatecan-style turkey leg). It's not gourmet, but it's tasty and you can't beat the atmosphere. A steady stream of customers keeps the pastry counter busy turning out house-made sweet breads.

**$–$$** **Los Almendros** (Calle 50A no. 493, at. Calle 57; ☎ 999/928-5459; daily 10am–11pm; cash only) is an institution, as it was the first place to offer tourists such Yucatecan specialties as *cochinita pibil* (marinated pork wrapped in banana leaves and baked in a pit) and *poc chuc* (pork slices marinated in sour orange and then grilled) and the less commonly encountered venison ($9–$9.50). The smaller items, such as the light, crispy fried tortillas topped with shredded chicken called *salbutes* ($6.50), are even better. A musical trio plays romantic traditional ballads every afternoon.

**$-$$$**    The *berenjenas al horno* at **El Pórtico del Peregrino** ★★★ (Calle 57 no. 501, btw. calles 60 and 62; ☎ 999/928-6163; daily noon–midnight; AE, MC, V), layers of eggplant, chicken, and cheese baked in tomato sauce ($7.50), reminds me of a hybrid between lasagna and moussaka and seems to personify Mérida's Italian and Lebanese influences. This unassuming entree is my favorite from a menu of finer fare with similar influences, from pastas ($7.50–$9), to poultry ($6.50–$7.50) including *pollo pibil*, enchiladas mole, and chicken liver shish kebob, to fish and seafood ($10–$18) with Yucatecan preparations with garlic.

**$$-$$$**    The fuchsia pink walls with peacock blue trim are very Frida Kahlo, but the food at **La Casa de Frida** ★★★ (Calle 61 no. 526, btw. calles 66 and 66a; ☎ 999/928-2311; Mon–Sat 6–11pm; cash only)is its own art. Chef Gaby Praget's version of *chiles en nogada* ($11), that mysterious concoction of up to 30 ingredients including apples, pecans, and plantains, is eyes-rolled-back-in-your-head good. Some menu items cost $8.50, but most are $12 to $13, and well worth it. Her habit of putting healthful, contemporary spins on regional dishes also produces some intriguing appetizers such as eggplant flan and *huitlacoche* crepes (made with a fungus that grows on corn and is eaten like mushrooms).

# WHY YOU'RE HERE: THE TOP SIGHTS & ATTRACTIONS

The natural place to begin exploring Mérida is the Plaza de la Independencia (more often called the Plaza Grande or Plaza Mayor), the fulcrum of city life. Best time to see the plaza and nearby streets is on Sunday, when vehicles are blocked off all day for **Mérida en Domingo** (p. 203) and the usual traffic frenzy is replaced by music, dancing, markets, and food and crafts stalls. Even when nothing is officially going on, the plaza is full of people sitting on benches, talking, and strolling.

Most of Mérida's other sights of interest lie north and east of the plaza, though the new city museum is in the old post office building in the market district south of town. If you need an orientation, or you just want to know more about Mérida, catch a **free walking tour** weekday mornings at 9:30am in front of the Palacio Municipal (City Hall), on Calle 62 between calles 61 and 63 on the Plaza Grande. Commentary is in English and Spanish.

Another option is to hire a *calesa,* one of the horse-drawn buggies that line up near the cathedral. The traditional hour-long tour, taking in downtown and Paseo de Montejo, costs $25, but you can ask for a double ($50), which lasts closer to two hours and takes in Avenida Reforma, the bullfight ring, the tropical Americas Park, tree-lined Avenida Colón, and the Paseo de Montejo and back to the plaza. You can also negotiate your own ride.

## PLAZA DE LA INDEPENDENCIA

Mérida's oldest buildings surround the plaza, and the most prominent is the hulking, fortresslike **Catedral de San Idelfonso** ★ (calles 60 and 61; daily 7–11:30am

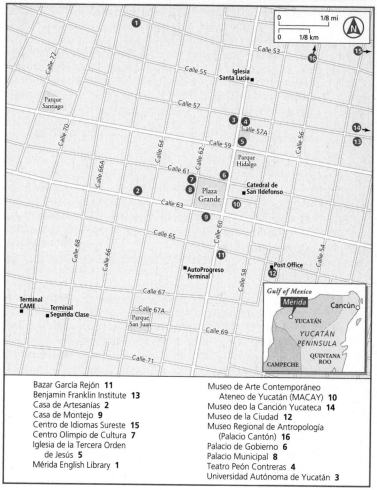

Bazar García Rejón **11**
Benjamin Franklin Institute **13**
Casa de Artesanías **2**
Casa de Montejo **9**
Centro de Idiomas Sureste **15**
Centro Olimpio de Cultura **7**
Iglesia de la Tercera Orden
    de Jesús **5**
Mérida English Library **1**

Museo de Arte Contemporáneo
    Ateneo de Yucatán (MACAY) **10**
Museo deo la Canción Yucateca **14**
Museo de la Ciudad **12**
Museo Regional de Antropología
    (Palacio Cantón) **16**
Palacio de Gobierno **6**
Palacio Municipal **8**
Teatro Peón Contreras **4**
Universidad Autónoma de Yucatán **3**

and 4:30–8pm). In fact, it was designed as a fortress as much as a place of worship—instead of windows, it has gunnery slits—affording protection to the
Spanish during the violent struggle to subdue the Maya. Even the interior is
severe, having been stripped bare during the Mexican Revolution. One of the
casualties, the black Cristo de las Ampollas (Christ of the Blisters), has been re-
created. The legend is that the original statue was carved from a tree in the village
of Ichmul, near today's Quintana Roo border, where it survived a fire unscathed
except for being blackened and covered by the blisters for which it is named. The
7m (23-ft.) replica might be the tallest Christ statue in Mexico, and it is the focus
point of a month-long festival beginning in mid-September. The cathedral is one
of the continent's oldest buildings, built from 1561 to 1598 on the site of a Maya
temple.

## A Grand Tour

For the advantages of a tour bus without that cattle-call feeling (or high price), take a circuit of the city on Mérida's **Turibus** (www.turibus.com.mx; $10 weekdays, $12 Sat–Sun and holidays, children 4–12 $5–$5.50; daily 9am–9pm). The red double-decker buses make a loop from the Paseo de Montejo and Avenida Colón (near the Fiesta Americana Hotel) and wind downtown to stop at the Plaza Grande near the cathedral. Heading back up Paseo de Montejo, they stop next at the Anthropology Museum. Continuing north, the third stop is the 15th-century church in the Itzimná neighborhood before going to the end of the Prolongación Montejo at the Gran Plaza shopping mall, Mérida's largest. They turn back down Paseo de Montejo for a final stop at the Monumento a la Bandera (Monument to the Flag) before returning to the starting point. You can ride the entire circuit (about 1 hr., 45 min.) for a city tour, or get off at any or all of the five stops for as long as you like. Another bus comes along every 45 minutes.

The former bishop's palace next door now houses the **Museo de Arte Contemporáneo Ateneo de Yucatán (MACAY)** ★★ (Pasaje de la Revolución 1907, btw. calles 58 and 60; ☎ 999/928-3236; www.macay.org; free admission; Wed–Mon 10am–5:30pm). The bright, cavernous building has the region's best modern art collection, with permanent exhibitions of world-renowned Yucatecan painters such as Gabriel Ramírez Aznar and Fernando García Ponce.

The opulent **Casa de Montejo** ★★ (Calle 63 at Calle 60; free admission; Mon–Fri 9am–5pm, Sat 9am–1pm), on the south side of the plaza, is recognizable by the gargantuan conquistadors carved into a Plateresque facade (a Spanish version of early Renaissance style), gripping spears and planting their feet on vanquished Maya rebels' heads. The palace was built in 1542 by Francisco de Montejo, who made the first attempt to conquer the Yucatán Peninsula before leaving it to his son to finish the job. His descendants lived here until the late 1970s, when it was converted into a bank. You can enter the courtyard to view the Montejos' restored wood-paneled dining room (in the back to the right).

Across the plaza from the cathedral, and next door to the impressive 17th-century **Palacio Municipal** (Calle 62, btw. calles 61 and 63; ☎ 999/928-2020; free admission; daily 9am–8pm), the porticoed but modern **Centro Olimpo de Cultura** ★ (Calle 62, btw. calles 61 and 63; ☎ 999/942-0000; Tues–Sun 10am–10pm) was built in 1999 to replace the old Olimpo, which the city tore down in the 1970s (a move that was later regretted). The new Olimpo, borrowing architectural details from the original, is a venue for free cultural events. The marble interior showcases international art exhibits, and the auditorium hosts classical music concerts, theater, and dance.

Completing the square, the **Palacio de Gobierno** ★★★ (Calle 61, btw. calles 60 and 62; ☎ 999/930-3101; free admission; daily 9am–9pm), the seat of state government, was built in 1892 on the site of the colonial governors' palace. The powerful murals by Fernando Castro Pacheco, whose strong colors show the

## City Museum Trades Up

"Small but interesting" was threatening to become part of the name of Mérida's city museum until late June 2008. The **Museo de la Ciudad** ★★★ (Calle 56 no. 529A, btw. calles 65 and 65A; ☎ 999/923-6869; free admission; Tues–Fri 9am–8pm, Sat–Sun 9am–2pm) moved from its old quarters at calles 61 and 58 to the majestic former Post Office building, built in 1908, which originally was the federal palace. Directed by Orlando Vega Carrillo (grandson of Felipe Carrillo Puerto, probably the most beloved of Yucatán's governors), the expansive new museum displays many items the old museum could not, including a cabinet with mementos and photos of the first immigrants from Lebanon and Korea and the scale model of the life-size statue of Carrillo Puerto that stands on Avenida Itzáes at the entrance to the city. Permanent exhibits focus on the pre-Hispanic city of Th'o (Mérida's Maya predecessor), colonial, 19th- and early-20th-century, and contemporary Mérida. Temporary exhibit rooms include galleries devoted to local artists' works. Guided tours are free and available in English; your guide might be Orlando Vega himself (whose face was the model for his grandfather's statue).

influence of famous Mexican muralists José Clemente Orozco and David Alfaro Siquieros, offer a chilling depiction of the bloody conquest of the Yucatán. Painted in the 1970s, they illustrate the Popul Vuh legend (in which man was created from corn), a jaguar with fierce Maya warriors in headdresses, the hands of a Maya *henequén* worker, and portraits of such heroes as Felipe Carrillo Puerto, the martyred revolutionary governor who instituted agrarian reform.

## BEYOND THE PLAZA

Calle 60, one of the city's main commercial streets, is lined with fancy hotels, restaurants, and many of the best crafts shops. It also boasts a series of beautiful colonial buildings. One block north of the plaza, **Parque Hidalgo** ★ (Calle 60, btw. calles 59 and 61) is a cozy park (officially Plaza Cepeda Peraza) lined on the south side by historic mansions reincarnated as hotels and sidewalk cafes. Marimba bands and street vendors do a brisk business at night, and live bands play for free all day during **Mérida en Domingo** (p. 203).

Just to the north is the **Iglesia de la Tercera Orden de Jesús** (Calle 59, btw. calles 58 and 60; Tues–Sat 8am–8pm, Sun 8am–2pm). Anchored by a copy of Renoir's *Madonna and Child* statue, the church was built in 1618 with limestone from a dismantled Maya temple. You can see the slanted, chain-line pattern common to many Maya ruins in some of the stones on the west wall. There's not much to see inside the church, but former convent rooms in the rear house the **Pinoteca Juan Gamboa Guzmán** art collection ($3). Striking bronze sculptures of indigenous Maya are more interesting than the portraits upstairs.

The enormous, ornate **Teatro Peón Contreras** ★★★ (Calle 60, btw. calles 57 and 59; ☎ 999/924-9290; daily 7am–1am) looks like it was dropped onto the wrong continent. The Italianate theater and art gallery, with a Carrara marble staircase and a dome covered with imported Italian frescoes, was commissioned from an Italian architect and built from 1900 to 1908, during Mérida's *henequén* heyday. Modeled after Europe's grand opera houses, the theater houses one of downtown's tourist information centers. Across the street is the **Universidad Autónoma de Yucatán** (Calle 60, btw. calles 57 and 59; ☎ 999/924-8000; www. uady.mx), a 400-year-old institution that is pivotal to the city's cultural and intellectual life. Check the bulletin boards inside the entrance for upcoming events.

Five blocks east of Calle 60, the **Museo de la Canción Yucateca** ★★ (Calle 57 at Calle 48; ☎ 999/928-3660; $3; Tues–Fri 9am–5pm, Sat–Sun 9am–3pm) is well worth the detour. Music is in the Yucatecans' very marrow, and the Yucatán even has its own musical style, the *trova* (trio). The small "Museum of the Yucatecan Song" is devoted to the region's music and musicians and traces pre-Columbian and Afro-Cuban influences on local *trovadores* (*trova* musicians). The gift shop is a good place to buy some romantic tunes.

Back on Calle 60, the small **Parque Santa Lucía** (Calle 60 at Calle 55) blossoms on Thursday nights, when people pack the square for Serenada, a 40-year-old tradition of romantic serenades; it also hosts a used-book fair on Sundays. The small church facing the park was built in 1575 for Maya residents, who weren't allowed to worship in many Mérida temples.

## PASEO DE MONTEJO

Nowhere are the fruits of Mérida's flirtation with fantastic wealth more evident than along the broad, shady Paseo de Montejo, where the *henequén* barons built the stately mansions that give Mérida its old-world appearance. The broad, tree-lined boulevard runs north starting at Calle 47, 7 blocks north and 2 blocks east of the Plaza Grande. Many of the palatial homes didn't survive the *henequén* bust after World War II, but the ornate French, Italian, and Moorish splendor of those that did provide eye candy enough to justify a cab (or *calesa*) ride.

Most of the survivors have been converted to restaurants, offices, and consulates. The exception is at the near end of Paseo de Montejo, where you can see how the upper crust lived inside the Palacio Cantón, home to the **Museo Regional de Antropología** ★★★ (Paseo de Montejo no. 485 at Calle 43; ☎ 999/923-0469; $3.50; Tues–Sat 8am–8pm, Sun 8am–2pm). Built for railway tycoon, general, and state governor Francisco Cantón Rosado by the same architect who designed the Teatro Peón Contreras, the eye-popping Beaux Arts palace presents a delicious irony: one of Mérida's most opulent examples of European architecture housing a tribute to the ancient civilization Europeans nearly extinguished. Today, the museum boasts one of the best displays on Maya culture outside of Mexico City. Limestone jaguars, skulls with jade-encrusted teeth, offerings recovered from Chichén Itzá's Cenote Sagrado, sacrificial instruments and offerings, and more are displayed against a backdrop of elegant cornice moldings, glowing chandeliers, turned-wood pillars, and oceans of marble. Temporary exhibits examine Mérida's history and specific archaeological sites. Most displays are in English and Spanish.

## BEYOND THE CITY

Mérida is at the epicenter of the Maya world; dozens of ruins, Maya villages, and haciendas are within day-trip range. (Most of these are covered in chapter 6.) The small archaeological site of **Dzibilchaltún,** though, is just 14km (9 miles) north of Mérida off the highway to Progreso, not much farther than Mérida's golf club (which was once a part of the grounds of Dzibilchaltún). The city was founded around 500 B.C., flourished around A.D. 750 and declined long before the Spanish reached the Yucatán. More than 8,000 structures have been mapped, but only about a half-dozen have been excavated. The main attraction is the **Templo de las Siete Muñecas (Temple of the Seven Dolls),** a low, trapezoidal temple in late Preclassic style with a *sacbé* (raised white road) connecting it to other structures; its doorways line up with the rising sun at the spring and autumn equinoxes. The site's **Xlacah Cenote,** with its bottle-green water, is a perfect way to cool off after hiking around the ruins. The small museum near the entrance, **Museo Pueblo Maya** ($6; Tues–Sun 8am–4pm), displays the strange, crude dolls that gave the temple its name, along with artifacts from other Yucatán sites, an exhibit on Maya culture, and, in the garden, several huge sculptures found on the site.

# THE OTHER MERIDA

It's hard to pass an elegantly decaying hacienda on Yucatán's narrow roads without wondering what it was really like to live there during the *henequén* boom days. Naturally, we envision ourselves as the lord of the domain, not as the Maya laborers who tended and harvested the stiff, thorny agave plants. At **Sotuta de Peón** (Municipio de Tecoh; ☎ 999/941-8639 or 121-1862; www.sotutadepeon.com; $25, $13 children 3–12, free for kids under 12; Mon–Sat 10am–4pm), 30 minutes south of Mérida on the Convent Route, you'll see hacienda life of a century ago from both sides.

The owners didn't just restore the house, they returned the hacienda to working order and put it into production, turning out 10 to 15 tons of *henequén* per month . . . and then opened it to visitors. You'll tour the beautiful, tile-festooned main house and sip lemonade on the breezy terrace, finger strands of *henequén* drying in the sun, and practice combing the dried fibers and spinning them into twine. The workers will show you how their machines—technological marvels of a century ago—rend fiber from the tough plants, stamp processed *henequén* into bales for export, weave fiber into rope and twine, and wrap it into balls. Some of the men were employed here as boys working alongside their fathers and grandfathers.

A mule-drawn "truck" (a cart on rails) takes you through acres of agave to a humble hut where Don Antonio, an elderly Maya man, has lived since he started working in the fields as a boy. He'll teach you how to plant an agave and demonstrate the dangers of harvesting the knifelike leaves. Then you have a chance to cool off in an underground cenote and buy lunch at the hacienda's restaurant, which excels at Yucatecan cuisine.

Tours are at 10am and noon and last about 4 hours, though guests are welcome to linger. It's an easy drive from Mérida on a good road, but the hacienda will also provide transportation for $20 per person. Practically any hotel in Mérida can also arrange tours, including transportation, for about $50.

Sure, the **Mérida English Library** (Calle 53 no. 424, btw. calles 66 and 68; ☎ 999/924-8401; www.meridaenglishlibrary.com; Mon 9am–1pm and 6:30–9pm, Tues–Wed 9am–1pm, Thurs 9am–1pm and 4–7pm, Sat 10am–1pm) has books to borrow, used books, and videos to buy ($1 apiece). But it's also an unofficial community center run by expat volunteers, and you don't have to live in Mérida to

# Living the Language

Mérida is the language-school capital of the Yucatán. Whether your primary goal is learning Spanish or getting to know Mérida, Spanish school provides a shortcut. Most schools also offer home stays with local families, which is your surest route to both: You're surrounded by Spanish at home as well as in class, and communicating with your hosts provides added motivation. A home stay may cost as little as $75 a week or as much as $275, depending on how many meals are included and whether rooms are shared or private or come with air-conditioning or private bathrooms. Sessions start on Mondays, and you can attend for as little as 1 week.

The granddaddy of Mérida's dozens of language schools is the **Benjamin Franklin Institute** (Calle 57 no. 474A, btw. calles 52 and 54; ☎ 999/928-6005; www.benjaminfranklin.com.mx; $12 per hr., $720 for 4 weeks), occupying a big old colonial building in the Centro Histórico. Teachers typically provide guided tours of local sights in addition to classroom work. The biggest language school, **Centro de Idiomas Sureste (CIS)** (Calle 52 no. 455, btw. calles 49 and 51; ☎ 999/923-0954; www.cisyucatan.com. mx; $305–$355 per week), has Mérida's longest-running Spanish program for English speakers. The most popular course is an intensive 5-hour-per-day class combining morning classroom work with cultural activities in the afternoons. Reports from people who have experience with these schools say Benjamin Franklin's management seems better organized than CIS, but its program is more formal and structured, which might not appeal to some short-term visitors.

Two other schools whose programs have special appeal to vacationers are located outside of the historical center, which gives you a chance to see another side of Mérida. Immersion training at the **Instituto de Lengua y Cultura de Yucatán** (Calle 13 no. 214, btw. calles 28 and 30, Col. García Gineres; ☎ 999/125-3048; www.ilcymex.com; $295–$370 per week) means including real-life activities, such as going to the bank or cooking a meal, to use what you've learned in the classroom. The newest school in town, **Ecora Spanish School** (Av. 50 no. 361, btw. calles 53B and 53F, Fracc. Francisco de Montejo; ☎ 999/953-4974; www.spanishschoolecora. com; $200–$390 per week) has a variety of nontraditional programs that include field trips to markets and museums and some purely recreational classes (no university credit). It will even send a teacher to you, for lessons or for day trips and tours.

benefit from their inside knowledge. Some of the library's activities are great opportunities for visitors to get a glimpse behind the curtain of the local culture. Each Monday at 7pm, "Conversaciones con Amigos" ("Conversations with Friends") gives English and Spanish speakers a chance to practice their second languages together in a relaxed social setting. It has become very popular with

Méridians and they are short on English speakers, so you don't have to be a library member to join in. (It's free, but donations are appreciated.) And all those fortresslike facades lining Mérida's streets that you just know are hiding gorgeous tiled terraces and courtyards full of tropical trees and flowers? If you're in Mérida from October through March, you can unleash your voyeuristic tendencies on the library's Wednesday morning "House and Garden Tours," getting a peek at some of the colonial beauties being rejuvenated by new owners. The cost was $20 in spring 2008, but call or e-mail for the 2009 rate.

On Saturdays at 10am, the library hosts "Story Hour" for children of all ages, but especially for 4- to 11-year-olds. And you can always drop by and check the bulletin board for information about services in Mérida.

## ACTIVE MERIDA

Compared with a place like Cancún, Mérida doesn't have much of a focus on organized outdoor activities. Golfers will be pleased, though. The 18-hole championship golf course at **Club de Golf de Yucatán** (Carretera Mérida-Progreso Km 14.5; ☎ 999/922-0053; daily 6:30am–6pm), about 14km (9 miles) north of the city on the road to Progreso, charges $97 for a round—less than the twilight rates on Cancún's courses. Better yet, they offer short-term memberships that really cut the fee. A 15-day family membership, for example, is $291, allowing you, your spouse, and kids to play as much as you want for 2 weeks.

To combine active pursuits with sightseeing, **Ecoturismo Yucatán** (Calle 3 no. 235; ☎ 999/920-2772; www.ecoyuc.com) is a reputable company focusing on protecting as well as sharing the region's natural assets. Trips focus on archaeology, birding, natural history, biking, and kayaking. An all-day bicycle tour to an underground cave, two archaeological sites, a *henequén* hacienda, and a swim in a cenote, for example, costs $116 and includes a 21-speed bike, helmet, water, and transportation from Mérida; a picnic lunch can be provided for an extra $7.

## ATTENTION, SHOPPERS!

Mérida is probably the best place in the Yucatán to buy hammocks; other major quarry for shoppers are *guayaberas* (lightweight men's shirts), Panama hats, and *huipiles* (traditional embroidered blouses and dresses). Prices are very reasonable, compared with the resort cities, and quality generally is high.

Stop first at the government-supported **Casa de Artesanías** (Calle 63, btw. calles 64 and 66 in the Casa de la Cultura Mayab; ☎ 999/928-6676; Mon–Sat 9am–8pm, Sun 9am–1pm). Though the exterior of the restored monastery looks tattered, the shop inside is beautiful, with rows of wooden display shelves and wall arches painted to contrasting colors. The quality of its crafts, which includes silver jewelry, is reliably high, though it doesn't have a large selection of clothing. You can get artful little trinkets here for $3 to $5, leather sandals for $20, and hammocks for $27 to $34. *Guayaberas* start at $20 and traditional embroidered blouses $19; the quality of the fabric and construction is good at lower prices, but the intricacy and beauty of the designs definitely increases with price.

Mérida's **Mercado Lucas de Gálvez** (calles 56 and 67; daily 5am–6pm), or Mercado Municipal, is two markets unto itself, surrounded by several blocks of more markets. You'll find everything from fresh fish to hand-tooled leather to stacks of scary-looking fruits and vegetables. For handicrafts, though, browse first

## Hammock Savvy

Hammocks might be the Yucatán's number-one shopping prize. If you plan to use it for more than a design accent, don't buy from a street vendor or even a market stall, where quality is lower. Most hammocks are made of nylon these days, because it is colorfast and dries faster in humid climates; cotton, on the other hand, is more comfortable. When comparing hammocks, be aware that the double-threaded weaves are stronger than single-threaded weaves. Hammocks are meant to be slept in at an angle, so make sure the width is be sufficient for your height.

in some reputable craft shops; market prices aren't necessarily better than in the shops unless you are an expert haggler. For something that won't languish in a closet, pick up a block of prepared adobo, a paste of ground *achiote* seeds, oregano, garlic, and other spices used in such dishes as *cochinita pibil.*

Two more crafts markets worth a look are the weekly handicrafts bazaar, or **Bazar de Artesanías** (Plaza Grande; Sun 9am–5pm), and the **Bazar García Rejón** (calles 65 and 60; daily 9am–6pm), with outdoor stalls selling leather goods, palm hats, and handmade guitars.

**Guayaberas Jack** (Calle 59 no. 507A, btw. calles 60 and 62; ☎ 999/928-6022; www.guayaberasjack.com.mx; Mon–Sat 10am–8pm) sells more than *guayaberas.* The store, attended by a helpful but not pushy staff, is almost half full of women's clothes. Men's *guayaberas* start at $32; dresses and blouses start at $25 and go up—sometimes way up—from there. These aren't the colorful embroidered *huipil* blouses, but a tailored design modeled after a *guayabera.*

For souvenirs that are both a delight and easy to pack, **Miniaturas** (Calle 59 no. 507A, btw. calles 60 and 62; ☎ 999/928-6503; Mon–Sat 10am–8pm) sells tiny ceramic figures, Día de los Muertos collections, dollhouse furniture, tinwork, and toy soldiers from different areas of Mexico. Prices are fixed at a fair level, so you don't need to bargain to start following this evolving folk art.

# NIGHTLIFE

You don't have to plan (or pay for) a single night out—the city has taken care of it for you, every day of the week. Mérida has a long tradition of sponsoring free nightly events that reflect a mixture of Spanish and Mayan cultures (see "Una Semana Yucateca," below). While visitors are welcome, these events are for Méridians, who live very much in the present but revere their roots. These couldn't be farther from Mexico Night in Cancún's restaurants: they are the best shows in town.

If you want to make your own little fiesta, there's plenty of commercial entertainment, too, from mariachi nights in hotel bars to salsa dancing in nightclubs. Méridians love to dance, but they also work hard, so many discos are open Wednesdays through Saturdays at most. The best dancing to DJ-spun salsa, merengue, and disco is **Mambo Café** (Plaza Las Américas, Calle 21 no. 327, btw. calles 50 and 52; ☎ 999/987-7533; Wed–Sat 9pm–3am), where 20-somethings mingle with an older crowd and a salsa band takes the stage later in the night.

# Una Semana Yucateca

The city of Mérida hosts cultural events at parks and plazas throughout the historical center, free of charge to both residents and visitors.

## Monday

**9pm:** Vaquería, Plaza Grande in front of Palacio Municipal on Calle 62 side. Outdoor concert with traditional Yucatecan cowboy music, dancing, and dress, dating from an early local festival celebrating the haciendas' branding of cattle.

## Tuesday

**9pm:** Remembranzas Musicales, Parque Santiago, Calle 59 at Calle 72. Big-band music of the 1940s with a Cuban beat in Santiago Park, with locals crowding in to show off their moves.

## Wednesday

**9pm:** *Trovas,* Auditorio del Olimpo, Calle 62 side of Plaza Grande. Traditional guitar trios and other presentations at the Olimpo Cultural Center.

## Thursday

**9pm:** Serenata Yucateca, Parque de Santa Lucia, Calle 60 at Calle 55. Open-air concert featuring Yucatecan music (*trovas,* boleros, ballads), dress, dance, music, and folklore.

## Friday

**9pm:** Serenata, Universidad Autónoma de Yucatán, Calle 60 at 57; $3. Typical regional dances performed by the University of Yucatán Ballet Folklórico in the main university building.

## Saturday

**7pm:** Noche Mexicana, Paseo de Montejo. Several performances of traditional Mexican music and dance, amateurs and professionals alike, with crafts booths and food stands selling great *antojitos* (finger foods), drinks, and ice cream.

**8pm–1am:** En El Corazón de Mérida, Centro Histórico, Plaza Grande and Calle 60 up to Calle 53. "Heart of Mérida" festival with several bands joined by stilt walkers, mariachis, and crafts and food stands in streets closed to traffic.

## Sunday

**9am–9pm:** Mérida en Domingo, Centro Histórico, Plaza Grande and up Calle 60 to Hidalgo Park, Calle 60 at Calle 59. "Mérida on Sunday" turns into a giant outdoor handicrafts market and food festival with live music all day and into the night, a flea market and used-book fair, children's art classes, educational booths, and bawdy comedy acts at Parque Hidalgo. Around 7pm, a large band plays mambos and rumbas and gets as many as 1,000 people dancing in the street; afterward, folk ballet dancers re-enact a typical Yucatecan wedding.

Wednesdays are free, and women pay $7 and men $15 for open bar on Thursdays; general cover is $6 on Fridays and Saturdays.

The place to see and be seen is the all-white, minimalist **El Cielo** (Prolongación Montejo at Calle 25, Campestre; ☎ 999/944-5127; Wed–Sat 9:30pm) lounge, which earns its name with its open-air rooftop perch. Music is mostly techno, with a little Spanish and English-language pop for good measure. Be prepared for long lines (hot blondes have the advantage). Depending on the night, women pay between nothing and $10 and men $3 to $15; cover is cheaper before 10:30pm. Thursdays and Saturdays are open bar. Another local in spot is **Slavia** (Calle 29 no. 490 at Calle 58; ☎ 999/926-6587; daily 7pm–2am), a restaurant and bar with eastern European flair near the Monumento a la Bandera (Monument to the Flag) on the Prolongación Montejo. This place is a magnet for the martini-and-wine set. Order a bottle of wine, and you get a bite from the restaurant on the house— all the better to soak in the glowing candlelit, beaded-curtain, mirrored wonder of it all.

The revolutionary-themed (think waiters in sombreros and bandoliers) **Pancho's** (Calle 59 no. 509, btw. calles 60 and 62; ☎ 999/923-0942; daily 6pm–2:30am), with its pricey but interesting modern-Mexican menu and lively night scene, has worked its way to a tourist must-see. Hip young Méridians and tourists mix it up to live salsa and English-language pop on the tiny but happening dance floor.

## The ABCs of Mérida

**American Express** The office is at Paseo de Montejo 492 (☎ 999/942-8200). It's open for travelers' services weekdays from 9am to 2pm and 4 to 6pm.

**Area Code** The telephone area code is **999.**

**Business Hours** Generally, businesses are open Monday to Saturday from 10am to 2pm and 4 to 8pm.

**Climate** From November to February, the weather can be pleasantly cool and windy. In other months, it's just hot, especially during the day. Rain falls any time of year, especially during the rainy season (July–Oct), and usually comes in the form of afternoon tropical showers.

**Consulates** The American Consulate has moved. It's now at Calle 60 no. 338-K, 1 block north of the Hyatt hotel (Col. Alcalá Martín; ☎ 999/942-5700). Office hours are Monday to Friday from 9am to 1pm.

**Currency Exchange** I prefer *casas de cambio* (currency exchange offices) over banks. There are many of these; one called **Cambios Portales,** Calle 61 no. 500 (☎ 999/923-8709), is on the north side of the main plaza in the middle of the block. It's open daily from 8:30am to 8:30pm. ATMs are also plentiful; one is on the south side of the same plaza.

**Hospitals** The best hospital is **Centro Médico de las Américas,** Calle 54 no. 365, between 33-A and Avenida Pérez Ponce. The main phone number is ☎ 999/926-2619; for emergencies, call ☎ 999/927-3199. You can also call the **Cruz Roja** (Red Cross) at ☎ 999/924-9813.

**Internet Access** Mérida has so many Internet access providers that you hardly have to walk more than a couple of blocks to find one.

**Newspapers & Magazines** Pick up a copy of the free monthly magazine **Yucatán Today** (www.yucatantoday.com), in English and Spanish, for a wealth of information on Mérida and beyond.

**Pharmacies** **Farmacia Yza,** Calle 63 no. 502, between calles 60 and 62 (☎ 999/924-9510), on the south side of the plaza, is open 24 hours.

**Police** Mérida has a special body of bilingual police to help tourists. They patrol the downtown area and the Paseo de Montejo. They wear brown pants and white shirts bearing the words POLICIA TURISTICA and they can tell you where to find consulates, hospitals, drugstores, restaurants, and tourist sites. Call ☎ 999/930-3200, ext. 40062, anytime. The regular municipal police are at ☎ 999/930-3200.

**Post Office** The *correo* is near the market at the corner of calles 65 and 56, with its own entrance separate from the new city museum. A branch office is at the airport. Both are open Monday to Friday from 8am to 7pm, Saturday from 9am to noon.

**Seasons** Tourism has two high seasons, but they aren't as pronounced as on the coast. One is in July and August, when Mexicans take their vacations, and the other is between November 15 and Easter Sunday, when Canadians and Americans flock to the Yucatán to escape winter weather.

**Telephones** Long-distance phone service centers are located at the airport and the bus station. In the downtown area is **TelWorld,** Calle 59 no. 495-4, between calles 56 and 58. To use the public phones, buy a Ladatel card from just about any newsstand or store. The cards come in a variety of denominations and work for long distance within Mexico and even abroad.

**Tourist Information** Mérida's city **tourist office** is in the Palacio Municipal facing the Plaza Grande on Calle 62, between calles 61 and 63 (☎ 999/942-0000, ext. 80119), and is open Monday through Saturday 8am to 8pm, Sunday 8am to 2pm. The downtown **state tourist office** is also on the plaza, in the Palacio de Gobierno, Calle 61, between calles 60 and 62 (☎ 999/930-3101; www.merida.gob.mx/turismo). The state also operates a **tourist information center** in the Teatro Peón Contreras at the corner of Calle 60 and Calle 57A (☎ 999/924-9290). Both are open daily from 8am to 9pm. Tourist information booths at the airport and the CAME bus station mostly offer hotel suggestions and coupons for lodging discounts.

# 6

# Yucatán State

## The Maya heartland

NEARLY 5 CENTURIES AGO, THE STATE OF YUCATAN HOSTED ONE OF THE world's great culture clashes. The collision of Maya and Spanish civilizations, cataclysmic as it was, gave rise to a unique culture that fascinated travelers decades before the Caribbean coast beckoned with groomed beaches and high-rise resorts. The legacies of those mighty civilizations still draw visitors to the remnants of ancient empires at Chichén Itzá and Uxmal, the colonial monuments of Mérida, and the grandly deteriorating haciendas that generated fortunes in centuries past. Most compelling of all, though, are the proud, gentle people who make Yucatán state like nowhere else.

Unlike the Aztecs of central Mexico or the Inca of Peru, Maya culture is still very much alive today. For centuries, Yucatecans were isolated from the rest of Mexico and had closer ties with parts of North America, the Caribbean, and Europe. The Maya are North America's largest indigenous population, who still speak their own language (in addition to Spanish). To truly appreciate what makes this part of the world unique, stop on your way between ruins, haciendas, and wildlife havens at the quiet clutches of thatch-roof huts where hammocks hang between narrow walls and women embroider elaborate floral borders on *huipil* blouses. Eat the food, listen to music, swing in a hammock, and you are in the Yucatán's beating heart.

## DON'T LEAVE YUCATAN STATE WITHOUT . . .

**FEELING THE WONDER**   Despite the crowds, Chichén Itzá's fabled ruins are all they're cracked up to be: a many-layered city encapsulating the evolution of a culture whose defining monument is akin to the world's largest sundial. See p. 227.

**GOING A LITTLE BIT COUNTRY**   Seemingly in the middle of nowhere, Hacienda Yaxcopoil is a former *henequén* (sisal) plantation that has been arrested in time rather than restored—except for a single guesthouse, where you'll have run of the place and live like a wealthy *hacendado* of times past. See p. 212.

**FOLLOWING THE FLOCK**   The vast majority of all the world's pink flamingos breed and nest on two estuaries at opposite ends of Yucatán's unspoiled Gulf coast. Fishing boats will take you through the estuaries to see them courting and feeding and raising their young. See p. 222.

**DIVING IN**   The clear blue waters of Cenote Dzitnup, deep in a cavern pierced by ethereal shafts of sunlight, is one of the Yucatán's most beautiful sights (and

## What's in a Name?

Several popular stories debate how Yucatán was named, all involving the *conquistadores'* misunderstanding of Mayan phonetics. In the most popular version, a Spaniard—usually identified as Diego Velázquez, Cortez's immediate superior—landed on the Yucatán coast and asked the inhabitants what they called their land. The Maya replied in their native tongue, "We don't understand your language." Thinking the reply was the name they were seeking, the explorers did their best to render the unfamiliar syllables into Spanish and came up with "Yucatán."

This story appears to originate with Cortez's first letter (of five recounting his exploits in Mexico, 1519–1526) to King Charles V of Spain. It might have been no more than one of numerous attempts to discredit Velázquez, then governor of Cuba and Cortez's political antagonist. The only certainty is that the name "Yucatán" originated during the Spanish Conquest.

most refreshing swims). If it gets too crowded for you, just cross the road to its still-secret twin, more recently discovered but equally beautiful. See p. 240.

**DISCOVERING YOUR OWN RUIN**    Since beginning work at Ek Balam in 1997, archaeologists have continually unveiled history-altering finds. They've excavated a pyramid 6m (20 ft.) taller than El Castillo on a site that rivals Chichén Itzá in size and importance . . . and almost nobody goes there yet. See p. 240.

**BEING A SMALL-TOWN GIRL (OR BOY)**    The village of Izamal, in Yucatán's interior, lives the legacy of three cultures, with ancient pyramids dotting the blocks around one of the largest monasteries the Spanish ever built in Mexico, and contemporary Maya artisans doing a brisk trade in their traditional crafts—all with unique, affordable lodgings nearby. See p. 231.

## LAY OF THE LAND

Yucatán state cuts a large, mostly flat, triangular swath through the middle of the Yucatán Peninsula, bordered on the east and southeast by Quintana Roo and the southwest by Campeche. Its unvarying carpet is a low, dense, semitropical jungle full of wild ginger and orchids, jaguars, monkeys, and tropical birds. Chichén Itzá, the biggest tourist attraction, is in the central part of the state. The region south of Mérida is studded with ruins, haciendas, and cenotes; flamingo preserves preside at opposite ends of the Gulf coast, Celestún in the west and Río Lagartos in the northeast. Along the 378km (235 miles) of coastline, only one 145km (90-mile) stretch of highway skirts the coast, from Sisal to Dzilam de Bravo.

A car is the most efficient and most flexible way to get around in Yucatán (although bus service is available to most popular sites; see individual sections in this chapter). The peninsula's spine is Hwy. 180, which links Cancún with

# Yucatán State

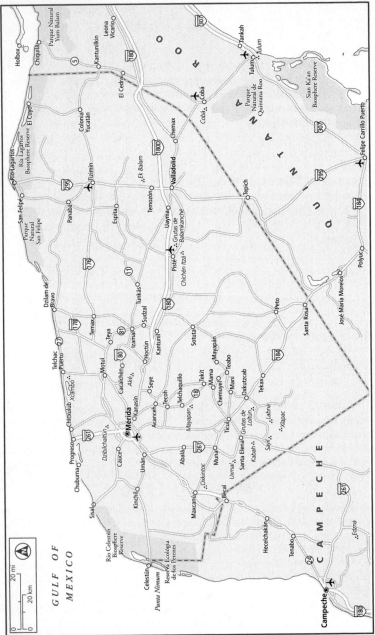

Mérida, about 322km (200 miles) to the west, before veering south into Campeche. For the more than 242km (150 miles) between Cancún and Kantunil (the turnoff for Izamal), you have the option of taking the fast toll road. The only exits are at Valladolid and Chichén Itzá, so if you want to stop and explore along the way, take the older, slower Hwy. 180 *libre,* which parallels the toll highway.

Hwy. 295, crossing Hwy. 180 at Valladolid, runs north through Tizimín to Río Lagartos on the Gulf of Mexico and south to Felipe Carrillo Puerto in Quintana Roo. In Mérida, Hwy. 261 extends north to Puerto Progreso (usually called simply Progreso) on the Gulf and south through Uxmal on its way to meet Hwy. 180 in Campeche state. Hwy. 184 breaks off of Hwy. 261 just before Uxmal, crossing the southern portion of the state along the edge of the hilly Puuc Route to end at Felipe Carrillo Puerto.

# A BRIEF HISTORY

Yucatán's history has been riddled with conflict between the Maya people, who began farming the region about 4,000 years ago, and a succession of invaders. And still they managed to give the world the concept of zero; create an accurate calendar; develop a written language; produce latex; cultivate chocolate, vanilla, and honey; and build some of the grandest monuments the world has seen.

Maya history is divided into three periods. During the **Preclassic period** (1800 B.C.–A.D. 250), they associated with the neighboring Olmecs, from whom they apparently got the jaguar god (Balam), a crude form of writing, and the foundation of their calendar system. At least one large Maya city, Dzibilchaltún, developed during this time.

The **Classic period** (A.D. 250–900)—around the time of the Roman Empire's decline—produced the famous temples and pyramids, along with stone monuments carved with hieroglyphs. These stelae, which introduced the only true written language of pre-Columbian times, weathered the centuries to provide a record of the Classic Maya civilization. For most of this period, Izamal was the greatest city in the northern Yucatán, rivaling Cobá in the east and Calakmul in the south. But around 800, Uxmal, in the Puuc hills, rose to power throughout the central and western Yucatán Peninsula and was as large as any European city of the time.

Perhaps through political upheaval, perhaps because of drought or some other catastrophe, the great cities of the Classic period were abandoned in the 9th century,

## On the Road

U.S. tourists might find Mexico's road nomenclature backward at first. Highways (*cuotas* or *autopistas*) are fast, divided toll roads, Mexico's closest equivalent to a U.S. freeway. If a local directs you to the "freeway" *(libre),* you'll follow the old two-lane roads that wind through the jungle, with an obstacle course of *topes* (speed bumps, some marked and some not) as they pass through every village along the way. The freeways are indeed free and since you pay to use the highways, it's hard to fault the terminology. Take the highway if you just want to make good time, the freeway if you have time to delve deeper into life in the Yucatán.

ushering in the **Postclassic period** (900–1521). Among the other groups that moved in were the Itzá, seagoing merchants who moved inland to build some of the Yucatán's most impressive cities. Chichén Itzá, the greatest of all, shows influence from the Toltecs, who dominated central Mexico. Toltec influence also introduced the worship of Quetzalcóatl (known to the Maya as Kukulcán, the Plumed Serpent god) and human sacrifice.

The last great city of the Postclassic period was Mayapán, built when Itzá/ Toltec rulers abandoned Chichén Itzá and moved south. Another clan, the Cocomes, ruled Mayapán until the Xiú Maya seized power in 1450. The Xiú were ruling over a deteriorating civilization of rival fiefdoms when the Spanish arrived.

Francisco de Montejo, a young Spanish nobleman, made several attempts to conquer the Yucatán beginning in 1527 but was repelled by ferocious Maya warriors. His son, Francisco de Montejo the Younger, finally succeeded in 1540, taking advantage of the feud between the Xiú and Cocom Maya. Montejo founded Mérida and built strongholds at Valladolid, Zací, and Chetumal in 1544. He brought most of the peninsula under Spanish rule and divided it into large estates where Maya natives were put to work as indentured servants. Franciscan friars relocated villagers to new missions built with stones from the rubble of Maya ceremonial centers toppled by the *conquistadores.* The friars' efforts to convert the natives to Catholicism produced a strange, hybrid folk religion that became the target of the Spanish Inquisition. The climax in the Yucatán came in 1562, when the Spanish bishop burned every Maya codex in the town of Maní.

Nearly 3 centuries of relative calm followed, interrupted sporadically by raids from such pirates as Francis Drake and Edward "Blackbeard" Teach. But after Mexico won independence from Spain in 1821, Maya natives were again enslaved, this time in debt peonage to rich landowners who had turned mission lands into huge tobacco, *henequén,* and sugarcane plantations. When General Santa Anna, of Alamo fame, moved in to subdue rebels bent on seceding from the new republic, he found ready recruits in Maya men eager to take up arms against their oppressors. The Maya militia remained after Santa Anna divided the peninsula into Yucatán, Campeche, and Quintana Roo territories.

In the midst of the revolution, New York writer John Lloyd Stephens and illustrator Frederick Catherwood came south to investigate rumors of lost cities in the jungle. Stephens's tales became worldwide bestsellers and are still in print today. But the frenzy of archaeological expeditions that would surely have followed was stymied by a massive Maya uprising in 1847, which touched off more than 60 years of warfare. The War of the Castes (from the Spanish word *casta,* or "race"), the longest and most devastating war in Mexico's history, halted travel to the Yucatán peninsula and reduced its population from about 500,000 to 200,000 by the turn of the century. It would be another 30 years before the territory of Quintana Roo came under official government control, and to this day some Maya do not recognize Mexican sovereignty.

In the 19th and early 20th centuries, Yucatán lands were taken over primarily by planters seeking their fortunes by growing *henequén* (also called sisal after the Gulf coast port from which it was shipped), the best natural fiber for making rope. Yucatán suddenly became the wealthiest territory in Mexico.

The end of the War of the Castes brought a stream of U.S. archaeologists to explore the world John Lloyd Stephens had unveiled 60 years earlier. Harvard archaeology student Sylvanus Morley's accounts in *National Geographic* were as

## The War of the Castes

Maya tradition holds that the world ends and a new one is created at regular intervals. The ancient calendar predicted 1847 would be one of those years.

The prophecy began to fulfill itself that July, when Maya deserters from the Mexican Army revolted, terrorizing *ladino* (white) residents of Valladolid. Government soldiers responded by burning and looting villages and forcing Maya residents to watch an accused conspirator's execution in Valladolid's plaza. All the Yucatán's Maya soldiers then took up arms and swept through the countryside, burning churches and sugar plantations and killing every Spaniard they saw.

By the spring of 1848, the rebels had seized Valladolid and soon drove every European from rural Yucatán. Mérida and Campeche were on the verge of surrender. But when the rainy season came, the rebels returned to their villages to plant their crops. The Yucatecan troops quickly made major advances, and thousands of Maya retreated into the jungles of Quintana Roo in a migration that would reshape the peninsula's economic and political landscape.

Violence continued sporadically for more than 60 years, with each side slaughtering members of the other wherever they found them. The war was officially declared over in 1901, though fighting in settlements that refused to acknowledge Mexican control continued on a reduced scale until 1915.

important as Stephens's books in revealing the Maya legacy to the world. Believing public interest would generate funding for archaeological digs, Morley proposed a plan to restore one of the great Maya ceremonial centers to inspire tourism. Chichén Itzá was chosen because it was the most accessible.

The development of synthetic rope fibers during World War II devastated the Yucatán economy, and the lavish haciendas were abandoned. Most of the Yucatán peninsula remained wild and empty, until the phenomenon known as Cancún. The past 2 decades have seen most of the peninsula's roads paved and even the most remote Maya villages fitted out with electricity. Young Maya people now leave the family cornfields to study at free national universities, mostly around Mérida. The courses most in demand are English, hotel and restaurant management, and a new college major, *turismo*.

# UXMAL & THE HILL COUNTRY

If Chichén Itzá is your main reference point for Maya culture, Uxmal will seem a city from a different civilization. Visiting the ruins of Uxmal is soothing rather than exhausting. In its graceful proportions and intricate stone work there is nothing to suggest military ambition or human sacrifice; its architects were preoccupied with man's relationship to nature, and their tools were intellect, science, and ceremony.

Deep in what is now one of the Yucatán's most sparsely populated areas, Uxmal ruled a thriving, widespread city-state, and it was second in size and influence only to Chichén Itzá. A network of *sacbeob* ("white roads"), raised causeways of cobbled limestone, connected the city to smaller ceremonial centers scattered through the rolling hills. Several of these satellite cities are connected today by paved roads designated the Ruta Puuc ("Hill" in Mayan), which winds its way east through the countryside.

## GETTING TO & AROUND UXMAL & THE HILL COUNTRY

Uxmal is about a 1½-hour drive south of Mérida. Take Hwy. 180 toward Campeche, then turn off at Umán to take the inland road (Hwy. 261) south, which passes through Muna. Uxmal is about 16km (10 miles) farther south. You can make a loop to all these sites, ending in the little town of Oxkutzcab or in the larger town of Ticul on Hwy. 184. To return to Mérida, continue west on Hwy. 184 to Muna and pick up Hwy. 261 north.

Virtually every hotel and travel agency in Mérida can arrange tours to Uxmal or the Ruta Puuc; the average rate is about $50. One highly recommended operator, **Mayan Heritage** (Calle 62 no. 471, btw. calles 55 and 57, Mérida; ☎ 999/924-8283; www.mayanheritage.com.mx), offers an afternoon tour of the ruins, dinner at a local restaurant, and a return to the sound-and-light show for $35, including transportation, guides, and dinner (but not admission to the ruins). Full-day tours including a visit to Kabah are also available.

If you'd rather go on your own but don't want to drive, the **ATS bus** line offers a Ruta Puuc excursion for about $12. It departs Mérida's second-class terminal (Calle 71, btw. 69 and 70) at 8am daily and takes 7 or 8 hours. You get a half-hour each at Labná, Sayil, Kabah, and Xlapak, and about 2 hours at Uxmal. This is just transportation—no guide or lunch—and it's a bit of a whirlwind, but it's easy on the budget. If you want to see only Uxmal, the bus will drop passengers there before continuing on to the smaller sites and pick them up on the return trip. This bus frequently fills up on Sundays, when admission to the ruins is free for Mexicans, so buy a ticket in advance if you plan to go that day.

## ACCOMMODATIONS, BOTH STANDARD & NOT

The ruins of Uxmal have no associated town. Budget lodgings are 5 to 15 minutes' drive away from the entrance, but if you have your heart set on staying at the Lodge at Uxmal or one of the other pricey hotels within walking distance, Mexican discount booking sites such as **Best Day Travel** (www.bestday.com; search Yucatán hotels) and **TravelYucatan.com** will give you a price break. If you're making a loop of Uxmal and the rest of the Ruta Puuc, staying in Oxkutzcab or Ticul increases your options.

### A Living Museum

**$$**    Instead of pouring millions of dollars into restoring an abandoned hacienda to its *henequén*-era grandeur, as luxury chains have taken to doing in recent decades, the owner of **Hacienda Yaxcopoil** ★★★ (Carretera 261 Km 186, 32km/20 miles south of Mérida; ☎ 999/900-1193; www.yaxcopoil.com; PayPal)ensconces you in a gracefully aging 17th-century plantation in a state of suspended animation. The hacienda is about midway between Mérida and Uxmal and its great

Moorish double arch at the entrance is impossible to miss. A single guesthouse is the only part of the estate that has been restored. Its two double beds, kitchen table, rocking chairs, and other simple furnishings are old-fashioned but not creaky, a perfect match for the decorative tile floor. The large room includes a sitting area, a kitchen (outdoor sink and grill), and a simple but modern bathroom. You can lounge on the back terrace or step out the front door to have run of the garden. And it costs just $60 for a double ($10 each for extra people). An optional $20 per person buys breakfast and a home-cooked traditional Maya dinner (*sopa de lima,* three types of tamales, seasonal fruit, and *horchata*), served at your convenience. Though you won't get air-conditioning, electric ceiling fans and good cross-ventilation keep the hacienda comfortable in all but the hottest weather.

With only one guesthouse (another was scheduled to open sometime in 2008), you'll have the estate to yourself in the evening and early morning. During the day, the hacienda is open for public **tours** (Mon–Fri 8am–6pm, Sun 9am–1pm; $5); guests get a private tour. Rather than remodeling the house, the owner arrested its decay and filled it with furnishings used during the height of the hacienda's late-19th-century splendor. A small museum displays Classic-period Maya artifacts recovered from ruins on hacienda grounds.

## Hotels & a Bed & Breakfast

**$**   The friendly market town of Oxkutzcab, on Hwy. 184 where the Puuc Route and Convent Route meet, is an especially good alternative if you're visiting both routes. The best choice is the newish motel-style **Hotel Puuc** ★ (Calle 55 no. 80 at Calle 44; ☎ 997/975-0103; cash only), whose good-size modest rooms are brightened by light wood furniture and wall murals of Puuc ruins. Bathrooms are small and walls are thin, but it's cheery and comfortable—a great value at $30 ($35 with air-conditioning). Its family-run restaurant, Peregrino, serves ample portions of tasty, simple international food.

**$**   Ticul, at the crossroads of highways 184 and 261, is one of the Yucatán's larger towns, known primarily for manufacturing women's dress shoes and embroidering *huipiles* (native blouses). The **Hotel San Antonio** ★★ (Calle 24A, btw. calles 26 and 26A; ☎ 997/972-1893; www.hotelsan-antonio.com; cash only), is a recent addition occupying a remodeled colonial-style building, 1 block off the central plaza. Modest rooms don't offer the traditional flourishes that grace public areas, but they are bright and offer air-conditioning, comfortable beds, and cable TV; many have small balconies overlooking a corner of the park. The restaurant serves good Yucatecan and Mexican food at low prices. Double rooms ($31–$37) come with a double, a king, or two double beds.

**$–$$**   The quiet but fetching town of Santa Elena, 15 minutes from Uxmal, is a good base for exploring the Puuc and Convent routes, and the **Flycatcher Inn B&B** ★★★ (Calle 20, Santa Elena; www.flycatcherinn.com; cash only), just off Hwy. 261, is an excellent place to lay your head. Spacious rooms tucked behind a broad colonnade offer simple, bright decor; queen-size beds with pillow-top mattresses; garden terraces; and lots of decorative ironwork forged by the owner. Double rooms are $45 (for the smallest room) to $55 a night, including an ample breakfast of tropical fruit and homemade breads. A larger suite, with a second bed and a marble bathroom, and a new private cottage rent for $65 a night ($10 per additional guest). Air-conditioning costs $10 extra in all rooms. A nature walk winds through lagoons, fruit trees, and wild woodland on the 8-hectare (20-acre) grounds.

**$$**  Perched grandly on a hill a 5-minute drive from the ruins, the resort-style **Hotel Misión Uxmal** (Carretera 261 Km 78; ☎ 997/976-2022; www.hotelesmision. com; AE, MC, V) boasts views of the surrounding jungle and the ruins beyond. The spacious guest rooms are a bit dated, and the beds (two doubles in each room) will be too hard for many tastes, but they are clean and pleasant, and all have balconies. Try for a room on the left side of the third floor, where you can see the glow from Uxmal's sound-and-light show at night. The rooftop solarium, with panoramic views of the rolling hills, is always open. Facilities include a large pool, a *temazcal* spa with bilingual staff, badminton and other sports areas, and a reasonably priced restaurant. The published rate is $82 per night, but you can get them for $62 to $65 on the discount sites.

**$$**  The best value among the hotels clustered around the ruins' entrance, **Villas Arqueológicas** ★★★ (Carretera 261 Km 76; ☎ 987/972-9300, ext. 8181 central reservations, or 997/974-6020; www.islandercollection.com; AE, MC, V) is a basic, two-story stucco quadrangle, admirably prettied up by lush vegetation, reproduction Maya statues, and a paint job with a semblance of traditional style. The bright, modern rooms are small and minimally furnished with wooden furniture and a double and a twin bed snuggled into their own niches (a potential challenge for tall people), but they offer ample storage and counter space. Public areas include a pool, tennis courts, and a well-used library with big-screen TV and plenty of books. You get most of the comforts available in the neighboring hotels at a much better price; though rack rates start at $106 for a double, discount sites have them for $74. *Note:* This is one of five hotels at major archaeological sites built by the Mexican government in 1977 and operated for years by Club Med. The group was recently taken over by Islander Collection, a new Mexican property management company. Changes so far have been limited to new labeling and fresh paint and varnish, but more could be on the way.

## DINING FOR ALL TASTES

Most visitors end up eating—and paying Cancún prices—at the hotels near Uxmal's entrance. Of these, the regional and international fare in the old-world atmosphere of **Villas Arqueológicas Uxmal**'s (daily 7:30am–10pm; see above) indoor restaurant is the best bet for dinner, at $7 to $20. The romantic restaurant at **Hacienda Uxmal** (Carretera 261 Km 78; ☎ 997/976-2011; www.mayaland.com; daily 7am–10pm; AE, MC, V) is more expensive but offers a set-price lunch for about $11. For more affordable dining, look in surrounding towns.

**$–$$**  Regional dishes from ultrafresh ingredients (grown and harvested by the staff) distinguish **Cana Nah** ★ 🧒 (Carretera 261, 4km/2½ miles north of Uxmal; ☎ 999/901-3829; daily 10am–7pm; cash only); its quality far outpaces that of the Rancho Uxmal hotel to which it is attached. The basic menu includes *sopa de lima, pollo pibil, poc chuc,* and other regional favorites, as well as Mexican *bistec* (steak) and such standbys as fried chicken, without topping $12. With its patterned red-tile floors and family-style tables, it's an appealing place to wait out the

2-hour closing time before Uxmal reopens for the evening light-and-sound show. Guests are also welcome to use the large pool in back or swing in a hammock under the trees.

**$–$$   Los Almendros** (Calle 22 at Hwy. 184; ☎ 997/972-0021; daily 9am–9pm; cash only), which now has branches in Mérida and Cancún, is in a new building at the southern entrance of Ticul. At the back is a pool for diners' use. The restaurant turns out an exemplary *poc chuc* (owners credit the original chefs with creating the dish); sample it along with *cochinita pibil* or *pavo relleno* (stuffed turkey). The menu is mostly Yucatecan, with a few other regional specialties for good measure (entrees $6.50–$11, daily specials $9–$11). When the restaurant isn't besieged by tour groups, you'll often have it practically to yourself.

## WHY YOU'RE HERE: THE TOP SIGHTS & ATTRACTIONS

The ancient Maya city of Uxmal, 80km (50 miles) south of Mérida, is the star of the Puuc (Hilly) Route, which includes the smaller sites of Kabah, Sayil, Xlapak, Labná, and the caves of Loltún. Since the road was paved to open the region to tourism in 1978, some structures at each site have been restored, while others remain in the maw of the jungle, much as early explorers and archaeologists found them. Either Uxmal or the smaller Ruta Puuc sites can be a reasonable day trip from Mérida or Campeche; but if you want to see them both, maybe in combination with the Convent Route (p. 219), you'll want to stay overnight.

### Uxmal

I would put the ruins of **Uxmal** ★★★ (Carretera 261, 80km/50 miles south of Mérida; $9.50 admission, $1 parking; daily 8am–5pm) ahead of Chichén Itzá on any must-see list. It's more tranquil, more beautiful, more purely Maya and distinct from other Maya sites in fascinating ways.

Uxmal dominated the entire Puuc region of southern Yucatán in the late Classic period, reaching its height between A.D. 700 and 900. Unlike other Maya cities, which were built on a flat plane, Uxmal's elegant architecture incorporates the varied elevations of the hilly landscape. Though the name means "thrice built" in the Mayan language, the city actually was built and rebuilt, layer upon layer, over hundreds of years, adding to its intriguing complexity.

Other cities depended on the Yucatán Peninsula's abundance of cenotes for fresh water. Because it stands about 30m (100 ft.) above sea level, Uxmal has no surface openings to the subterranean water. Instead, engineers devised a system of

---

### Shine the Light

Don't write off the nightly **Luz y Sonido** (included with regular admission, $3 light show only; 8pm summer, 7pm winter), or light-and-sound show, as theme-park hokum. The play of lights over the friezes of the Nun's Quadrangle to a narration mixing ancient legend with accounts of archaeological discoveries makes a mesmerizing dramatization of Uxmal's final days. The narration is in Spanish, but translation devices are rented for $2.50.

# Uxmal

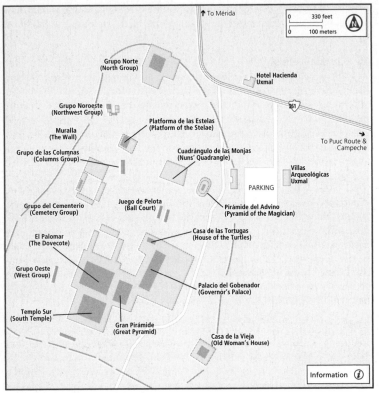

To Mérida

0 — 330 feet
0 — 100 meters

Grupo Norte
(North Group)

Hotel Hacienda
Uxmal

Grupo Noroeste
(Northwest Group)

Platforma de las Estelas
(Platform of the Stelae)

Muralla
(The Wall)

Cuadrángulo de las Monjas
(Nuns' Quadrangle)

Grupo de las Columnas
(Columns Group)

To Puuc Route &
Campeche

Villas
Arqueológicas
Uxmal

PARKING

Grupo del Cementerio
(Cemetery Group)

Juego de Pelota
(Ball Court)

Pirámide del Advino
(Pyramid of the Magician)

El Palomar
(The Dovecote)

Casa de las Tortugas
(House of the Turtles)

Grupo Oeste
(West Group)

Palacio del Gobernador
(Governor's Palace)

Templo Sur
(South Temple)

Gran Pirámide
(Great Pyramid)

Casa de la Vieja
(Old Woman's House)

Information ⓘ

*chultunes* (cisterns) to collect and hold rainwater to support a population estimated at 25,000. The scarcity of water also made Chaac, the rain god, supreme in Uxmal, and his image is ubiquitous in the city's carved stone facades.

Uxmal is considered the finest and most extensively excavated example of Puuc architecture, characterized by low, elongated palaces with intricate cornices, corbeled arches (also called Maya or false arches), rows of columns, and upper walls covered with geometric stone mosaics and friezes. There is no sign of the interior murals common to most Maya architecture; the artistry is all in the stonework.

Rising before you as soon as you enter the ruins is the back of the majestic and slightly strange **Pirámide del Adivino (Temple of the Magician),** the city's tallest structure at 38m (125 ft.). Its refined, rounded profile, visible throughout the site, is a marked contrast to the angular, stepped pyramids typified by Chichén Itzá. At the top of the stairway on the west, or front, side, the gaping mouth of a giant mask of Chaac forms the doorway leading to two temples at the summit. Rebuilt five times on the same foundation, the temple has yielded artifacts from several different kingdoms.

West of the pyramid, the **Cuadrángulo de las Monjas (Nun's Quadrangle)** was named by Spaniards because its 80 or so small chambers reminded them of a convent in old Spain. In fact, the complex probably was a training ground for soldiers,

## Hours & Admission

The archaeological sites along the Ruta Puuc charge $3 admission and are open daily from 8am to 5pm.

healers, astrologers, or priests. The four palaces surrounding the large plaza were built on slightly different elevations, their upper levels festooned with masks, geometric patterns, and representations of coiling snakes. Chaac, with his long, curling nose, is prominent among them—there's even a totemlike stack of Chaac faces on one corner. Entering through a corbeled arch in the south building, you are facing the north temple, the tallest and probably oldest building, with a view from the top that takes in all the city's major buildings. While Chaac and other elements appear on all four structures, each has a distinct look. The east palace is etched with latticework; a Quetzalcóatl motif marks the top of the west palace, suggesting influence from central Mexico.

South of the Nun's Quadrangle, the long, low **Palacio del Gobernador (Governor's Palace)** was built on a raised plaza that covers 2 hectares (5 acres). While surrounding buildings face west, this one faces east, most likely to allow observation of the planet Venus. As is typical of Puuc architecture, the lower level is smooth and plain, while upper levels display sculptures of Chaac, serpents, and astrological symbols that must have kept hundreds of masons and sculptors busy over many generations. The best place to take in this extraordinary facade is from the huge double-headed jaguar throne in front of the palace.

Behind the palace to the south, the raised platform descends in terraces to another large plaza dominated by the 32m (105-ft.) **Gran Pirámide (Grand Pyramid).** This pyramid is only 6m (20 ft.) smaller than the Temple of the Magician, which has been closed to climbers. You can climb its restored north face to a temple and lofty views on top.

Other buildings worth exploring include the **Casa de las Tortugas (House of the Turtles),** whose symbols were associated with rain; **El Palomar (The Dovecote),** with roof combs rarely seen in Puuc architecture; and **Casa de la Vieja (Old Woman's House),** a small structure best known for the large stone phallic images in front of it.

### Ruta Puuc

The well-marked Puuc Route includes four main sites southeast of Uxmal, each smaller and largely unexcavated but worth visiting for their unique characteristics. Kabah is 27km (17 miles) southeast of Uxmal on Hwy. 261, beyond Santa Elena, and the other sites are within a few kilometers of one another. These sites can be combined with Uxmal on a day-trip loop, but you'll get more out of it if you stay overnight in the area and break up your visits.

If you do visit the entire Puuc Route in a day, I'd recommend doing the loop in reverse. Starting at Loltún Caves in the morning, you won't risk running out of time before the last tour, and you'll reach Uxmal in the afternoon, giving you the option of staying for the evening light-and-sound show.

One of the most interesting small sites is **Kabah** ★★ (23km/14 miles south of Uxmal on Carretera 261), the region's most important ceremonial city after Uxmal. The site straddles the highway, but most of the restored ruins are to the east. The most important buildings were built between A.D. 600 and 900, during the later part of the Classic period. The most famous is the **Palacio de los Mascarones (Palace of the Masks),** to the right of the entrance. The facade, unique in Maya architecture, is covered in nearly 300 three-dimensional stone Chaac masks. The palace's modern Maya name, Codz-Poop (Rolled Mat), might have been a reference to the Chaac faces' long, curled-up noses, most of which have broken off. The two male figures (one headless) on the east side of the Codz-Poop are among the few three-dimensional human figures appearing among Maya sites.

**El Palacio (The Palace),** directly in front of you as you enter the ruins, displays the distinctive Puuc architectural decorative columns on the upper part of the facade; a trail through the jungle behind it leads to the **Templo de las Columnas (Temple of the Columns),** with more impressive columns. Across the highway, past what was once the **Templo Mayor (Great Temple),** is a lofty but crumbling arch thought to be the center of the city and the entrance to the *sacbé* (white road), now mostly overgrown, that led to Uxmal in one direction and Labná in the other.

To reach **Sayil** ★ (9km/5½ miles south of Kabah on Carretera 31E), which means "place of the ants," you turn off Hwy. 261 about 4km (2½ miles) south of Kabah and go another 4km (2½ miles) east. This site and tiny Xlapak (which otherwise doesn't have a lot to recommend it), on the way to Labná, are the least restored Puuc sites. The main attraction, the majestic **Gran Palacio (Great Palace),** stands on a hill. Its 90 rooms once housed as many as 350 people. Animals and other figures adorn the facade, which stretches across three terraced levels with rows of columns recalling ancient Greek palaces. Claiming its own modest measure of fame is Stele 9, in the jungle beyond a small temple. The fertility god carved here brandishes a phallus of hugely exaggerated proportions.

Four buildings have been restored in **Labná** ★★★ (9km/5½ miles south of Sayil on Carretera 31E), once a city of as many as 3,000 people. To support such numbers in the arid hills, water was collected in 60 to 70 *chultunes,* a few still visible today. You first come to **El Palacio,** one of the longest Puuc structures, with much of its decorative stone carvings still intact. On the west corner, the serpent's head with a human face peering out from between its jaws is believed to be the symbol of Venus. The lower level has a series of well-preserved Chaac masks, and the upper level contains a large *chultún* that still holds water. The view from here, of the site and the hills beyond, is impressive.

A reconstructed *sacbé* leads from the palace to the site's most striking structure, a well-preserved corbeled arch with exuberant latticework. **El Arco Labná,** nearly 6m (20 ft.) high, is flanked by two chambers and probably was the entrance to a religious ceremonial site. Beyond the arch is **El Mirador,** a pyramid (mostly rubble) topped by a temple with a roof comb etched against the sky.

One of the Yucatán's largest and most fascinating cave systems—and a welcome break from ruins and heat—lies beyond orchards, bananas, and palm groves. Carbon-dated artifacts recovered inside suggest Maya people used the **Grutas de Loltún** (19km/12 miles northeast of Labná; $5; daily 9am–5pm) for ceremonies as early as 800 B.C. Murals of hands, faces, and animals visible as recently as 20 years ago have been all but erased by curious visitors' hands. Still, the limestone stalactites, stalagmites, and formations with such names as Cathedral and Ear of Corn make a fascinating ½-mile walk. The only way to see the caves is by guided tour, offered at 9:30 and 11am, and 12:30, 2, 3, and 4pm. Guides work for tips, so be generous. (**Note:** If you start your tour here rather than at Uxmal, turn left on your way south from Mérida at Muna and follow Hwy. 184 toward Oxkutzcab, following the signs to Loltún.)

## SIDE TRIP FROM UXMAL: THE CONVENT ROUTE

Moving a few centuries forward in time, the Convent Route takes you through colonial churches, convents, and cenotes in the heart of the Yucatán. The only practical way to make this trip is by car. If you are combining it with a Puuc Route tour, stay overnight in **Oxkutzcab** or **Ticul.** In the morning, take the road to Maní, then follow Route 18 north toward Mérida through **Chumayel, Mama, Tekit, Telchaquillo, Tecoh, Acanceh,** and **Kanasín.** Your time at each stop will vary from 15 to 45 minutes. Churches are open daily from 10am to 1pm and 4 to 6pm.

Many people also make this a day trip from Mérida; start with a full tank of gas and get on the road by 8am. Take the *periférico* (beltway) to Route 18 (signs will say Kanasín), and follow the signs to Acanceh and on south from there. (To return to Mérida from Maní, head to Ticul and take Hwy. 184 to Muna, then follow Hwy. 281 north to Uman and on to Mérida.)

The first stop, and historically the most important, is **Maní** (Mah-*nee*). Now a humble village of about 4,500 descendants of ancient Mayapán, it was the capital of the Maya Xiú empire in the 16th century. The dynasty surrendered to the conqueror Montejo and joined the Spanish in fighting the rival Cocom clan, only to be enslaved to build the massive stone church and monastery you see today. It contains a working church with remnants of colorful religious paintings on plaster walls that witnessed the slaughter of 200 Maya during the War of the Castes. As the seat of the Spanish Inquisition in the Yucatán, Maní was the site of Bishop Diego de Landa's infamous *auto-da-fé* in 1562, which destroyed thousands of idols, 13 altars, 27 deerskin scrolls, and nearly 200 vases with hieroglyphs that, in combination, recounted Maya history. The scrolls were the first books of the New World, predating any in Europe. (The contrite bishop later recorded all he could remember in a book, *Relation of Things in the Yucatán.*) Today, you'll see a large church, convent, and museum with explanations in English.

Continuing 12km (7½ miles) to **Teabo** (Teh-*ah*-boh), known for its hand-embroidered *huipiles* and stately 17th-century temple, veer left and continue another 4km (2½ miles) to **Chumayel** (Choo-mah-*yel*) where the famous Maya document "Chilam Balam," chronicling the rise of Chichén Itzá, was written. Ten kilometers (6 miles) farther in the village of **Mama** (Mah-*mah*), you'll find the oldest church on the route, with massive bell gables, wall frescos, and a baroque altar. Six kilometers (4 miles) father on, in the prosperous village of **Tekit** (Teh-*keet*) the Moorish-style temple of the San Antonio De Padua parish houses ornate statues of saints in individual wall niches.

About 26km (16 miles) up the road, is the turn to **Mayapán** ✩✩✩ ($2.50; daily 8am–5pm), the last of the great city-states. The walled city, with a population of about 12,000, was equal in size to Chichén Itzá, and it has a smaller version of the Pyramid of Kukulcán. The city was demolished in 1450, presumably by war. A half dozen of 4,000 jungle-covered mounds have been excavated—royal palaces, round observatories, and the temple of Kukulcán with its vivid red and orange murals—and archaeologists are still at work.

Continuing north, you'll come quickly to **Telchaquillo** (Tel-chah-*kee*-yoh), with its small, austere chapel and a cenote in the plaza. Another 23km (14 miles) down the road, the ornate church and convent dedicated to the Virgin of the Assumption in **Tecoh** (Teh-*koh*) has three carved *retablos* (altarpieces) covered in gold leaf. The hill that the complex is built on actually is the base of a large Maya pyramid that was dismantled to provide stones to build the church.

The central plaza in the bustling village of **Acanceh** ★★ (Ah-con-*keh*, "moan of the deer"), 8km (5 miles) farther, boasts an interesting Maya ruin, the Grand Pyramid, overlooking a colonial church. A caretaker may offer to take you to see the large stucco deities at the top of the pyramid; admission is $2.50. Ask around to find the Templo de los Estucos (Temple of the Stuccoes), a ruin about 4 blocks away. Its murals, discovered in mint condition in 1908, have deteriorated somewhat. Villagers are accustomed to this, and someone will give you directions; if someone leads you there, tip 10 pesos or so.

# PROGRESO & THE GULF COAST

In profound contrast to the march of development down Mexico's Caribbean coast, the Yucatán's Gulf of Mexico coastline remains a wonderland of undiscovered white sands and mangrove-fringed estuaries. Mérida residents have built summer homes east of Progreso, the only coastal city, but the rest of the 378 seafront kilometers (235 miles) stretching from near Isla Holbox to Celestún belongs to a few fishing villages and a whole lot of flamingos.

The challenge for would-be beach bums is access. Except for about 72km (45 miles) of coastal road out of Progreso, the only way to get to the beaches is by driving long narrow roads from the interior highways. Separate roads radiate out from Mérida to Celestún, the fishing village of Sisal, and the port of Progreso. Getting to Río Lagartos, the other flamingo haven, requires a long trek east and then due north (it's best reached from Valladolid and will be covered in that section).

Lodging and restaurants in most of these places can't be called anything but basic, and shopping consists of little more than buying fresh fish off a boat. But those who take the time will find the villages at the ends of these roads full of local residents who are hip to the ecotourism agenda and eager to welcome travelers.

## CELESTUN

On a spit of land separating Celestún's *ría* (estuary) from the Gulf of Mexico, Celestún is the gateway to the **Reserva Ecológica de los Petenes,** a wildlife reserve with extensive mangrove forests and one of North America's largest flamingo colonies. As one of the first places on the Gulf coast to be gathered into the ecotourism fold, it has more tourist comforts than the rest of the coast, while still remaining a tranquil and humble fishing village.

### Getting to & Around Celestún

Celestún is an easy 90-minute drive out of Mérida. Take the *periférico* (beltway) to the exit south toward Umán, and keep right when you reach the Y at Umán's main plaza. After 2 blocks, turn right to Hwy. 281 toward Kinchil and Celestún. When you cross a bridge, you're at the entrance to the flamingo reserve; the center of town is a few blocks farther north.

Buses leave Mérida's Terminal Noroeste 15 times a day ($4) between 5am and 8pm, and take about 2 hours. Return buses run on a similar schedule.

Celestún is a popular day-trip destination, and any hotel can book a tour. One of the best companies is **Ecoturismo Yucatán** (Calle 3 no. 235, Col. Pensiones; ☎ 999/920-2772; www.ecoyuc.com); its staff has a passion for Yucatán's culture and natural history and a stellar track record. Full-day tours including transportation, a tour guide, lunch (excluding drinks), park fee, and boat tour cost $50 per person. Reservations must be made 72 hours in advance.

## Accommodations, Both Standard & Not

Though the flamingo reserve is an easy day trip from Mérida, staying overnight in Celestún allows you to see the flamingos early in the morning, the best time to catch them in flight. Flamingo tourism has spawned a couple of $100-a-night-plus resorts, but the small beachfront hotels along Calle 12 in the center of town are still a trove for budget travelers.

**$** The most colorful, in more ways than one, is **Hotel Sol y Mar** ★ (Calle 12 no. 104 at Calle 11; ☎ 988/916-2166; cash only). The multihued, flag-festooned property looks like a '50s-era Florida transplant—perhaps because that's just what the owner is. Cuban-American Geraldo Vásquez is a worldwide adventurer and a gregarious storyteller. His two-story hotel offers large, sparsely furnished rooms with two queen-size beds, a table and chairs, TV, and, in some, a small fridge. Upstairs rooms, starting at $32, are fan cooled but get sea breezes (and views). Downstairs rooms (about $40) are air-conditioned. The hotel is a block off the town beach and has a rooftop bar overlooking the ocean.

**$$** Two stories of Moorish arches rise over the beach at **Ecohotel Flamingos Playa** (Calle 12 no. 67, btw. calles 3 and 5; ☎ 988/916-2133; ecohotel_flamingo.tripod.com; cash only), about 3 blocks north of the town square. The arches frame ocean and sunrise views from the patterned tile corridors running in front of basic, well-kept guest rooms (air-conditioning, two beds, table and chairs, satellite TV). A small pool overlooks the clean, white beach (shared with the pricey Hotel Manglares next door). Standard rooms ($50) have one double and one single bed; junior suites ($60) have two double beds (up to two kids stay free).

## Dining for All Tastes

Celestún is known for its inexpensive seafood restaurants, which specialize in crab, octopus, and a variety of fresh fish. A handful of small places planted in the sand offer outdoor tables on the beach and similar menus and prices ($6–$10)—or pack up a kilo of fresh shelled crab to go for about $10. (There are rumors, which I can't confirm, of people getting ill at some of the cheaper places, so stick with restaurants that have been recommended.) Note that some places will close earlier in low season.

**$–$$** The original beachside joint, a quaint place with seascape murals, is **La Playita** ★★ (kids) (beach just past foot of Calle 11; daily 9am–5pm; cash only), known for its large portions of fresh seafood, and particularly for its ceviche ($4). A full dinner starring sautéed crab or *filete relleno* (stuffed fish filet, big enough for two) will come to about $12.

**$$–$$$**    Of more recent vintage, **La Palapa** ✦✦✦ 🅺 (Calle 12 no. 105, btw. calles 11 and 13; ☎ 988/916-2063; daily 11am–7pm; AE, MC, V), departs from rustic Celestún style with modern architecture featuring a conch-shell facade and Caribbean atmosphere. The house specialty is *camarones a la palapa* (fried shrimp coated with a smooth garlic cream and served over fettuccini), but the fantastically varied menu also offers crab, lobster, octopus, sea bass, red snapper, and other fresh fish in infinite variations. This is Celestún's fine dining spot, and some entrees are upwards of $20, but there's plenty in the $7 to $12 range. You can also choose from beef and poultry dishes, and kids get not only their own menu but a play area with swings, doll houses, and sand toys.

## Why You're Here: The Flamingo Reserve

Celestún is the gateway to the **Reserva Ecológica de los Petenes** ✦✦✦, a 40,500-hectare (100,000-acre) wildlife reserve famous for its flamingo colony. The long, shallow estuary, where salty Gulf waters mix with fresh water from 80 or so cenotes, is sheltered from the open sea by a narrow strip of land, making it an ideal breeding ground for flamingos and many other species of waterfowl. The estuary extends into northwestern Campeche state, bordered by mangrove forests and sporting islets and white-sand beaches. Pink clouds of flamingos soar overhead all year, but the months to see them in the greatest numbers are April through July.

The reserve is also one of the Gulf's largest duck wintering grounds, hosting at least 15 species, along with hundreds of other types of waterfowl and birds of prey. The estuary also has a large sea-turtle population; other endangered species in residence include ocelot, jaguar, and spider monkey.

The time-honored tactic of finding a fishing boat under the bridge to hire for a tour has been supplanted by a modern visitor center, just to the left after you cross the bridge entering town. Facilities include a small museum, a snack bar, clean bathrooms, and a ticket window. Prices are fixed at about $50 for a 75-minute tour for up to six people (about what the old grab-a-fishing-boat method cost). You can join another group and split the price if you don't have a boatload yourself.

You'll definitely see flamingos on your tour; nonbreeding flamingos remain here year-round. Pelicans, spoonbills, egrets, frigate birds, and sandpipers also feed on shallow sandbars all through the year. Tour boats also skirt the mangroves for close-up views and stop for swimming in the sweet, transparent waters of a cenote burbling up from under the ground. A longer tour ($75) includes a stop at one of the white-sand beaches.

---

## In the Pink

The eye-catching pink plumage that makes such a spectacle when flamingos take flight isn't a birthright. There is no such thing as a pink flamingo chick—they are born downy white. As flamingos grow, they feed on crab and shrimp larvae dredged from the shallows. Accumulated carotene from the crustaceans eventually gives the birds their characteristic pink-orange color, becoming more vivid as they mature.

*A reminder:* The *ría* is a fragile ecosystem. Boatmen are required to keep 91m (300 ft.) away from flamingos while using their motors and 46m (150 ft.) while poling. Do not ask them to go any closer, and don't make abrupt moves or noises that could startle the birds. Flamingos spend half their time eating, and if they are disrupted, they might leave for other, less suited habitat. If you swim, don't use sunblock, except for special biodegradable formulas.

## PROGRESO

Progreso is Mérida's escape valve. When the heavy summer heat verges on the unbearable, Méridians flock to the coastal city's well-groomed white-sand beach. If you're traveling in summer, you might want to follow their lead; otherwise, there's not much to keep you for long in this former fishing village. Progreso has been the Yucatán Peninsula's main port of entry since the 1870s, when *henequén* crops were the major economic force; today it's a major stop for cruise ships. For the cruise-ship crowd, it's a jumping-off point for a quick trip to Mérida. For most of the rest of us, it's a jumping-off point for exploring the northern coastline.

### Getting to & Around Progreso

To reach Progreso from Mérida, take Paseo Montejo or Calle 60 north. Either street will funnel you onto Hwy. 261, a fast four-lane highway that goes straight to Progreso and ends at the beach 32km (20 miles) later.

The **Transportes AutoProgreso** (Calle 62, btw. calles 65 and 67) runs buses every 12 to 14 minutes, daily 5am to 10pm, out of its station in Mérida. A direct trip (50 min.) costs about $1.50 each way. The trip with stops along the way takes almost 2 hours and only costs about 25¢ less, but you can catch it along Calle 60 if you want to avoid going to the station. In Progreso, the bus station is on the west side of Calle 82, a block north of the main plaza and 3 or 4 blocks from the beach.

Progreso's even-numbered streets run north and south; odd-numbered streets are east and west. The central plaza straddles Calle 80 between calles 31 and 33, 6 short blocks from the waterfront Malecón.

### Accommodations, Both Standard & Not

Although close enough to Mérida to be an easy day trip, Progreso itself can be a base for day trips along the virtually tourist-free coast. The past few years have brought in some B&Bs and small hotels that make it a pleasant place to stay.

$ Basic is the word at **Hotel Embajadores** (Calle 64 no. 130C, btw. calles 21 and 23; ☎ 969/935-5673; www.progresohotel.com/eng-rooms.htm; cash only) but for about $30 a night ($25 with fan only) you get exceptionally friendly proprietors, air-conditioning, a fully equipped communal kitchen, the beach across the street, and a ride from the bus station if you need it. Rooms come with one or two queen-size beds and a small TV. Most have ocean views, and the rooftop lounge area has all the ocean view you could want. For $40 a night, the larger, air-conditioned oceanview suite with sitting area and refrigerator is considerably more attractive (but there's only one, so it might be hard to get).

**$$** Ensconced in a grand, century-old house a few steps from the beach, the Canadian-owned **Casa Isadora** ★ 🌟 (Calle 21 no. 116; ☎ 969/935-4595; www. casaisidora.com; AE, DISC, MC, V, PayPal) offers six spacious, simple, airy guest rooms with 4m (14-ft.) ceilings and restored ceramic-tile floors. Two have small private patios; two more open onto the pool patio. Each has two double beds ($75 a night) and is big enough for one more ($15). Continental breakfast is served in the dining room or by the pool. A breezy, oceanview dormitory room on the second floor is available for large groups; rates depend on meal plans and number of guests. The hotel also operates a restaurant and a bar and grill on the street side (the pool patio bar is just for guests). If you don't stay here, come by for excellent hamburgers, chicken burgers, and fries, and margaritas and beer regardless.

**$$** The elegant, old-world **Hotel Yakunah** ★★★ 🌟 (Calle 23 no. 64, btw. calles 48 and 50, Colonial Ismael García; ☎ 969/935-5600; www.hotelyakunah. com.mx; AE, DISC, MC, V; PayPal) is a former aristocrat's summer home. Occupied until 2006 by the Casa Quixote B&B, it is now owned by a multilingual Dutch family who renovated the property, added three rooms, and reopened as a hotel. (A light continental breakfast is included, but full breakfasts cost extra.) The quiet location is a 10-minute walk from the central plaza but just across the street from the beach. Guest rooms have a romantic feel with large beds, Mexican rugs, armoires, and easy chairs, and include cable TV and gleaming tiled bathrooms with large showers. Doubles are $65 a night, $15 for each extra person over 12. Rooms with two double beds are $75. A two-bedroom, two-bathroom garden apartment with fully equipped kitchen and private terrace is also available for $120. One of the owners is a chef who turns out breakfasts and dinners (extra charge) that could save you the trouble of finding a restaurant.

## Dining for All Tastes

**$$** A popular expat hangout, **Flamingos** ★ (Calle 19 no. 144-D at Calle 72; ☎ 969/935-2122; daily 7am–10pm; MC, V) is a large place with an open kitchen and an ocean view. Its frozen margaritas are among the best, and it doesn't hurt that they come with hearty *botanas* (snacks) such as ceviche, *sikil-pak* (pumpkin seed, roasted tomato, and cilantro dip), and fresh jicama strips with lemon juice and chili powder. Some of the main dishes fall short of sublime (shrimp in a white sauce with melted cheese, onions, and bacon?), but the large, breaded, and lightly fried fish filets approach perfection. Plus, you'll find it's a challenge to spend more than $10. The location, cleanliness, and attentive service get full marks.

**$$–$$$$** Generous fish dishes at moderate prices and a *palapa* terrace with sea views are the reasons to go to **Restaurant Los Pelicanos** ★★ (Malecón at Calle 70; ☎ 969/935-0798; daily 8am–10pm; cash only), in the Hotel Real del Mar. You could eat a meal in the time it takes to read the menu, which leans toward Mexican/Yucatecan with a few international favorites. Salads, soups, and pastas top out at $6.50; ceviche (shrimp, snail, octopus, fish, or mixed) are $6 to $14. Oh, and did we mention the fish? Spicy, *a la plancha* (on a wood plank), Veracruz style, baked in a banana leaf, au gratin . . . all between $6 and $7. Shrimp, which is prohibitively expensive in much of the Yucatán, is prepared at least 10 ways, for $8.50 to $10.

## Why You're Here: The Top Sights & Attractions

Though Progreso can get hectic when a cruise ship is in port, most passengers are going to hop a bus to Mérida for the day, anyway. Still, the main attractions are outside of town.

### PROGRESO WATERFRONT

When it hit the cruise-ship map, Progreso got busy sprucing up **El Malecón,** its 16-block seaside promenade. Though fancy restaurants have been added and vendors have started selling handicrafts and T-shirts along the beach, it's still a pretty tranquil place most of the time. With no currents or tides, the long white beach is inviting to sunbathers and safe for swimmers. As with other Gulf beaches, the water is murky compared with the Caribbean, but it is clear and bathtub warm. The Malecón is the best place in town for people-watching, especially in the evenings when local families gather to gossip, exercise, and solve the world's problems.

One curiosity along the Malecón is the *muelle* **(pier),** so long that it seems to disappear. Extending 7km (4½ miles) out to sea, it is the world's longest pier. The limestone shelf that supports the entire peninsula slopes very gradually out to sea, leaving a long expanse of water far too shallow for large ships. The pier was built—the first section in 1942 and the rest within the past 10 years to accommodate cruise ships—to meet ships past the shelf. Even so, the water at the end of the pier is only about 9m (30 ft.) deep.

### NEARBY FISHING VILLAGES

Just west of Progreso is a slice of the "real Mexico" in everyone's imagination. **Chelem,** 9km (5½ miles) away by the coast road, is a peaceful fishing village with a traditional central plaza surrounded by lots of seafood restaurants and some good beaches. Located between the Gulf of Mexico and the Estero (Estuary) Yucalpetén, Chelem's residents are close to nature. If your Spanish is serviceable, you can find fishing captains just south of the main plaza and arrange an hour-long boat ride into the *ría* (about $25 for up to six people) to see flamingos and turtles at a freshwater cenote. The boats are very basic, but they are safe.

In Chelem and in **Chuburna** 🐟 another 11km (7 miles) west, local fishing captains are beginning to offer organized walking, kayaking, and cycling tours combined with a boat trip through the mangroves for about $35. This is eco-tourism in its infancy, and you won't find websites or even phone numbers, but you can ask the **Progreso Tourist Office** (Casa de La Cultura, Calle 80, btw. calles 25 and 27; ☎ 969/935-0104) for help setting up a trip.

### THE EMERALD COAST

The 120km (75 miles) of Yucatán's northern coast along Hwy. 27 from Chuburna to the village of Dzilam de Bravo is dubbed La Costa Esmeralda (the Emerald Coast), after the clear, green Gulf waters. Although many people from Mérida and other inland towns have built summer homes here, the beautiful scenery and varied bird life are barely touched by tourism.

To increasing numbers of snowbirds and expats, the sleepy beach town of **Chicxulub,** about 8km (5 miles) east of Progreso, is their own private paradise. To scientists, it is the site of a buried impact crater, about 161km (100 miles) in diameter, from a meteor that smashed into the earth 65 million years ago. Researchers believe this meteor strike created the Yucatán's cenotes, which form a ring around the crater's rim—the only visible signs of its existence. The meteor impact also coincides with the sudden extinction of the dinosaurs, and scientists are still debating whether the two events are related.

At **Uaymitun** ✹, less than 10km (6 miles) beyond Chicxulub, a large wooden tower looms over the right side of the road. This is an observation post for viewing a new colony of flamingos that migrated here from Celestún several years ago. The state agency CULTUR operates the tower and provides binoculars free of charge.

A short inland detour is in order about 11km (6½ miles) after leaving Uaymitun. The signs say X'TAMPU, but they lead to the Maya site of **Xcambó** ✹, down a road through marshes and coconut plantations. A tinge of iodine hangs in the air since Xcambó was (and still is) a salt production center, supplying Chichén Itzá, Uxmal, and Izamal in a day when salt was more valuable than gold. The site is still under reconstruction, and only two plazas have been restored so far. From the top of the Pyramid of the Cross, you can see the coast in the distance and the wide reach of amorphous rock outcroppings that reveal how big the city once was. Restoration work began only about 8 years ago, but the site has been no secret to local villagers, who collected the white rocks to build their fences, homes, and churches. In fact, a rough-hewn Catholic church, complete with altar, flowers, and statues, rises from some of the ruins, presenting a curious fusion of two eras—and some welcome shade.

Past Telchac Puerto, the largest village on the coast (which offers some decent restaurants if you're hungry), the picturesque village of **San Crisanto** ✹✹✹ is home to a group of fishermen who have carved out several kilometers of trails through the mangrove forests, connecting a number of crystal-clear cenotes that were formerly closed to the public. For about $3, they will paddle you along shallow canals through mangroves, where small labels in English and Spanish tell you what you're seeing, to an open-air cenote. You'll have time to swim, and perhaps even indulge your inner Tarzan by swinging on one of the vines hanging over the water. Buy a ticket at the Ejido de San Crisanto office. When you get to the intersection at San Crisanto, turn right and go about half a block; the office is across the street from the baseball field.

The coast road ends 108km (67 miles) east of Progreso at **Dzilam de Bravo,** the final resting place of the "gentleman pirate" Jean Lafitte; a gleaming white memorial plaque stands on the beach, facing the sea. Local fishermen recently formed a cooperative called **Dzayachuleb** ✹ (east end of town, next to Port Captain's office; ☎ 991/912-2520; ecoturyucatan.com.mx) to offer a wide range of boat tours into the nearby Parque Natural San Felipe, one of the Yucatán's most unspoiled bird-watching areas. One of the closest stops is a lagoon where hundreds of flamingos, herons, egrets, and other waterfowl breed, close by the resident crocodiles. Early morning is the best time to see flamingos, which take off for other feeding grounds later in the day. The shorter tours include a trip to a cenote, as well as a walk through flocks of pelicans and shorebirds into mangrove marshes. Longer tours visit more distant lagoons and the offshore Bocas islands. Prices range from $50 to $100 per boatload (up to eight passengers).

# CHICHEN ITZA & THE MAYA INTERIOR

The fabled ruins of Chichén Itzá, by far the most visited of all Maya sites, is all that many travelers see of Yucatán's vast interior. Worthy though they are, the monumental ruins are only one aspect of Yucatán's largely tourist-free core, with its traditional Maya towns and pockets of colonial elegance.

Chichén Itzá's "New World Wonder" status, unfortunately, has made the great city harder to appreciate. Somehow, seeing dozens of plastic El Castillo key chains and night lights in every souvenir shop and standing in line to get an unobstructed photo of the pyramid cuts sharply into the awe factor. Wandering through the towns where real life still carries on, and visiting some of the lesser ruins with their mystery still intact, will enhance a visit that might otherwise feel like a cattle call.

At the very least, spend a night near Chichén Itzá to get a shot at seeing the site in peace before the tour buses arrive. Better yet, base yourself in the picturesque and historical town of Izamal or the seriously underrated colonial city of Valladolid to mingle with local Maya people, explore remote cenotes and haciendas, and discover some of the little-known ruins for yourself.

## GETTING TO & AROUND CHICHEN ITZA

Chichén Itzá is on the old Hwy. 180 *(libre)* between Mérida and Cancún. The fastest way to get there from either city is to take the Hwy. 180 *autopista,* or *cuota* ($7 from Mérida, $22 from Cancún). It's about a 1½-hour trip from Mérida, 45 minutes from Valladolid, and 2½ hours from Cancún. The Chichén Itzá exit deposits you on the road to the village of Pisté, where you'll come to a T junction at Hwy. 180 *libre;* turn left to get the ruins, less than 2km (about a mile) away. The exit for the hotel zone is a little beyond the entrance to the ruins, at Km 121.

First-class buses run from Mérida's CAME station, Cancún, and Valladolid to Chichén Itzá several times a day. Tours also are widely available from Mérida ($50–$60) and Cancún ($60–$80).

## ACCOMMODATIONS, BOTH STANDARD & NOT

Your choices are between the handful of expensive hotels immediately east of the ruins or along the main street of Pisté, less than 2km (about a mile) west of the site. The expensive hotels all have beautiful grounds, and you can walk from them to the back entrance of the ruins. Pisté doesn't have much to recommend it except affordable lodging.

### Chichén Itzá

**$$** A longtime favorite with budget travelers, **Hotel Dolores Alba** ★ (Hwy. 180 *libre* Km 122; ☎ 985/858-1555; www.doloresalba.com; cash only), about 2½km (1½ miles) east of the ruins, is a motel kind of place that tries hard—and mostly succeeds—in creating a hacienda atmosphere. Large, air-conditioned rooms with two double beds have lots of colorful tile accents and satellite TV with English stations. Even with mismatched sheets, the $52 double rate is a bargain for what you get. The grounds have two pools—one into a natural spring—and hammocks hanging under *palapas.* The hotel provides transportation to the ruins, but you'll have to flag down a bus to get back or mooch a ride from another visitor. If you're traveling by car, it's probably worth paying the parking fee. It has a decent restaurant with moderate prices.

**$$$**   Like its sister property at Uxmal, **Villas Arqueológicas Chichén-Itzá** ★★★ (east entrance to ruins; ☎ 987/972-9300, ext. 8181, or central reservations 985/ 851-0034; www.islandercollection.com; AE, MC, V) was recently taken over from Club Med by Islander Collection. It's not as lavish as its more upscale neighbors but is a pleasant place with everything you need. The building surrounds a patio pool with a cocktail bar. The rooms are modern and comfortable, except for tall people—each bed is in its own alcove with walls at the head and foot. Most have one double (smaller than standard) and one twin bed. The entrance to the ruins is a 5- to 10-minute walk on a peaceful road. Rooms start at $106 but are available from discounters for about $86—DoCancun (www.docancun.com) has doubles starting at $84 for room only. Buy bottled water in town and bring it with you; when you run out of the one that comes with your room, the price of buying more is steep.

## Pisté

**$-$$**   An economy-priced sibling of the luxury Mayaland resort at the ruins' entrance, the **Hotel Chichén Itzá** ★ (Calle 15A no. 45; ☎ 800/235-4079 toll-free U.S., or 998/887-2495; www.mayaland.com; AE, MC, V) is a great deal if you stick with its standard double rooms, which come with two double beds and are uncluttered and comfortable in a pared-down colonial style. You can get them starting at $40 a night on local discount booking sites such as DoCancun. The superior doubles, which have been remodeled with pink marble tile and fancier furnishings, aren't worth the $30 leap in price, especially if you're just there to get an early start at the ruins.

## DINING FOR ALL TASTES

This isn't a culinary hot spot by any stretch, but there is decent food if you keep it simple. The restaurant at the ruins' visitor center does a pretty good job with light fare, and the hotel restaurants around the entrance are good, if more expensive than they should be. The **Hotel Villas Arqueológicas** achieves the best balance between price and quality, but you might want one meal (lunch is a better value) at the **Hacienda Chichén,** specializing in Mexican and Yucatecan food, just for its lush, romantic surroundings. Down the road, the **Dolores Alba**'s restaurant is better than average, and you can use the hotel pool if you eat there.

In Pisté, **Las Mestizas,** a block east of the Hotel Chichén Itzá and across the street, gets high marks for its regional cuisine.

## WHY YOU'RE HERE: THE TOP SIGHTS & ATTRACTIONS

Even though it is the world's most famous Maya site, what makes **Chichén Itzá** ★★★ ($10, free for kids under 12, parking $1; daily 8am–5pm) an archaeological marvel is its departure from Maya tradition. The old highway that once passed through Chichén Itzá is now a path dividing the ruins into two distinct parts. Chichén Nuevo (New Chichén), built after A.D. 925, shows strong Toltec influence through its huge ball court and in its emphasis on human sacrifice and military glory. Chichén Viejo (Old Chichén) was established around A.D. 300 and

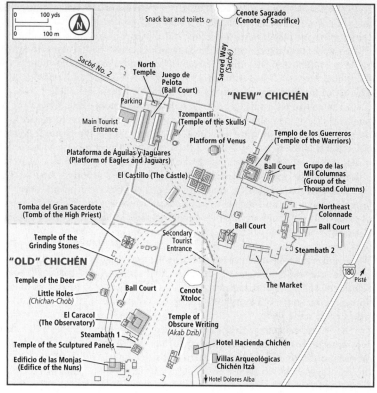

built before the Itzá clan, with their Toltec alliances, came to power, in a style more reminiscent of the Puuc ruins.

Most of the important structures are in New Chichén, but if you have time (and energy), the older structures are worth seeing. The entire site occupies 6½ sq. km (2½ sq. miles), and it will take most of a day to see it all. Even if you don't try to see everything, plan to get there early in the morning, as the midday heat can be brutal.

What draws the crowds, of course, is **El Castillo (The Castle),** or more fully, El Castillo del Serpiente Emplumado (Castle of the Plumed Serpent, a favorite deity in Mesoamerican cultures, also known as Kukulcán). Though its 24m (79-ft.) height no longer makes it the Yucatán's tallest (Ek Balam's more recently discovered Acrópolis outreaches it), it easily dominates the surroundings. Its relatively unadorned bulk, rising alone in the center of a great grassy plaza, appears simple, but embedded in Castillo is an intricate stone calendar: Each staircase has 91 steps, which, added to the single step at the temple's main entrance, amounts to 365; each side of the temple contains 52 panels aligned with the sun. During the spring equinox, the phenomenon of the stairway's shadow slithering down a corner of the pyramid to the giant serpent's head at the bottom draws hordes of worshipers and admirers every year.

El Castillo has been closed to climbers, but you can climb down instead, into the pyramid beneath the pyramid (if you're not too claustrophobic); the Maya commonly built new structures over the old. Enter through a tunnel at the back of the upper temple and descend the cramped, hot, and humid staircase formed by the outside wall of the inner pyramid (check at the entry gate for hours when the tunnel is open). You'll come to a chamber with a Chac Mool statue and the **Throne of the Red Jaguar,** an altar painted red and inlaid with jade.

Just beyond El Castillo is the largest **Juego de Pelota (Ball Court)** in the Americas. Maya men played pok-ta-pok, a game whose goal was to propel a ball through stone rings mounted on a wall 7m (23 ft.) above the ground. A major difference between pok-ta-pok and its modern successors of soccer and basketball is that captain of the team who made the first successful shot was decapitated as a sacrifice to the gods. The 166m-long (545-ft.) court's acoustics render a clap audible from one end of the court to the other, echoing exactly seven times.

The grassy plaza on which El Castillo sits was the focus of Chichén Nuevo; all its important buildings are here, along with a *sacbé* leading to **Cenote Sagrado (Cenote of Sacrifice),** where archaeologists have retrieved bones of sacrificial victims, including children. This natural well signified life as well as death to the Maya, and it gave the city its name (literally "at the edge of the well of the Itzá"). Sacrifices may also have been carried out at the **Plataforma de Aguilas y Jaguares (Platform of Eagles and Jaguars),** with its reliefs of eagles and jaguars holding human hearts, and the **Tzompantli (Temple of the Skulls),** carved on every side with leering stone skulls.

The Toltec influence is particularly evident on the eastern edge of the plaza. The **Templo de los Guerreros (Temple of the Warriors),** lined on two sides by the **Grupo de las Mil Columnas (Group of the Thousand Columns),** recalls the great Toltec site of Tula, with its almost Greco-Roman columns portraying more than 200 battle-garbed warriors. The temple is rife with feathered serpents, warriors, jaguars, and eagles devouring human hearts, as well as the undeniably Maya masks of the curly-snouted rain god Chaac. On top—visible only at a distance now that the temple has been closed to climbers—is the famous Chac Mool altar, with two superb figures of the Maya god, reclining with hands cupping a plate on his stomach that awaits the hearts ripped from live sacrifices.

One of Chichén Itzá's most intriguing structures is in the old part of the city. From a distance, the rounded tower of **El Caracol** (The Snail, for its shape), sometimes called the Observatory, looks like any modern observatory. Quite unlike other Maya buildings, the entrances, staircases, and angles are not aligned with one another. Four doors lead into the tower, where a spiral staircase leads to the upper level. The slits in the roof are aligned with the sun's equinoxes.

The admission fee includes the **Luz y Sonido,** the light-and-sound show, held at 7pm in winter or 8pm in summer. It's worth seeing mainly for the spectacle of the lights showing off the ancient city's remarkable geometry. Narration is in Spanish, but headsets can be rented ($2.50) in several languages. You can use your ticket to reenter on the same day. The modern visitor center at the main entrance includes a museum, an auditorium, a restaurant, bathrooms, and a bookstore.

It's worth hiring a bilingual guide, who will point out architectural details you would miss on your own and explain their significance. Guides usually wait at the entrance and charge about $45 for a group of up to six people. Don't be shy about asking other visitors who speak your language if they want to share a guide.

## Grutas de Balamkanché

Just 6km (3½ miles) east of Chichén Itzá on the highway to Valladolid and Cancún, the Throne of the Jaguar Caves, as the name translates from Mayan, make a dank, dark contrast to Chichén Itzá's sunlit heights. The **Grutas de Balamkanché** ($5, free for children 6–12; no children under 6; tours in English at 11am, 1, and 3pm), used as a hiding place during the War of the Castes, originally were a temple for the worship of Chaac, the rain god. This is the easiest of any of the Yucatán's cave tours to negotiate, but it is hot and humid. The entry fee includes a tour with a minimally helpful taped commentary. It leads past vases, jars, and incense burners once used in sacred rituals, as well as stalactites, stalagmites, and side caves enhanced by colored lights. At the end is the cenote where Maya priests worshiped Chaac, and a round chamber with a huge rock formation resembling a *ceiba,* the Mayas' tree of life, with clay pots in the shapes of gods' faces and other offerings around its base. There's a six-person minimum, but the ticket vendor sometimes will admit as few as two.

# IZAMAL

A pocket of picturesque Maya towns and villages, all overlaid with orderly Spanish town plans around a central plaza and church, lie east of east of Mérida and north of Hwy. 180. Most picturesque of all is Izamal, with an entire city center—the market, the huge monastery, all the colonial buildings—painted a glowing ochre-yellow. Besides the cobblestone streets and iron lampposts, a set of Maya pyramids are right in town. Take the scenic route through the villages of Tixkokob and Cacalchén, and you can stop in Aké, an intriguing juxtaposition of a Maya ruin and a resuscitated *henequén* hacienda. Although it's an easy day trip from Mérida, Izamal also makes a quieter, slower-paced base for exploring the Yucatán.

## GETTING TO & AROUND IZAMAL

Izamal is about 45 minutes from Mérida by car. Take the *periférico* (beltway) to the Tixkokob exit. At Tixkokob, you can veer right (southeast) to Aké, 12km (7½ miles) away, or continue on through Cacalchén and Citilcum to Izamal.

Buses run every half-hour from Mérida's **Terminal Noroeste** (Calle 50, btw. calles 65 and 67; ☎ 999/924-7868; $2.50) and take about an hour and 15 minutes.

Horse-drawn buggies *(calesas)* are your taxis in Izamal, as they are for its residents. A leisurely 20-minute *paseo* around the town will cost about $5.

## ACCOMMODATIONS, BOTH STANDARD & NOT

Hotels in Izamal are few and humble, but you'll also find some great alternatives.

$–$$ Staying at **Macanché Bed & Breakfast** ★★★ 🧒 (Calle 22 no. 305, btw. calles 33 and 35; ☎ 988/954-0287; www.macanche.com; cash only), 4 blocks east of the central plaza, is like having your own private jungle camp, only with comfy digs and congenial neighbors. Free-standing cottages are tucked within luxuriant gardens filled with bamboo, bird of paradise, and bougainvillea. Each has its own theme (an Asian room with a Chinese checkers board and origami decorations; a safari room with artifacts from Mexico and Africa). Some have skylights; some have porches with hammock chairs; some sport quirky *trompe l'oeil;* and others have sturdy colonial decor. The hotel has a natural rock-bottom swimming pool and offers massages and yoga classes. Double rooms go for $38 with fans, $50 to $55 with air-conditioning. Rooms vary widely in size, decor, and layout; there are minisuites, family suites, and houses ($62–$75), and one house that can accommodate six people ($130). Rates include a full breakfast of local fruits, fresh-baked bread, and a hearty main course.

## A Hacienda of One's Own

**$–$$$**    The only problem with staying at **Hacienda San Antonio Chalanté** ★★★ **(2km/1½ miles east of Sudzal; ☎ 813/636-8200 U.S., or 999/132-7411; www. haciendachalante.com; cash only)**, 6km (4 miles) outside of Izamal, is that you might never be motivated to get out and see the rest of the area. The secluded hotel occupies a colonial hacienda built on the site of an ancient Maya ceremonial center. Like other haciendas, it was a virtual city unto itself, and the grounds offer miles of private hiking and horseback trails, Maya ruins, a cenote, and an 18th-century church that once anchored a hacienda community of 600 people.

Owner Diane Dutton Finney, who formerly owned Macanché, has trodden lightly on the hacienda's heritage, making guest rooms modern and comfortable while leaving their character intact. The 10 air-conditioned rooms and suites (two more were due for completion by the end of 2008) range from simple to elaborate and rent for $50 to $80 a night (an additional $10 each for more than two people). Occupying two manor houses and former workers' cottages, each is unique, though they have high ceilings, antique furniture, and modern bathrooms in common. Some open onto the colonnaded garden patio in the main house; others are in the imposing High House, a second manor built in the 18th century. One occupies the quirky little cottage where Finney lived during renovations. While adding a *temazcal* and a beautiful new pool modeled after a cenote, she left most of the grounds—set in the midst of a 356-hectare (880-acre) nature preserve—as she found them. The stables, managed by Finney's Maya husband, Victor Manuel Tuyub, belonged to the original hacienda. Some horseback rides include visits to the next hacienda down the road, whose owner has lived there since he was born 91 years ago.

## DINING FOR ALL TASTES

Izamal has a few simple restaurants that serve hearty regional food. **Los Mestizos** ★ **(Calle 33 behind the market; ☎ 988/954-0289; cash only)** is popular with locals as well as visitors, offering good regional dishes such as *salbutes, panuchos,* and chicken and turkey entrees, for less than $10. **Kinich Kakmó** ★ (Calle 27 no. 299; ☎ 988/954-0489; cash only), at the entrance to the pyramid of the same name, is a perennial favorite for Yucatecan classics served in a pretty, shaded garden ($10–$20); you can watch your tortillas being made on the patio.

**$$–$$$    Macanché Bed & Breakfast** ★★ (Calle 22 no. 305, btw. calles 33 and 35; ☎ 988/954-0287; Mon–Sat 5–10pm; cash only) has opened its highly regarded restaurant to the public for dinner, offering Yucatecan-influenced international dishes. The restaurant changes daily to take advantage of seasonal ingredients but includes Yucatecan specialties (*poc chuc, pollo pibil,* fish filet cooked in garlic), Mexican standards (chile rellenos and enchiladas), and international favorites (*camarones* and New York steak), all for $12 to $18.

# WHY YOU'RE HERE: THE TOP SIGHTS & ACTIVITIES

Before it was an exceptionally scenic colonial town, Izamal was an ancient center for the worship of Itzamná, the Maya god of creation and mythical founder of the city. A few of the dozen or so pyramids devoted to him and other gods are still scattered around the center of town. It might have been this patent expression of religious fervor that provoked the Spanish to impose the enormous Franciscan monastery, which dominates the heart of town today, upon the people of Izamal.

The **Ex-Convento y Iglesia de San Antonio de Padua** ✹✹ (daily 8am–9pm), just as ocher-yellow as the rest of the city and trimmed with 75 white archways, anchors two main squares, one in front of the church and one at its side. Walking along its colonnades and looking out over the plaza and town streets is a heady experience, and you can easily imagine priests believing they were touched by the hand of God. Bishop Fray Diego de Landa, who would later wreak the brutal *auto-da-fé* upon Maní, leveled a Maya pyramid here to make room for the massive monastery and church. Inside is a beautifully restored altarpiece, the stained-glass window of St. Francis of Assisi, and many statues—primary among them the Nuestra Señora de Izamal, brought here from Guatemala in 1652. During a festival every August, pilgrims climb the *convento*'s broad staircase on their knees to ask her for miracles. The town still basks in the glory of Pope John Paul II's 1993 visit.

The gigantic, porticoed atrium, said to be second in size only to the Vatican's, presents a 30-minute **light-and-sound show** (Tues, Thurs, and Sat 8:30pm; $4.50) called "Light of the Mayas." While similar to shows at many ruins, this one incorporates incense, strolling monks, music, and projected images. (Buy tickets at the site a half-hour early.)

Across the square from the Ex-Convento is a new **Centro Cultural y Artesanal** ✹✹ (Calle 31 no. 201; ☎ 988/954-1012; $2; Mon–Sat 10am–8pm, Sun 10am–5pm). You'll get an excellent introduction to Izamal's handicrafts in 11 galleries, with signs in English as well as Spanish, that highlight works from local artists and others from around the country. Its good-size shop sells fine-quality hammocks, clothing, bags, and mats, all marked with the name of the artist, his or her village, and the material. This is one of many places to get a free map of folk art workshops you can visit in town (see below).

On the other side of the square, **Hecho a Mano** ✹ (Calle 31 no. 308 at Calle 32; ☎ 988/954-0344), sells carefully selected collectible folk art—everything from Mexican wrestling masks to *rebozos* from Oaxaca, *henequén* mats and hammocks, and museum-quality lacquered gourds—that owner Jeanne Hunt buys and commissions directly from the artisans.

Most of the pyramids that dotted the Maya city at its height, between A.D. 250 and 600, have been reduced to bumps in the surrounding countryside, but several survive within the city. The grandest, **Kinich Kakmó** (Calle 28 at Calle 25; free admission; daily 8am–8pm), covers about 4 hectares (10 acres)—the largest pre-Hispanic building in the Yucatán—just a couple of blocks north of the central plazas. It impresses with sheer size rather than quality of architecture or detail, but it's so close to everything else that you wouldn't want to miss it. The mostly unrestored pyramid looks like a freakishly symmetrical hill, but there are stairs on the south face. At the top, you'll find a view of the cathedral and a welcome fresh breeze.

# THE OTHER IZAMAL

If you've ever picked up a piece of embroidery or an intricate woodcarving in a crafts shop and wondered, "How in the world did someone do that?" you're in the right place. Izamal, one of Yucatán's best-known crafts centers, has created a self-guided **Cultural and Folk Art Route** to bring visitors into local artisans' home workshops.

You'll definitely want to visit **Esteban Abán** (Calle 26, btw. calles 45 and 47), whose family workshop uses thorns from *henequén* leaves and cocoyol seeds (a palm whose fruit is made into candy) to create striking, very contemporary jewelry set in silver. You can drop in on **Agustín Kanún Colli** (Calle 19 btw. calles 24 and 26), who makes some of Yucatán's famous hammocks on the type of vertical wooden frame that has been used for centuries to interweave the threads by hand, using different weaves for cotton, crochet, or nylon fibers.

Other humble home workshops produce cross-stitch embroidery, tin work, animal figures, papier-mâché butterflies and dragonflies, and miniatures created from recycled materials. You get a two-fer of needlework and healing arts from **María Ligia Pech Canché and Feliciano Patrón** (Calle 29 btw. calles 38 and 40) and their five daughters. The entire family creates embroidered clothing with techniques passed from generation to generation. From Feliciano, the town's herbal doctor, you can also learn the art of creating relaxing and curative brews.

The idea, of course, is that you'll want to buy one of these creations in exchange for being welcomed into the artisans' homes. Rest assured, you'll get the very best prices.

Pick up the bright yellow "Routes, Walking Tours and Festivals" map brochure at the **Centro Cultural y Artesanal** (see "Why You're Here," above). The tour is

---

## The Other Aké

Intermingled with the ruins of Aké is a working *henequén* plantation, **Hacienda San Lorenzo de Aké** (www.ruinasake.com), where visitors are welcome to watch the *henequén*'s progress from cactus leaf to ball of twine. Even with the introduction of shredding and rope-making machines at the turn of the 20th century, it's a laborious process. First the tough, thorny leaves must be cut, peeled, and crushed. Workers hand inspect the leaves before putting them into the *planta desfibradora,* or shredding machine, to render the fibers. The pale-green strands dry in the sun until they turn the color of straw and the texture of a horse's tail. The fiber is then combed by hand before it is spun into twine.

You can see the whole operation from start to finish, if you like, but you won't be led by the nose. This is a pretty casual operation; you can poke around the hacienda and the machinery, and wander over to the Maya site next door if you like. There are no formal reservations or even regular hours; you just have to stop by and see if it's a good time. The owner's family still uses the Casa Principal as a part-time home, but the Casa Maquina (machine house) and other working areas are open to the public.

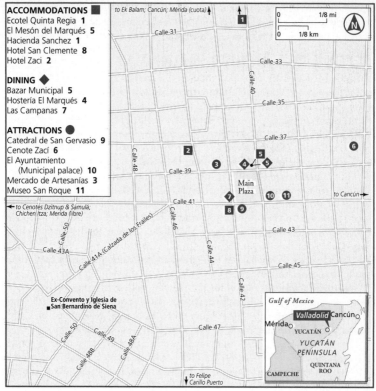

**ACCOMMODATIONS** ■
Ecotel Quinta Regia **1**
El Mesón del Marqués **5**
Hacienda Sanchez **1**
Hotel San Clemente **8**
Hotel Zaci **2**

**DINING** ◆
Bazar Municipal **5**
Hostería El Marqués **4**
Las Campanas **7**

**ATTRACTIONS** ●
Catedral de San Gervasio **9**
Cenote Zací **6**
El Ayuntamiento
    (Municipal palace) **10**
Mercado de Artesanías **3**
Museo San Roque **11**

*to Ek Balam; Cancún; Mérida (cuota)*
Calle 31
Calle 33
Calle 40
Calle 35
Calle 37
Calle 48
Calle 39
Main Plaza
Calle 41
*to Cancún*
*to Cenotes Dzitnup & Sámulá;
Chichen Itza; Merida (libre)*
Calle 50
Calle 43
Calle 46
Calle 41A (Calzada de los Frailes)
Calle 44
Calle 43A
Calle 45
Ex-Convento y Iglesia de
■San Bernardino de Siena
Calle 42
Calle 47
Calle 50
Calle 49
Calle 48A
Calle 48B
*to Felipe
Carillo Puerto*

0    1/8 mi
0    1/8 km

*Gulf of Mexico*
*Valladolid* Cancún
Mérida  YUCATÁN
YUCATÁN
PENÍNSULA
CAMPECHE  QUINTANA
ROO

walkable, but workshops are spread out enough that you probably won't want to walk it all in 1 day. If you don't have more than 1 day, hire a *calesa* at the main square and ask the driver to follow the folk art route.

## A SIDE TRIP TO AKE

The seldom-visited ruins of **Aké** ($3; daily 9am–5pm)lie halfway between Mérida and Izamal on the back road via Cacalchén. The city, dating from the Postclassic era, is linked to Izamal by one of largest *sacbeob* (Maya roads) in the Yucatán and was probably its ally. By far the most impressive feature is a palace structure with rows of more than 20 stone columns—if you saw it out of context, you'd swear it was in Greece.

You'll want a car for this jaunt, or you can hire a taxi in Mérida for $12 to $15 an hour—about $30 each way. If you make it part of a longer day trip, you can negotiate a lower rate for a half or full day.

# VALLADOLID

Despite its turbulent history as one of the first Spanish strongholds and the crucible of the War of the Castes (p. 211), Valladolid still has handsome colonial buildings and 19th-century structures that make it a pleasant place to soak up the real Yucatán. With a small but appealing selection of affordable hotels and decent restaurants, Valladolid is close enough to Chichén Itzá to beat the crowds, and it makes a good base for trips to Ek Balam and Río Lagartos to the north.

## GETTING TO & AROUND VALLADOLID

Valladolid is less than 2 hours from either Mérida or Cancún on the Hwy. 180 toll road, or *cuota* (about $18 from Cancún, $10 from Mérida). The exit deposits you at Hwy. 295 just less than 2km (over a mile) north of the city. Hwy. 180 *libre* (free) takes considerably longer. From the *cuota,* Hwy. 295 enters downtown Valladolid on Calle 42, which runs along the west side of the main plaza (it's one way; you'll take Calle 40 when you leave town). Hwy. 180 *libre* enters town on Calle 39 from the east or Calle 41 from the west.

Direct buses run to and from Mérida's CAME station 12 times a day and Cancún five times. Either trip costs about $12. Valladolid's main bus station is 1½ blocks west of the plaza at calles 39 and 46, but many first-class buses stop at La Isleta, a station on the toll highway, where shuttles complete the 10-minute ride into town. Second-class buses leave Valladolid's station for Chichén Itzá every hour and sometimes on the half-hour, but for about the same price ($1.50), you can catch a faster *colectivo* (kind of a cross between a bus and a taxi, used for local transportation) across the street on Calle 44.

Valladolid's layout is typical for the Yucatán, with even-numbered streets running north and south, odd numbers east and west. The main plaza, Parque Francisco Cantón Rosado (more often called El Centro) is bordered by Calle 39 on the north, 41 on the south, 40 on the east, and 42 on the west.

The small **tourism office** in the Palacio Municipal on the southeast corner of the plaza (Mon–Sat 9am–8pm, Sun 9am–1pm) is a pretty casual operation and not always attended, but it has maps and details about its in-house tour operator, **Viajes Valladolid** (Calle 42 no. 206, Apt. 2; ☎ 985/856-1857; www.mexonline. com/viajes-valladolid.htm).

## ACCOMMODATIONS, BOTH STANDARD & NOT

Valladolid is a balm for the budget. You can choose from a good selection of simple lodging and even the best hotels won't strain your wallet. For higher-priced hotels, meaning over $50 a night here, check **Best Day Travel** (www.bestday. com), **YucatanTravel.com, DoCancun** (www.docancun.com), or **Cancun.com** for discounted rates.

**$**   One of the most pleasant budget hotels is **Hotel San Clemente** ★ 🧒 (Calle 42 no. 206, btw. calles 41 and 43; ☎ 985/856-2208; www.hotelsanclemente.com. mx; MC, V), a great value right on the corner of the plaza. The modern, three-story motel-style building is rescued from blandness by such colonial-style details as tile floors, arches, and wrought-iron railings and light fixtures. The 60 rooms are unremarkable but clean, cool, and comfortable. Each has two firm double beds and good-size bathrooms with somewhat worn but well-scrubbed tiles. Air conditioners are old and a bit noisy but quite efficient. Doubles rent for $38 (two children under 13 stay free), triples are $45, and quadruples $53. The hotel is across the street from the cathedral, so be prepared for bells tolling early in the morning.

**$** A lot of Mexican travelers stay at the friendly **Hotel Zaci** (Calle 44 no. 191, btw. calles 37 and 39; ☎ 985/856-2167; www.hotelzaci.com; cash only), another modern place overlaid with colonial style and built around a quiet, sunny courtyard. The flowery ruffled bedspreads are a bit fussy and the lighting somewhat dim, but rooms have substantial wood furniture and a tranquil atmosphere. Hotel employees go out of their way to help visitors find their way around. The location, around the corner from the bus station and a block from the plaza, is convenient, though you might occasionally hear the station's departure announcements (but not at ungodly hours). Standard rooms (one double bed plus a double or single) are $40 a night; king "suites" with a Jacuzzi are $60.

**$–$$** Only a remnant of the original hacienda remains at **Hacienda Sánchez** ★★ 🅺🅸🅳🆂 (Calle 23, btw. calles 40 and 42; ☎ 985/856-5212; www.hotel haciendasanchez.com.mx; MC, V). The hotel is all new construction, but the quirky historical park is endearing. A modern hotel wing with standard double rooms is tucked discreetly behind the restaurant (Yucatecan specialties) that occupies the original hacienda fragment, framed by huge Moorish arches. In front, tiny villas with clay-tile roofs stand in for houses surrounding a large, grassy plaza anchored by a stone fountain, replicating a little colonial pueblo. There's even a miniature but suitably ornate *capilla* modeled after the Franciscan mission chapels. Standard doubles are a cut above average, with hair driers, cable TV, and Wi-Fi ($48 a night for two adults; two children stay free). Villas ($58) are larger and have terraces looking onto the plaza. Two-room villas ($77–$96 for two to four adults) and villa suites ($96–$135 for two to six) are also available. Discount sites offer standard rooms and villas for $40 to $48, larger villas for $65 to $81. The parklike grounds also contain an antique-car collection, a working 18th-century *noria* (horse-drawn water wheel), and a historical exhibit of paintings, furniture, and arms from colonial and revolutionary times. This place is at the southern entrance to town, so it's best for those traveling by car.

**$–$$$** The doyen of Valladolid's plaza is **El Mesón del Marqués** ★★★ (Calle 39 no. 203, btw. calles 40 and 42; ☎ 985/856-2073; www.mesondelmarques.com; AE), built in the remains of a lovely early-17th-century house. The original porticoed patio, lush with hanging plants and bougainvillea, is the centerpiece of the excellent restaurant, which occupies most of the original house. More recent construction in back melds gracefully, though not seamlessly, with the old and incorporates a pretty swimming pool and garden shaded by mature trees. Rooms are more modest than the original house, varying from bland to fairly charming with heavy hand-carved furniture. Most come with two double beds. Large thick towels, hair dryers, and a full complement of toiletries add a touch of luxury for $64 (standard double) to $79 (superior) a night, though you can get them for $46 to $54, including breakfast, on discount sites. Discount rates for the more expensive larger suites range from $77 to $137.

**$$–$$$** With its cheerful gold-and-melon-colored facade topped by a tiled dome roof, the **Ecotel Quinta Regia** ★★ (Calle 40 no. 160A at Calle 27; ☎ 985/856-33472; www.ecotelquintaregia.com.mx; AE, MC, V) is a happy blend of modern and traditional style; I doubt that any colonial building ever had more pillars and arches. Modern rooms with Wi-Fi access and great lighting sport brick archways, wrought-iron fixtures, and carved-wood furniture. The rooms are supremely comfortable (though with the heavy doors and tiled corridors that echo every footstep, you have to hope your neighbors won't pull up stakes too early in the morning). Facilities include a lovely pool patio and well-maintained tennis court. The grounds are what make the place, though: Room wings are separated by paths to an arboretum with local tropical plants, and each room has a balcony or terrace, angled to provide views of vegetation rather than other rooms. The hotel gets some tour groups but is a peaceful oasis most of the time. Doubles rent for $71 and junior suites $100, but discount rates range from $57 to $89.

## DINING FOR ALL TASTES

You can eat well on any budget in Valladolid. In addition to Yucatecan cooking, its own regional cuisine includes *lomitas de Valladolid* (Mayan-style chili made of chopped tenderloin pork), *chicken escabeche* (chicken in a spicy vinegar broth), and *longaniza* (a spicy local sausage); you might think twice, though, about *mondongo,* made from beef intestine. Taco stands around the plaza sell delicious, cheap *cochinita pibil, carnitas,* and *lechón asado* (all pork dishes) until early afternoon. Side streets are full of little *loncherías* selling simple, savory *tortas* (sandwiches) of succulent pork and other fillings for $1 to $2. Note that restaurants often include a 10% *propina* (tip), so check your bill before settling up.

$    The stalls in the bright, clean **Bazar Municipal** (Calle 39 at Calle 40; daily 7am–9pm; cash only), next to the Mesón del Marqués, are full of locals eating cheap, hearty Mexican breakfasts ($2–$3) and varied *comidas corridas* (set meals, $3–$8) for lunch and dinner. Huge tumblers of delicious, fresh-squeezed orange juice cost about $1.50, or you can take it to go in a plastic bag with a straw.

$$    My favorite place to linger over a simple meal is **Las Campanas** ★★ (corner of calles 41 and 42; daily 8am–2am; cash only), in a colonial mansion cater-corner from the cathedral. It's a good place to share several side orders (peppers stuffed with cheese, twice-baked potatoes with delicious fillings, cowboy bean soups, or roasted onions, $4–$7). The house specialty is *arrachera* steak, marinated and cooked with prickly pear cactus, onion, cheese, pepper, beans, and avocados ($10). If you go crazy with the huge and varied menu of Mexican and international dishes, a full dinner with drinks and dessert can hit $20. Blaring amplified music can make the place noisy during the afternoons; in the evenings, its 6m (20-ft.) wood-beam ceilings, patterned tile floors, and artwork in illuminated wall niches make a delightful place to enjoy live guitar music.

$$–$$$    The best restaurant in town is the **Hostería El Marqués** ★★★ (in the El Mesón del Marqués, above), an almost unbearably romantic setting for a candlelight dinner to live music. One standout on the excellent menu is Zac Kol de Pollo, spicy chicken cooked in a thick corn puree with chunks of tomato, raisins, olives, capers, and chilies, for $7.50. International dishes and Yucatecan classics such as *sopa de lima* and *poc chuc* share the menu with regional specialties such as

*escabeche de Valladolid* and the local *longaniza* ($7–$9). Fish and seafood dishes, though, cost as much as $18.

# WHY YOU'RE HERE: THE TOP SIGHTS & ATTRACTIONS

Simply spending an afternoon wandering Valladolid's central plaza, surrounded by colonial buildings and full of Maya villagers in traditional dress who come to town to sell their crafts and do their shopping, is an immersion in living history. The town's unhurried pace allows leisurely exploration of colonial and natural attractions a little farther afield.

## The Main Plaza

Lazing in the leafy **Main Plaza** ★★★ (btw. calles 39 and 41, to the north and south, 40 and 42 east and west) is an almost perfect afternoon. This is where Maya women hang their embroidered *huipiles*, woven bags, and *guayabera* shirts on the north fence to entice shoppers, workers fortify themselves at food carts, and couples smooch in the concrete S-shaped *confidenciales*, or lovers' seats.

The thick stone walls of the **Iglesia de San Gervasio** (Calle 41 at 42; daily 7am–1pm and 4–8pm) on the south side of the plaza weren't enough to hold back the Maya rebels who sacked it in the starting volley of the War of the Castes in 1847, but you'll still find an impressive *retablo* (painting on carved wood) towering over the altar. This cathedral was built 1706 to replace the church built in 1545. On the east side, climb the worn steps of **El Ayuntamiento** (Calle 40 at 41; daily 8am–8pm), the municipal building, for a bird's-eye view of the plaza. The second-floor wall murals portray the region's history, including a scene of a Maya priest foretelling the Spanish Conquest. On Sunday evenings, the municipal band plays elegant *jaranas* and other traditional music under the arcade while locals waltz around the plaza's bandstand.

Valladolid is fertile ground for handicraft shoppers, and one of the Yucatán's finest shops stands at the northeast corner of the square. **Yalat** ★ (Calle 39 at 40; Mon–Sat 9am–8pm, Sun 10am–8pm) looks more like a gallery but sells unique folk art from throughout Mexico, specializing in Yucatecan tapestries, ceramics, jewelry, black pottery, and, of course, *huipiles*. After embroidery, leatherwork is the city's most important craft—this has been cattle country since colonial times. You'll find inexpensive huaraches and leather bags a block west of the square at the **Mercado de Artesanías** (Calle 39, btw. calles 42 and 44; Mon–Sat 8am–8pm, Sun 8am–2pm), along with woodcarvings, *huipiles, guayabera* shirts, jewelry, and hammocks.

For an overview of arts and crafts from surrounding Maya villages, seek out the pink, fortresslike building that houses the unmarked **Museo San Roque** ★ (Calle 41, btw. calles 38 and 40; free admission; Mon–Sat 9am–9pm), a block east of the plaza (signs in Spanish only). The reverential atmosphere inside might come from the building's origins as a 16th-century hospital chapel, or it might come from the display of ancient stone masks, pottery, and bones unearthed at the nearby Ek Balam architectural site—a group of tiny infant bones found with jade offerings in an *olla* (pot) is particularly compelling.

## Around Town

Named for the original Maya town where the *conquistadores* built Valladolid, **Cenote Zací** (Calle 36, btw. calles 37 and 39; $1.50; daily 8am–5pm) provided ancient people with fresh water. Today it's the centerpiece of a park, 3 long blocks from the main square, that also holds traditional stone-walled thatched houses, a handicraft shop, and a decent *palapa* restaurant. Even if you don't take the plunge, descending the broad, Indiana Jones–style stairs through the partially open cave's stalactites and hanging vines to the water's edge will cool you off.

For one of the most beautiful strolls in all the Yucatán, start at the corner of calles 41 and 46 and follow Calle 41A, the cobblestone street running diagonally to the southwest. The **Calzada de los Frailes (Walkway of the Friars)** is lined by huge clay planters and passes elegantly painted colonial homes on its way (about 1km/½-mile) to the **Ex-Convento y Iglesia de San Bernardino de Siena ★★** (calles 49 and 41A; Wed–Mon 9am–noon and 5–8pm; Mass daily 6pm). This Franciscan monastery complex was built in 1552 by the same architect who built the original cathedral. Despite being sacked during the War of the Castes, a fine baroque altarpiece and some striking 17th-century paintings remain.

Well worth the short trip outside of town, **Cenotes Dzitnup and Samulá ★★★** (5km/3 miles west of Valladolid off Hwy. 180; $3; daily 7am–6pm) flank the old highway to Chichén Itzá. Dzitnup, also called Cenote Xkekén, must be the most-photographed cenote in the Yucatán. A short but tricky stone stairway leads to the deep, clear pool at the bottom. It's bathed in light streaming through openings in the huge cave's ceiling. You can swim with the tiny blind catfish (if you can stand the ice-cold water) or just absorb one of the Yucatán's most beautiful sights. Dzitnup is hugely popular and sometimes crowded, but you can always go across the road to the smaller and less developed, but equally beautiful, Samulá (daily 8am–5pm; $3). Both caverns are well lit, and claustrophobics will be glad to know they have high ceilings and plenty of air.

# SIDE TRIPS FROM VALLADOLID
## Ek Balam

Archaeologists began work at **Ek Balam ★★★** (off Carretera 295, 29km/18 miles north of Valladolid; $3.50; daily 8am–5pm) only in 1997, and excavations continue to unveil astonishing finds. The city, whose name means "black jaguar" in the Mayan language, has one of the northern Yucatán's longest records of human occupation, from as early as A.D. 100 until the Spanish Conquest. It reached its height in the late Classic period and might have been a satellite to Chichén Itzá, which rose to power as Ek Balam waned.

No matter how many ruins you've seen, you'll be gape-jawed at the sight of the recently uncovered **Templo de los Frisos,** with its elaborately carved and astonishingly preserved stucco friezes about three-fourths of the way up the site's main pyramid. A phenomenal mask of the underworld god Balam crowns the temple, his open, toothy mouth forming the entrance to the tomb of the powerful 9th-century ruler King Ukit-Kan-Lek-Tok. The entrance incorporates other statues and carvings of angels, animals, and other figures so finely detailed that you can see the braids in their hair. About 85% of the frieze is original, unretouched plaster.

The massive **Acrópolis** pyramid is phenomenal in itself, rising nearly 30m (100 ft.) from the jungle—easily surpassing Chichén Itzá's Kukulcán. Like other Maya pyramids, the Acrópolis is superimposed on earlier ones, and its six different levels housed governors and other dignitaries. Climbing to the top, you will see two large, untouched ruins rising like jungle-covered hills to the north, and all the way to the tallest structures of Cobá, 48km (30 miles) to the south.

Though known primarily for the quality and uniqueness of its sculpture, Ek Balam is unusual in other ways. Two concentric walls enclose 45 structures in the ceremonial heart of the site, a rarity in Maya cities; whether they were defensive or symbolic remains unclear. You can begin to appreciate the city's full reach beyond these walls if you climb the Acrópolis and see the jungle-covered mounds spreading far and wide. An unrestored network of *sacbeob,* the raised causeways that linked ancient Maya cities, is still visible as raised lines penetrating the tropical jungle in all directions. Most Maya cities had these roads, but few are distinguishable today.

Perhaps best of all, this site is uncommonly peaceful and mysterious because it gets so few visitors. That will surely change; a new road already makes it easier to get there, and as new discoveries are revealed Ek Balam is likely to rival any Maya city in the Yucatán.

To get to Ek Balam, take Calle 40 north out of Valladolid to Hwy. 295; go 19km (12 miles) to the well-marked turnoff, and continue 13km (8 miles). An air-conditioned bus ($4.50) departs Valladolid's main square daily at 9am, allowing a couple of hours at the ruins, and returns at 1pm. *Colectivos* on Calle 44 also go to the ruins. Ask at the site's ticket desk about hiring a guide (about $35 for a small group) who has worked on the excavations; the many rich details are worth it.

## Río Lagartos

After the flamingos of Celestún (p. 222) have completed their courtship rituals, they take flight around April. Their destination, 225km (140 miles) northeast of Celestún, is the **Parque Natural Ría Lagartos,** where they make their nests, lay their eggs, and prepare their young for the return journey in October. According to the Nature Conservancy, 89% of all pink flamingos in the world migrate to Celestún and Ría Lagartos.

At one end of the 50,000-hectare (123,500-acre) Ría Lagartos refuge, established in 1979 to protect the North America's largest nesting population of flamingos, is Río Lagartos, a small fishing village that supplements its income by squiring the occasional tourist through the flamingos' domain. The nesting area, a good distance east of town, is off limits, but boat tours allow you to see plenty of flamingos noshing at their many feeding sites and congregating on the sandy shores. You'll also see some of the 300 other species of birds that frequent the estuary, including herons, ducks, spoonbills, and migratory wading birds from the United States and Canada.

---

## Río or Ría?

Even though they are widely confused, and often misprinted even on otherwise reliable maps, the name of the village is Río Lagartos, but the name of the wildlife refuge is Ría Lagartos. In Spanish, *río* means "river," and *ría* means "estuary." The body of water where the flamingos nest is an estuary, protected from the Gulf of Mexico by an 80km-long (50-mile) barrier island.

---

Río Lagartos is about 80km (50 miles) north of Valladolid on Hwy. 295. If you aren't swarmed by offers of boat tours to see the flamingos, find your way to the waterfront Restaurante-Bar Isla Contoy (Calle 19 at *malecón*), where licensed guides offer day tours for $50 to $60 for two to three people. (The town has no bank or ATM, so be prepared.) They also offer night excursions, on which you might see some of the crocodiles for which Río Lagartos was named. From May through September, sea turtles are fairly easy to spot.

If you want to stay overnight so you can see the flamingos early in the morning, try **Posada Leyli** (Calle 14, 2 blocks north of the waterfront; ☎ 986/862-0106) for rooms at $35 a night with a fan only) or the air-conditioned **Hotel Villa de Pescadores** (Calle 14 at *malecón;* ☎ 986/862-0020) with rooms at $45 a night.

# 7 Campeche

## The walled city

CAMPECHE IS ONE OF ONLY THREE WALLED CITIES THE EUROPEANS BUILT in the Western Hemisphere—along with Quebec City in Canada and Cartagena in Colombia—and it must be the most beautiful city . . . that hardly anyone visits. Most of those who do find their way here are Mexicans interested in their own culture and heritage. The smattering of foreign tourists—mostly European—are seeking an antidote to the beach-and-beer vacation or stopping on their way to or from somewhere else. They invariably have the same reaction: Why is this fascinating city being ignored?

At its outskirts, Campeche looks suspiciously like any other small (about 275,000 residents) Mexican industrial city, but its splendidly preserved historic core is a baroque fantasy of 18th- and 19th-century mansions, domed churches, and remnants of ancient fortification walls that call Córdoba or Seville to mind. Since being declared a UNESCO World Heritage Site in 1999, Campeche has restored hundreds of its colonial mansions, houses, and government buildings. Recoated in their original confectionery pastel hues trimmed in white, they now house shops, restaurants, coffeehouses, and museums, bathed at night by an amber glow from wrought-iron street lamps. Nary a crumbling facade nor a pile of rubble can be found in the entire 44 blocks. The narrow, diligently swept cobblestone streets and underground wiring keeps the postcard perfection intact. It's not hard to figure out why director Steven Soderbergh chose Campeche to stand in for the Havana of Che Guevara's time in *The Argentine,* starring Benicio Del Toro. Your camera, too, will get a workout.

If that were all Campeche had to offer, it would be reason enough to visit. But there's more to warrant lingering longer. You'll likely never see a better sunset than the celestial conflagration that stops joggers and strollers and squealing children in their tracks every evening on the modern *malecón,* or seafront boulevard, just outside the old wall's path. The city's residents, mostly Maya and mestizo, are exceedingly warm and hospitable even by Mexico standards, making it evident in every conversation that they really want you to like their city.

As capital of the state of the same name, Campeche is also a launchpad for trips to haunting restored haciendas and some of the Yucatán Peninsula's most impressive Maya ruins. Campeche is the Yucatán's largest state in terms of area but has a population of only 800,000—fewer people than live in Mérida alone. It's the only Mexican state with two World Heritage cities: Campeche and the archaeological zone/biosphere reserve of Calakmul. More archaeological sites are open to the public here than any other state in the Maya world.

Campeche's tourism industry is still in its infancy, and the city remains a secret. The lack of commercialization spares you from throngs of tourists, hawkers, and timeshare hustlers, but it also presents some challenges. Many of its attractions, and a few of its hotels, have no Internet presence. Many store clerks and restaurant workers speak little or no English, and most signs are in Spanish only; you'll definitely need some rudimentary language skills to explore beyond the capital. And then there's that thing about the beach. Despite being a seafront city, Campeche itself has no swimming beach; for that you must take the coastal road to the south.

Even with its flaws, Campeche remains an undiscovered gem . . . for now. Cancún-like luxury developments are already taking hold in Ciudad del Carmen, the island city to the south that until now has been known primarily as the hub of the petroleum industry. More coastal resorts are on the drawing boards, and American and European investors have been buying historic buildings for potential bed-and-breakfast inns, restaurants, and second homes. There's no way to predict when the scale will tip. So, like the man said, get it while you can.

## DON'T LEAVE CAMPECHE WITHOUT . . .

**GOING BACK IN TIME**    Even if you've visited all the famous Maya archaeological sites, Edzná's elegant architecture and lack of tour buses will give you an entirely new experience of that ancient world. See p. 261.

**WALKING THE LINE**    Atop the only remaining chunk of the old wall that once surrounded colonial Campeche, you can walk 8m (26 ft.) above street level for incomparable views of the new as well as the old city. The breezy seafront *malecón* is another excellent stroll, bringing locals and visitors together at all times of day. The best time is sunset, when the waning sun bathes the city in a celestial glow. See p. 245 and 255.

**ANTEING UP**    The Lotería tables in the main square each weekend night welcome visitors to lay down their pesos and join in a bingo game with a Campachean twist. See p. 259.

## A BRIEF HISTORY

As in the rest of the Yucatán, Campeche was first occupied by Maya civilizations that flourished and then inexplicably declined. Campeche, founded in the 3rd century A.D., was the principal town of the Maya kingdom of Ah Kin Pech ("Place of Serpents and Ticks"). Explorer Francisco de Córdoba, the first Spaniard to arrive, stopped nearby in 1517 to replenish his water supply but was killed, along with his entire crew, when they didn't move on quickly enough. Native resistance kept the Spanish at bay until Montejo the Younger (founder of Mérida) gained a foothold in 1540 and established the Villa of San Francisco de Campeche. As the only populated harbor, and with easy inland access, Campeche fueled Spanish expansion into the Yucatán and soon became one of new Spain's richest ports, funneling local timber, gold, and silver mined in other regions and other Yucatecan products to Spain.

The bounty did not escape the notice of Spain's rivals, and Campeche quickly became a favorite lair for pirates. Beginning with an attack by French pirates in 1559, the list of pillagers who descended on Campeche well into the 18th century reads like a casting call for *Pirates of the Caribbean,* from the famous Dutch buccaneer Peg Leg, from whom so many fictional one-legged pirates are descended;

to the Frenchman called El Olonés, infamous for his unrelenting butchery; to British privateers Henry Morgan and Francis Drake (a knight by any other name . . .). After a century of being plundered and burned, Campeche prevailed upon the Spanish Crown to build a 3m-thick (11-ft.) wall around the city. The irregular hexagonal wall, with *baluartes* (bulwarks) at each vertex, enclosed all the government buildings and the Spanish elite's residences. Four gates opened to the outside world. Moat-and-drawbridge forts were later added on the hills flanking the city.

The wall, completed in 1668, eventually succeeded in fending off the pirates, and the city flourished on maritime trade and farming. When prosperity waned, Campeche, like the rest of the Yucatán, found salvation in *henequén,* the fiber from the agave cactus that became known in the New World as sisal, in great demand for producing hammocks, dense fabrics, ropes, and ship cables until the end of World War II. Today's economy is largely driven by offshore oil fields in the Bay of Campeche and shrimp exports (much of it to the United States), whose profits helped to fuel the historic restoration. Tourism is a small but accelerating force in the state's economy.

# LAY OF THE LAND

Campeche stands on the edge of the Gulf of Mexico, about 177km (110 miles) from Mérida by Hwy. 180. Most of the wall, having done its job in ending the pirate scourge, has been razed and its stones reused to pave city streets. Seven of the eight *baluartes* still stand along Avenida Circuito Baluartes, which rings the historical center along the path of the old wall. Outside the seaward wall, which once stood at the water's edge, reclaimed land has displaced the sea to make room for severely modern hotels and office towers. Here, around Plaza Moch-Couoh, is where you find most of the government buildings, known by such nicknames as El Tocadiscos (The Jukebox) and El Platillo Volante (The Flying Saucer). The saving grace is the seafront boulevard running several miles along Campeche's shore. It changes names as it runs north and south to connect with Hwy. 180—it's called Avenida Adolfo Ruiz Cortínez where it skirts the city center—but it is best known simply as *el malecón.*

The original city of Campeche was divided into several barrios, including Guadeloupe and San Francisco to the north, where the Maya population lived; San Román in the south, where mestizos and mulattos lived; and the walled city, home to the Spanish elite. Such distinctions no longer apply, but the neighborhoods still have their own personalities.

Within the Circuito Baluartes, the old city's even-numbered streets (from Calle 8 to Calle 16) run north and south, while odd-numbered streets (Calle 51 to Calle 65) run east and west. Two of the wall's four old gates still stand. The Puerta de Mar (Sea Gate), at Calle 8 and Calle 59, no longer opens to the sea but to Circuito Baluartes and the government offices and hotels built on landfill. The Puerta de Tierra (Land Gate) stands at the other end of Calle 59.

The main routes in and out of town run north and south. Hwy. 180, a toll road for part of the way, bypasses Campeche and runs by the airport. One confusing quirk: A separate road, also labeled Hwy. 180, runs east out of Campeche and meets Hwy. 261, which passes the turnoff to Edzná on its way south. (Take

# Campeche State

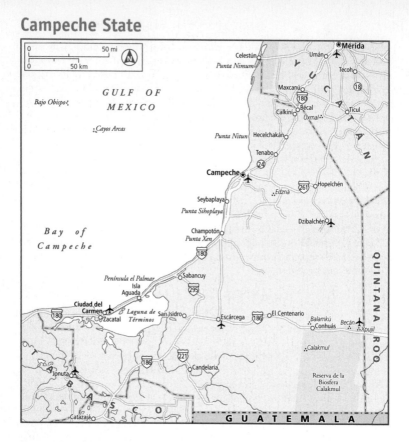

Av. Gobernadores, which joins Circuito Baluartes at the Baluarte San Pedro traffic circle, to reach this east-west road.)

South of Campeche, the highway splits at Champotón. Hwy. 180 continues along the Gulf shore to Ciudad del Carmen and eventually into the southern state of Chiapas. Hwy. 261 veers south to Escárcega, and to the east-west Hwy. 186 to Calakmul, the Río Bec region and straight across the peninsula to Quintana Roo.

## GETTING TO & AROUND CAMPECHE

### BY AIR

Campeche has a small airport which, so far, has no international flights—although it's officially named **Campeche Ingeniero Alberto Acuña Ongay International Airport.** It's about 8km (5 miles) southeast of the historical center. The only airline serving the United States that flies into Campeche is **Aeromexico** (☎ 800/237-6639 toll-free U.S.; www.aeromexico.com), via its regional carrier Aeroliteral. Any flight booked from the U.S. to Campeche requires a plane change in Mexico City. If you're already in Mexico, Aeromexico flies from dozens of cities to Mexico City for the connection to Campeche. **Click Mexicana** (☎ 800/112-5425 toll-free Mexico; www.clickmx.com) flies through Mexico City and several other destinations into Ciudad del Carmen, about 225km (140 miles) south of Campeche.

It frankly makes more sense to fly to Mérida, a 2½-hour drive from Campeche. Not only is it a lot cheaper ($523 round-trip as opposed to $640 from San Francisco, $515 instead of $593 from New York, and $413 instead of $553 from Los Angeles, on a sampling of fares for the same day in spring), the fact is few tourists come to Mexico just to visit Campeche; if you're on this side of the peninsula, you're probably going to be visiting Mérida anyway.

If you do fly into Campeche, there are no convenient bus routes to or from the airport. A taxi takes about 15 minutes and costs about $10.

## BY CAR

Hwy. 180, known as the *vía corta* ("short route") goes south from Mérida, passing near the basket-making village of Halacho and near Bécal, known for its Panama hats. Take the shortcut by exiting right at Tenabo (Hwy. 24) and heading toward the coast, where you can enter town along the *malecón*. The *vía larga* ("long route") from Mérida is Hwy. 261, which veers east past Uxmal and through the Puuc region, but either way will take about 2½ hours.

## BY BUS

First-class buses run from Cancún, Mérida, Chetumal, and points south to Campeche's **ADO** bus station (Av. Patricio Trueba 237; ☎ 981/816-2802), less than a kilometer (about ½-mile) from the Puerta de Tierra. The trip from Mérida, scheduled four times daily, costs about $15 each way and takes 2½ hours. Three buses a day make the 7-hour run from Cancún for about $41 each way.

## GETTING AROUND

Most of Campeche's sights, restaurants, and hotels are inside the walls of the historical center or within a short walk. And walking is the superior form of transport in the old city, where parking is scarce along the narrow streets. If you've arrived in town by car and your hotel doesn't offer private parking, find a street space as close as you can and park it there until you leave town. Figuring out the local buses, which are hot, crowded, and in varying states of repair, is a challenge that could take longer than you'll be in town. To get to the forts or other places beyond walking range, do yourself a favor and take a taxi; fares within the city range from $3 to $10. You can also hire taxis for longer excursions for about $15 an hour.

# ACCOMMODATIONS, BOTH STANDARD & NOT

In general, lodging prices are reasonable in Campeche. The historical center does have a few hostels, and their private rooms provide the lowest-priced lodging you'll find. You'll have to do without air-conditioning, though, so you'll probably want to upgrade if you visit in the hot, humid summer months. Both of the hostels that follow rent bikes and arrange a wide range of tours with an emphasis on adventure and ecotourism.

## HOSTELS

$  Campeche's newest hostel, **Hostal La Parroquia** ★★★ (Calle 55, btw. calles 10 and 12; ☎ 981/816-2530; www.hostalparroquia.com; MC, V), occupies a splendid 16th-century mansion half a block from the Parque Principal. Guest rooms,

# Campeche

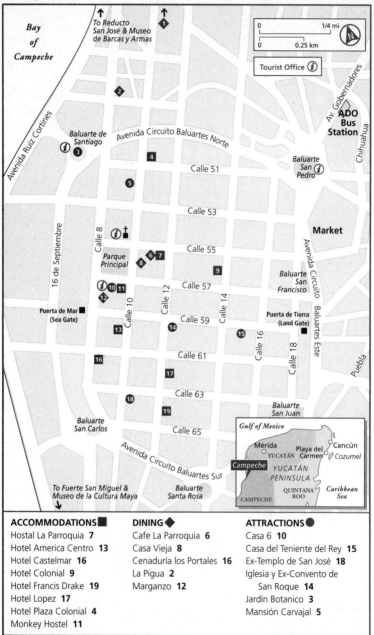

**ACCOMMODATIONS** ■
Hostal La Parroquia **7**
Hotel America Centro **13**
Hotel Castelmar **16**
Hotel Colonial **9**
Hotel Francis Drake **19**
Hotel Lopez **17**
Hotel Plaza Colonial **4**
Monkey Hostel **11**

**DINING** ◆
Cafe La Parroquia **6**
Casa Vieja **8**
Cenaduría los Portales **16**
La Pigua **2**
Marganzo **12**

**ATTRACTIONS** ●
Casa 6 **10**
Casa del Teniente del Rey **15**
Ex-Templo de San José **18**
Iglesia y Ex-Convento de
San Roque **14**
Jardín Botanico **3**
Mansión Carvajal **5**

with their original stone walls and high, beamed ceilings, flank a grand hallway that gives the place the air of a romantic European movie set in the 1940s. Guests have use of a fridge, microwave, and dishes in the colorful, light-flooded kitchen, which opens on to a patio and tidy lawn. Plain, clean double rooms with shared bathroom are 200 pesos (about $19); dorm beds are 90 pesos ($8.50) per person. Prices include continental breakfast next door at Cafe La Parroquia; guests receive discounted meals there and at two other restaurants. The friendly staff keeps the place so clean that it almost looks new. The only problem is that just two private double rooms are available. Better have a backup plan.

$ The atmosphere at **Monkey Hostel** ✦ (Calle 57 no. 6 Altos, at Calle 10; ☎ 800/ CAMPECHE [226-7324] toll-free Mexico, or 981/811-6605; www.hostalcampeche. com; cash only) is more frat house than European romance, but its lively international social scene around the bar is fueled by a friendly staff dedicated to showing visitors the best of Campeche. The old city's first hostel and still the best known, it enjoys a vantage point right on the plaza. From the worn sofas in the common room, the glow of the cathedral and adjacent arcade fills the large window at night. In addition to five dorm rooms (85 pesos/$8 per person in a six-bed room, 80 pesos/$7.60 in an eight-bed room), six sparse but brightly painted private doubles rent for 200 pesos ($19) a night, including continental breakfast in the green courtyard; one has its own bathroom. The hostel's information center offers a wealth of info about Maya ruins and volunteer opportunities.

## HOTELS

$ The **Hotel Colonial** (Calle 14 no. 122; ☎ 981/816-2222; cash only) is one of Campeche's former King's Lieutenant's houses, converted in 1947. The original tiles, colored with swirls and geometric patterns, and wrought-iron balcony railings exude character, and it has a loyal following among travelers who treasure its quirks. Rooms are scrupulously clean but decidedly basic, from the hard mattresses to the tired furniture to the small bathrooms with archaic (though surprisingly robust) plumbing. The 30 rooms, going for $25 double ($35 with air-conditioning), all overlook the tiled inner courtyard.

$ Unique among Campeche's converted mansions, the **Hotel López** ✦✦✦ (Calle 12 no. 189; ☎ 981/816-3344; www.hotellopezcampeche.com; MC, V) is all Art Deco verve, with curlicued ironwork topped by polished wood railings swooping around layers of curved walkways floating above an oval-shaped, open-air courtyard. Looking vaguely like the interior of the old *Queen Mary* ocean liner, it makes you want to dress for dinner. Yet doubles go for just $46, including continental breakfast. Built in 1950, the López was rehabilitated 3 years ago into a stylish hotel with gleaming tile bathrooms, a waterfall pool, free Wi-Fi throughout the property, and a small cafe. The illusion of grandeur dissipates somewhat with the guest rooms, which are comfortable but unremarkable. Still, this three-story, 45-room hotel is a great value and a welcome addition to the old city's budget offerings.

$ Stately in an unpretentious way, the **Hotel América Centro** ✦✦ 🅺🅸🅳🆂 (Calle 10 no. 252, btw. calles 59 and 61; ☎ 981/816-4588; www.hotelamericacampeche.com;

MC, V), another converted colonial home, wears its original floors of marble and painted tiles proudly. At its center, arcaded corridors of grand proportions surround a courtyard where a complimentary breakfast is served. The night I was there, tables throughout the public areas were full of families playing games and eating food from takeout bags. Doubles cost $48, and family packages allow two children up to 18 to stay free. Rooms are simply decorated in a kind of modernized colonial style, and the beds are comfortable, but lighting is on the dim side; rooms also have Wi-Fi. Some rooms on the second floor have balconies, and they're appealing but sometimes noisy.

**$$**  With just 24 rooms and a touch of upscale comfort, the pretty **Hotel Francis Drake** ★★ 🅺 (Calle 12 no. 207, btw. calles 63 and 65; ☎ 981/811-5626 or 811-5627; www.hotelfrancisdrake.com; AE, MC, V) has all the grace of a boutique hotel. Marble-tile floors and sponge-painted walls lend elegance to the spacious rooms, and the modern bathrooms have large showers with amenities running the gamut from face cloths to shampoo. Service is attentive, if not overly warm by Campeche standards. The initial impression of formality in the hotel's restaurant is softened by a whimsical sky scene painted in the ceiling coves, and it serves fine examples of local dishes at budget prices (you can easily have dinner for less than $10). Double rooms are $75, suites $90.

**$$**  The **Hotel Castelmar** ★★★ (Calle 61 no. 2, btw. calles 8 and 10; ☎ 981/811-1204; www.castelmarhotel.com; AE, MC, V) is a remarkable transformation of a former $5-a-night backpackers' flophouse, restored and reopened in 2006. Some of the preserved architectural details—pillars, archways, and tall, narrow wooden doors—resemble Starwood's $220-plus-per-night Hacienda Puerta de Campeche. A double at the Castelmar, booked through its website, is $68. The original floor plans and tiles—with different patterns in each room—remain, and all the rooms are different shapes and sizes. But the bathrooms are brand new (with such elegant details as monogrammed towels and fine hair dryers), as are the sleek swimming pool and sun deck. This is where Steven Soderbergh bunked while filming his two-part epic movie about Che Guevara (though the star, Benicio Del Toro, stayed at the Puerta de Campeche).

**$$$**  The **Hotel Plaza Colonial** ★ (Calle 10 no. 15, at Calle 51; ☎ 981/811-9930; www.hotelplazacolonial.com; AE, MC, V), reclaimed from another derelict mansion in late 2006, is the offspring of the pricier Plaza Campeche Hotel across Circuito Baluartes. Except for the lobby, with black-and-white marble tiles and an abundance of potted plants, the 41-room hotel's interior is modern and angular. Spacious guest rooms with solid furnishings somehow remain dignified despite rooms striped in bold, sometimes startling, colors. Some of the parent property's upscale touches find their way here, such as telephones, shampoo, hand towels, and room safes. The hotel's website quotes $80 for a double, though Best Day Travel's website (www.bestday.com) had it for a special rate of $66. The large junior suites rent for $94.

# DINING FOR ALL TASTES

As a fishing town surrounded by fishing villages, Campeche is known for the freshness of its seafood. In addition to that staple, restaurants also offer a range of

## Campechano Cuisine

You'll find many Yucatecan classics, such as *cochinita pibil* (pit-baked pork in *achiote* sauce) and *panuchos* (fried tortillas stuffed with beans and topped with chicken or turkey), in Campeche. But this city and state has specialties all its own, a marriage of Spanish cuisine, recipes brought by pirates from all over the world, and the region's own exotic fruits and vegetables. Here are some of the best known:

- ◆ *Pan de Cazón* (**Baby Shark Casserole**): Though *pan* means "bread" in Spanish, Campeche's most famous specialty looks more like a layer cake. Three tortillas are spread with refried beans and a mixture of cooked *cazón* (baby shark), stacked up and smothered with tomato sauce.
- ◆ *Pulpo* (**Octopus**): In season (Aug 1–Dec 15), restaurants serve octopus in a wide variety of preparations: cooked in its ink, in garlic, in *escabeche* (pickled onions), fried, and in ceviche.
- ◆ *Camarones al Coco* (**Shrimp with Coconut**): Shrimp is breaded in shredded coconut and corn crumbs, deep fried to a crisp, and served with an apple compote.
- ◆ *Pámpano en Escabeche* (**Pompano in Pickled Onions**): Grilled fish is simmered in a piquant *escabeche* sauce of sliced onions, oil, garlic, chilies, herbs, and sour orange juice.
- ◆ *Pollo Entomatado* (**Chicken in Capers**): This traditional Campeche dish has its roots in Spanish cuisine. Chicken is roasted in a sauce of fresh tomatoes, onions, chilies, peppers, saffron, olives, capers, and raisins.
- ◆ *Dulce Papaya Verde* (**Sweet Green Papaya**): Throughout the state, papaya is cooked in lime water, rinsed, cooked again in a syrup of sugar and honey, then preserved in glass jars.

pork, chicken, turkey, and beef dishes similar to those found throughout the Yucatán. For an inexpensive introduction to *campechano* cuisine, sample the home-cooked fare at the food stalls that spring up around the Parque Principal on Saturday and Sunday evenings. The offerings include *pibipollo* (chicken tamales traditionally cooked underground) and the ever-popular *pan de cazón*. Or breach the city wall to snack at the city's main market at Circuito de Baluartes across the street from Baluarte de San Pedro.

**$–$$$**    Especially good for breakfasts and the daily lunch specials, **Cafe La Parroquia** ★★★ 🧒 (Calle 55 no. 9; ☎ 981/816-8086; MC, V; daily 24 hr.) is a popular local hangout at any hour of the day or night. The classic coffeehouse atmosphere includes brisk, white-coated waiters tending to tourists, workers in traditional *guayabera* shirts, and tables filled with families. Lunch specials may be pot roast, pork or fish with rice or vegetable, beans, and tortillas; Cafe La Parroquia also offers a wide range of regional favorites such as *pollo en escabeche*. Breakfast and lunch start at about $5; dinner entrees are $12 to $15.

**$–$$**    Venture a short way beyond the city walls to join local families flocking to the **Cenaduría los Portales** ★★★ kids 💷 (Calle 10 no. 86, at Portales San Francisco; ☎ 981/811-1491; daily 6pm–midnight; cash only) for a light supper on a wide colonial veranda under stone arches alongside the Plazuela de San Francisco in the barrio of the same name. It's the city's oldest neighborhood, adjacent to the historical center to the north. This most traditional of restaurants specializes in such dishes as *sopa de lima, panuchos,* and sandwiches *clavetado* (honey-and-clove-spiked ham), which taste that much better for being eaten on plastic tablecloths in the open air. *Antojitos* (finger foods) cost less than $2 each; a session of noshing should run $5 to $10. The *horchata*, a sweet, milky, rice-based drink flavored here with coconut, is practically mandatory.

**$–$$$**    Though it seems to be increasingly catering to tour-bus groups, the creative blend of Cuban and Yucatecan cuisine at **Casa Vieja** (Calle 10 no. 319; ☎ 981/811-1311; Tues–Sun 9am–2am, Mon 5:30pm–2am; cash only) still holds interest. A nondescript door leads upstairs to a large, inviting space in the arcade overlooking the main square. The walls are filled with contemporary artwork, and live Cuban music sometimes serenades you while you dine on pastas, salads, and Cuban and Campechean dishes that range from $7 to $18. But the real reason to eat here remains the broad terrace where you can catch the breezes while looking down over the plaza's action.

**$$–$$$$**    Not only do many locals tout **La Pigua** ★★ (Av. Miguel Alemán no. 179A; ☎ 981/811-3365; www.lapigua.com.mx; daily noon–6:30pm and 7:30–11pm; AE, MC, V) as Campeche's finest restaurant, the place has one of the Yucatán's most distinctive settings—a modern rendition of the traditional Maya oblong house, but with walls of glass crowded by plants. The menu is devoted to seafood—*camarones al coco, pan de cazón,* fish stuffed with shellfish, rice with squid—ranging from $10 to $25. Not a cheap meal, but well prepared, as fresh as you could wish and a legitimate dining "experience."

**$$–$$$$**    It's not quite the bargain it once was, but **Marganzo** ★ (Calle 8 no. 267, in front of the Sea Gate; ☎ 981/816-3899; www.marganzo.com; daily 7am–11pm; MC, V) is still a great place to go for an early breakfast. You can choose anything from cereal to eggs to *panuchos* (about $4–$7), plus a variety of juices that includes carrot and beet. The rest of the day, the focus is on an extensive choice of seafood, including such specialties as stuffed pompano and *pan de cazón*, which can push the tab to $20.

# WHY YOU'RE HERE:
# THE TOP SIGHTS & ATTRACTIONS

Campeche's primary lure is the restored old city, most of which lies within the razed wall's boundaries. With no buses on its narrow streets, it's a peaceful place to explore, preferably on foot. I'd go so far as to say it's the most walking- (and breathing-) friendly capital in Mexico. Calle 10 was the old city's *calle de comercio*,

## Time Passage

For a special treat, stop for dinner at **Hacienda Uayamon** ✖✖✖ (Carretera China-Edzná Km 20; ☎ 800/325-3589 toll-free U.S./Canada, or 981/829-7526; www.haciendasmexico.com; daily public hours 7–10pm; AE, MC, V) on the way back from a visit to the Maya ruins at Edzná. With room rates starting at $220 and rising quickly from there, a stay at this unusual hacienda hotel isn't in the cards for most budget travelers, but prices at its stellar restaurant—especially for the regional dishes—are well within reach, ranging from empanadas with cheese for about $7 to *chile relleno de cazón* (*xcatic* pepper stuffed with baby shark meat) for $16.

Dinner guests have a chance to see much of what makes this hacienda unique. Unlike many of the Yucatán's other haciendas, which were substantially (or thoroughly) restored for the conversion into a hotel, Uayamon still looks like a ruin when you approach, darkened by time and missing pieces here and there. The sense of arrested decay is strangely calming in the hush that prevails throughout the grounds. Within the crumbling walls, though, interiors are modern, air-conditioned, and in perfect repair, and the staff provides service to match. More than any other hacienda I've visited, Uayamon places you in two eras at once and keeps both firmly in the present.

or main street, where wealthy merchant families operated their stores out of the ground floor and lived above. With more than 1,600 refurbished facades and hundreds of completely renovated buildings, the grand mansions, monumental government buildings, and ornate churches can be sampled in half a day or savored, along with forays to nearby beaches and architectural sites, over a week.

## THE COLONIAL CENTER

Sixteenth-century Campeche's military camp is today's central plaza, officially named Plaza de la Independencia but commonly called the **Parque Principal** ✖✖✖ (btw. calles 8 and 10 and calles 57 and 55). The modest but exceedingly pretty square is enclosed by an ironwork fence and ringed by tiled benches. On weekend evenings, the plaza comes alive as the surrounding streets are closed, the sombreroed and panchoed municipal band takes the stage in the rococo gazebo, and food and bingo tables are set up in front of the cathedral. It's a beguiling place for rest stops as you explore the city's historic streets.

On the north side of the square, the **Catedral de Nuestra Señora de la Purísima Concepción** ✖✖ (Calle 55, btw. calles 8 and 10), whose crown-shaped bell towers dominate the plaza, stands on the site of the lime-and-pebble, thatch-roof chapel that Montejo ordered built in 1540. Two centuries later, it was replaced by this sober baroque edifice with one tower on the land side, called La Española. It took another hundred years to add the water-side tower, La Campechana. Though repeatedly sacked by pirates for its gold decorations, the interior is an imposing vision of marble, stone, and gold leaf. Seek out the collection of carvings of saints used in religious parades and the colonial-era paintings lining the nave. Campechana's clock, added in 1916, still keeps Campeche's time today, and Sunday Mass fills the cathedral to capacity.

For a look at life as lived by the Spanish elite during colonial times, cross the plaza to **Casa 6** ★★★ (Calle 57, btw. calles 8 and 10; ☎ 981/816-1782; free admission; daily 9am–9pm). One (unconfirmed) legend is that the 17th-century home belonged to Francisco Montejo the Younger, Campeche's founder and the Yucatán's conqueror. Wander through the courtyard with Moorish arches atop Doric columns, a sitting room furnished with Cuban period pieces, a bedroom with a patch of the original wall exposed, and a traditional kitchen of stucco and terra-cotta tile in an arrangement many *campechanos* still use today. The front of the house, where the owners' store would have been, is now a cultural center with a patio restaurant and a bookstore specializing in Campeche's history and music. One bedroom exhibits local artists' paintings, and a "Campechana's Serenade" of Yucatecan *trova* (trio) music is performed on Friday nights. Casa 6 also hosts a tourist information center and rents audio guides to the city in English ($11).

Two other remarkable colonial houses are worth seeking out. The **Mansión Carvajal** ★ (Calle 10, btw. calles 51 and 53; free admission; Mon–Fri 9am–3pm), a beautiful example of early-19th-century civil architecture, belonged to Rodrigo Carvajal Iturralde, one of the Yucatán's wealthiest *hacendados* (he also owned the Hacienda Uayamon, p. 253, between Campeche and Edzná). It was a hotel and a dance hall before being restored. Its most famous feature is a massive Carrara marble stairway, but also impressive are the ornate iron railings and black-and-white checkerboard tile floors stretching toward Moorish archways whose white outlines against the pastel walls look like a Victorian wedding cake. Today it houses government offices but is open to the public on weekdays.

The **Casa del Teniente del Rey** (Calle 59, btw. calles 14 and 16; $3; Tues–Sat 8am–2pm and 5–8pm, Sun 9am–1pm), the "House of the King's Lieutenant," is one of four homes built for the Spanish king's right-hand men, charged with overseeing the city in the governor's absence. This one belonged to Col. Don Leandro Poblaciones, who held the post in the early 1800s. On the ground floor of the two-story house, columns are built into the facade on either side of the large framed door to support a large second-floor balcony. The small interior courtyard is surrounded by arches.

The house of a later king's lieutenant, Juan José de León y Zamorano, stands at the corner of calles 10 and 51. Calles 55, 57, and 59 are other good areas for ogling handsome colonial homes.

As the reigning queen of Campeche's religious architecture, the cathedral has some worthy attendants. An especially striking example is the **Ex-Templo de San José** ★ (Calle 10, btw. calles 63 and 65; $2.50; Tues–Sun 9am–3pm and 4–8:30pm), a massive, baroque church built by the Jesuits just before they were expelled from the New World. With its block-long facade and portal covered by blue-and-yellow Talavera tile, it would look more Moorish that anything else—were it not for the lighthouse, topped by a weather vane, that crowns one of its spires. Built in 1756, it eventually became state property and is now part of the university next door. The deceptively plain exterior of **Iglesia y Ex-Convento de San Roque** (calles 12 and 59; free admission; daily 8:30am–noon and 5–7pm) harbors an elaborate, carved main altarpiece that was restored inch by inch a few years ago. Built in 1565, it was originally called Iglesia de San Francisco and is still affectionately

## The Tourist Trolley

The best, and certainly the easiest, way to get an overview of the historical center and its fortifications is the **Tranvía de la Ciudad** ★★ (betty mena@yahoo.com.mx; $7; daily every hour 9am–1pm and 5–9pm). These colorful trams, which leave from the Parque Principal on the Calle 10 side, have a history of their own. They are named after the trams conceived in the late 1800s to provide local transportation on train tracks standing idle after a local entrepreneur's rail line went out of business. Today's motorized trams offer three routes, all lasting about 45 minutes, with commentary in Spanish and English. The red Tranvía de la Ciudad tours the historic town center, including visits to the most important colonial quarters, a circuit of city walls, and a jog down the *malecón*. The green El Guapo (The Handsome One) tram visits the historical center as well as Fuerte San Miguel to the south, while Super Guapo visits the historical center and Fuerte de San José. Schedules and tickets are available at the booth just inside the plaza next to the trolley stop.

called San Francisquito today. During my last visit, students from a Mexico City school for professional restoration specialists were in the middle of peeling back 16 or 17 layers of paint applied over 300 years, and undoing the damage from repeated attacks by gold-hungry pirates, to finally bring the little church back to its original condition.

## THE BALUARTES

Two main entrances connected the protected city to the outside world. The **Puerta del Mar** (near calles 8 and 59), or Sea Gate, opened onto a wharf where small craft delivered goods form ships anchored farther out. The gate you see today is a reconstruction of the original, which was knocked down in the late 1800s. The old city walls also were reconstructed running east from the Sea Gate to the Plaza Muoch-Cuouh on the north side of the walls.

On the opposite side, the **Puerta de Tierra** (calles 59 and 18, at Circuito Baluartes/Av. Gobernadores), or Land Gate, is the original, which opened in 1732 to admit *campechanos* living in the suburbs. Today, it houses a small museum displaying arms, including a 5-ton French cannon from the 18th century, and portraits of pirates and city founders. The Land Gate hosts a popular Luz y Sonido (light-and-sound) show several times a week (see "Nightlife in Campeche," later in this chapter).

Seven of the eight original bastions that connected the wall's six sides still stand, and four of these minifortresses house small museums. **Baluarte San Pedro** (calles 18 and 51, Circuito Baluartes; free admission; daily 9am–9pm) now stands in the center of a huge traffic circle. A steep ramp leads to the rooftop gunnery slits, watchtower, and an escape-proof prisoner hold exposed to full sun. Downstairs, the **Museo y Galería de Arte Popular** ★★★ (free admission; daily 9am–4pm) displays folk art from all over the state and illustrates techniques and tools used by Campeche's finest craftsmen to make *jipi* hats (woven of *jipijapa* palm fibers) from Bécal, items of bull horn (which are replacing tortoiseshells), and other works.

**Baluarte de Santiago** (calles 8 and 49, Circuito Baluartes; free admission; Tues–Fri 8am–2pm and 5–8pm, Sat–Sun 8am–2pm), the last to be built, was completed in 1702. What you see today is a reconstruction of the original, which was demolished at the turn of the 20th century, and all it defends is the **Jardín Botánico X'much Haltún** ★. Among the more than 200 species of tropical plants growing in the courtyard is the enormous *ceiba* tree, which symbolized the link between heaven, earth, and the underworld to the Maya.

The largest bastion, built to protect the Puerta del Mar, is **Baluarte de Nuestra Señora de la Soledad** (Calle 8, btw. calles 55 and 57), named for the patron saint of sailors. Standing with no supporting walls like a Roman triumphal arch, its ramparts offer views of the cathedral, municipal buildings, and old houses along Calle 8. Inside, the **Museo de la Cultura Maya** ★★ ($2.50; Mon 8am–2pm, Tues–Sun 8am–8pm) has four rooms of artifacts from throughout Campeche, including columns from Edzná and a sculpture of a man in an owl mask. Some of the stelae are worn but are accompanied by line drawings and English commentaries. One of Campeche's most worthwhile museums, it is a splendid overview of Maya writing, sculpture, and architectural style.

At the southwestern corner of the old wall, the **Baluarte de San Carlos** (Calle 8, btw. calles 63 and 65, Circuito Baluartes; $2.50; Tues–Sun 9am–1pm and 5–9pm) was named after the Spanish king of the time, King Carlos II. Inside, the centerpiece of the small but intriguing **Museo de la Ciudad (City Museum)** is a model of the city during colonial times showing its fortification system; other displays include some excellent ship models, muskets, and a ship's figurehead.

The smallest of the seven, **Baluarte San Juan** (free admission; Calle 18, btw. calles 63 and 65; Tues–Sun 8am–7:30pm) has an exhibition on the history of the bulwarks, but even more intriguing is the stairway down to an old well, underground storage area, and dungeon. The only remaining chunk of the old city wall connects this bastion with the Puerta de Tierra. For an incomparable view of the new as well as the old city, walk along the crenellated wall, 8m (26 ft.) above the street, from San Juan to the gate.

## THE FORTS

The bastions and walls surrounding Campeche stopped the pirates from sacking and burning the city, but ships anchored offshore were sitting ducks. Campeche

---

## Tourist Information

The **State of Campeche Office of Tourism** (Plaza Moch-Couoh, Av. Ruiz Cortínez s/n; ☎ 981/816-6767; www.campechetravel.com) is open daily 9am to 9pm. Other offices are located at **Casa 6** (Calle 57, btw. calles 8 and 10; ☎ 981/811-3990 or 811-3989); **City Hall** (Calle 55 no. 3, next to the cathedral; ☎ 981/811-3990 or 811-3989); **Baluarte San Pedro** (calles 18 and 51, Circuito Baluartes); and in the **botanical garden** at Baluarte Santiago (corner of calles 8 and 49).

was the Yucatán's primary port until the mid-1800s, and these ships were laden with *palo de pinto* dyewood, mahogany, *henequén, chicle* (the latex of the *sapodilla* tree, used to make chewing gum), and other products bound for Europe, or returning with European furniture and Chinese silks. It took two large forts, finally erected in the early 19th century, to make Campeche's cargo ships safe.

Campeche's most imposing colonial fort, **Fuerte San Miguel** (Av. Francisco Morazán s/n, Cerro de Buenavista), faces the sea about 3km (2 miles) southwest of the historical center, where Avenida Ruiz Cortínez (the *malecón*) winds to the top of a 61m (200-ft.) hill. Designed on a pentagonal ground plan, it still retains its moat, drawbridge, watchtowers, and cannons. Even the S-shaped entrance passage was part of the defense plan, making attack difficult by hindering projectiles' path. Built between 1779 and 1801, the fort was positioned to blast enemy ships out of the Bay of Campeche, but the long-range cannons lining the roof deck were fired only once, in 1842, when Santa Anna commandeered the fort to put down a revolt by the region's Yucatecan separatists.

The fort, which is also an ecological park, now houses the **Museo de la Cultura Maya** ★★★ ($3.25; Tues–Sun 9am–7:30pm), whose 10 halls display findings from archaeological sites throughout the state, including Calakmul, Edzná, and Jaina, an island to the north that the Maya used as a connecting point between the Gulf of Mexico and the Caribbean and as a burial site for Maya aristocracy. Jewelry, masks, pottery, stucco heads, stelae, and bones are grouped thematically around Maya concepts of the afterlife, cosmology, gods, and war. Most of the small figures and pottery on display were offerings recovered from tombs. Some of the star attractions include haunting jade burial masks from Calakmul and the mummified remains of Yichak Kak, one of Calakmul's most important kings, wrapped with gum and covered in jade. Also intriguing are alabaster from Honduras, articulated dolls that look like wizards and witches, and skulls with their foreheads pressed into an unnatural slope and indentations in the teeth where jade was once embedded.

San Miguel's northern counterpart, **Reducto de San José el Alto** (Av. Escénica s/n, Cerro de Bellavista), sits atop the Cerro de Bellavista, where its flat roof commands a view of the city ending at the mangroves stretching away to the north. During the day, the sloping lawns are ideal for a picnic; as sunset approaches, the cannons on the hillside are crawling with children and the grass is dotted with strollers and snuggling couples. To reach the redoubt, completed in 1792, you cross a drawbridge over a moat. Inside, the **Museo de Barcas y Armas** ★ ($2.50, free Sun; Tues–Sun 9:30am–5:30pm) illustrates the port's maritime history through displays in former soldiers' and watchmen's rooms, focusing, as its name suggests, on boats and weapons. Exhibits include model ships, ships in bottles, an ebony rudder carved in the shape of a hound, the oldest cannon in Mexico, and a gallery profiling what must be every pirate who ever sailed the seas.

The easiest way to reach either fort is by taxi, which will cost about $4. If all you're interested in is the view, the El Guapo tram (p. 255) goes to the forts but doesn't stop long enough to visit the museums within them before returning to town.

## MORE BEYOND THE CITY WALLS

Though it has nothing to do with the city's storied past, Campeche's *malecón* ★★★ at sunset belongs at the top of any must-do list. The broad, palm-lined boulevard and sea walk, completed in 2000, is both a major thoroughfare and an escape valve for locals and visitors alike. It runs about 3km (2 miles) along the water from the Justo Sierra Méndez monument in the south to Avenida Joaquín Musel in the north, punctuated by fountains, cannons, exercise equipment, statues, and gardens. Directly on the shore, a wide concrete walk with a separate jogging and bike path bustles with energetic locals, especially in the cooler early morning hours but also late into the night.

A series of monuments honors figures and events that loom large in Campeche's history. At the beginning of the *malecón* southwest of Plaza Moch-Couoh is a statue of Campeche native Justo Sierra Méndez, credited with founding Mexico's modern educational system. Heading north, other sculptures represent Campeche's two forts and symbolize the wall's four gates. A block north of the Hotel Del Mar is a monumental sculpture of Pedro Sainz de Baranda, a local boy instrumental in defeating the Spanish and ending the war of independence. The girl gazing out to sea near the Convention Center is the Novia del Mar, who is said to have fallen in love with a foreign pirate and forever awaits his return.

Campeche's San Román neighborhood, just south of the old city's walls, was part of the historic district's restoration effort and has its own share of picturesque charm. Its major attraction is the **Iglesia San Román** (Calle Bravo, btw. calles 10B and 12, in front of Parque San Román; free admission; daily 7am–1pm and 3–7pm), for its *Black Christ*, a 2m (6-ft.) ebony image of Jesus that was carved in Italy and shipped to the humble church in about 1565. Worship of the *Black Christ* is the most important cult in the Yucatán, Chiapas, and Tabasco; this is one the few originals of many brought from Europe to Mexico during colonial times. Though generally wary of Christianity, the subjugated Indians associated the *Black Christ* figure with miracles. The most-repeated of numerous legends holds that a ship that refused to carry the statue was lost at sea, while the one that accepted it reached Campeche in record time. The annual Feast of San Román, when worshippers carry a black-wood Christ and silver cross through the streets on September 14, is still celebrated with both pomp and earnestness.

Campeche is a coastal city, but if it ever had beaches, they were long ago obliterated by pirate-proof walls and landfill. The closest good swimming beach, is **Playa Bonita,** about 13km (8 miles) south of town just past the fishing village of Lerma. The public beach is on a small cove backed by a line of palms and a big recreational pavilion. It's a friendly place where you can laze under a *palapa,* stroll 3km (2 miles) of soft sand, buy refreshments, and swim in calm, warm water that tends more toward green than blue.

Playa Bonita is easy enough to reach by taxi or local bus along the waterfront, but if you're driving, you can find miles of undeveloped, white-sand beaches along the coastline between Campeche and Ciudad del Carmen. Some beach areas are restricted to protect sea turtle populations. When leaving Campeche, follow the old coast road, which hugs the coastline, instead of the new toll road. Other beaches to try include **Seybaplaya,** a pretty little fishing village about 29km (18 miles) from Campeche, and **Sihoplaya,** 39km (24 miles) away. The larger fishing village of **Champotón,** about 64km (40 miles) from Campeche, earned its place in history when the Maya killed Córdoba and his crew there in 1517. It boasts excellent seafood restaurants overlooking the ocean. About 26km (16 miles) farther south, Punta Xen is a lovely beach with gentle waves that is also a hawksbill turtle nesting site and sanctuary. The research station there, which operates a turtle adoption program, is fun to visit.

## TOURS

Much of what Campeche has to offer is sparsely documented and hard to find, especially when you want to explore beyond the city. This is one place where taking a guided tour can make more sense than trying to do it yourself.

**Operadora Turística Edzná** (Av. Miguel Alemán s/n, at Calle 49C; ☎ 981/811-7711; www.edzna.com.mx) is an especially good local tour operator with friendly, knowledgeable, English-speaking guides. Their offerings include comprehensive city tours by day or night (the latter includes the light show at the Land Gate) for about $67 per person and half-day guided tours of Edzná for $60. A full-day tour of the Chenes Route to the northeast, including three archaeological sites and the Xtacumbilxunáan Caves, costs $112. It's a fascinating look at how people in a land with no surface water revered the caverns and wells *(chenes)* upon which their lives depended, incorporating them into architecture characterized by facades profusely decorated with immense stone masks. I wouldn't recommend the marathon trip to Calakmul and Balamkú, a small ruin close to the Calakmul turnoff that is known for the quality of its architectural reliefs. Leaving at 5am and returning around 7pm, you'll spend more time in the van than at the ruins. Overnight trips to Calakmul and the Río Bec sites beyond are less punishing but expensive at about $360 per person. (To give these sites their due, rent a car and go on your own; see "Calakmul" on p. 262.) The office is behind the Hotel Plaza Campeche and across the street from the botanical garden.

**Xtampak Tours** (Calle 57, btw. calles 10 and 12; ☎ 981/811-6743; www.xtampak.com; Mon–Sat 8:30am–3pm and 5–9pm), one of the historical center's most highly recommended agencies, offers a similar lineup at comparable prices.

If you don't find exactly what you're looking for among the tour offerings, I can recommend **Erik Mendicuti** (☎ 981/121-0892; emobile2@hotmail.com), a local guide with varied experience in the tourism industry and a passion for Campeche. He works closely with the state tourism office and with Operadora Turísta Edzná and is also available for private hire. The fee depends on distance and travel times but generally averages about $30 for the first hour and $20 per additional hour for a half-day or less, for up to five people.

## THE OTHER CAMPECHE

With so few tourists in Campeche, you'll find yourself surrounded by *campechanos* during your time here no matter what you do. The sense of division that arises in most tourist destinations is far less of a factor. To be a part of local life, just go where the locals do.

A kind of kooky—but really fun—way to dive into local life is to join in **La Lotería** at the Parque Principal on a weekend evening (or during most festivals). This is basically bingo, but with pictures (a barrel, a shrimp, a deer . . .) instead of letters. The caller, operating a manual *tómbola,* will call out "nine barrels," for example, or "13 rabbits." Tables go up in front of the cathedral on weekend evenings at about 6pm, and you may play as many cards as you handle for a peso each. Don't worry if your Spanish is limited—other players will keep an eye on your card and prompt you if necessary. And you just might end the evening a few pesos richer.

# ATTENTION, SHOPPERS!

Shopping isn't a major tourist activity in Campeche, but if it's handicrafts you're after, the state-run **Casa de Artesanías Tukulná** (Calle 10 no. 333, btw. calles 59 and 61; ☎ 981/816-9088; www.tukulna.com; Mon–Sat 10am–8pm; AE, V), occupying a lovely colonial building, has top-quality examples of items produced throughout the state. It's not the best place for trinkets, but it charges reasonable prices for top-quality Panama hats and other *jipi* palm articles from Becál, Tepakán pottery, colorful embroidered dresses and blouses in traditional styles that wear well with contemporary clothing, hammocks, and locally produced furniture. An elaborate display of regional arts and crafts in the back is a veritable museum, including not only a display showing a *henequén* hammock in the making but also reproductions of a mud-walled Maya house. For more casual shopping, including lamps, clothes, picture frames, or other gifts and souvenirs, try the **Bazar Artesanal** (Plaza Ah Kim Pech on the *malecón;* daily 10am–10pm; cash only), where the wares are sold directly by the artisans. One section features demonstrations of traditional craft techniques. Prices here are set, so haggling will get you nowhere.

The bustling **Mercado Principal** (Av. Circuito Baluartes Este, btw. calles 51 and 53; daily 7am–5pm; cash only), just outside the city walls, will feel rustic in contrast to the tidy confines of the historical center, but this is the place to bargain. Especially intriguing are the array of spices and herbs, exotic fruit, and chilies. And if you have any bargaining skills at all, you can get a better price on a traditional *huipil* or *guayabera* here than at the handicraft shops.

# NIGHTLIFE

Campeche's bars and clubs are open Thursday through Saturday, generally until 2am. It's pretty quiet the rest of the week.

Locals favor clubs along the waterfront, including—go figure—the pirate-themed **Restaurant Bar Lafitte** (51 Av. Ruiz Cortínez; ☎ 981/811-9191; dinner 7pm–midnight, disco midnight–3am) in the Hotel del Mar, where you walk a plank to enter. For a mellower time, **Rum** (Av. Ruiz Cortínez; ☎ 981/127-1628) is a stylish newer bar on the inland side of the waterfront.

For a drink steeped in atmosphere, head for the lush courtyard at **La Iguana Azul** (Calle 53, btw. calles 10 and 12; ☎ 981/816-3978; free–$5; Fri–Sat 11am–2am), a restaurant opposite La Parroquia that hosts local bands and has jazz combos on weekends. The most appealing nightspot in town is the rooftop terrace lounge at **Hacienda Puerta Campeche** (Calle 59 no. 71, btw. calles 16 and 18; ☎ 981/818-7535; no cover; Fri–Sat noon–midnight). You can drink in glittering city views along with your libations at Campeche's finest luxury hotel, created by reconfiguring several 17th-century mansions.

For my money, the best show in town is weekends in **Parque Principal** ★★★ 🇰🇮🇩🇸 when the streets close to traffic, beginning at 6:30pm. You never know exactly what kind of entertainment you'll get on Saturday—a rock band, a traditional dance troupe, a celebrity impersonator—but the Sunday night show begins with the state band's rendition of classic *campechano* songs, marches, and show music.

The 2-hour **Luz y Sonido** 🎦 (Puerta de Tierra; $4; Tues and Fri–Sat 8:30pm; daily in spring, summer, and Christmas holidays) is a variation on the sound-and-light shows that have become hugely popular at many of the Yucatán's archaeological sites. This one, reenacting pirate tails from Campeche's rich lore, is a little campy with all the cannon blasts and flashing lights, but it's somehow appropriate to the subject matter and, naturally, a hit with kids.

# SIDE TRIPS FROM CAMPECHE

## EDZNA

Just because you've seen Chichén Itzá, Tulúm, or other well-known ruins, it would be a mistake to think you don't need to see **Edzná** ★★★ (Carretera 261, east from Campeche City for 43km/27 miles to Cayal, then Carretera 188 southeast for 18km/11 miles; $3.50; daily 8am–5pm). Despite its relative obscurity in the tourist world, archaeologists consider Edzná one of the Yucatán's most important ruins. It's the closest archaeological site to Campeche—less than 45 minutes—and easy to get to, but it gets fewer visitors in a year than Chichén Itzá does in a day. Because of that, you'll take in the natural beauty and the magnificence of the architecture, and of the civilization that accomplished it, on a whole different level.

Edzná was founded between 600 and 300 B.C. as a small agricultural settlement. It grew into an economical, political, and religious force in the Maya world, rising to its height as a grand regional capital between A.D. 600 and 900.

The city, abandoned in the 14th century, lay hidden for 500 years. Although archaeologists discovered the ruins in 1907, no one returned for 20 years, and excavation didn't begin until the late 1950s, and not in earnest until the mid-1970s. After 40 years, only 5% of what proved to be a vast city has been uncovered. If archaeologists intended to excavate the whole city—which they don't—it would take 800 years, about the time it took the Maya to build it in the first place.

Edzná's architects were a clever lot. Given a region with no lakes, no rivers, no water of any kind, they built 100 cisterns, or *chultunes,* throughout the city for domestic use. They built canals and lakes for agriculture—from the air, you can still see them etching the shape of a wheel into the landscape.

The city was a crossroads between cities in today's Chiapas and Yucatán states and Guatemala, and influences from all of them show up in Edzná's elegant architecture. Its roof combs and corbeled arches resemble those of Palenque, and giant stone masks are characteristics of the Petén style made famous by Guatemala's ruins of Tikál. The relationship between Edzná and Tikál, in fact, it seems, was a standoff between two huge powers not unlike the United States and Russia during the Cold War.

The best place to survey Edzná is from the 31m-tall (102-ft.) **Pirámide de los Cinco Pisos (Five-Story Pyramid),** built on the raised platform of the **Gran Acrópolis.** Ponder whether those green mounds you see spreading around you, seemingly into infinity, are just jungle growth or temples and tombs overgrown with vegetation. Campeche state has more than 2,000 known ruins, and new ones are discovered every year. Only 18 are open to visitors, and most will never be disturbed.

You can also plot out other major buildings to explore, such as the **Plataforma de los Cuchillos (Platform of the Knives),** where flint knives were recovered inside, and the **Templo de los Mascarones (Temple of the Big Masks),** flanked by twin sun-god masks with protruding crossed eyes (a sign of elite status), filed teeth, and earplugs favored by Maya gentry.

Informational signs are printed in English as well as Spanish and Mayan, and Edzná, far more than sites receiving busloads of tourists every day, lets you absorb a remarkable amount of insight simply by osmosis. But there are always things you won't notice or can't know. The *palo de pinto* tree that grows in profusion all over Edzná, for example, was the source of the red paint the Maya used to color their buildings—none were white or gray as we see them today. The tree became Campeche's main export during colonial times, and the target of the infamous pirate attacks. That irregular line of white rocks in the ground is actually the remnant of *sacbé*—a raised causeway connecting Maya villages and kingdoms. For other such details, hiring a guide is the best investment you can make (p. 259).

## CALAKMUL

Still half buried by jungle, **Calakmul** ★★★ (Carretera 186 to Km 97 at Conhuás, then south for 50km/31 miles; $3.80 biosphere reserve plus $3.70 archaeological site; Tues–Sun 7am–5pm) is both a vast Maya archaeological zone (about 70 sq. km/27 sq. miles) and a 70,000-hectare (172,900-acre) biosphere reserve taking up about 13% of Campeche state's entire territory. The Yucatán's tallest pyramid is here, and continuing research might prove Calakmul to be the largest site in the Maya world, more than equal to Guatemala's Tikál.

The city was first spotted from an airplane in 1931 but not explored until 1982. Nearly 7,000 buildings have been mapped since excavation began. As work continues, the surrounding jungle is being left in its natural state, full of howler monkeys who scold you as you walk among the ruined tombs and palaces.

Calakmul was populated as early as 500 B.C. and is believed to have had 60,000 residents at its height; this was the leading city of the vast Kingdom of the Serpent's Head from about A.D. 542 to 695. Its decline began with Tikál's defeat of the king called Jaguar Claw, whose shrouded body has been the archaeologists' most significant discovery. Most of the stelae (about 120, more than at any other Maya site) that have yielded so much information about the city date from A.D. 364 to 810. By the time of the Spanish Conquest in 1519, Calakmul's population had dwindled to fewer than 1,000.

From the ticket booth at the end of the road, the ruins are about a kilometer (½-mile) walk through tropical forest, its tree canopy higher than the typical Yucatán jungle. Arrows guide you to a short, medium, or long path, all leading eventually to the immense Gran Plaza with its twin pyramids, prosaically known as Structure II and Structure VII. At 53m (175 ft.), Structure II is the Yucatán's tallest Maya building. If you're up to the climb, you'll be able to see across 50km (31 miles) of forest to the ruins of El Mirador, Calakmul's sister city in Guatemala. You'll also see Structure VII, where one of Calakmul's most recognizable jade masks was found, across the plaza to the north, and the photogenic Structure I, Calakmul's second great pyramid, rising above the jungle to the southeast.

More than 800 tropical plant species grow in the surrounding rainforest, which was designated a biosphere reserve in 1989 (Mexico's second-largest, after

Sian Ka'an in neighboring Quintana Roo). Spider and howler monkeys, deer, and hundreds of exotic birds, orchids, butterflies, and reptiles thrive here, along with five of the six wild cats found in Mexico. Come early in the day to spot them.

Calakmul is less than 322km (200 miles) from Campeche, but the last 60km (37 miles), after you Hwy. 186 just east of the town of Conhuás, is nearly 1½ hours on mostly one-lane (but well-paved) road. It's not an ideal candidate for a day trip, although tour companies will do it. If you drive on your own, you need to rent a car (p. 275) and avoid the wet months of June to October, and bring food and water; the only place to buy a meal is near the entrance to the ruins. To get an early start and maximize your chances of seeing wildlife, consider staying overnight at **Puerta Calakmul** (Carretera 185 Km 98; ☎ 998/887-0799; www.hotelpuertacalakmul.com), inside the reserve on the road to the ruins (but still 50km/31 miles away), with doubles at $140 a night. Another possibility, especially if you'll be going on to the Río Bec sites farther east, is **Río Bec Dreams** (Carretera 186 Km 142; ☎ 983/124-0501; www.riobecdreams.com), 12km (7½ miles) west of the town of Xpujil, a village with its own tiny Maya site almost at the Quintana Roo border. Doubles cost between $40 and $75.

# 8 The Essentials of Planning

*by Jeanne Cooper & Christine Delsol*

"I'LL GET TO THAT *MAÑANA...*" IS A FINE ATTITUDE TO HAVE ON VACATION— especially in the Tropics, where trying to cram too much into one sunny day can lead to an involuntary slowdown from heat exhaustion. However, taking the time for some careful planning before your trip will help you make the most of your vacation budget. This chapter summarizes the basics to consider before you go.

## WHEN TO VISIT

You won't have to worry whether it's "sweater weather" when packing for your trip. The average temperatures in Cancún, similar to those elsewhere in the Yucatán, range between 27° and 35°C (81°–95°F), with days of sunshine virtually year-round. Even at night in the cooler months, air temperature rarely drops below 20°C (68°F), when a light jacket will suffice. As for the water? It's bath temperature by European standards, and generally pleasant for Americans: 23° to 27°C (73°–80°F) in winter and spring, and around 29°C (84°F) in summer and fall.

The peak travel periods of the November to April **high season** correspond with United States vacation schedules and Christian holidays: late November (around Thanksgiving), mid-December through the first week of January (especially Christmas week), and Easter (the week before and after). For Cancún and nearby islands, U.S. college students' spring break (floating weeks in Mar, which often overlap with Easter) and the week around Presidents' Day (the third Mon of Feb) also bring out the crowds and bring up prices, although booking packages—or last-minute—can help keep costs down (see "Air/Hotel Packages" on p. 16 for information and tips on booking a package tour).

Cancún and Playa del Carmen are notorious for their volatile lodging rates, with as many as six or eight price ranges throughout the year; low-season rates may be less than half of the high-season prices. At the other end of the spectrum, the least visited areas often charge the same rate year-round.

It's not just holidays and student vacations that make November through April the high season (which conveniently rhymes with "dry season"). Those are the coolest months, with highs averaging 30° to 32°C (86°–89°F)—ideal for exploring Maya ruins and colonial cities. In terms of actual rainfall, March and April are the driest. The region's infamous humidity, which can be oppressive, also tapers off some in late spring; in winter, northern trade winds add additional cooling to coastal sites. Inland destinations, however, may feel sweltering when it's breezy at the beach.

May through October is the wet season, and therefore the **low season;** the most rain typically falls in September and October, frequently in intense downpours that give way to azure skies later in the day. But vacationing families with schoolchildren are willing to put up with rising temperatures and humidity in June and July, so the population (and prices) tends to swell again during those months. Summer is also when divers find the best underwater visibility, anglers go after the big-prize fish, and wildlife-watchers spot the greatest number of critters.

# The Yucatán's Visit-Worthy Annual Events

Maya traditions, Catholic feast days, and Mexican history have created numerous annual events worth incorporating into your visit—or avoiding, if parades, crowds, and closed banks aren't your thing. In Cancún, the Riviera Maya, and Mérida, promoters have also come up with music, film, and food festivals, as well as sporting events, to entice tourists. The best sources of information on these themed events are the regional tourism promoters (see "Online Resources" on p. 286) or your accommodations provider.

## January

**Three Kings' Day.** The Día de los Santos Reyes, also known as the Feast of Epiphany, commemorates the arrival of the wise men in Bethlehem on January 6 with gift giving. Some restaurants offer Rosca de Reyes, a special cake with a Christ Child figurine inside.

**City of Mérida Festival.** Mérida throws itself a big, art-themed birthday party starting the first week of January and running 10 days or more; the 2008 edition involved more than 170 events and 1,000 artists.

## February

**Candlemas.** Candle-lit processions herald the end of the Christmas season on February 2, Día de la Candelaria. Look for special meals of tamales and hot chocolate or *atole* (a corn drink) in local restaurants or homes, if you're invited. Campeche's festival includes fireworks and dancing.

**Carnaval.** The widespread partying known as Carnaval starts 5 days before Ash Wednesday (date varies), with major street celebrations in Mérida (home to five parades, including a children's procession), Campeche, Cozumel, and, increasingly, Cancún.

**Flag Day.** Purchase a Mexican flag from a street vendor to put on your rental car February 24 for Día de la Bandera; in Cancún, children host a special ceremony for the occasion.

## March

**Spring Equinox.** The shadow of serpent god Kukulcán appears to crawl down El Castillo pyramid at Chichén Itzá close to sunset on March 21 (as well as a couple of days before and after). Around 5am March 21, the sun shines through a special opening in the Temple of the Seven Dolls at Dzibilchaltún, north of Mérida. Maya ceremonies and large crowds are part of both events, with similar observances at Uxmal.

**Benito Juárez's Birthday.** The beloved 19th-century reformer and president, born March 21, is honored with a national holiday on the third Monday in March. Cancún, municipal seat of Quintana Roo's Benito Juárez municipality, celebrates his Día de Nacimiento with street parties.

## April

**Holy Week.** Semana Santa, the week between Palm Sunday and Easter Sunday (dates vary; it sometimes starts in Mar), prompts religious processions, re-enactments, and ceremonies throughout the country. Passion plays, dramatizing Christ's crucifixion, take place on Good Friday, with an especially elaborate one in Acanceh, near Mérida. Holy Week and the week after is also a top travel time for Mexicans.

**Honey Festival.** The 3-day Feria de la Miel in Hopelchén (Campeche) in mid-April includes traditional dances, fireworks, and a street fair.

## May

**Holy Cross.** In Cancún, the celebration of the Santa Cruz feast day on May 3 can stretch into a week of festivities. Construction workers nationwide put crosses on unfinished buildings and hold mini–street fairs, while Hopelchén (Campeche) celebrates with the traditional dance known as Cabeza de Cerdo (pig's head).

**El Cedral Fair.** Cozumel's signature *feria* at the beginning of May commemorates Mexico's first Catholic Mass and highlights the rustic traditions of the Maya settlement of El Cedral. Events include bullfights, rodeos, food vendors, and the Baile de las Cabezas de Cochino—another dance of the pigs' heads. Festivities may start in late April.

**Primero de Mayo.** A national holiday, May 1 is Mexico's equivalent of Labor Day.

**Cinco de Mayo.** May 5 marks Mexico's defeat of the French Army at the Battle of Puebla in 1862 (and not Independence Day, which is in Sept). Though the date is observed nationwide, don't expect the margarita-fest that the date has become in the United States, except possibly at Señor Frog's in Cancún. Celebrations are especially low-key in the Yucatán, which was far removed from the battle. You'll probably find music, dancing, and great food in the nearest *zócalo*; if you're lucky, you might come across a military parade.

## June

**Navy Day.** The Día de la Marina on June 1 honors Mexico's naval forces and those lost at sea, with marine parades, fishing tournaments, and fireworks. Progreso's (Yucatán state) celebration includes a waterfront fair.

**Corpus Christi.** Religious processions revering the Body of Christ mark the Catholic feast day in mid-June.

**Saints Peter & Paul.** Cozumel, among other communities, celebrates the June 29 feast day of San Pedro y San Pablo with a street fair.

## July

**Tunich Municipal Handicraft Fair.** This 3-day regional festival highlights Mérida's traditional crafts and local artisans, typically drawing 50,000 visitors.

**Our Lady of Carmen Festivals.** Playa del Carmen (Quintana Roo) and Ciudad del Carmen (Campeche) honor their patroness, Nuestra Señora del Carmen, in mid-July. The Ciudad del Carmen festivities last 2 weeks, including music, traditional dances, and parades.

## August

**Assumption of the Virgin Mary.** The Catholic feast day is celebrated nationwide with special Masses and religious processions in mid-August, with special emphasis in Oxkutzcab, Izamal (Yucatán), and Calkiní (Campeche).

**Fundación de Isla Mujeres.** Parades and street fairs on August 17 mark the founding of Isla Mujeres.

**Maní Festival.** The Fiesta de Maní commemorates the 1562 burning of Maya cultural treasures in Maní (on Yucatán's Convent Route) by a Spanish bishop with an exuberant celebration of all things Maya: food, arts, music. It takes place in the town's central square, around August 20.

## September

**San Román Festival.** Campeche's San Román neighborhood spends 2 weeks in September (dates vary) celebrating its statue of Cristo Negro, housed in a church built after a locust plague in 1565. The fiesta includes a parade of the ebony statue of Christ on Campeche's feast day (Sept 14) and a street fair.

**Mexican Independence Day.** Street revels take place in Mérida, Cancún, Isla Mujeres, and anywhere there's a city hall on the evening of September 15, when Mexicans relive Father Hidalgo's call for *independencia* from Spain in 1810. September 16 is a national holiday, with a major military parade in Cancún, among other sites.

**Christ of the Blisters Festival.** Labor groups stage colorful parades around Mérida's cathedral during a month-long festival honoring Cristo de las Ampollas, beginning mid-month.

**Fall Equinox.** The shadow of serpent god Kukulcán appears to crawl down El Castillo pyramid at Chichén Itzá the afternoon of September 21 (and a couple of days before), accompanied by Maya ceremonies and hordes of spectators.

**Fiesta de San Miguel Arcángel.** The patron saint of Cozumel, the archangel St. Michael, gets a week of festivities at the end of September, with parades, street fairs, and a waterfront ceremony honoring lost sailors.

## October
**Fundación de Campeche.** The October 4 fair celebrating the founding of Campeche overlaps with special Masses and processions honoring St. Francis of Assisi.

**Día de la Raza.** Columbus's arrival in the Americas, which led to the Mexican *raza*, or race, is marked throughout the region October 12 with bullfights, dancing, and processions.

## November
**Day of the Dead.** As elsewhere in Mexico, families and organizations visit cemeteries and erect altars with colored candles, sugar skulls, and such traditional foods as *mucbil pollo* (chicken and pork potpie) to honor their dead on November 1 (All Saints' Day and Día de los Angelitos, remembering saints and "little angels," or children) and November 2 (All Souls' Day, or Todos los Santos, honoring everyone else). Mérida's main plaza hosts numerous altars made by Maya villagers and other groups beginning October 31.

**Yucatán State Fair.** The 23-day Feria Yucatan in Xmatkuil, 6km (4 miles) south of Mérida, began as a cattlemen's trade show but has evolved into an exposition of traditional and contemporary Yucatecan culture. In addition to cattle and horse shows, rodeos, folkloric dance performances, and crafts displays, it also has bicycle acrobats, dolphin shows, and even hip-hop bands.

**Mexican Revolution Day.** A national holiday recalling the 1910 uprising, it's marked by parades on the third Monday in November.

**Bird Festival of Yucatán Toh.** Bird-watchers alight on various sites (2008's are Mérida and Uxmal) for this annual event with workshops, conferences, and a 28-hour "bird-a-thon" over a 3-day weekend in late November. For information, and for the 2009 locations, see www.yucatanbirds.org.mx.

## December
**Immaculate Conception.** The December 8 feast day honoring the Virgin Mary, patron saint of Isla Mujeres, is cause for celebrations there, while Yucatecan faithful head to Izamal, home to a revered statue of Our Lady of Izamal, the Yucatán's patroness.

**Virgin of Guadalupe.** December 12 is the feast day of Mexico's patron saint, Nuestra Señora de Guadalupe, and thus a huge event nationwide. Churches are packed for Masses, followed by public novenas, musical tributes, and private celebrations throughout the day.

**Christmas Season.** Lively candlelit processions called *posadas* kick off the Christmas season December 16, with nightly reenactments of Joseph and Mary's search for lodging in Bethlehem. Following midnight Mass on Noche Buena (Christmas Eve), December 25 is a national holiday and a breather for everyone, but Nativity scenes and the festive atmosphere remain through Three Kings' Day on January 6.

**New Year's Eve.** Fireworks, street revelry, and all-night parties herald the start of *el año nuevo.*

## Hurricane Season

The official hurricane season is June 1 through November 30, although the greatest chance of storms is in September and October. Hurricane Wilma, the most destructive in recent memory, struck in October 2005, although storms can hit earlier: Hurricane Dean menaced the area in August 2007. **The U.S. National Hurricane Center** (www.nhc.noaa.gov) posts advisories and tracks storms for the Atlantic region (including the Gulf of Mexico and Caribbean Sea) on its website; information for each season generally is not posted until the season starts, unless there's exceptionally early bad weather. When a hurricane is on the way, the **Hurricane Cancún** (www. hurricanecancun.com) blog is a great source of local information, commiseration, advice, and damage reports. Tourist authorities are quick to point out that major storms are likely to hit only once every 12 years, but you may want to consider travel insurance (p. 277) with weather-related coverage if you're set on a low-season visit, just to avoid possible financial hassles.

# ENTRY REQUIREMENTS

It's a bit easier to enter Mexico than it is to leave—at least if you're returning to the United States, where the Department of Homeland Security continues to roll out changes in travel regulations.

**Arriving by Air:** Citizens of the U.S., Australia, Canada, Ireland, New Zealand, and the United Kingdom, among others, need only show a passport and a tourist permit known as an FMT, to enter Mexico. The same is true for permanent legal residents of the U.S. and Canada. You'll get the form from your travel agent, from your airline (at check-in or on board), or at the airport when you land. Canadian and U.S. citizens also have the option to present a certified birth certificate, voter registration card, or naturalization certificate in lieu of a passport, along with a government-issued photo ID (such as a driver's license) and the FMT, but bringing your passport will speed entry—and all travelers must have one to enter the U.S. (that goes for U.S. citizens returning home, and foreign travelers with a layover in the U.S.).

Tourists can stay up to 180 days in Mexico with an FMT, so your passport should be valid for at least 6 months after your arrival. The fee for the FMT (about $20) is included in your airfare.

Hang on to the lower half of the FMT to present at the airport when you leave; if you lose it during your trip, go to the local office of the **Instituto Nacional de Migración** (☎ 998/881-3560 in Cancún, 999/925-5009, ext. 217, in Mérida, 981/816-0369 in Campeche; www.migracion.gob.mx) for a replacement. Technically, you'll need a police report confirming the loss or theft of your FMT, along with your passport or proof of identity as outlined above, although anecdotal evidence says you may be able to skip the report. Either way, you'll pay a fee of about $40 for a new FMT. For updated and detailed information, including a directory of local offices, see the website mentioned above (click on "English," then "I want to travel to Mexico as tourist"). The Cancún and Mérida airports also have small migration offices.

**Arriving by Sea:** Currently, Mexico does not require tourist permits or visas to enter a port in Mexico; your cruise line will already have made arrangements and will let you know which documents to bring.

**Arriving by Land:** While it's unlikely that you'll be driving or busing all the way to the Yucatán Peninsula, you are subject to the same document requirements as those arriving by air. You'll also need to pay the FMT fee and complete the tourist permit form at the immigration checkpoint.

Whatever your method of departure, you'll need to **return the lower half of your tourist permit.** Mexico also levies an airport tax (about $26) on all international departures, which U.S. and Canadian airlines are supposed to include in your airfare. However, some tours and charters have been known to exclude this tax to keep their prices low, so ask to make sure. If it's not included, you'll have to pay the tax in cash (pesos or dollars) at the airport.

And for U.S. citizens, returning from Mexico is no longer a matter of saying, "Yup, I'm an American," or flashing a driver's license to the immigration officer. For updates on the latest requirements, and information on obtaining documents, contact the **U.S. State Department** (☎ 888/407-4747; travel.state.gov, click on "Travel to Canada, Mexico and the Caribbean"). Here are the current guidelines:

**Returning by Air:** All U.S. citizens, including children, must present a passport at the airport. Permanent residents may use their Alien Registration Card (form I-551). Note that all persons traveling to the United States, even if only for a layover in an airport, must present a valid passport and possibly a visa. Residents of other countries who plan to visit the United States immediately after a stay in Mexico should contact the **U.S. State Department** (☎ 888/407-4747; travel. state.gov, click on "Visas for Foreign Citizens"). The U.S. State Department has a **Visa Waiver Program (VWP)** allowing citizens of certain countries (mainly European, Australian, and New Zealand citizens) to enter the United States without a visa for stays of up to 90 days. For the most up-to-date list of countries in the VWP, consult www.travel.state.gov/visa. Canadian citizens may enter the United States without visas; they will need to show passports (if traveling by air) and proof of residence.

**Returning by Sea or Land:** Currently, U.S. and Canadian citizens ages 19 and over must present a passport, passport card, or enhanced driver's license denoting citizenship (if available) to enter the United States from Mexico via sea or land. If you don't have one of those documents, you can show a driver's license or military or government ID with photo, plus one of the following: U.S. or Canadian birth certificate, U.S. naturalization or citizenship certificate, U.S. or Canadian citizen ID, or Canadian citizenship certificate. U.S. and Canadian citizens 18 and younger will need to show a passport or a government-issued birth or naturalization certificate. U.S. permanent residents must use the I-551 form.

The rules for sea and land crossings from Mexico into the United States (part of the Western Hemisphere Travel Initiative) will tighten again on June 1, 2009. U.S. citizens will need a passport, passport card (a new document set for launch in summer 2008, not valid for air travel), a trusted traveler card (valid at limited entry points), enhanced driver's license, or certain military documents. Only U.S. and Canadian children younger than 16 will be able to present just a birth certificate or other proof of citizenship to enter from Mexico; Canadian citizens 16 and older will need a passport or enhanced driver's license. (A special exemption will allow people 18 and younger to enter with just proof of citizenship.) The U.S. State Department website has details about the initiative.

## CUSTOMS REGULATIONS

Strict regulations govern what can and cannot be brought into and taken out of Mexico.

### What You Can Bring into Mexico

To state the obvious, don't bring anything that's generally illegal, particularly drugs or firearms. Have your doctor's prescription handy for medications, especially psychotropic drugs. Don't bring multiple computers, cameras, CDs, or anything it looks like you might try to sell; for the exact number of specific items allowed for personal use, see the Mexican Customs website, **Aduana México** (www.aduanas.sat.gob.mx, click on "English," then "Passengers arriving by airplane" or "Passengers arriving by land"). A few examples of what's allowed: 12 rolls of film, 10 DVDs, two cellphones, one laptop. For visitors over 18, current regulations allow for 20 packs of cigarettes, 25 cigars, or 200 grams of tobacco; up to 3 liters of "alcoholic beverages"; and 3 liters of wine.

You'll have to fill out a Customs Declaration form at the airport (available on board or at the Customs information counter when you land) or, if arriving by land, your point of entry. Going through Customs in Mexico is a breeze; if you have nothing unusual to declare, press the green button to pass through without inspection (although officials have the right to inspect your luggage regardless). Pressing the red button will hail an inspector.

Cruise passengers who enter the country at a port of call do not have to worry about clearing Customs; in most cases, they simply disembark the ship and head straight into town (or onto the beach). Getting back on ship, however, usually requires an official ID (driver's license or passport) and a passenger ID issued by the cruise line. Your cruise line will alert you to its specific protocol.

### What You Can Take Home from Mexico

If you're returning to the **United States** from Mexico, you'll fill out a Customs Declaration form on the plane, at the airport or border crossing. Citizens are allowed an $800 personal exemption, including up to 200 cigarettes and 100 cigars (except Cuban cigars), and 1 liter of alcoholic beverage. Family members may combine their exemptions (except for alcohol or tobacco, in the case of children). Besides the usual drugs and guns, U.S. Customs agents are on the lookout for fresh fruits and vegetables, exotic animals or animal skins, Cuban cigars, and prescription medicines bought over the counter. Fines can be substantial. For details, including rules for international visitors, contact **U.S. Customs and Border Protection** (☎ 202/927-1770; www.cpb.gov, click on "Travel," then "Know Before You Go").

For **Canadian** customs regulations, request the booklet "I Declare" from the **Canada Border Services Agency** (☎ 800/461-9999 in Canada, or 204/983-3500; www.cbsa-asfc.gc.ca). For **United Kingdom** regulations, contact **HM Customs & Excise** (☎ 0845/010-9000 in the U.K., or 020/8929-0152; www.hmce.gov.uk). Travelers returning to **Ireland** should contact the **Customs Information Office** (☎ 353-1/877-6222; www.revenue.ie). **Australia**'s consulates and Customs offices offer a "Know Before You Go" brochure; contact **Australian Customs Service** (☎ 1300/363-263; www.customs.gov.au). **New Zealand** details its regulations in "New Zealand Customs Guide for Travellers, Notice No. 4"; contact **New Zealand Customs** (☎ 04/473-6099 or 0800/428-786; www.customs.govt.nz).

# GETTING TO & AROUND CANCUN & THE YUCATAN

## BY AIR

Of the airports in the region, Cancún—the second-busiest in the nation—has the cheapest and most nonstop international flights, and the broadest selection of rental-car agencies, and other services. Its lower airfares often justify the extra time you might spend on the road to a farther-flung destination. For example, comparing one-stop flights from San Francisco for midsummer turned up $510 for Cancún, compared with $778 for Cozumel and $816 for Mérida. Note that prices usually drop for two-stop flights (lowering in this case to $447 Cancún, $692 Cozumel, $718 Mérida), but travel times can increase substantially. For a discussion of finding the best airfare to Cancún, see "Getting to & Around Cancún" on p. 14. Also, the difference between airfares to Cozumel and Cancún can be less dramatic in high season; if you're planning to spend most of your time in the former, it may make sense to fly there instead—see "Getting to & Around Cozumel" on p. 108.

Cancún is the travel hub of the entire peninsula, so even if your main destination has its own airport, you might still save money by flying into Cancún and traveling by bus or even rental car to your main destination. Be sure to read "Getting Around the Yucatán," later in this chapter and the "Getting To" section for each individual city and town for the scoop on traveling the peninsula. For a rundown of driving times in the Yucatán, see the inside front cover.

To get the lowest airfares, fly midweek and late at night. The Big Three online travel agencies, **Travelocity, Orbitz,** and **Expedia,** often produce lower fares than individual airlines because they aren't limited to a single flight route or schedule. The new generation of price-comparison engines such as **Kayak** (www.kayak.com), **Mobissimo** (www.mobissimo.com), **Sidestep** (www.sidestep.com), **Momondo** (www.momondo.com), and **BookingBuddy** (www.bookingbuddy.com) sometimes come up with lower fares than the Big Three by searching hundreds of travel providers' sites and using different combinations of flights and airlines.

## Discount Airlines Spread Their Wings

Since Mexicana Airlines spun off its "no-frills" **Click Mexicana** (☎ 55/ 5322-6262; clickmx.com) in 2005, seven more discount airlines have jumped into the Mexican domestic market. Only two of the low-fare carriers serve U.S. airports, so they make the most sense if you're starting your Yucatán vacation in another part of Mexico. But if you can grab a good fare to one of these airlines' hubs, you might beat the cost of booking your entire flight from a U.S. airport.

Click Mexicana, for example, flies nonstop from Mexico City to four airports in the Yucatán: Chetumal, Ciudad del Carmen (south of Campeche city), Cozumel (its closest service to Cancún), and Mérida. Take the following example: advance-purchase, midweek, round-trip flights for summer low season, including taxes and fees, cost about $340 for Chetumal, $345 for Ciudad del Carmen, $420 for Cozumel, and $170 for Mérida.

In this example, the lowest price for one-stop round-trip flights from San Francisco to Mérida on Orbitz was $867. By flying to Mexico City ($533) and then Click Mexicana to Mérida, you'd pay a total of $725, saving $142 per ticket. Using the same strategy from New York was less dramatic but still saved $94 per ticket.

It does take some work to figure out which of these airlines suit your itinerary and to find the lowest price; they don't appear on the search sites, and some of their websites are in Spanish only. *Another caveat:* Fares initially displayed don't include taxes and fees; select specific flights to see the final total.

## Booking Packages to Cancún & the Yucatán

Cancún and the Riviera Maya are staples for travel packagers, which bundle airfare, lodging, and optionally car rentals (and sometimes other extras) at a discount, often a significant one. If that's where you're headed, begin your research with the packagers to give you a point of comparison (for complete details, see "Air/Hotel Packages" on p. 16). The big U.S.-based companies mentioned in that section don't venture into other parts of the Yucatán, but you can find packages to Mérida and Ciudad del Carmen through **Mexicana Vacations** (☎ 800/ 380-8781 toll-free U.S./Canada; www.mexicanavacations.com), **Best Day Travel** (☎ 800/593-6259 toll-free U.S., or 998/287-3674; www.bestday.com), and **DoCancun** (☎ 998/881-7206; www.docancun.com); the latter two also offer packages to Campeche. These Mexican companies generally have more hotel choices and include more budget properties than the U.S. companies.

If you find a great package deal to Cancún, that doesn't necessarily lock you into the area for the duration. Fly-drive packages for at least two people will still cost less than purchasing the airfare and car rentals separately—and many air/ hotel packages allow you to stay a night or more in Cancún or the Riviera Maya and leave the remaining nights open for more offbeat lodgings along the road.

These aren't dilapidated puddle jumpers but efficient airlines with courteous, well-trained crews, new equipment, and free drinks, entertainment, and sometimes meals; their on-time records beat most U.S. or European carriers (faint praise though that may be). Here are six more low-fare airlines serving the Yucatán:

- **Aladia** (☎ 818/228-9290; www.aladia.com) flies to Cancún from its hub in Monterrey.
- **Alma de México** (☎ 888/811-2562 toll-free U.S., 333/836-0770; www.alma.com.mx) flies to Cancún, Chetumal, Mérida, and Ciudad del Carmen from its hub in Guadalajara.
- **Aviacsa** (☎ 866/246-0961 toll-free U.S., 998/887-4211; www.aviacsa.com) flies to Cancún and Mérida from its hub in Mexico City; it also flies from Las Vegas to Mexico City and Monterrey.
- **Interjet** (☎ 866/285-9525 toll-free U.S., 722/273-5271; www.interjet.com.mx) flies to Cancún, and Ciudad del Carmen from Toluca (64km/40 miles southwest of Mexico City).
- **Viva Aerobus** (☎ 888/935-9848 toll-free U.S., 818/215-0150; www.vivaaerobus.com) flies to Cancún, Cozumel, and Mérida from its hub in Monterrey; it also flies from Austin, Texas, to Cancún and Monterrey.
- **Volaris** (☎ 866/988-3527 toll-free U.S., 551/102-8000; www.volaris.com.mx) flies to Cancún and Mérida from its hub in Toluca (with free shuttle service to Mexico City International Airport). It was scheduled to begin service to Campeche in summer 2008.

## BY CAR

Taking your own car to the Yucatán involves a lot of time, money, and effort. Consider the following: The drive is a minimum of 26 hours from the Texas border to Cancún (not including well-advised overnight breaks); you have to buy Mexican insurance (U.S. insurance is invalid), post a bond (up to $400) in cash or on a credit card, and pay the temporary car-importation fee; and you must present a pile of paperwork (driver's license, original registration, copy of the title, tourist permit) at the Banjercito office at the nearest Customs office before you can get the temporary car-importation permit. You'll also want to check with your local Mexican consulate for any updated rules.

Perhaps you've already dealt with the hassle and brought your car into Mexico. From Mexico City to Campeche—the first major Yucatán-area destination you'd encounter—it's a minimum of 11 hours driving and about $88 in tolls (for more on toll roads, see p. 275). From Villahermosa (the capital of neighboring Tabasco), it's 4 hours and about $15 to Campeche; from the Gulf of Mexico port of Veracruz, 8½ hours and $53. Continuing onto Cancún from Campeche adds another 5 hours and $12 in tolls. In most cases, flying into the region and navigating by car or bus once they're there is both cheaper and easier.

## BY BUS

While long-distance buses serve every city in Mexico, the remoteness of the Yucatán from other major Mexico travel destinations makes it less likely that visitors will want to arrive by motorcoach from central Mexico, much less the distant U.S. border. Even with infrequent stops, it takes just under 17 hours to reach Campeche, the regional gateway, from Mexico City; add on another 7 hours for Cancún. Both cities are served by the luxury bus line ADO, as is Mérida (a little over 19 hr. from Mexico City). The length of the trips require overnight journeys, which U.S. authorities discourage for solo travelers (particularly women) for safety reasons. The price, however, may be right: From Mexico City, it costs about $80 to Campeche, $90 to Mérida, and $100 to Cancún on standard ADO buses, $10 to $15 more for the cushier ADO GL buses.

From relatively closer starting points, intercity buses make more sense. From Villahermosa, the 6-hour trip on either ADO or MTS costs about $25; from Veracruz, an ADO GL bus offers the fastest route, 11 hours and 40 minutes, for about $62. The website www.ticketbus.com.mx will allow you to compare trip lengths and prices as well as book tickets. For more on intercity bus travel, see p. 275.

## GETTING AROUND THE YUCATAN
### By Car

You don't need a car to enjoy Cancún, Mérida, and other resort areas or cities, or even to make extensive side or point-to-point trips, thanks to the panoply of reasonably priced public buses, affordable small-group tour operators, and helpful taxi drivers whom you can hire by the day. But adventurous types who want to stick to their own schedule while exploring the interior or remote stretches of the coast will want to hire a car—if they can afford the tariffs, which include mandatory insurance with steep deductibles. You'll find all the major American car-rental companies—Advantage, Alamo, Avis, Budget, Dollar, Hertz, National, Payless, and Thrifty—plus international and Mexico-based companies such as Caribetur, Easy Way Rent A Car, and Europcar. They all have online booking sites, but it's easier to do comparison via the major travel portals (Orbitz, Expedia, and such) or Mexico travel sites such as mexicocar.net. You'll usually get a better rate if you reserve before you leave home. Go with whichever company is cheapest (it changes week to week). If you really need to save on rental costs, make a reservation but continue your online searches up until your departure date. If you find lower prices, cancel your initial reservation (you don't turn over your credit card number until you show up to claim your car) and book again. Base rates in Cancún are slightly higher than renting in Mérida or Playa del Carmen. On the other hand, Cancún has a greater selection of vehicle types not available elsewhere. Most companies have both automatic- and manual-transmission vehicles on hand, although some may charge you $1 to $10 more per day for an automatic.

Whatever the rate, the important thing to keep in mind is that it's only about half of what you'll end up paying. Mexico's mandatory insurance costs about $17,

$35, or $50 a day on an average economy-car rental, depending on the level of coverage. Technically, you can decline to buy any insurance, but you will be breaking Mexican law. If you have an accident, you won't be allowed to leave the country until you pay the damages, and you may be put in jail until you settle up.

You can pick up a **rental car** at the airports in Cancún, Cozumel, and Mérida, and in all major cities. You must be at least 25 years of age and have a valid driver's license and credit card, with sufficient funds for insurance and a security deposit beyond the daily rental fee.

Before you set off, check the gas tank; rental-car companies typically send you out with half a tank (expecting you to return it with the same amount), and remote areas like Uxmal have no gasoline services. It's best to fill up as soon as you can. Also note carefully any chips, dings, or scratches on the car on a special form before you leave the rental lot, to prevent being charged for them when you return; it's unlikely to be a problem when renting from U.S. companies such as Hertz or Avis, but some online resources have reported complaints from travelers. Don't drive at night, particularly in rural areas, since roads and vehicles may not have lights, and hazards, from the notorious *topes* (speed bumps) to pedestrians and farm animals, may appear without warning.

If you get into an accident, you must file a police report; both drivers may be taken into custody until the police determine who is at fault, and the at-fault driver must pay damages before being released from custody. It's important to carry your proof of Mexican insurance and to keep the emergency assistance number of your car rental agency handy.

For other roadside emergencies, call the **Green Angels** *(Angeles Verdes)* fleet at ☎ **078.** The bilingual crews on these radio-dispatched green trucks can provide mechanical help, first aid, and protection, and will only charge you for parts, gas, and oil (as needed). From dawn to sunset daily, the Green Angels also patrol main highways—nearly 3,200km (2,000 miles) over a total of 21 routes throughout Campeche, Quintana Roo, and Yucatán—looking for drivers in trouble. If you can't call for help, pull over in a safe spot and lift the hood of your car.

For intercity trips, unless you have plenty of time to savor the scenery (and patience to tolerate speed bumps), you'll want to opt for a toll road (called a *cuota autopista,* or *carretera de cobro*), which allow for much faster and safer travel. The *libre* (free) roads are local roads that meander through villages and towns and are frequently pocked with speed bumps of every size—they will slow you down considerably and cause undue stress on your car. Toll charges reflect distances traveled; you'll pay 319 pesos (about $30) to travel from Cancún to Mérida, but only 65 pesos (about $6) from Mérida to Campeche. Most drivers consider the tolls worth the expense—at least in one direction. If your itinerary includes a round-trip route, consider taking the *cuota* one way and the *libre* in the other to vary your views. But do not drive the *libre* roads at night since hazards, such as people, speed bumps, other cars, and livestock, are rarely lit, and no one wants to deal with a breakdown on a deserted road at night.

## By Bus

**Buses** are convenient for travel within and between cities. Intercity buses *(camiones)* come in several classes. First-class and *lujo* (luxury) buses are clean and modern, usually including air-conditioning, TVs, toilets, and sometimes cafeterias. Second-class buses may be almost as nice, or fairly dilapidated; they cost less,

## Fill 'Er Up

**Pemex (Petroleras Mexicanas),** the government-owned oil company, has a monopoly on gasoline and gas stations. Pull up to a green-handled pump for Magna, Pemex's 87-octane unleaded gas, or to a red-handled pump for Premium, its higher-octane version (90–93 octane; the Pemex website is coy on the subject). Diesel pumps have black handles labeled "Diesel." To ask for a fill-up, say *"Llene* (yeh-*neh), por favor."* Gas stations are full service; watch to make sure the attendant resets the counter to zero before he or she starts pumping. Although this is a time-honored admonition, I've driven thousands of miles in Mexico and never had a problem.

Pemex sells gas by the liter (about a quart, or 3.78 liters, to the gallon); it's trying to crack down on franchisees who adulterate their gas or shortchange drivers on the amounts, but some fraud may still occur. More stations are accepting credit and debit cards, though few have the credit card readers found in the United States and Europe; you'll give your card to the attendant, who'll come back with a slip to sign (check the amount carefully). You may offer a small tip (5 pesos or so) to the attendant, although it's not required; do tip the windshield washer or bathroom attendant, if you use their services—3 to 5 pesos is fine.

---

but tend to spend more time picking up passengers en route. **Ticket Bus** (☎ 800/702-8000 toll-free Mexico, 55/5133-2424; www.ticketbus.com.mx) culls fares on intercity lines; you can also purchase tickets with reserved seats (you may be required to buy the tickets at least 6 hr. in advance). At press time, taking the ADO or ATS lines from Cancún to Campeche cost 324 to 408 pesos ($31–$40), depending on the quality of the bus; the trip lasts nearly 7 hours with local stops. A trip from Cancún to Mérida cost 246 pesos ($24) on ADO's first-class buses, 290 pesos ($28) on its luxury ADO GL buses, or 390 pesos ($38) on the UNO luxury line, which includes bed seats with blankets and pillows, and four flat-screen video screens. Trip time varies from 4 to 4½ hours. Although the U.S. State Department has no specific warnings against bus travel in Cancún and the Yucatán, it recommends daylight hours and first-class buses for travel in Mexico in general.

Inexpensive *colectivos* and *combis*—usually minivans—often run between smaller towns, including the route from Cancún to Tulum. You wave them down (the driver will often flash his headlights to signal he has room in the van); you also need to let the driver know where you want to get off. *Colectivos* are generally safe, although standard caution should apply when traveling after dark. The comfort level varies by region: In tourist zones, *colectivos* are likely to be new, air-conditioned vans; off the beaten path, they might be much older models without air-conditioning, or even pickup trucks.

The *colectivo* from Cancún to Playa del Carmen, which runs about every 5 to 15 minutes between 5am and 10pm, costs 40 pesos (less than $4) one-way; from Playa del Carmen to Tulum costs another 20 pesos ($2). You can catch the *colectivo* anywhere on Hwy. 307 from Cancún to Tulum, in downtown Cancún at La

Comercial Mexicana (Av. Tulum) or in Playa del Carmen at Calle 2 Norte between avenidas 15 and 20.

Cancún, Mérida, Campeche, and Chetumal have municipal bus services with traditional bus stops; your hotel will have the current schedule. Depending on your time, the size of your party, and the distance involved, taxis might be more efficient or economical. Cancún has one of the best bus systems in the country (p. 15), and Mérida's (p. 186), while tricky, has a couple of routes useful to visitors. In other destinations, you're not likely to need a local bus except for the occasional day trip, such as Valladolid's service to Chichén Itzá (p. 235).

## By Taxi

Taxis are a reasonable, and often preferable, alternative to bus tours for day trips. The prevailing hourly rate is $15, and you can often negotiate a lower price for a half- or full-day excursion. You need to have only two passengers to meet or beat the cost of a tour bus. Drivers often prove to be excellent guides. They aren't as polished as the official guides, but they will steer you to places where locals go, if you ask them, and they follow no schedule but yours. Taxis are also an option for transportation to towns that are difficult to reach by bus, but keep in mind that you'll need to pay them for their return time after they drop you off.

# TRAVEL INSURANCE

Before you buy travel insurance, check with your credit card provider and home insurance agency to see if you're already covered for lost or stolen luggage, canceled flights, or other expenses related to travel mishaps. Then, once you know what is and isn't covered, get quotes from a number of providers, who charge a small percentage of your trip, at **InsureMyTrip.com,** but review any exclusions carefully. If you're traveling during hurricane season, make sure your policy includes weather-related costs. No matter what your medical insurance says it will cover—and not all policies do cover expenses incurred abroad—be prepared to pay any doctor or hospital fees upfront in Mexico, and collect a refund from your company later. **Medex** (☎ 800/537-2029 toll-free U.S.; www.medexassist.com) offers short-term medical insurance with up to $100,000 in expenses, 24-hour assistance, and emergency medical evacuation starting at $4 a day. **MedToGo** (☎ 866/633-8646 toll-free U.S.; www.medtogo.com) also makes recommendations of several companies' policies for travel and health insurance in Mexico. If

---

## Auto Insurance

It doesn't matter what policy you already have: If you're renting a car, you need to buy Mexican car insurance, or risk being in violation of the law. Rental-car agencies will offer you collision and damage insurance to cover damage to your car and to others, in cases where you're at fault, and personal accident insurance to cover damage to you or anyone in your car. Proof of this insurance can be critical: If you're in an accident, you'll be taken into custody and kept there until police determine who is at fault and your ability to pay for damages, if liable.

---

you're planning any "extreme" activities, like scuba diving, ziplining, or parasailing, you'll probably need to buy an optional "hazardous sports" rider, and not every company offers these.

If you're renting a condo or home, rather than staying at a hotel, you may want to consider trip-cancellation or trip-interruption insurance—policies that refund at least part of your costs if you can't make the journey or need to return home early. While most hotels usually let you cancel a stay without penalty with 24 hours' notice, and let you depart early with a day's penalty at most, not so with vacation rentals, which tend to be individually owned. **TravelSafe** (☎ 888/885-7233 toll-free U.S.; www.travelsafe.com) offers policies that will let you cancel for any reason—not just medical emergencies or deaths in the family; rates vary based on your age and the percentage of your trip's costs that you choose to insure.

# MONEY MATTERS

Cancún is not the bargain destination that Mexico is generally reputed to be; except in El Centro, expect to pay at least what you would in the United States for just about everything. Prices have also crept up along the Riviera Maya, though there are bargains sprinkled among the pricier tourist-oriented hotels, restaurants, and shops. The rest of the Yucatán, though, is made for the budget traveler.

Mexico's unit of currency is the **peso,** with 100 **centavos** (cents) per peso. **Bank notes** come in 20-, 50-, 100-, 200-, 500-, and 1,000-peso denominations, with several versions in circulation over the last decade (see "Currency Conditions," p. 282). **Coins** come in 1-, 2-, 5-, and 10-peso versions—worth hanging on to for small tips—plus the rarer 100-peso coin. There are also 5-, 10-, 20-, and 50-centavo coins, but only the latter is common.

Though the dollar hasn't taken the drubbing in Mexico that it has in the rest of the world, it has slipped in the past year. At press time, the exchange rate was 10.39 pesos to the dollar, down from 10.75 in late 2007.

Be prepared to hear *"no hay cambio"* ("no change") from bus drivers, marketplace vendors, and shops outside of tourist zones, especially if you're trying to break a larger note. Try to assemble as many small bills and coins as you can from mainstream establishments, so you can pay with exact change when possible. For tipping, American dollar bills will do in a pinch, but remember the recipient will lose money on the exchange, and might also have to wait in one of those long bank lines you wisely avoided.

You'll be able to use **credit cards,** generally Visa, MasterCard and, less often, American Express, at more upscale hotels, restaurants, and shops. Plan to use cash at more affordable venues, in local markets, on public transit, and in taxis. Smaller hotels that don't take credit cards are beginning to accept payment online through **PayPal,** which gives you the option of charging the transaction to your credit card or taking it directly from your bank account.

To avoid the problem of variable hours (often limited to weekdays), time-consuming protocols, and the resulting long lines at Mexican banks, it's easiest to get your pesos at **ATMs.** They're at many banks throughout the region, and at grocery stores in the major cities and tourist destinations—use them with the same precautions you would at home. Fees will vary, but are usually a small percentage of your withdrawal; as with **credit card purchases,** your home bank may charge an additional currency conversion fee as well as an ATM transaction fee. The

## Dollars or Pesos?

Sometimes it can be hard to tell what the price is, if the vendor only uses the $ sign. In this book, $ signifies U.S. dollars, but if you're in Cancún or another touristy area, it could mean either dollars (which most places accept) or pesos. Look for the abbreviations MX or MN to indicate Mexican pricing, or US for American pricing—or just ask (in Spanish, *"Es el precio en pesos?"*) In the interior and less visited cities, the $ sign generally denotes pesos, but it never hurts to practice your Spanish by double-checking. *Important note:* Paying in pesos usually gives you the better deal.

exchange rate is generally the wholesale banking rate, which even with the conversion fee is normally as good or better than you'd find on your own.

Before you go, check with your **debit and credit card** providers to find out your withdrawal limits (per transaction and per day). You will also need a four-digit PIN (personal identification number), since most ATMs in Mexico will not accept longer PINs. Cards on the Cirrus and Plus networks will work at overseas ATMs with those logos, which are easily found in tourist and metropolitan areas. If you're planning more remote travel, you can find listings in advance from **Cirrus** (☎ 800/424-7787; www.mastercard.com) and **Plus** (☎ 800/843-7587; www.visa.com). You may also wish to inform card issuers that you plan to use the card in Mexico, in order to prevent a "hold" based on suspicious activity. As a precaution, carry the toll-free numbers for alerting providers of your cards' theft or loss separately from where you carry the cards.

Travelers' checks are not recommended, since they're generally much less convenient to use (particularly outside of Cancún) or to convert into pesos. If you must exchange cash or travelers' checks, *casas de cambio* **(foreign-exchange offices)** have longer hours and sometimes offer better rates than banks. Banks often have limited hours for money exchange, so go in the morning just to be safe (they are also quite fussy about the condition of the bills if you're exchanging cash). Although the exchange booths at the airport in Cancún seem pricey, those in some towns can offer reasonable deals. The larger hotels will also offer foreign exchange, but usually take a bigger cut than banks or *casas de cambio.* Using an ATM will most often give you the better exchange rate, unless you need a large amount of cash. Most Mexican ATMs limit cash withdrawals to 3,000 pesos (about $300), so making numerous withdrawals, each incurring transaction fees, will eventually outpace the one-time cost of converting a large amount at a *casa de cambio* or bank.

# HEALTH & SAFETY

Exercising the same common sense you would at home will allow you to avoid most hazards in the region, with a few notable exceptions.

## STAYING HEALTHY

The most common medical problems for visitors, which fortunately can be easily prevented, are sunburn, dehydration, and digestive ailments such as traveler's

## Taxing Issues

Mexico imposes a value-added tax (*impuesto de valor agregado,* or IVA) on nearly everything you pay for; it's 15% in most parts of the country, although only 10% in Cancún and Cozumel (among other ports of entry outside the region). Hotels generally add a local bed tax of 2%, for a total of 12% to 17%, depending on your location. Posted prices normally include tax.

Tourists departing through certain airports, including Cancún and Mexico City, can claim a refund for the IVA on merchandise (not meals or lodging) purchased anywhere in the country, as long as the total amount of purchases is at least 1,200 pesos (about $115). At the airport kiosk, you'll need to present your passport and receipts for purchases from approved stores (if you don't see a sign, ask the sales help where you're shopping if that store is eligible). The purchase must be made in cash or with a credit or debit card issued outside of Mexico. You'll get half of your IVA refund in pesos (up to 10,000, or about $955); the rest will be credited to your card or bank account within 40 days. Note that this is a brand-new program for 2008—expect some kinks in the system initially. The program will expand to other airports and cruise ports beginning in 2009.

diarrhea (it's impolite to call it Montezuma's Revenge—and inaccurate, since Mexicans traveling outside their country are prone to it as well).

To prevent diarrhea, drink only bottled or purified water. Hotels and restaurants in Cancún and other resort areas will generally serve purified water (*agua purificada*) and ice made from purified water. If you're uncertain, feel free to ask, or just stick to canned or bottled beverages. You should also avoid salads and unpeeled fruit outside of resort restaurants. In addition, the **U.S. Centers for Disease Control** (www.cdc.gov) recommends washing hands often with soap and water or an alcohol-based hand gel; drinking only bottled or boiled water, or carbonated drinks in cans or bottles; and avoiding food purchased from street vendors, undercooked food, and dairy products, unless you know they have been pasteurized. **MedToGo** (www.medtogo.com)—see "Travel Insurance," p. 277—sells a Mexico-oriented first-aid kit for $24 that includes electrolyte replacement tablets, which are key to combat a severe case of diarrhea; it also posts a list for do-it-yourself kits that includes a description of how to use antibiotics, Tums, or other drugs for diarrhea prevention and remedy.

When outside during the day (even when it's cloudy), regularly apply waterproof sunscreen with a high SPF (sunburn protection factor) to exposed skin, and wear a hat and sunglasses. Keep in mind that some cenotes and snorkeling sites in the Yucatán require swimmers to either not wear any sunblock or lotions or to wear only biodegradable formulas (p. 119). Remember that the sun is more intense in the Tropics, and the reflection from water at the beach or in the swimming pool will magnify the effect of ultraviolet rays. To avoid heat exhaustion, stay hydrated with bottled water and juices; if you're prone to heavy perspiration, bring salt tablets or an electrolyte replacement. Wearing lightweight, long-sleeved shirts and pants will also help prevent sunburn and decrease bug bites that might also cause illness and irritation. Although the risk of contracting malaria or dengue fever from mosquitoes is very low (the CDC considers only a small area of Quintana Roo on the border with Belize and Guatemala to be at risk for malaria), it's wise to minimize bites from mosquitoes and gnats. Bring an insect repellent that contains DEET to apply to exposed skin (try it at home first to be sure you aren't allergic) and bug spray to kill any flying insects in your hotel room. Repellents are readily available in Mexico but are more expensive than in the United States.

## AVOIDING ACCIDENTS

The sensible traveler should have little difficulty staying safe in Cancún and the Yucatán. Still, the **U.S. State Department** (☎ 888/407-4747; travel.state.gov) website's safety information for Mexico notes that "standards of security, safety, and supervision may not reach those expected in the United States." Its report cites fatal incidents such as automobile accidents, falls from balconies, drowning in the ocean and hotel pools, and mishaps involving parasailing and personal watercraft tours. It should be obvious, but assume you have the primary responsibility for your (and your children's) safety.

Specific problems for this region, according to the State Department, include a strong undertow in Cancún, along the beach from the Hyatt Regency south to Club Med, and several drownings and near drownings on the east coast of Cozumel, particularly in the Playa San Martín–Chen Río area. Moped-rental companies in Cancún and Cozumel often carry no insurance and do not conduct safety checks; avoid those who don't provide a helmet with a rental. Drivers should also exercise special caution on the expressway south of Cancún, especially between Playa del Carmen and Tulum, as it is narrow and poorly maintained.

## CIRCUMVENTING CRIME

Car break-ins and petty theft are the major crime concerns in the Yucatán. Avoid wearing or displaying valuables, and make use of your hotel room safe. For Mexico in general, the State Department warns of pickpocketing on public transit, and recommends drivers use toll roads when they have the option. Women

## Recommended Vaccines

While no vaccinations are required to enter Mexico, the **U.S. Centers for Disease Control** (www.cdc.gov) recommends that travelers who have not already had a hepatitis A or immune globulin (IG) vaccine to get one before going to Mexico. It considers Mexico to have "an intermediate or high level" of hepatitis A infection, and exposure occurs through food or water, not just off the beaten path, but also in standard tourist settings. The CDC also recommends vaccinations for typhoid, "especially if visiting smaller cities, villages, or rural areas and staying with friends or relatives where exposure might occur through food or water."

## Currency Conditions

Before you travel, familiarize yourself with the current design of peso notes and coins to prevent potential fraud. Some Americans have been arrested for passing on counterfeit money they received in change, according to the State Department. You can find pictures of valid currency online at the **Bank of Mexico** (www.banxico.org.mx) website under "Billetas y monedas" (if you can follow the links in Spanish), or at **Mexperience** (www.mexperience.com) in the "Money Guide" link under "Travel Essentials." If you somehow end up with outdated currency, banks will exchange versions dating back to 1993 (including the now old *nuevo,* "new"), for the same value as today's peso. Currency issued earlier than 1993, however, is worth substantially less: A 2,000-peso note from 1992, for example, will net you only two of today's pesos. The Mexico Tourism Board also notes that the 20-peso coin is not accepted everywhere; it's no longer being minted.

should be particularly cautious when traveling alone, and all solo visitors should avoid travel at night. The State Department says "a significant number" of rapes have been reported in Cancún and other resort areas, many taking place at night or in the early morning, on deserted beaches or in hotel rooms. Often acquaintances are involved, but hotel workers, taxi drivers, and security personnel have also been implicated. If you're hitting the clubs in Cancún, keep an eye on your drink as well. But don't let this kind of common-sense caution—which could apply to nearly any urban or less affluent travel destination—deter you from exploring the region. As long as alcohol doesn't cloud your judgment, and you don't routinely advertise your belongings as ripe for the picking, you should be fine.

## PACKING

With airlines adding fees for checked luggage and increasing the cost for oversize or overweight bags, you want to pack as efficiently as you can. Traveling around by taxi, bus, or other shuttles will also be easier—and possibly cheaper—if you bring fewer bags.

Outside of the beach resort areas, Mexico is fairly conservative when it comes to dress. Pack a **light pair of pants** (or a **light dress** or **modest skirt,** for women) to wear instead of shorts when touring churches, colonial cities, and Maya villages, or when going out for dinner. A **light jacket** will protect you from winds at the coast or cool evenings in winter, and makes a great cover-up for a sleeveless shirt that's fine by itself during the day. For walking up stone pyramids or around cobblestone streets, you'll want cool, sturdy **walking shoes** or **hiking sandals** (like Tevas); flip-flops will wear the soles of your feet out.

If you like to read in bed, a small, battery-operated **book light** will foil the inadequate lighting that often plagues budget lodgings and can double as a flashlight in a pinch. A travel-size roll of **toilet paper** or stash of tissues invariably comes in handy. Public restrooms may be clean but in need of toilet paper, and carrying a small **hand sanitizer** (like Purel) will fill possible voids in soap and water. Likewise, a supply of **zip-top plastic bags** will be invaluable in ways you've never thought of.

A simple **first-aid kit** stocked with your favorite brand of pain reliever, an antacid or heartburn remedy (like Tums), an anti-diarrhea agent (Imodium A-D) and electrolyte replacement (Pedialyte), a seasickness remedy (Dramamine) if you're planning any boat trips, and plastic bandages (Band-Aids), can save you a trip to a pharmacy or the expense of a hotel gift shop. You can buy sunscreen in Mexico, but it's generally cheaper to bring it with you; choose a high sunburn protection factor (SPF). If you plan to visit an eco-park like Xcaret, or swim in any cenotes or among the whale sharks of Isla Holbox, look for a biodegradable formula such as those made by Mexitan, Kiss My Face, or Hawaiian Tropic.

Keep all **medications,** especially prescribed medicines, in their original containers, with a copy of the prescriptions. Don't assume you'll be able to refill any prescriptions or simply buy what you need over the counter (although it helps if you know the generic name of prescribed drugs or favorite remedies). Mexican pharmacies do sell several drugs over the counter, including antibiotics, that are available in the United States only by prescription, but U.S. authorities don't look kindly on anyone bringing back undocumented or suspiciously large supplies.

Make copies of **important papers**—your passport, driver's license, vouchers for airport transfers, rental-car or hotel confirmations, bus tickets, and a list of emergency phone contacts, for example—to keep separately from the originals.

You might need an electrical **adapter** (see "Electricity" in "The ABCs of Cancún & the Yucatán" on p. 288). Most laptops sold in the last few years have their own built-in electricity converter.

# SPECIALIZED TRAVEL RESOURCES

## FAMILIES

As in the rest of Mexico, children will receive a warm welcome here, but plan on bringing your own collapsible crib if you're not staying at a large hotel and a car seat if you'll be driving, since they may not be available for rent.

Double rooms in most hotels have two double beds, and many hotels allow up to two children ages 12 and younger to stay for free with up to two adults. Expect to pay $10 to $15 for rollaway beds and cribs. In larger resorts with all-inclusive meal plans, children may be allowed to eat free, as well; many have simple children's menus with the basics (spaghetti marinara, chicken nuggets, grilled cheese). Note that hotels may reduce children's discounts during peak seasons, and policies vary, so confirm before you make a reservation.

The larger resort hotels will also book babysitters and offer children's activities. The less touristy lodgings and restaurants will generally not have special programs, but feel free to ask the proprietors for help or recommendations: Given the cultural benevolence accorded children, they'll try to accommodate you. For excursions, children's discounts are widely available and can come to about 50% off the standard rate. Where fees are smaller, discounts are more modest—along the lines of 10 pesos ($1) off a 40-peso ($3.85) adult admission. Discounts are usually based on age, but occasionally height will be the deciding factor (as at theme park Xcaret).

## Parental Permission

The greatest number of children abducted from the United States by a parent end up in Mexico. To prevent such abductions, Mexican law requires any non-Mexican citizen under the age of 18 to carry a notarized letter of permission from any parent (or guardian) not traveling with the child. This letter must include the name of the parent, the child, and anyone traveling with the child, and the notarized signature(s) of the absent parent(s). The U.S. State Department recommends that the letter also include a travel itinerary and a brief description of the purpose of the trip. The child must carry the original letter—not a facsimile or photocopy— as well as proof of the parent/child relationship (usually a birth certificate) and an original custody decree, if applicable.

The **Family Travel Forum** (www.familytravelforum.com) offers a wealth of advice and ideas on general travel issues, as well as hundreds of articles about Mexico from a family perspective, including a hefty selection on Cancún and the Yucatán. Registered users can submit specific questions for customized trip planning advice. The Family Vacations section of **About.com** (http://travelwithkids.about. com) has a variety of informative reports on its "Mayan Riviera/More Mexico" link under "Topics," and its forums (scroll to the link at the bottom of the left-hand frame) have a section on the Caribbean and Mexico.

## TRAVELERS WITH DISABILITIES

Mexico has few laws requiring facilities to have wheelchair access or other accommodations for the disabled, so only the larger, upscale resorts tend to provide services or permit assistance animals. Fortunately, a private company, **Cancún Accesible** (Bl. Kukulcán Km 8.5; ☎ 998/883-1978; www.cancunaccesible.com) has stepped in to bridge the gap. It can arrange for wheelchair and motorized chair rentals, transportation in adaptive vans, and oxygen therapy, and provides hotel care for people with special needs at their hotel. The company also offers special guided tours (in English and Spanish) in Cancún and the Riviera Maya. At press time, the website was only in Spanish, but the company, founded in 2005, serves English-speaking customers; it also has plans to offer sign-language interpretation and dialysis services in Cancún and Playa del Carmen. **Access-Able Travel Source** (☎ 303/232-2979; www.access-able.com) shares readers' referrals and posts business listings for Cancún lodgings and attractions. The U.S.-based website wrongly puts Mexico under the heading of Central America, a common mistake, but is generally considered reliable.

## SENIORS

Mexicans treat older citizens—*la tercera edad,* or "third age"—with great respect. While the prices in Cancún and the climate of the Yucatán haven't made them popular retirement destinations like Puerto Vallarta or San Miguel de Allende, senior travelers should have no issues. Senior discounts are not common, but starting at age 60 (in some cases, 62) you might find a few discounts similar to those in the United States at attractions and hotels (look for the abbreviation "*3a. edad*"); always inquire first.

Members of **AARP** (www.aarp.org) can take advantage of discounts on flights on **Mexicana** (☎ 888/291-1757; www.mexicana.com) and at numerous chain hotels; check the website for details. Depending on the accommodations and flights, however, a travel company's air/hotel package might beat those discounts, so compare prices before booking. **Elderhostel** (☎ 800/454-5768; www.elder hostel.org), the nonprofit educational tour operator for adults over 55, organizes all-inclusive trips that focus on Maya history and birding.

## GAY & LESBIAN TRAVELERS

Although not as rainbow colored as Puerto Vallarta or Mexico City, Cancún and Playa del Carmen are the most gay-friendly destinations in the region, with a sprinkling of gay nightclubs, discos, and beaches; Mérida's growing gay population is not quite as "out." Particularly outside of the resorts, remember that socially conservative Mexico is influenced by traditional Catholic teachings; generally, it's wise to avoid public displays of physical affection, although women may walk hand in hand.

Travel providers **MexGay Vacations** (www.mexgay.com), based in Los Angeles, and **Arco Iris Tours** (☎ 800/765-4370; www.arcoiristours.com), based in San Diego, can arrange packages including stays at gay-owned or gay-friendly lodgings. **Gay.com Travel** (☎ 415/644-8044; www.gay.com/travel) is a worthy online successor to the popular *Out & About* travel newsletter, with up-to-date information on gay-owned, gay-oriented, and gay-friendly lodging, restaurants, and attractions in major worldwide destinations, including Cancún, Mérida, and Playa del Carmen.

## BRIDES & GROOMS

Marriage requirements in Mexico vary from state to state, but passports, licenses, witnesses, and blood tests—performed in Mexico—are normally part of the process. It's simpler to have a symbolic ceremony in Mexico and a civil (or legal religious) ceremony back home, but the major resort hotels all have wedding coordinators who can help you with the paperwork as well as the festivities.

---

## Calling All Cells

Those who call cellphones in Mexico are generally the ones who pay for the privilege. To call a Mexican cellphone from a landline within the same area code, you need to dial (044) before the area code (two or three digits) and phone number (seven or eight digits). To call a Mexican cellphone with a different area code, dial (045) before the area code and phone number. When calling Mexican cellphones from outside the country, use your international access code and the country code (52), followed by 1 and the cellphone's area code and number. Fortunately, when calling from one Mexican cellphone to another, you can just use the area code and number.

---

## Online Resources

Finding reliable, up-to-date visitor information online can be a bit of a challenge: "Official" sites often aren't, Internet connections can be tenuous, and English translations shaky, when they exist at all. These are some of the most comprehensive privately produced websites and the most useful government tourism sites:

◆ **www.asur.com.mx:** Official site of Aeropuertos Del Sureste (Airports of the Southeast); useful information for Cancún, Cozumel, and Mérida airports, among others.

◆ **www.campechetravel.com:** Official Campeche state tourism site; basic listings of hotels, restaurants, guides, and other "touristic services," and engaging articles on folklore, handicrafts, and history.

◆ **www.cancun.info:** Official Cancún Convention and Visitors Bureau site; broad directories of hotels and "experiences" (everything else) with plenty of photos and videos. Individual listings are not very detailed but include addresses, phone numbers, and websites.

◆ **www.cozumelmycozumel.com:** Produced by an expat couple who have lived on the island for 10 years, with lots of insider tips and hugely informative message boards.

◆ **www.mapchick.com:** Nitty-gritty practical advice from creator of the best maps available for Cancún, the Riviera Maya, and Chichén Itzá (with a link to her online store).

◆ **www.mexperience.com:** One of the best general Mexico travel sites, with articles divided between "Travel Essentials" and "Travel Guides"; includes the humorous and compelling Foreign Native blog.

Independent wedding coordinators include **Cancun Weddings** (☎ 800/444-6967; www.cancunweddings.com), a division of U.S.-based Weddings on the Move, and **Cancun Mexico Weddings** (Av. Kohunlich 42, Cancún; www.cancunmexicoweddings.com).

## STAYING WIRED WHILE AWAY

**Cellphones** are ubiquitous in Mexico, but it can be complicated, not to mention costly, to bring your own with you. To use your cellphone in Mexico, you need a tri-band model (to access the Global System for Mobiles network) and an account that permits international calling; contact your provider in advance if you're not sure what you have. Roaming charges are substantial; if you're planning to make a number of calls, it may make more sense when you arrive to buy a prepaid SIM card (to swap with your phone's existing memory chip) or a phone kit (a phone, card, and short-term calling plan, good only in Mexico; rates start at 415 pesos/$40 for the kit, but expect high per-minute rates). You'll find cellphone providers at the Cancún airport and in downtown areas; hotels can also point you to local services. Another cheap alternative, if you have a laptop and headset with

+ **www.locogringo.com**: Maintained by a U.S. couple living in Akumal since 1992; advice, bookings, and voluminous forums focusing on the Riviera Maya and Costa Maya.
+ **www.sac-be.com**: Online arm of excellent monthly travel guide; articles, reviews, travel tips, and events listings tilted toward nature and culture.
+ **www.thisiscozumel.com**: Privately run tourism site with listings and online bookings as well as balanced news stories on Cozumel development and, in "Tourist Info," useful tips.
+ **www.travelyucatan.com**: Comprehensive practical information for destinations throughout the Yucatán; includes short tips and detailed articles by travelers and English-speaking residents with helpful photos of things like bus stations, not just glamour shots of beaches and ruins. It also offers bookings for hotels and hotel/air packages at competitive rates.
+ **www.yucatanliving.com**: Destination and cultural articles produced by and for expatriates; excels at in-depth listings of events in Mérida and the Yucatán.
+ **www.yucatantoday.com**: One of the least commercial privately run sites; well-written cultural notes, detailed maps, transportation advice, and lists of hotels, restaurants, and events in Yucatán state by editors of a stellar monthly magazine.

microphone, is to download **Skype** (www.skype.com) or another program using Voice over Internet Protocol, or VoIP, which charges a few cents per minute.

**Internet cafes** (sometimes called *cybercafés*) are plentiful in most towns and all resort areas throughout the Yucatán. While modern hotels (and many older ones now, too) offer Wi-Fi *(inalámbrica)* access, Internet computers are becoming harder to find. Restaurants and other public sites are also adding *inalámbrica* in droves. Internet cafes offer connections of varying bandwidth, from poky dial-up to high-speed DSL; outside of Cancún's Hotel Zone, prices can be as low as $1.50 an hour. Providers are generally centrally located in towns and cities; for suggestions in Cancún, see "The ABCs of Cancún" on p. 67. Exercise the same theft precautions you would at home: Don't leave your laptop, cellphone, or other electronic devices unattended in public areas or in plain view in your vehicle, and take advantage of hotel safes when offered.

## RECOMMENDED READING

Not surprisingly, the mysteries and marvels of Maya culture, rather than the region's colonial history or contemporary developments, have long fascinated writers, beginning with explorer John L. Stephens' classic *Incidents of Travel in Yucatán*. First published in two volumes in 1841, his accounts of discovering Maya ruins are available in historical reprints from Dover Publications and the University of Michigan. More current works that expand on Stephens' insights, all available in paperback, include:

- *The Forest of Kings: The Untold Story of the Ancient Maya,* by Linda Schele and David Freidel (Harper Perennial, 1992). This well-illustrated, well-documented text is nevertheless engagingly accessible for the average reader.
- *The Maya,* by Michael D. Coe (7th ed., Thames & Hudson, 2005). Written in a more scholarly style, this traces the ancient civilization's rise and fall, but includes a guide for travelers and updated interpretations of hieroglyphics and other archaeological data.
- *The Ancient Maya,* by Robert Sharer and Loa Traxler (6th ed., Stanford University Press, 2005). This 931-page, 3.2-pound tome, which earned praise from scholars and laypeople for its definitive and comprehensive approach, should probably stay home for you to consult before or after your trip.

## The ABCs of Cancún & the Yucatán

**Area Codes** The three-digit codes in this region, which you'll need to use when calling between cities (see "Telephones," below), sometimes cross state borders.

In **Campeche,** the namesake city code is 981; most towns to the northeast and southeast share 996, while 982 covers most towns to the southwest. Two important exceptions: **Ciudad del Carmen,** 938; and **Xpujil,** 983.

In **Quintana Roo,** the area code for **Cancún, Isla Mujeres,** and **Puerto Morelos** is 998, while **Cozumel** uses 987; most other nearby visitor destinations, including **Akumal, Isla Holbox, Playa del Carmen, Tulum,** and **Xcaret,** require 984. In the southern part of the state, including the capital of **Chetumal,** the code is 983.

In **Yucatán,** 999 covers **Mérida** and nearby towns; **Valladolid** and **Chichén Itzá** (near **Pisté**) use 985, while **Progreso's** code is 969. **Acanceh** and **Izamal** in the interior and **Celestún** on the Gulf coast share 988; the Maya-centric town of **Maní** has 997. On the Emerald Coast, **Chicxulub** requires 999, **Dzilam de Bravo** takes 991, and **Río Lagartos** uses 986.

**American Express** Offers travel services at offices in **Campeche, Cancún, Ciudad del Carmen, Cozumel,** and **Mérida;** hours and functions vary widely (not all cash travelers' checks, for example). For a list of addresses, hours, and services, consult the directory at www.americanexpress.com, under "Travel." For emergency card replacements in Mexico, call the main office in Mexico City at ☎ 55/5326-2522.

**ATMs** See "Money Matters" on p. 278.

**Business Hours** Most stores in Cancún's Hotel Zone are open 10am to 10pm daily. Downtown Cancún hours are similar to those in Mérida and other nonresort towns, where stores are open 10am to 2pm and 4 to 8pm Monday through Saturday. Banks are primarily open Monday to Friday from 9 or 9:30am to anywhere between 3 and 7pm, with some open Saturday mornings.

**Doctors** Embassies and consulates (see below) and hotels can recommend competent doctors and dentists, usually English speaking. But be prepared to pay first and try to collect from your insurance company later (see "Travel Insurance" on p. 277).

**Drinking Laws** The legal drinking age in Mexico is 18, hence the college crowds in Cancún at spring break. Drinking in the streets or inside a vehicle is illegal.

**Electricity** Mexico uses the same 110-volt standard as the United States and Canada, although occasionally it cycles more slowly (best to keep your hair dryer on medium or low speed). Since many outlets do not accept polarized plugs (where one prong is larger) or three-prong plugs, you may still need to bring an adapter, as will travelers from Europe, Australia, and New Zealand.

**Embassies & Consulates** The United States, Canada, and the United Kingdom have consulates in or around Cancún:

The main office of the **U.S. consulate** is in **Mérida** (Calle 60 no. 338-K; ☎ 999/942-5700; http://merida.usconsulate.gov; Mon–Fri 7:30am–12:30pm, closed the second and fourth Wed of the month). It also staffs consular agencies in **Cancún** (Plaza Caracol 2, Bl. Kukulcán Km 8.5, 3rd floor, Loc. 320-323; ☎ 998/883-0272; Mon–Fri 9am–2pm); **Cozumel** (Villa Mar Mall in the Main Plaza, Av. Juárez at Av. 5 Norte; ☎ 987/876-0624; Mon–Fri noon–2pm); and **Playa del Carmen** (The Palapa, Calle 1 Sur, btw. avs. 15 and 20; ☎ 984/873-0303; Mon, Wed, and Fri 10am–1pm). These offices may have limited hours for walk-in services and observe both Mexican and U.S. national holidays, but citizens may call 24 hours a day for help in case of life-or-death emergencies.

Also in Cancún's Hotel Zone are consulates for **Canada** (Plaza Caracol 2, Bl. Kukulcán Km 8.5, 3rd floor, Loc. 330; ☎ 998/883-3360; Mon–Fri 9am–5pm) and the **United Kingdom** (Royal Sands Resort, Bl. Kukulcán Km 13.5; ☎ 998/881-0100, ext. 65898; Mon–Fri 9am–3pm). Canadians may also call the emergency toll-free line to Ottawa at ☎ (001) 800/514-0129.

Citizens of other English-speaking countries in need of assistance while on the Yucatán Peninsula should call their embassies in Mexico City: **Australia,** ☎ 55/51101-2200; **Ireland,** ☎ 55/5520-5803; **New Zealand,** ☎ 55/5283-9460; **South Africa,** ☎ 55/5282-9260.

**Emergencies** Dial ☎ **060** for the police (similar to 911 service in the United States), ☎ **080** to call the fire department and ambulances, and ☎ **065** for the Red Cross (Cruz Roja), for first aid. For **Air Ambulance (Global Ambulance)** service, call ☎ **01-800/305-9400** toll-free in Mexico. For roadside emergencies, call the **Green Angels (Angeles Verdes)** fleet at ☎ **078,** which connects to the Mexican Ministry of Tourism's toll-free 24-hour tourist hot line at ☎ **01-800/903-9200.** The region's top destinations have special cadres of **English-speaking police** *(policía turística)* to help travelers and patrol popular areas. In Cancún, call ☎ **998/885-2277;** in Mérida, call ☎ **999/925-2555.** Mexico's **national tourist security hot line,** based in Mexico City, is ☎ **55/5250-0123.**

The national **Consumer Protection Agency** (Procuraduría Federal del Consumidor, or Profeco) has a branch in Cancún (Av. Cobá 9–11, above Fénix drugstore; ☎ **998/884-2634;** Mon–Fri 9am–3pm), and Isla Mujeres (☎ **998/887-3960**). The **Tourist Legal Aid** agency (Procuraduría del Turista) has a 24-hour hot line based in Mexico City at ☎ **55/5625-8153.** For other assistance, contact your country's nearest consulate or embassy (see above).

**Holidays** National public holidays when banks, government offices, and many businesses close include **New Year's Day,** January 1; **Constitution Day,** February 5 (or the Mon closest to it); **Benito Juárez's Birthday,** celebrated the third Monday in March; May 1 (the equivalent of Labor Day, it's simply known as **Primero de Mayo**); May 5 (commemorating the Battle of Puebla, it's known as **Cinco de Mayo**); **Independence Day,** September 16; **Revolution Day,** the third Monday in November; and **Christmas,** December 25. You can also expect widespread closures the week before Easter, and especially Maundy Thursday and Good Friday; November 1 and 2 (All Saints' and All Souls' days, or Día de los Muertos), December 12 (the feast day of the Virgin of Guadalupe) and on other religious and civic holidays (see also "The Yucatán's Visit-Worthy Annual Events," p. 265).

Hospitals In Cancún and neighboring resorts, hospitals and clinics are used to treating Americans and other English-speaking tourists—although that doesn't guarantee you'll find English-speaking staff, and few will accept American insurance. Larger facilities will accept credit cards for payment; others may require cash. Some recommended facilities:

**Cancún: American Medical Care Center** (beside Plaza Quetzal in front of the Presidente Hotel, Blvd. Kukulcán Km 8, ☎ 998/883-0113) and the 24-hour **American Hospital** (Calle Viento 15; ☎ 998/884-6068).

**Cozumel: Médica San Miguel** (Calle 6 Norte, btw. avs. 5 and 10; ☎ 987/872-0103) has an intensive-care unit and other services.

**Isla Mujeres: Hospital de la Armada** (Av. Rueda Medina at Ojón P. Blanco; ☎ 998/877-0001), ½-mile south of town; **Centro de Salud** (Av. Guerrero, near the *malecón;* ☎ 998/877-0117) for less urgent care.

**Costa Maya: General Hospital** (Av. Andrés Quintana Roo 399, Chetumal; ☎ 983/832-1977).

**Mérida: Centro Médico de las Américas** (Calle 54 no. 365, btw. 33-A and Av. Pérez Ponce; ☎ 999/926-2619 or, for emergencies, 999/927-3199).

**Campeche: Hospital General de Campeche** (Circuito Baluartes and Central; ☎ 981/816-0920). If you have time to travel, Mérida's facilities are more comprehensive.

Language English might serve most of your needs in the coastal resorts and bigger cities, but mastering basic Spanish phrases and courtesies will smooth your way; in the interior and smaller towns, they will be essential. A Mayan phrasebook can also help you break the ice with traditionally reserved Maya villagers, but politely broaching a conversation in Spanish is acceptable. See p. 299.

Mail **Sepomex** (Servicio Postal Mexicano; www.sepomex.gob.mx) is the national postal agency. It's fine for sending nonurgent letters and cards home (expect at least 1 week for air mail to U.S. and Canadian destinations, 2 weeks for other destinations overseas). International rates start at 10.50 pesos (about $1) for postcards and letters to North and Central America, 13 pesos for Europe and South America, and 14.50 pesos for everywhere else. For packages and crucial deliveries, you may want to use **FedEx** or other courier services; your hotel's front desk can also usually assist you, or at the least direct you to the nearest *correo* (post office). Some of the larger ones in the region and their hours:

**Campeche:** In the Edificio Federal (corner of Av. 16 de Septiembre and Calle 53; ☎ 981/816-2134), open Monday to Saturday 7:30am to 8pm.

**Cancún:** See "The ABCs of Cancún" on p. 67.

**Cozumel:** On the south of town (Av. Rafael Melgar at Calle 7 Sur; ☎ 987/872-0106), open Monday to Friday 9am to 3pm, Saturday 9am to noon.

**Mérida:** At the airport and in the Palacio Federal (near the central market, corner of Calle 65 and Calle 56; ☎ 999/928-54-04), both open Monday to Friday 8am to 7pm, Saturday 9am to noon.

Newspapers & Magazines Of English-language newspapers, the *Miami Herald* is the easiest to find at newsstands. Hotel gift shops, larger bookstores, and newsstands in metropolitan areas will also carry major English-language magazines.

Pharmacies **Cancún** has 24-hour pharmacies (see "The ABCs of Cancún" on p. 67), as does **Mérida** (**Farmacia Yza;** Calle 63 no. 502, btw. calles 60 and 62; ☎ 999/924-9510). Normal pharmacy hours are Monday through Saturday 8am to 8pm; in areas with more than one pharmacy, the *farmacia de turno* will be open during off hours when the others are closed.

Smoking Mexico City's comprehensive 2008 ban on smoking in all enclosed public areas—including bars, restaurants, offices, stores, buses, and taxis—is expected to spread throughout the country, where smoking and nonsmoking sections already exist in many establishments. But outside of resort areas, enforcement of the ban may come more slowly in the Yucatán.

**Restrooms** Restaurants (particularly fast-food chains), Pemex gas stations, and upscale hotel lobbies are your best bets for public toilets. If there's an attendant, leave a small tip (about 5 pesos).

**Taxes** In addition to the value-added IVA tax of 10 or 15%, which can be refunded on purchases of goods over 1,200 pesos (see "Taxing Issues" on p. 280), hotel rates generally include a local bed tax of 2%. Posted prices should already include the IVA (pronounced "Ee-vah") and bed tax, but ask if you're not sure.

**Telephones** If you're calling a Mexican land line from outside the country, dial your international access number (011 in the United States and Canada), then the country code, **52,** before the area or city code (in the Yucatán Peninsula, they all have three digits; see "Area Codes," above) and the local number (seven digits for this region). In Mexico, dial 01 before the city code and local number for a long-distance call to a domestic land line. (For calling cellphones, see "Calling All Cells," p. 285.) To call the United States and Canada from Mexico, dial 001 before the area code and phone number; to call other countries, dial 00 before the country code, city code, and phone number.

If you don't have a mobile phone that works in Mexico or access to Skype (see "Staying Wired While Away," p. 286), you can use a long-distance phone service center or a public phone. For the latter, you'll need a Ladatel card, which you can buy at newsstands and many other stores. For directory assistance, generally only in Spanish, dial ☎ **040;** for operator assistance, dial ☎ **090** for international calls, ☎ **020** for domestic calls.

**Time** The entire Yucatán Peninsula is on Central Time (6 hr. earlier than Greenwich Mean Time), as are Mexico City and neighboring states; the country as a whole observes daylight saving time from the first Sunday in April to the last Sunday in October.

**Tipping** As in the United States, it's standard to tip waiters (10%–15% of the bill), bellhops (10 pesos per bag, up to 20 pesos in Cancún), skycaps (10 pesos per bag), tour guides (15%–20% of the tour price and valet parking attendants (10–20 pesos). You'll also find bathroom attendants, who expect a small tip (3–5 pesos). Unlike in the States, taxi drivers usually don't count on tips, unless you've hired them as a guide or asked for other special services. You may distribute tips in U.S. dollars if necessary (see "Money Matters," p. 278), but don't give U.S. coins, since the recipient usually can't exchange them.

**Tourist Information** Government-funded tourist bureaus have offices in central locations of visitor destinations; few have an online presence, and hours and services vary. Some main sites: **Campeche** (Plaza Moch-Couoh, Av. Ruiz Cortínez; ☎ 981/816-6767); **Cancún Convention and Visitors Bureau** (Cancún Center, Bl. Kukulcán Km 9; ☎ 998/881-2745 or -2774; cancun.travel); **Cancún Municipal Tourism Office** (Av. Cobá at Av. Tulum; ☎ 998/887-3379); **Cozumel** (Av. Benito Juárez at Av. 5 Norte; ☎ 987/872-0972); and **Isla Mujeres** (Av. Rueda Medina, no. 130; ☎ 998/877-0767). The **Quintana Roo State Tourism Office** is also in Cancún (Cancún Center, 1st floor, Bl. Kukulcán Km 9; ☎ 998/881-9000; www.qroo.gob.mx). **Mérida** has a city visitor information office on the ground floor of the Ayuntamiento building facing the main square (Calle 62; ☎ 999/942-0000, ext. 801119). The **Yucatán State Tourism Board** (☎ 999/924-9290; www.mayayucatan.com.mx) has two Mérida locations, in the Teatro Peón Contreras by Parque de la Madre and in the Palacio Gobierno on the main plaza. For other sources of travel information before you go, see "Online Resources" on p. 286.

# 9 Useful Terms & Phrases

## ENGLISH-SPANISH PHRASES

| ENGLISH | SPANISH | PRONUNCIATION |
|---|---|---|
| Good day | **Buen día** | Bwehn *dee*-ah |
| Good morning | **Buenos días** | *Bweh*-nohs *dee*-ahs |
| Good afternoon | **Buenas tardes** | *Bweh*-nahs *tahr*-dehs |
| What's your name? | **¿Como se llama?** | *Koh*-moh seh *yah*-ma |
| My name is . . . | **Me llamo . . .** | Meh *yah*-moh |
| Pleased to meet you | **Mucho gusto** | *Moo*-choh *goos*-toh |
| How are you? | **¿Cómo está?** | *Koh*-moh eh-*stah* |
| Very well | **Muy bien** | Mwee byehn |
| Thank you | **Gracias** | *Grah*-syahs |
| You're welcome | **De nada** | Deh *nah*-dah |
| Goodbye | **Adiós** | Ah-*dyohs* |
| Please | **Por favor** | Pohr fah-*vohr* |
| Yes | **Sí** | See |
| No | **No** | Noh |
| Excuse me | **Perdóneme/** | Pehr-*doh*-neh-meh/ |
| | **con permiso** | kohn pehr-*mee*-soh |
| Can you tell me . . . ? | **¿Puede decirme . . . ?** | Pweh-deh deh-*seer*-meh |
| Give me | **Déme** | *Deh*-meh |
| Where is . . . ? | **¿Dónde está . . . ?** | *Dohn*-deh ehs-*tah* |
| the station | **la estación** | lah eh-stah-*syohn* |
| a hotel | **un hotel** | oon oh-*tehl* |
| the bank | **el banco** | el *bahn*-koh |
| the ATM | **el cajero** | el *kah*-hehr-oh |
| | **automático** | ow-toh-*mah*-tee-koh |
| the store | **la tienda** | lah *tyehn*-dah |
| the museum | **el museo** | el moo-*seh*-oh |
| the hospital | **el hospital** | el oh-spee-*tahl* |
| the market | **el mercado** | el mehr-*kah*-doh |
| the central plaza | **el zócalo** | el *zoh*-kah-loh |
| a gas station | **una gasolinera** | *oo*-nah gah-soh-lee-*neh*-rah |
| a restaurant | **un restaurante** | oon res-tow-*rahn*-teh |
| the bathroom | **el baño** | el *bah*-nyoh |
| a good doctor | **un buen médico** | oon bwehn *meh*-dee-coh |
| the road to . . . | **el camino a/hacia . . .** | el cah-*mee*-noh ah/*ah*-syah |
| Is this the way to get to . . .? | **¿Por aquí vamos a . . . ?** | Pohr ah-*kee vah*-mos ah |
| To the right | **A la derecha** | Ah lah deh-*reh*-chah |
| To the left | **A la izquierda** | Ah lah ee-*skyehr*-dah |
| Straight ahead | **Derecho** | Deh-*reh*-choh |

| ENGLISH | SPANISH | PRONUNCIATION |
|---|---|---|
| On the corner | En la esquina | Ehn lah eh-*skee*-nah |
| Here | Aquí | Ah-kee |
| There | Allí (near), allá (far) | Ah-*yee*, ah-*yah* |
| In front of | Frente a | *Frehn*-te ah |
| Behind | Detrás de | Deh-*trahs* deh |
| Up | Arriba | Ah-*rhee*-bah |
| Down | Abajo | Ah-*bah*-hoh |
| I would like . . . | Quisiera/ | Kee-*syeh*-rah/ |
| | me gustaría . . . | meh goos-tah-*ree*-ah |
| a newspaper | un periódico | oon peh-*ryoh*-dee-koh |
| soap | jabón | hah-*bohn* |
| more towels | más toallas | mahs *twah*-yahs |
| paper | papel | pah-*pehl* |
| I want . . . | Quiero . . . | *Kyeh*-roh |
| to eat | comer | koh-*mehr* |
| something to drink | algo para beber/ | *ahl*-goh pah-rah beh-*behr*/ |
| | tomar | toh-*mahr* |
| Do you have . . . ? | ¿Tiene usted . . . ? | *Tyeh*-neh oo-*sted* |
| the key | la llave | lah *yah*-veh |
| a dictionary | un diccionario | oon deek-syoh-*nah*-ryoh |
| I don't have . . . | No tengo . . . | Noh *tehn*-goh |
| How much is it? | ¿Cuánto cuesta? | *Kwahn*-toh *kwehs*-tah |
| When? | ¿Cuándo? | *Kwahn*-doh |
| What? | ¿Qué? | Keh |
| Which? | ¿Cuál? | Kwahl |
| Who? | ¿Quién? | Kyen |
| How? | ¿Cómo? | *Koh*-moh |
| There is | Hay . . . | Eye |
| (Is there . . . ?) | (¿Hay . . . ?) | |
| What is there? | ¿Qué hay? | Keh eye |
| What's going on? | ¿Qué pasa? | Keh *pah*-sah |
| Yesterday | Ayer | Ah-*yehr* |
| Today | Hoy | Oy |
| Tomorrow | Mañana | Mah-*nyah*-nah |
| Now/right now | Ahora/ahorita | Ah-*oh*-rah/ah-oh-*ree*-tah |
| Later | Más tarde | Mahs *tahr*-deh |
| Big | Grande | *Grahn*-deh |
| Small | Pequeño, chico | Peh-*keh*-nyoh, *chee*-koh |
| Good | Bueno | *Bweh*-noh |
| Bad | Malo | *Mah*-loh |
| Better (best) | (Lo) Mejor | (Loh) Meh-*hohr* |
| More | Más | Mahs |
| Less | Menos | *Meh*-nohs |
| Stop | Alto | *Ahl*-toh |
| No smoking | Se prohibe fumar | Seh proh-*ee*-beh foo-*mahr* |
| Insect repellent | Repelente contra | Reh-peh-*lehn*-teh *cohn*-trah |
| | insectos | een-*sehk*-tohs |

# MORE USEFUL PHRASES & QUESTIONS

| ENGLISH | SPANISH | PRONUNCIATION |
|---|---|---|
| Do you speak English? | ¿Habla usted inglés? | *Ah*-blah oo-*sted* een-*glehs* |
| Is there anyone here who speaks English? | ¿Hay alguien aquí que hable inglés? | Eye *ahl*-gyehn ah-*kee* keh *ah*-bleh een-*glehs* |
| I speak a little Spanish. | Hablo un poco de español. | *Ah*-bloh oon *poh*-koh deh eh-spah-*nyohl* |
| I don't understand Spanish very well. | No (lo) entiendo muy bien el español. | Noh (loh) ehn-*tyehn*-doh mwee byehn el eh-spah-*nyohl* |
| I don't know. | No sé. | Noh seh |
| The meal is good. | Me gusta la comida. | Meh *goo*-stah lah koh-*mee*-dah |
| What time is it? | ¿Qué hora es? | Keh *oh*-rah ehs |
| It is one (two) o'clock | Es la una (son las dos) | Ehs la *oo*-nah (sohn lahs dohs) |
| May I see your menu? | ¿Puedo ver el menú (la carta)? | *Pweh*-doh vehr el meh-*noo* (lah *car*-tah) |
| Is the tip included? | ¿Está incluida la propina? | Ehs-*tah* een-*klwee*-dah lah pro-*pee*-nah? |
| The check, please. | La cuenta, por favor. | Lah *kwehn*-tah pohr fa-*vorh* |
| What do I owe you? | ¿Cuánto le debo? | *Kwahn*-toh leh *deh*-boh |
| Do you have change? | ¿Tiene cambio? | *Tyeh*-neh *kahm*-byoh |
| What did you say? | ¿Mande? (formal) ¿Cómo? (informal) | *Mahn*-deh *Koh*-moh |
| I want (to see) . . . | Quiero (ver) . . . | *kyeh*-roh (vehr) |
| a room | un cuarto or una habitación | oon *kwar*-toh, oo-nah ah-bee-tah-*syohn* |
| for two people | para dos personas | *pah*-rah dohs pehr-*soh*-nahs |
| with (without) bathroom | con (sin) baño | kohn (seen) *bah*-nyoh |
| We are staying here only . . . | Nos quedamos aquí solamente . . . | Nohs keh-*dah*-mohs ah-*kee* soh-lah-*mehn*-teh |
| one night | una noche | oo-nah *noh*-cheh |
| one week | una semana | oo-nah seh-*mah*-nah |
| We are leaving . . . | Partimos (Salimos) . . . | Pahr-*tee*-mohs (sah-*lee*-mohs) |
| today | hoy | oy |
| tomorrow | mañana | mah-*nyah*-nah |
| Do you accept . . . ? | ¿Acepta usted . . . ? | Ah-*sehp*-tah oo-*sted* |
| traveler's checks? | cheques de viajero? | *cheh*-kehs deh *byah*-heh-roh |
| credit cards? | tarjetas de crédito? | tar-*heh*-tahs deh *creh*-dee-toh |
| I am ill. | Estoy enfermo (a). | Eh-*stoy* ehn-*fehr*-moh (mah) |
| Is there a laundromat . . . ? near here? | ¿Hay una lavandería . . .? cerca de aquí? | Eye *oo*-nah lah-vahn-deh-*ree*-ah *sehr*-kah deh ah-*kee* |
| Please send these clothes to the laundry. | Hágame el favor de mandar esta ropa a la lavandería. | *Ah*-gah-meh el fah-*vorh* deh mahn-*dahr* eh-stah roh-pah a lah lah-bahn-deh-*ree*-ah |

## Numbers

| | | | |
|---|---|---|---|
| 1 | **uno** (*ooh*-noh) | 17 | **diecisiete** (dyeh-see-*syeh*-teh) |
| 2 | **dos** (dohs) | 18 | **dieciocho** (dyeh-*syoh*-choh) |
| 3 | **tres** (trehs) | 19 | **diecinueve** (dyeh-see-*nweh*-beh) |
| 4 | **cuatro** (*kwah*-troh) | 20 | **veinte** (*bayn*-teh) |
| 5 | **cinco** (*seen*-koh) | 30 | **treinta** (*trayn*-tah) |
| 6 | **seis** (says) | 40 | **cuarenta** (kwah-*ren*-tah) |
| 7 | **siete** (*syeh*-teh) | 50 | **cincuenta** (seen-*kwen*-tah) |
| 8 | **ocho** (*oh*-choh) | 60 | **sesenta** (seh-*sehn*-tah) |
| 9 | **nueve** (*nweh*-beh) | 70 | **setenta** (seh-*tehn*-tah) |
| 10 | **diez** (*dyehs*) | 80 | **ochenta** (oh-*chehn*-tah) |
| 11 | **once** (*ohn*-seh) | 90 | **noventa** (noh-*behn*-tah) |
| 12 | **doce** (*doh*-seh) | 100 | **cien** (syehn) |
| 13 | **trece** (*treh*-seh) | 200 | **doscientos** (doh-*syehn*-tohs) |
| 14 | **catorce** (kah-*tohr*-seh) | 500 | **quinientos** (kee-*nyehn*-tohs) |
| 15 | **quince** (*keen*-seh) | 1,000 | **mil** (meel) |
| 16 | **dieciseis** (dyeh-see-*says*) | | |

## DAYS OF THE WEEK

Monday   **lunes** (*loo*-nehs)
Tuesday   **martes** (*mahr*-tehs)
Wednesday   **miercoles** (*myehr*-coh-lehs)

Thursday   **jueves** (*hueh*-vehs)
Friday   **viernes** (*byehr*-nehs)
Saturday   **sábado** (*sah*-bah-doh)
Sunday   **domingo** (doh-*meen*-goh)

## MONTHS

January   **enero** (eh-*neh*-ro)
February   **febrero** (feh-*breh*-roh)
March   **marzo** (*mahr*-zoh)
April   **abril** (ah-*breel*)
May   **mayo** (*mah*-yoh)
June   **junio** (*hoo*-nyoh)
July   **julio** (*hoo*-lyo)

August   **agosto** (ah-*goh*-stoh)
September   **septiembre** (sehp-*tyehm*-breh)
October   **octubre** (ohk-*too*-breh)
November   **noviembre** (noh-*byem*-breh)
December   **diciembre** (dee-*cyehm*-breh)

## TRANSPORTATION

| ENGLISH | SPANISH | PRONUNCIATION |
|---|---|---|
| Airport | **Aeropuerto** | ah-eh-roh-*pwehr*-toh |
| Arrival | **Llegada** | yeh-*gah*-dah |
| Baggage | **Equipajes** | eh-kee-*pah*-hehs |
| Baggage claim area | **Recibo de equipajes** | reh-*see*-boh deh eh-kee-*pah*-hehs |
| Bus | **Autobús** | ow-toh-boos |
| Bus stop | **Parada del autobús** | pah-*rah*-dah deh ow-toh-*boos* |
| Customs | **Aduana** | ah-dwah-nah |
| Departure | **Salida** | sah-*lee*-dah |
| First class | **Primera** | pree-*meh*-rah |
| Flight | **Vuelo** | *bweh*-loh |
| Highway | **Carretera** | cah-reh-*teh*-rah |
| Immigration | **Inmigración** | een-mee-grah-*syohn* |

| ENGLISH | SPANISH | PRONUNCIATION |
|---|---|---|
| Intercity | Foraneo | foh-rah-*neh*-oh |
| Lane | Carril | kah-*reel* |
| Luggage storage area | Guarda equipaje | *gwar*-dah eh-kee-*pah*-heh |
| Nonstop (bus) | Directo | dee-*rehk*-toh |
| Nonstop (flight) | Sin escala | seen eh-*skah*-lah |
| Originates at this station | Local | loh-*kahl* |
| Originates elsewhere | De paso | deh *pah*-soh |
| Rental car | Arrendadora de autos | ah-rehn-da-*doh*-rah deh *ow*-tohs |
| Second class | Segunda | seh-*goon*-dah |
| Speed bump | Tope | *toh*-peh |
| Stops if seats available | Para si hay lugares | *pah*-rah see eye loo-*gah*-rehs |
| Ticket | Billete, boleto | bee-*yeh*-teh, boh-*leh*-toh |
| Ticket window | Taquilla | tah-*kee*-yah |
| Toilets | Sanitarios | sah-nee-*tah*-ryohs |
| Toll highway | Cuota | *kwoh*-tah |
| Truck | Camión | ka-*myohn* |
| Waiting room | Sala de espera | *sah*-lah deh eh-*speh*-rah |

# DINING TERMS

| ENGLISH | SPANISH | PRONUNCIATION |
|---|---|---|
| Breakfast | Desayuno | Deh-sah-*yoo*-noh |
| Lunch | Almuerzo | Ahl-*mwehr*-zoh |
| Dinner | Cena | *Say*-nah |
| A table | Una mesa | Oo-nah *meh*-sah |
| Fixed-price menu | Comida corrida | Koh-*mee*-dah koh-*ree*-dah |
| A bottle of . . . | Una botella de . . . | Oo-nah boh-*teh*-yah deh |
| A cup of . . . | Una taza de . . . | Oo-nah *tah*-sah deh |
| A glass of . . . | Un vaso de . . . | Oon *bah*-soh deh |
| Water (purified) | Agua (purificada) | Ah-gwah (poo-ree-fee-*kah*-da) |
| Beer | Cerveza | Sehr-*beh*-sah |
| Bread | Pan | Pahn |
| Salt/pepper/sugar | Sal/pimienta/azúcar | Sahl/pee-*myehn*-tah/ah-*soo*-kahr |
| Fork/knife/spoon | Tenedor/cuchillo/cuchara | Teh-neh-*dohr*/koo-*chee*-yoh/koo-*chah*-rah |
| Dish | Plato | *Plah*-toh |
| Napkin | La servilleta | Lah sehr-bee-*yeh*-tah |
| Enjoy! | Buen provecho | Bwehn proh-*beh*-choh |
| The bill (check) | La cuenta | Lah *kwehn*-tah |

# MENU TERMS

**Achiote**   Small red seed of the annatto tree.

**Antojito**   Typical Mexican supper foods, usually made with masa or tortillas and having a filling or topping such as sausage, cheese, beans, and onions; includes such things as tacos, tostadas, *sopes,* and *garnachas.*

**Botana**   An appetizer.

**Buñuelos**   Round, thin, deep-fried crispy fritters dipped in sugar.

**Carnitas**   Pork deep-cooked (not fried) in lard, then simmered and served with corn tortillas for tacos.

**Cebolla en escabeche**   Red onions pickled in sour orange juice, chilies, and spices. Traditional topping for *cochinita pibil,* often served as a condiment with other dishes.

**Ceviche**   Fresh raw seafood marinated in fresh lime juice and garnished with chopped tomatoes, onions, chilies, and sometimes cilantro.

**Chaya**   Spinachlike vegetable added to soups, sauces, scrambled eggs, casseroles, and drinks.

**Chayote**   A vegetable pear or mirliton, a type of spiny squash boiled and served as an accompaniment to meat dishes.

**Chile rellenos**   Usually poblano peppers stuffed with cheese or spicy ground meat with raisins, rolled in a batter, and fried.

**Chipotles**   Smoke-dried jalapeño chilies.

**Churro**   Tube-shaped, breadlike fritter, dipped in sugar and sometimes filled with *cajeta* (milk-based caramel) or chocolate.

**Cochinita pibil**   A Yucatecan specialty of pork wrapped in banana leaves, pit-baked in a *pibil* sauce of *achiote,* sour orange juice, and spices; served with pickled red onions.

**Enchilada**   A lightly fried tortilla dipped in sauce, usually filled with chicken or white cheese, and sometimes topped with mole (*enchiladas rojas* or *de mole*), or with tomato sauce and sour cream (*enchiladas suizas*—Swiss enchiladas), or covered in a green sauce *(enchiladas verdes),* or topped with onions, sour cream, and guacamole *(enchiladas potosinas).*

**Escabeche**   A lightly pickled sauce used in Yucatecan chicken stew.

**Frijoles refritos**   Pinto beans mashed and cooked with lard.

**Garnachas**   A thickish small circle of fried masa with pinched sides, topped with pork or chicken, onions, and avocado, or sometimes chopped potatoes and tomatoes, typical as a *botana* in Veracruz and Yucatán.

**Gorditas**   Thick, fried corn tortillas, slit and stuffed with choice of cheese, beans, beef, chicken, with or without lettuce, tomato, and onion garnish.

**Horchata**   Refreshing drink made of ground rice or melon seeds, ground almonds, and cinnamon, and lightly sweetened.

**Huevos mexicanos**   Scrambled eggs with chopped onions, hot green peppers, and tomatoes.

**Huitlacoche**   Sometimes spelled *cuitlacoche.* A mushroom-flavored black fungus that appears on corn in the rainy season; considered a delicacy.

**Lomitos**   Steak sautéed in a tomato, onion, and chipotle sauce.

**Manchamantel**   Translates to "tablecloth stainer." A stew of chicken or pork with chilies, tomatoes, pineapple, bananas, and jicama.

**Masa**   Ground corn soaked in lime; the basis for tamales, corn tortillas, and soups.

**Mixiote**    Rabbit, lamb, or chicken cooked in a mild chili sauce (usually chili ancho or pasilla), then wrapped like a tamal and steamed. It is generally served with tortillas for tacos, with traditional garnishes of pickled onions, hot sauce, chopped cilantro, and lime wedges.

**Mole**    A dark, spicy, chocolate-based sauce, usually served over chicken.

**Naranja agria**    A local bitter orange used often in marinades.

**Pan de cazón**    Campeche's most famous dish. A stack of three tortillas, each covered with refried beans and a mixture of cooked baby shark, smothered with tomato sauce.

**Pan de muerto**    Sweet bread made around the Days of the Dead (Nov 1–2), in the form of mummies or dolls, or round with bone designs.

**Panuchos**    Tortillas stuffed with black beans, fried crisp then topped with shredded turkey or chicken, tomato, lettuce, and onions. Without the bean stuffing, they are called *salbutes*.

**Papadzules**    Tortillas stuffed with hard-boiled eggs and seeds (pumpkin or sunflower) in a tomato sauce.

**Pibil**    Pit-baked pork or chicken in a sauce of tomato, onion, mild red pepper, cilantro, and vinegar.

**Pipián**    Also *pepián*. A sauce made with ground pumpkin seeds, nuts, and mild peppers.

**Poc chuc**    Slices of pork with onion marinated in a tangy sour orange sauce and charcoal broiled; a Yucatecan specialty.

**Pozole**    A soup made with hominy in either chicken or pork broth, served with an array of condiments.

**Relleno negro**    A regional specialty made with chilies, green pepper, and *achiote* served over shredded turkey or pork and a hard-boiled egg.

**Quesadilla**    Corn or flour tortillas stuffed with melted white cheese and lightly fried.

**Queso relleno**    "Stuffed cheese," a mild yellow cheese stuffed with minced meat and spices; a Yucatecan specialty.

**Recado**    Marinade made from lime, grapefruit, orange, or sour orange juice with a variety of chilies, garlic, and spices, including saffron, cumin, cinnamon, oregano, and *achiote*.

**Salsa verde**    An uncooked sauce using the green tomatillo and puréed with spicy or mild hot peppers, onions, garlic, and cilantro; it's found on tables countrywide.

**Sopa de flor de calabaza**    A soup made of chopped squash or pumpkin blossoms.

**Sopa de lima**    A tangy soup made with chicken broth and accented with fresh lime; popular in Yucatán.

**Sopa de tortilla**    A traditional chicken broth–based soup, seasoned with chilies, tomatoes, onion, and garlic, served with crispy fried strips of corn tortillas.

**Sope**    Pronounced "soh-*peh*." An *antojito* similar to a *garnacha,* except topped with refried beans, crumbled cheese, and onions.

**Tacos al pastor**    Thin slices of flavored pork roasted on a revolving cylinder dripping with onion slices and juice of fresh pineapple slices. Served in small corn tortillas, topped with chopped onion and cilantro.

**Tamal**    Incorrectly called a tamale (tamal singular, tamales plural). A meat or sweet filling rolled with fresh masa, wrapped in a corn husk or banana leaf and steamed.

**Tikin xic**   Also seen on menus as *tik-n-xic* and *tikik chick*. Charbroiled fish brushed with *achiote* sauce.

**Torta**   A sandwich, usually on *bolillo* bread, typically with sliced avocado, onions, and tomatoes, with a choice of meat and often cheese.

**X'catic**   A mild chili frequently used in marinades and sauces.

**Xtabentún**   Pronounced "shtah-behn-*toon.*" A Yucatecan liquor made of fermented honey and flavored with anise. It comes *seco* (dry) or *crema* (sweet).

**Zacahuil**   Pork leg tamal, packed in thick masa, wrapped in banana leaves and pit-baked, sometimes pot-made with tomato and masa; a specialty of mid- to upper Veracruz.

# MAYAN TERMS & PHRASES

Hundreds of thousands of Maya living on the Yucatán Peninsula today speak at least some of their mother tongue. Most speak Yucatec Maya (commonly called simply "Maya"), one of more than 30 Mayan languages used today that can be traced back about 4,000 years to a single language believed to have originated in northwestern Guatemala. You will see numerous spelling variations around the peninsula. *Note:* The term "Mayan" is reserved for Mayan languages. The noun or the adjective for the people is "Maya."

Mayan vowels are pronounced very much as they are in Spanish. Double vowels are pronounced like their single counterparts but are held longer. The "x" is pronounced "sh," as in "ship"; the "j" sounds like "h," as in "home." Consonants that come before an accent (') are glottalized. Though the difference is hard for a newcomer to discern, glottalized consonants have a harder, more emphatic sound. Accents in Mayan words usually fall on the last syllable (unlike Spanish, which emphasizes the second-to-last syllable unless an accent mark indicates otherwise). Plurals in Mayan are formed by adding the suffix –ob.

| ENGLISH | MAYAN | PRONUNCIATION |
|---|---|---|
| Hello | Ola | *oh*-lah |
| How are you? | Biix a beel? | Beesh a bell |
| So long | Tu heel k'iin | Too heel k-*een* |
| See you tomorrow | Asta sa'amal | Ahs-*ta* sah-ah-*mahl* |
| Okay (fine, well) | Ma'aloob | Mah-ah-*lohby* |
|  | He'le' | Hey-*leh* |
| No | Ma' | Mah |
| I don't understand | Min na'atik | Meen na-ah-*teek* |
| Thank you | Dyos bo'otik | Dee-*yos* boh-oh-*teek* |
| Stop | Wa'alen | Wah-ah-*lehn* |
| You're welcome | Mixba'al | Meesh-bah-*ahl* |
| I'm hungry | Wi'hen | Wee-*hehn* |
| I'm going home | Kin bin tin nah | Keen been teen nah |
| Bon appetit | Hach ki' a wi'ih | Hach kee ah wee-*ee* |
| Let's (go) | Ko'ox (tun) | Koh-*osh* (toon) |
| Take care/Good luck | Xi'ik tech utsil | Shee-*eek* tech oot-*seel* |
| Take care/Be careful | Kanantaba | Kahn-ahn-tah-*bah* |
| Where is the beach? | Tuxan há? | Too-*shan* hah |

# A BASIC MAYAN GLOSSARY

**Ahau**   God or high king.

**Ah kin**   A high priest.

**Aktun**   Cave.

**Atl-atl**   Spear-throwing device.

**Bacab**   A class of important gods.

**Balam**   Jaguar spirit that keeps evil away.

**Cán**   Serpent.

**Cenote**   A natural waterhole created by the collapse of limestone caves; corruption by the Spanish of the Maya word *dzonot.*

**Chaac**   God of rain and agriculture.

**Ch'en**   Pool.

**Chicle**   The juice of the sapodilla tree, used in the making of chewing gum.

**Chilan**   A soothsayer or medium.

**Chultun**   A bottle-shaped, underground cistern.

**Corte**   Indian woman's traditional full-length skirt.

**Há**   Cacao seed.

**Huipil**   A traditional Maya wraparound, woven cotton dress, worn leaving the shoulders bare.

**Ixchel**   Goddess of fertility, the moon, and medicine

**Kayab**   A turtle-shell drum.

**Kayem**   Ground maize.

**Kin**   The sun, the day, unity of time.

**Kukulcán**   Quetzal serpent, plumed serpent god.

**Manta**   A square of cloth, used as a cloak or blanket; still worn by the Maya today.

**Milpa**   A cornfield.

**Muxubbak**   Tamale.

**Nohoch**   Important, big.

**P'ac**   Tomatoes.

**Palapa**   Traditional thatched-roof Maya structure built without nails.

**Pok-a-tok**   A Maya ball game.

**Pom**   Resin of the copal tree, used for rubber, chewing gum, and incense.

**Quetzal**   A rare Central American bird, now almost extinct, prized by Maya kings for its long, brilliant blue-green tail feathers.

**Sacbé**   Literally "white road," a raised limestone causeway linking Maya buildings and settlements.

**Xibalbá**   The Maya underworld.

# Index

See also Accommodations and Restaurant indexes, below.

## GENERAL INDEX

**AARP,** 285
About.com, 284
Abyss (Playa del Carmen), 145
Acanceh, 220
Access-Able Travel Source, 284
Accidents, avoiding, 281
Accommodations. *See also*
Accommodations Index
  Akumal, 159–161
  Campeche, 247–250
  Cancún, 16–34
    air/hotel packages,
      16–18, 20–21
    as attractions, 49–50
    booking services, 27
    condos and vacation
      rentals, 21–25
    El Centro, 30–34
    fluctuating prices, 27
    money-saving tip, 27
    Zona Hotelera, 27–30
  Celestún, 221
  Chichén Itzá, 227
  Cozumel, 110–113
  dive courses at resorts, 59
  Isla Holbox, 98–100
  Isla Mujeres, 76–80
  Izamal, 231–232
  Mérida, 188–193
  Playa del Carmen, 138–141
  Progreso, 223–224
  Puerto Morelos, 150–151
  Sian Ka'an Biosphere
    Reserve, 179
  Tulum, 168–170
  Uxmal and the hill country,
    212–214
  Valladolid, 236–238
Acrópolis (Ek Balam), 240–241
Active pursuits
  Akumal, 165–166
  Cancún, 53–61
  Cozumel, 124–125
  Isla Mujeres, 88–91
  Mérida, 201
  Playa del Carmen, 145–147
  Tulum, 172–174
Aduana México, 270
Aeropuerto Internacional de
  Cozumel, 108

Ah Cacao (Playa del Carmen),
  148
Air Ambulance, 289
Air travel
  Campeche, 246–247
  Cancún, 108
  Cozumel, 108
  Mérida, 185
Aké, 235
Akumal, 134, 158–166
  accommodations, 159–161
  active pursuits, 165–166
  getting to and around, 159
  restaurants, 161–162
  sights and attractions,
    162–165
Akumal Bay, 162, 166
Akumal Dive Adventures, 166
Akumal Dive Center, 165–166
Akumal Dive Shop, 165, 166
Akumal Rentals, 160
Akumal Tours, 159
Akumal Travel, 159, 160
Akumal Vacations, 160
Aladia, 273
Albatross Charters (Cozumel),
  125
Alienet (Cancún), 68
Alltournative, 50, 144
Alma de México, 273
Alma Libre Bookstore (Puerto
  Morelos), 150, 157–158
Almost Heaven Divers (Puerto
  Morelos), 155, 156
*Aluxes,* 164
Ambar Lounge, 127
American Airlines Vacations, 20
American Cetacean Society, 57
American Express
  Cancún, 67
  Mérida, 204
American Hospital (Cancún), 68
American Medical Care Center
  (Cancún), 68
Amigos De Los Animales (Isla
  Mujeres), 88
Angeles Verdes, 289
Apartment rentals, Isla Mujeres,
  76–78
Apple Vacations, 20–21
Aqua Fun (Cancún), 54

Aquarium, Interactive (Cancún),
  47, 56–57
Aqua Safari (Cozumel), 118
Aquatours (Cancún), 55
AquaWorld (Cancún), 55–56
Archaeological sites and ruins.
  *See also specific buildings and
  structures*
  Acanceh, 220
  best, 4
  Calakmul, 262–263
  Cancún, 47–49
  Chichén Itzá, 228–230
  Cobá, 174–176
  Cozumel, 120
  Dzibilchaltún, 199
  Edzná, 261–262
  Ek Balam, 240–241
  Grutas de Balamkanché, 231
  Grutas de Loltún, 218–219
  Izamal, 233, 234
  Kabah, 218
  Labná, 218
  Maní, 219
  Mayapán, 219
  Tulum, 171–172
  Xcambó, 226
Area codes, 288
  Cancún, 67
  Mérida, 204
Artesanías Arcoíris (Isla
  Mujeres), 94
Assumption of the Virgin Mary,
  266
Asterix Tours (Isla Contoy), 93
Atkun Chen, 163
Atlantis Submarines (Cozumel),
  123
ATMs, 278
Australia, customs regulations,
  271
Auto insurance, 277
Aviacsa, 273
Ayuntamiento (Valladolid), 239
Azúcar (Cancún), 65

**Balamkanché, Grutas de,** 231
Ball Court (Juego de Pelota;
  Chichén Itzá), 230
Baluarte de Nuestra Señora de
  la Soledad (Campeche), 256

301

# RESTAURANTS